LIFE AND DEATH
IN A GERMAN TOWN

LIFE AND DEATH IN A GERMAN TOWN

Osnabrück from the Weimar Republic to
World War II and Beyond

PANIKOS PANAYI

Tauris Academic Studies
London · New York

Published in 2007 by Tauris Academic Studies, an imprint of I.B.Tauris & Co Ltd
6 Salem Road, London W2 4BU
175 Fifth Avenue, New York NY 10010
www.ibtauris.com

In the United States of America and Canada distributed by Palgrave Macmillan
a division of St. Martin's Press, 175 Fifth Avenue, New York NY 10010

This publication has been made possible by a grant from the Scouloudi Foundation
in association with the Institute of Historical Research.

International Library of Twentieth Century History 10

ISBN: 978 1 84511 348 3

A full CIP record for this book is available from the British Library
A full CIP record is available from the Library of Congress

Library of Congress Catalog Card Number: available

Printed and bound by Thomson Press (I) Ltd.
From camera-ready copy edited and supplied by the author

This book is dedicated to the memory of Osnabrück residents killed by Nazi policies and Allied bombs.

CONTENTS

LIST OF TABLES

ACKNOWLEDGEMENTS

This book has emerged over many years during which I have accumulated a series of debts. First of all, I must thank De Montfort University, which granted me two periods of leave for the purpose of working on Osnabrück. Second, I would like to thank the three funding bodies, which supported this project. In the first place, the Alexander von Humboldt Foundation, which supported six months of research in Osnabrück. The Leverhulme Trust gave me a research grant allowing further trips to Osnabrück, Freiburg, Hanover, Berlin and London. The support of the Humboldt Foundation and the Leverhulme Trust also covered the transcription of interviews. The Research Leave Scheme of the Arts and Humanities Research Board meant that my one semester free from teaching became two, which proved crucial in the completion of a sensible first draft of this book. Earlier versions of chapters 7 and 9 appeared as articles in the *European History Quarterly* and *Journal of Contemporary History* respectively, both published by Sage, while a version of chapter 8 appeared in *Patterns of Prejudice* (Taylor and Francis).

I would also like to mention the administrative back up I received, particularly in Osnabrück. The archivists at the Niedersächsisches Staatsarchiv in Osnabrück were extremely helpful, especially Manfred Brockel, Tanja Rathsmann, Gerd Steinwascher and Sonja Wahlbrink. Oskar Reese and Isa Blönker delivered documents with perfect efficiency, while Heinrich Kampmeyer copied thousands of papers for me. At the Institut Für Migrationsforschung und Interkulturelle Studien, where I was based while carrying out research in Osnabrück, I would especially like to mention Sigrid Pusch and Jutta Tiemeyer who offered wonderfully efficient secretarial help and transcribed my interviews. At De Montfort I am extremely grateful to John Mackintosh and Steve Gamble for assistance with the maps and the typesetting of the book.

I would also like to thank a number of academic colleagues who have supported this project from its inception. Michael Burleigh gave initial encouragement after reading the first proposal, as did Stefan Berger, who has offered help throughout. Similarly, Tony Kushner has also taken an interest and offered support. Others I would like to mention include Kathy Burrell, Frank Caestecker, Neil Gregor, Donald MacRaild, John Martin, Jochen Oltmer, Colin Richmond, Gurharpal Singh and Johannes Dieter Steinert. I would like to single out Klaus Bade for his help from the start. Richard Evans has been with the project since its inception and has given much of his time, in various ways over the years, for which I am very grateful.

Finally I would like to express my gratitude to my family and friends. First of all, as ever, my parents, who looked after my house while I was away in Germany. Of friends, I would especially like to thank Andreas Demuth and Gerda Spellmeyer. It was through Gerda that I obtained a significant number of my interviewees, as her aunt, Renate Schlechtriem, still kept in touch with her classmates, from St Ursula in Osnabrück, who graduated just before the outbreak of World War Two. I obtained a list from Gerda and wrote to everybody on it. Andreas and Gerda also offered great friendship during all of my stays in Osnabrück. Above all I would like to thank my wife, Mundeep, who supported and encouraged me throughout.

Panikos Panayi
Oadby, Leicestershire

PREFACE

This book has the central aim of describing the continuities and discontinuities in the everyday life of all ethnic groups in the Lower Saxon town of Osnabrück between 1929 and 1949. These years witnessed a series of crises in the form of the collapse of the Weimar economy, the transformations of the peacetime Nazi years, the impact of World War Two and the consequences of post-War dislocation. The volume argues that all ethnic groups experienced great hardship during these years but recognizes the differences between native ethnic Germans, refugees, Jews, Romanies and foreigners established in post-War historiography.

The book has three distinct features, two of which are unique. First, it takes the perspective of *Alltagsgeschichte*, in an attempt to demonstrate everyday realities for people living in one German location in the years 1929-49. It is rooted in many of the standard histories, which have taken this approach, including the work of Detlev J. K. Peukert.[1] It uses a similar methodological approach to Robert Gellately[2] and Ian Kershaw,[3] amongst many others, who have focused on the local to inform the national, and is based on a wide range of official and unofficial sources. Nevertheless, like these, the centre remains the focus of the book. While the historiography helps to root the text, events in Osnabrück carry the narrative forward.

Its second, unique, feature lies in the time scale taken. Most works about Germany in the second quarter of the twentieth century focus purely upon the Nazi period, whether they consist of local or national studies. Some include the Weimar Republic, particularly its final years. But I have not found any studies that cover the period from the end of the Weimar Republic to the immediate aftermath of World War Two, which allows the narrative to trace the experiences of all of those who lived through the crises of the years 1929-49 in Osnabrück. In this sense, the book is broader in conception than the studies of Gellately or Kershaw, which focus on the relationship between the Nazis and the populace, or of the volumes of William Sheridan Allen[4] or Walter Struve,[5] which have the political history of the Third Reich at their core. My own volume traces all of the economic, social and political aspects of everyday life before, during and after the Nazis.

Equally unique is the study of all ethnic groups in one German town, or even in Germany, during this period.[6] Despite the centrality of race in Nazi ideology, I have found no study which has looked at the experiences of the differing ethnic groups in Germany during this period: native ethnic Germans (by which is meant German Roman Catholics and Protestants), German Jews, Romanies, foreign workers and prisoners of war, and German refugees from eastern Europe. The book examines the individual experiences of these groups over two decades (its main concern) as well as the relationships between them.

The volume therefore has two basic themes, which drive the narrative forward. First, the whole point of choosing the years 1929-49 is to illustrate issues of continuity and discontinuity in the everyday lives of Osnabrückers during four small periods when dramatic short term change deeply impacted upon their experiences. These periods consist of: the final years of the Weimar Republic, when the economic and political systems established in 1918, collapsed; the peacetime Nazi years, when the new regime instituted dramatic economic, social and political changes; World War Two, when mobilization and Allied bombing had a profound impact upon the residents of Osnabrück and other German towns; and the immediate post-War crisis, when Germans came to grips with the consequences of defeat.

The chapters on ethnic minorities pay particular attention to the impact of Nazi racial policy upon them. They also tackle, in addition to the issue of continuity and discontinuity, which varied from one group to another, the theme of inter-ethnic relations. State policy towards minorities changed under the Nazis, but how did this impact upon the ways in which individuals from different ethnic minorities interacted with the majority population?

The volume divides into four parts and ten chapters. Part I, introductory in nature, has two chapters. 'National and Local History in Germany' elaborates upon the central concepts of the volume and then moves on to discuss the unique features of Osnabrück, its history before 1929 and the historiography of the town during our period. 'The Economic Crisis and the Rise of the Nazis' is again introductory in nature, placing Osnabrück against the background of national events. It outlines the collapse of the national and local economy and then traces the rise of the NSDAP, focusing particularly upon electioneering, propaganda and violence in Osnabrück, which are themes covered in detail by local police reports.

Part II of the book tackles the experiences of ethnic majorities. Chapter 3 examines 'The Establishment of a New Society, 1933-39', under the three issues of 'Social and Economic Transformation', 'Propaganda' and 'Repression', which illustrate the changes which took place in Osnabrück and other German towns during these years. While real transformation did occur, it came with the elimination of opposition and a campaign of persuasion. The fourth chapter has the consequences of Allied bombing as one of its core themes. It further argues that mobilization went a considerable way towards denting the economic and social gains made before 1939, and also demonstrates how repression intensified. The fifth chapter turns to the aftermath of defeat, demonstrating how Osnabrück, in common with the rest of the country, had, by 1949, gone a significant way towards recovery from the trauma of Nazism and War in social, economic and political terms, but also illustrates the uncertainties and shortages of these years. The final chapter in Part II looks at the experiences of German refugees who arrived in Osnabrück after the War. Although they had a harder time than natives, the support of local institutions meant that they did not face the hostility experienced by ethnic minorities.

Part III examines these ethnic minorities. It begins with the experience of Jews, demonstrating how the relatively integrated group of the early 1930s, despite the antisemitism which existed, faced elimination as a result of Nazi racial policy, which led most of the Osnabrück community to leave by 1939. Those who remained faced deportation to eastern Europe during the War. Unlike communities in other German towns, Osnabrück Jewry re-established itself after the War, albeit on a smaller scale. Chapter 8 tackles the experience of Romanies by looking at the small number of files which have survived in the local archive. As the title suggests, the chapter specifically focuses upon 'The Continuity of Anti-Romany Discrimination', recognizing that it intensified under the Nazis, but demonstrating that it existed before 1933 and after 1945. The chapter on 'Foreign Workers and Prisoners of War' looks at the experience of the thousands of people who moved to Osnabrück from locations throughout Europe after 1939, making the town more 'multicultural', on a surface level, than it has ever been. The chapter demonstrates how Nazi racial policy marginalized and exploited these forced migrants. At the end of the War they took revenge on natives, even though many of the latter displayed sympathy towards them.

The 'Epilogue' places the history of Osnabrück in the years 1929-49 against the background of its development after 1949. It argues that those who survived the crises, moved from 'pain to prosperity', to experience the 'German economic miracle'. The Epilogue also deals with inter-ethnic relations, tracing the interaction of the different ethnic minority populations with the ethnic majority during the years 1929-49 and making comparisons with relations between Germans and ethnic minorities under the Federal Republic.

LEADING PERSONALITIES IN OSNABRÜCK, 1929-49

Berning, Wilhelm (1877-1955)
Born in nearby Lingen, Berning became the Roman Catholic Bishop of Osnabrück in 1914, holding the position throughout the Weimar Republic, the Third Reich and the first post-War decade.

Day, Geoffrey Herbert (1905-77)
Born in Worcester, this British colonel served as chief of the British Military Government in Osnabrück from April 1945 until September 1947.

Gaertner, Erich (1882-1973)
Born in Neckarbischofsheim, Gaertner became Mayor of Osnabrück in 1927 and held his position until the end of the Third Reich, when he faced arrest.

Karwehl, Richard (1885-1979)
Karwehl studied theology in Tübingen, Göttingen and Berlin, displayed sympathy for socialist ideas and became pastor of the *Paulskirche* in the working class Osnabrück area of Schinkel in the 1920s, opposing Nazi ideology during the following two decades.

Kolkmeyer, Erwin (1889-1961)
This native born watchmaker was one of the leading Nazis and antisemites in Osnabrück, joining the NSDAP in 1929 and serving as *Ortsgruppenleiter* of Osnabrück Altstadt from 1933-45.

Kühling, Karl (1899-1985)
This native-born leading journalist in Osnabrück during the Third Reich subsequently went on to write standard local histories of the town in the period between 1925-45, as well as a series of other more specific studies.

Landwehr, Ludwig (1897-1981)
A leading figure in the Osnabrück KPD during the Weimar Republic, he faced arrest for high treason in March 1933 and subsequently served a prison sentence of 15 months, after which he moved to Stuttgart. At the end of the War he found himself in the concentration camp in Buchenwald.

Marxer, Otto (1896-1942)
Born in Augsburg, this dentist took over as leader of the NSDAP in Osnbrück in 1925, but lost this position after a conflict with *Gauleiter* Carl Röver in 1933. He moved to Munich in the summer of that year, where he held a more senior position. He died on the Eastern Front in 1942.

Petermann, Johannes (1886-1961)
This member of the Catholic Centre Party, had served as deputy mayor of Osnabrück from 1926-38 and found himself appointed as the new Mayor after the arrival of the British Army in 1945. He held this position for just a few months as a result of promotion to *Regierungspräsident*, which he retained until 1951.

Rißmüller, Julius (1863-1933)
Born in Münden in Hanover, Rißmüller served as Mayor of Osnabrück from 1901-27.

Schierbaum, Heinrich (1883-1934)
Born in Voxtrup, just outside Osnabrück, this quack doctor founded the antisemitic *Stadtwächter* party, which poisoned civic politics in the town at the end of the Weimar Republic.

Map 1: Location of Osnabrück within the Nazi Gau Division

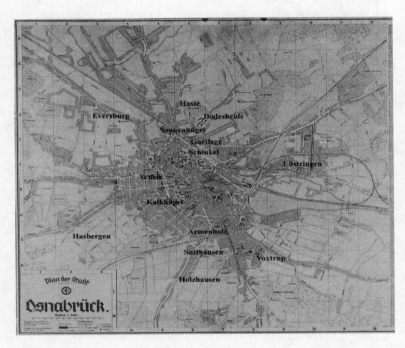

Map 2: Areas of Osnabrück

Map 3: Osnabrück City Centre During the Late 1930s.

PART I

INTRODUCTION

1

NATIONAL AND LOCAL HISTORY IN GERMANY, 1929-1949

Yet Another Book on the Nazis?

In his award winning volume on *The Third Reich*, Michael Burleigh wrote that the 'subject of one chapter in this book is the subject of over 55,000 titles, and many of the other chapters concern issues covered with something approaching this density'.[1] Virtually every subject area in the history of Nazism has received a significant amount of attention from scholars writing decades later and from contemporaries, both within Germany itself and also in Europe and the USA. Every aspect of the regime and every geographical region have received attention. By the early twenty first century, local and professional historians have dissected the experiences of virtually every ethnic group in a medium sized German town such as Osnabrück and have also covered nearly every aspect of the social history of the town in this period.

Do we therefore need another book on the history of the Third Reich? This seems a rather bizarre question in view of the time frame covered by the volume. It does not deal with the years 1933-45, but extends backwards to 1929 and forwards to 1949. While the core of the project clearly consists of the Nazi period, it is about the history of everyday life in Germany, as illustrated by the experiences of one German town, in the years 1929-49. The years before 1933 created the circumstances which allowed the Nazis to come to power, while the period after 1945 represented the aftermath of the defeat and collapse of the Third Reich.

From an *Alltagsgeschichte* perspective the first half of the twentieth century is a period of constant upheaval and trauma in Germany. Locations throughout the country went through a series of seemingly never ending crises from the upheavals of the First World War, the economic catastrophe of the Weimar Republic, the rise of the Nazis and the consequences of their political and racial cleansing, the horrors of the Second World War and the aftermath of the total defeat following total war.[2] The period 1929-49 witnessed the most traumatic events in central European history since the Thirty Years War three hundred years earlier.[3]

The present study contains, at its core, a case study of an individual medium sized German town. The experiences of its residents, both majorities and minorities, resemble those of other people who lived within German borders during the years 1929-1949. While the archival and other primary source material concentrates entirely upon Osnabrück, the historiographical context focuses upon Germany as a whole.

The volume can therefore be read as a narrative of one location, but also as a story of Germany between 1929-49. The local case study approach I am taking mirrors that used by other scholars studying Nazi Germany. For instance, the work of Robert Gellately, which concentrated on Würzburg and Düsseldorf as examples of the way in which the Gestapo operated.[4] The case studies of William Sheridan Allen dealt with the experience of Northeim in Hanover between 1922 and 1945[5] while Walter Struve tackled Osterode in the Harz mountains between 1918 and 1945.[6] All of these works, like the present one, accept that their centres have unique features. While they might represent 'German' experiences, they do not efface the centre upon which they focus.

Nevertheless, the present study differs from those of Allen and Struve because while they concern themselves mainly with political history, which I certainly do not ignore, I take a micro-historical approach which looks at individual lives and experiences, as well as focusing upon events which occurred in the town, particularly those which remain etched on the popular memory. This book is therefore an example of social history, of history from below, the ways in which tumultuous and traumatic events impacted upon one German town and its inhabitants. However, it is an example of one particular form of social history, which developed especially in Germany and which has had a particular focus upon the Nazi period, in the form of *Alltagsgeschichte*, the history of everyday life. This approach helps us to place ourselves at ground level within the minds of the individuals who experienced the events of the years 1929-49.

The book fits into a tradition which has counted some of the leading German historians within its ranks. The most important of these include Detlev J. K. Peukert, who produced several books which took this approach, using, once again, local case studies.[7] He concentrated especially upon opposition and did much of his work on the Ruhr.[8] *Alltagsgeschichte* has now become, in the German language historiography, a fairly conventional approach amongst both professional and popular historians. Some volumes have taken a national perspective, particularly the more populist ones,[9] while most focus upon particular locations[10] or themes, including women,[11] the consequences of Nazi medical policies,[12] and the local experience of the educational policies of the Third Reich upon elementary schools.[13]

How old is *Alltagsgeschichte*, how does it work and what disadvantages does it have? Some scholars have asserted that this form of history represents a reaction to the structuralism which characterized social and economic approaches, which had become dominant in alternative history by the 1970s, rooted in the Marxist tradition, which offered little scope for individuals to make themselves heard.[14] We could see the emergence of *Alltagsgeschichte* as part of the process of the death of the grand narrative which has happened as a result of the growth of postmodernism from the 1970s. The *Alltagsgeschichte* approach would encapsulate this process because it allows individual voices to make themselves heard.[15] On the other hand, one of its main practitioners, Peukert, would not have recognized this description, as he saw himself as a Marxist, pointing to the fact that a variety of alternative approaches had emerged by the 1980s.

Alltagsgeschichte focuses upon the micro, which helps to illustrate the macro. It almost takes an anthropological approach,[16] which centres 'on the actions and sufferings of those who are frequently labelled "everyday, ordinary people". What is foregrounded is their world of work and nonwork. Descriptions detail housing and homelessness, clothing and nakedness, eating habits and hunger.'[17] In essence, the historian attempts to reconstruct everyday realities for ordinary individuals.

In terms of sources, *Alltagsgeschichte* does not differ fundamentally from other social history. It uses a wide range of sources.[18] In his book on the 'Edelweiss Pirates', a youth opposition group in the Ruhr, Peukert's material includes Gestapo files. Stefan Riesenfellner has pointed to the importance of contemporary accounts, especially newspaper articles, in helping to reconstruct everyday life.[19] *Alltagsgeschichte* allows members of the group under scrutiny to speak for themselves. Oral history represents a major source for practitioners of *Alltagsgeschichte* because of its central aim of describing the experiences of ordinary people. 'The history of everyday life has also directed historians to look in a new way at sources such as diaries, memoirs, petitions from ordinary people, sermons and church visitations. Historians have been encouraged to look at them from the perspective of those involved'.[20] The personal memoir actually represents a central source for the history of everyday life. A few have survived on Osnabrück for our period.[21] Clearly, many of the individual sources described above would prove problematic in themselves because they often present the views of individuals. They therefore need balancing against other material.

Does the *Alltagsgeschichte* approach have any disadvantages, particularly when dealing with the Third Reich? A volume on this subject, originated from a colloquium in Munich attended by Martin Broszat, Detlev Peukert, Klaus Tenfelde and Heinrich August Winkler, all of whom agreed on the value of this approach.[22] Broszat, for instance, asserted that the relationship between politics and society could only be understood at the microhistorical level.[23] Winkler pointed out that, in a society in which free speech had disappeared, historians need to turn to new sources and new forms of research to get inside the minds of people who lived under the Nazis. *Alltagsgeschichte* especially allows a study of dissent and resistance under the Third Reich,[24] a point stressed by Peukert in the introduction to *Inside Nazi Germany*.[25]

Nine years after the colloqium in Munich the 39th *Historikertag* held a plenary session attended by 800 people which asked: 'What comes after the history of everyday life?'. The discussants, including Wolfgang Hardtwig, Jürgen Kocka, Hans Medick, Ute Daniel and Alf Lüdtke, reaffirmed their faith in the progress which the history of everyday life had made over the previous decade focusing upon specific methodological issues. Hardtwig looked at the pluralization of historical research and the increasing importance of the study of individuals. Medick stressed the importance of micro-historical studies in illustrating broader themes.[26] The 1992 *Historikertag* also provided impetus for a volume edited by Brigitte Berlekamp and Werner Röhr reassessing the importance of *Alltagsgeschichte* for the Third Reich. One essay in the volume focused especially upon the regional and local importance of this approach, with a section containing essays on individual locations.[27]

The present study represents a history of everyday life in one specific town between 1929 and 1949. It is not yet another book on the Third Reich because of its original features. The first of these consists of the *Alltagsgeschichte* approach. It will examine all aspects of the lives of Osnabrückers during the years under consideration. It will consider their economic situation, their social lives and their attitudes towards politics. It will also focus upon the changes which took place as a result of the rise and fall of the Nazis in political terms, such as the suppression of opposition, the elimination of racial undesirables, and the arrival of Allied troops. While I will provide background about the national and local level bureaucratic changes, my main concern consists of the consequences of these changes for ordinary people, i.e. ethnic cleansing through the eyes of a Jew or Romany, or the arrival of the British as experienced by a native German. The project also allows for the examination of the consequences of specific developments during these years such as the introduction of non-Hippocratic medical practices and, above all, the issue which impacted most upon the majority population, Allied bombing. I am therefore attempting to produce a portrait of the totality of life under the Nazis, using one town as the case study, with the aim of reconstructing the realities of German life between 1929 and 1949. The *Alltagsgeschichte* approach means that one of the central aims of the book, following Broszat, consists of the relationship between political developments and the individual's reaction to them. The volume aims at reconstructing the realities of the traumatic events of the years 1929-49. The *Alltagsgeschichte* approach may therefore not be original, but the totality of the approach is. In this way, the project differs from the single town studies of Allen and Struve, which primarily concerned themselves with politics.

A second departure of the project lies in its examination of the experiences of all ethnic groups in Osnabrück, an approach which does not seem to have been attempted elsewhere.[28] By dealing with the different ethnic groups on this local scale, we can compare the experiences which they endured and also examine the relations between them. The project proceeds along the ethnic lines drawn up by the Nazis in the form of German Aryans, Jews, Slavs and Romanies.[29] The present project also deals with the German refugees expelled from eastern Europe at the end of the Second World War, millions of whom made their way westward, with a small number finding their way to Osnabrück. By the time they had arrived the racial categories devised by the Nazis had disappeared.

But ethnic divisions in Germany neither originated with the Nazis nor ceased to exist with the collapse of the regime. The differences between Germans and Jews had established themselves from the medieval period as part of the legacy of Christianity and continued throughout the process of industrialization, despite emancipation and intermarriage.[30] At the same time, Romanies had faced persecution since their arrival in Germany in the fifteenth century.[31] Similarly, direct continuities exist between the persecution of eastern European workers during the Second World War and the history of German policies in eastern Europe, especially after the partitions of Poland at the end of the eighteenth century, when the future German state had acquired territory which it would hold until the end of the First World War.[32] The German nation state had imported labour, from both eastern and western Europe, from the end of the nineteenth century, shortly after its formation. All of the leading scholars on the history of labour importation have recognized the continuities in the history of this process, which continued after the end of the Second World War.[33]

This book therefore deals with the experiences of differing ethnic groups in a particular location through four political systems from the late Weimar Republic through the Third Reich, the Allied occupation to the foundation of the Federal Republic in 1949. It does not argue that each ethnic group experienced the same levels of persecution, exploitation or loss as a result of the rise of the Nazis. The vast amount of literature on Nazism stresses the differing experiences of racial insiders and outsiders, the latter clearly coming off worse than the former. This project does not challenge this assertion. What it does is to focus upon the everyday life of the differing populations to illustrate that everybody living on German soil between 1929 and 1949 experienced major upheaval.

Of course, no ethnic group in Germany had a uniform experience during the first half of the twentieth century and it would be erroneous to speak of sections of the population as if they consisted of monoliths. This applies more to the ethnic majority than the ethnic minorities. For the former, individual experiences varied according to two factors in particular in the form of political persuasion, which could mean imprisonment immediately after the Nazis came to power, and health, which could lead to sterilization or death. In addition, members of the ethnic majority could make choices about their relationship to the regime, usually determined by their family's allegiance. Thus, those from left wing backgrounds often opposed the Nazis in various ways, while a small percentage actively worked on behalf of the regime. In the ashes of 1945, all members of the ethnic majority found themselves losers, although at least they had survived and would witness a relatively quick recovery. In the immediate post-War period those German refugees who moved from the east faced greater problems than natives.

The experience of ethnic minorities remained more monolithic in the sense that they had fewer choices, although this applied more to some groups than others. The majority of Jews in Osnabrück actually managed to emigrate before the *Kristallnacht* pogrom of November 1938. Only a small minority therefore faced deportation to concentration and death camps after 1939. But the majority of Osnabrück Romanies went to Auschwitz in March 1943. The experience of foreign workers from both east and west transported to Osnabrück remained overwhelmingly bleak in the sense that they had to endure bad living conditions, working long hours hundreds or thousands of miles away from their families.

While this project revolves around the ways in which the different ethnic groups reacted to the crises which confronted them, particularly the Nazi regime, Section III also deals with relations between them. The examination of the attitudes of the majority towards the minority proves easier, however, than vice versa. Oral history and archival material allow us to achieve this task. The situation is more complicated in reverse because we know less about the attitudes of ethnic minorities towards Germans.[34] This interethnic approach will demonstrate, as the previous literature has done, that the actions of Germans towards minorities were complex.

The ethnic approach means that the project does not concern itself with the history of Osnabrückers born and living or having lived in the town between 1929 and 1949. Instead, the central focus, as the above discussion has made clear, consists of the lives of individuals who found themselves in the town in these years. This means that the experiences of Osnabrück males fighting on the eastern front do not concern us, unless these experiences affected relatives who remained in Osnabrück. But the project will reconstruct the lives of foreign workers in the town, as well as those of the ethnic majority and the refugees, in detail. In short, to reiterate, this is a history of the town of Osnabrück and those who lived within it between 1929 and 1949.

The timeframe of the project also makes it unusual and perhaps unique. Clearly, by picking the period 1929-49, Nazism remains at its core. But why go back and forward to the dates mentioned? On the one hand, we can see that the beginning and end of the project simply confirm the centrality of Nazism in the book. The late Weimar crisis represents the background to the rise of the Nazis, while the period 1945-9 forms the aftermath of the Third Reich. On the other hand, we can also see the years 1929-49 as a period during which three of the major crises of the first half of the twentieth century affected Germany. In a sense much of the nineteenth century in Germany, until 1914, represented a time of economic and political upheaval and transformation due to industrialization and political unification.[35] The second half of the twentieth century, on the other hand, became a period of extraordinary stability for West Germans, if not for those in the east who had to face the economic disaster caused by the collapse of communism and reunification during the 1990s.[36] But the first half of the twentieth century represents a period of constant crisis. In fact, we can count six crises, causing varying degrees of upheaval, which affected the German population between 1900 and 1949, four of which this book covers. First, the Great War, which resulted in the collapse of *Kaiserreich* and economic hardship.[37] Second, its aftermath, which meant extreme economic dislocation.[38] Third, the late Weimar crisis, which saw the end of democracy and high levels of unemployment. The peacetime Nazi years represent the next crisis, a period during which the new regime transformed the nature of German economy, society and politics. The Second World War is the most dramatic period in German history during the first half of the twentieth century. During these years the country experienced extreme dislocation, especially as a consequence of Allied bombing. There then followed the final crisis of the immediate post-War years when people rebuilt their lives.[39]

As well as a social history of Nazism, its immediate origins and its aftermath, the book also examines how a single town and the individuals within it coped with crisis of the most extreme kind, whether they formed part of a minority or the majority. The former could face loss of civil rights, exploitation, humiliation and deportation, while the latter would experience the consequences of Allied bombing. Although the book may attempt to deal with discontinuity in German history, it is, however, also concerned with continuities, examining the ways in which individuals survived the crises outlined above as well as tackling changes and continuation in local, regional and national economic, social and political development.

Two projects carried out during the course of the 1980s and 1990s would seem to question some of the original features suggested above for the present study. The first, under the leadership of Lutz Niethammer, focused upon the Ruhr[40] and the second tackled the Saarland, led by Klaus-Michael Mallmann and Gerhard Paul.[41] The former resulted in three volumes spanning the years 1930-60. Based upon more than 150 interviews, it aimed to trace personal experiences of residents of the Ruhr, a much larger area than Osnabrück town, from the end of the Weimar Republic to the first decade of the Federal Republic. In this way the project aims to examine 'people's histories and social culture',[42] with the aim of demonstrating the most important experiences in individual lives as perceived by individuals themselves. There are clear differences between this project and my own. First, and most obviously, the time period is different. I have chosen to end in 1949 because my core concern remains the impact of Nazism, unlike Niethammer, who tells us that he is trying to understand the history of the Federal Repubic by placing it in its immediate Nazi background.[43] Secondly, the methodology is highly dependent upon oral history because the Ruhr project was concerned with establishing how people saw the decades from 1930-60. However, this is just one way of tackling the history of everyday life. Peukert, Gellately and others have relied just as heavily upon written sources. Finally, the Ruhr project does not deal with ethnic minorities to any great extent, with the exception of one essay by Ulrich Herbert, examining attitudes towards foreign workers. The events in the Ruhr between 1930 and 1960 are seen through the eyes of the ethnic majority.[44] The project led by Paul and Mallmann is also different from mine. Again, it concerns itself with a significantly larger area, the Saarland. The chronology only covers the years 1935-45. It has, as its core, the theme of relationships between individuals and the Nazi state, with the three volumes covering different aspects of this theme. It pays considerable attention to racial issues. The project is concerned with reconstructing the realities of the time and therefore uses oral history along with other available written material. In these last three ways my own work follows a similar path, if not in its geographical and chronological coverage.

In terms of sources the present volume takes a more traditional approach, but tries to use as much material as possible in an attempt to give a balanced picture. The most important information consists of the archival documentation held in the *Niedersächsisches Staatsarchiv* in Osnabrück, the repository for information on the town and the administrative district of which it formed the centre. The main sources consist of governmental records of all descriptions on both the municipal and regional level, divided amongst different departments. Regional police records proved of particular importance for all manner of developments from the surveillance of Nazi activity at the end of the Weimar Republic through the observation of illegal activity during the Third Reich, to reports about criminality in the depression which followed the end of the regime.[45] The archive also contains some *Gestapo* documentation, but not of the nature of material extant in Würzburg or Düsseldorf used, for instance, by Gellately and Peukert. The Osnabrück archive does, however, contain a card index.[46] Gerd Steinwascher, the former archive director edited for publication the regular reports written by all branches of the local security apparatus, including the *Gestapo*, which he gathered from a variety of locations.[47] The archive in Osnabrück holds a particularly good set of medical records, which allow a detailed reconstruction of the processes of sterilization.[48] The other useful regional records include a series of miscellaneous legal cases.[49] This documentation covers the whole administrative region.

In addition, the archive holds numerous records simply concerned with the city itself, including an official miscellaneous group covering a vast time period.[50] Within this overarching category we can find useful and detailed documentation left by the local air raid police, with precise descriptions of every attack which took place and the damage caused, which allows us to reconstruct the day to day experience of the Air War, especially as it intensified during 1944 and 1945.[51] The NSO also houses miscellaneous unofficial records belonging to various individuals and organizations during our time period.[52]

The project also used other repositories. Within Osnabrück the archive of the Roman Catholic Bishopric of Osnabrück contains details of the charitable activities of the Church, as well as information on the controversial Archbishop Wilhelm Berning. The headquarters of the Lutheran Church in Hanover provided some details on ecclesiastical resistance to the Nazis. Some of the most interesting information used for this study consists of court records held in Münster and Hanover. The regional archive in the former contains the proceedings of the public prosecutor's office in Hamm in the Ruhr, which tried suspected Communist and Socialist activity throughout north and west Germany for the crime of high treason. Equally interesting is the documentation of the special court in Hanover, which tried cases of *Heimtücke* (treachery against the homeland) and *Volksschädlinge* (racial pests) under wartime legislation passed by the Nazis.[53]

As with other *Alltagsgeschichte* projects, archival information proves central for this project. The range of documentation available, some of it described above and most of it official, allows the reconstruction of everyday life in Osnabrück. Court and medical records give a clear account of the consequences of Nazi policy during our period, from the point of view of both the state and individual. In many cases archival documentation gets us into the minds of people who lived in the town during our period, because many files allow local people to speak for themselves.

The project also used newspapers, mostly held in the local archive, although, as the town came under British rule at the end of the War, the British Library in Colindale also contains those published in this period. The leading Osnabrück newspapers before 1945 consisted of the following: *Osnabrücker Tageblatt*, described as without political allegiance before 1933, but this changed under the Nazis and the Allies; the *Osnabrücker Zeitung*, an organ of the *Deutschnationale Volkspartei* before 1933, which survived until 1936; the *Osnabrücker Volkszeitung*, linked with the Catholic Centre party before 1933, which lasted until 1937; the Social Democratic *Freie Presse*, which survived until 1932; and the anti-Semitic *Stadtwächter*, linked to an eponymous local party. During the Third Reich the National Socialist *Neue Volksblätter* became the leading newspaper in Osnabrück. The newspapers which covered Osnabrück after 1945, licensed by the British, included the *Neues Tageblatt, Niederdeutscher Kurier, Niedersächsischer Kurier, Nordwest Nachrichten* and *Nordwestdeutsche Rundschau.*[54] The Nazi press clearly creates problems because of the issue of censorship. Although newspapers do not prove as useful as other sources used for this project, they provide some factual information. Those covering the Nazi years offer important information about how propaganda worked on a local scale.

The project also uses 26 interviews carried out with 33 people who lived in the town during the period under consideration. From the point of view of getting into the minds of individuals these would appear to represent one of the best of all possible methodological approaches. Nevertheless, interviews represent a complex source which needs to be treated with caution. The first problem consists of representation. The reminiscences of 33 people need contextualization against the wide ranging documentation used for the project. They essentially provide illustrative material. Unlike the project by Niethammer, this is not simply a narrative based upon oral testimonies. Interviews make up one of many sources. The sample I used is slightly skewed. Eleven interviewees consisted of women born between 1920 and 1923 who had attended the private Roman Catholic St. Ursula School. These women were contacted because they continued to have class reunions. The rest of the interviewees remain rather miscellaneous, although they do represent a reasonable cross section of the population of Osnabrück in the years with which the project deals. Most of them responded to an advert placed in the *Neue Osnabrücker Zeitung.* These interviewees consisted mostly of men, with a variety of social and political backgrounds and relationships with the Third Reich, as well as birth dates throughout the 1920s and 1930s. In addition to these fairly mainstream individuals, the research also involved talking to outsiders in the form of several socialists and communists, as well as one Jewish woman. The latter came by appealing to the local headquarters of the Jewish community and the former through academic contacts at the University of Osnabrück. The St Ursula graduates came from another academic contact at the University. After writing to 38 of the 39 people on a list (the other one had already died) I carried out eight interviews.

The Typicality of Osnabrück

Having spent much time discussing the methodology and chronology of the project, we can now turn to its geographical centre, Osnabrück. Why not choose any other town or city in Germany? What makes this medium sized town in north west Germany any different from any other location in the country? Why not choose another town in south or east Germany, for instance? What are the typical features of Osnabrück?

The main reason for choosing the town actually consisted of a purely practical, but very important, one. I already had considerable previous knowledge of it, at least of its contemporary situation because I had, by the time I began substantially working on this project, already lived in Osnabrück, on and off, for the previous nine years including one period of ten months based at the *Institut für Migrationsforschung und Interkulturelle Studien* at the University. This did not simply mean familiarity with the town, but also with the research material available.

It also made sense to focus upon Osnabrück because it reflects other towns of a similar size throughout Germany, despite its individual features. We could argue that Osnabrück resembles more German towns than either Osterode, chosen by Struve, or Northeim, used by Allen, both quite small in scale.[55] We could not, however, go as far as to say that Osnabrück is more typical of the German experience than the large industrial area of the Ruhr used by Peukert, although, it may not be less typical. The Ruhr contained several towns of over 400,000 including Dortmund, Essen, Düsseldorf, Duisburg and Wuppertal.

With a population of 94,700 in 1930, Osnabrück remains much smaller than these large cities. Nevertheless, it does represent a typical medium sized town, resembling others in Germany in the second quarter of the twentieth century. In 1931 the German Statistical Office divided German urban settlements into three categories. Group A, with 27 locations, counted towns with over 200,000. Group B listed twenty settlements of between 100,000 and 200,000. Group C counted 43 locations with populations of between 50,000 and 100,000 residents. Osnabrück housed the fifth largest number of people in this list in 1930. While a large percentage of Germans lived in major urban locations of over 100,000 people in the second quarter of the twentieth century, the experience of living in a medium sized town remained equally typical during these years.[56] In 1940 the German statistical office divided urban settlements into five categories. Group A1 simply consisted of Berlin with a population of 4,356,000 in 1939. Group A2 counted eleven locations with between 500,000 and 2 million, which, by this time, included Vienna. Group A3 consisted of seventeen settlements between 200,000 and 500,000. At number 63 stood Osnabrück, the smallest location of the 21 towns in Group B counting between 100,000 and 200,000. There then followed a further 49 locations with between 50,000 and 100,000 residents.[57] In 1949 the west German statistical office listed 427 towns with populations of more than 10,000. Group A1 consisted of Berlin and Hamburg, both counting more than 1 million residents. Group A2, Munich, Essen and Cologne, had more than 500,000. Group A3 listed sixteen locations with population counts of between 200,000 and 500,000. Osnabrück fitted into group B (at number 46 with a population of 97,745 in 1948) which listed 59 settlements of between 50,000 and 190,000. Group D counted 117 towns of between 20,000 and 50,000, while group E listed 227 locations of between 10,000 and 20,000.[58] The statistical evidence points to Osnabrück as, what we can describe as, a medium sized German town.

We might also regard Osnabrück as a good case study because of its denominational make up. Although it lies in Lower Saxony, it does not, like most settlements in this part of Germany, have an overwhelmingly Protestant majority. Instead, it divides fairly evenly between Catholics and Protestants. In 1925 it counted an evangelical population of 61 per cent and a Roman Catholic one of 36.9 per cent.[59] This reflects the history of the town as the centre of a Roman Catholic Archbishopric and also as one of the two cities, along with Münster, in which the Treaty of Westphalia was signed to end the Thirty Years War in 1648.

This leads us on to the size of ethnic minority communities in the city. The 435 Jews in 1933 would appear to make up a small percentage of the population of Osnabrück. Just 0.45 per cent, in fact. This remains considerably lower than that for the bigger cities, where members of this minority concentrated. Nevertheless, the Osnabrück figure resembles the overall percentage of Jews in the population in 1933, which stood at 0.76.[60] Similarly, the 54 Romanies residing in Osnabrück in the early 1940s,[61] reflect the fact that just 30,000 lived in the expanded German Reich in 1939.[62]

The Uniqueness of Osnabrück

While we might regard Osnabrück as a typical medium sized German town, we must also recognize that it has its own unique history and its own particular topographical, economic, social and political features. The town lies in the north west of Germany about forty five miles from the Dutch border and one hundred miles from the North Sea coast, giving it particularly north German characteristics, with damp winters and a temperate climate. It remains relatively isolated, surrounded by countryside (and the Teutoburger Forest to the south), with the nearest substantial settlements consisting of Oldenburg, Bremen, Bielefeld and Münster, the last two of which are the closest at nearly fifty miles away. In this sense it can certainly be regarded as provincial, as well as being medium sized; the nearest large cities, Bremen and Dortmund, lie over 60 miles away (see Map 1).

Within Osnabrück itself, the centre of the town, the *Altstadt*, has had an ecclesiastical heart, the seat of a Roman Catholic Archbishop, since the ninth century. By the twentieth century this heart consisted of the Roman Catholic Cathedral, the *Rathaus* and the Lutheran *Marienkirche* (see Map 3). The middle classes lived both to the north (Westerberg) and the south of this location (Großestraße and Johannisviertel). The centre of working class settlement consisted of Schinkel to the east of the city centre, with the railway station as a focal point. Beyond these two central areas of the *Altstadt* and Schinkel, lay the mixed social districts of Sonnenhügel and Gartlage to the north, and Wüste and Kalkhügel to the west and south, all of which expanded due to a housing boom during the 1920s[63](see Map 2).

An important landmark in the early history of Osnabrück came at the beginning of the ninth century when it became the seat of a Bishop. Its economic activities in the medieval and early modern period included metal work. In addition, it also became part of the Hanseatic League. The Thirty Years War tore it apart and it experienced occupation by Sweden, witch hunts and trials, as well as destruction. In fact, the signing of the Treaty of Westphalia in the town hall in 1648 represents the most significant landmark in the early modern history of Osnabrück. Tolerating both Catholicism and Protestantism, the Treaty meant that the two religious groups could live side by side in the town, in fairly equal numbers, even though, until the beginning of the twentieth century, they remained fairly distinct.

During the eighteenth century the town reached a low point in demographic terms, when its population fell to 5,923 at the end of the Seven Years War. From 1780 Osnabrück experienced a 'Golden Age', which involved economic growth in the linen and tobacco industry. One of the most important figures in the history of the town, Justus Möser, was born in 1720, writing his *Osnabrücker Geschichte*, 'the first German social and constitutional history' in the words of his twentieth century successor, Ludwig Hoffmeyer. The town underwent several significant developments during the Revolutionary and Napoleonic Wars. In 1795 Prussian troops moved in but French troops entered in 1803, finally leaving in November 1813. Two years later Osnabrück became the centre of a Hanoverian region, ultimately under Prussian control from 1866.

Table 1.1: The Employment Structure of Osnabrück in 1907

Employment Sector	Percentage of Osnabrück's Population Involved
Agriculture	2.58
Mining and Industry	47.01
Trade and Commerce	21.29
Domestic Service	1.62
Military, Administration and Professions	10.60
Pensioners and Unemployed	16.66

Source: Günther Höfelmann, Wilhelm van Kampen and Alfred Lindner, 'Industrialisierung und Arbeiterbewegung in Osnabrück vor dem Ersten Weltkrieg', in Wilhelm van Kampen and Tilman Westphalen, eds, *100 Jahre SPD in Osnabrück, 1875-1975: Ausgewählte Kapitel zur Geschichte der Arbeiterbewegung in Osnabrück* (Osnabrück, 1975), p. 21.

The nineteenth and early twentieth centuries witnessed the development of Osnabrück into the modern industrial town which it had become by the Weimar Republic, involving several major changes. In the first place, it experienced significant population growth, increasing from less than ten thousand in 1810 to over 70,000 by 1914. This formed the basis of industrialization, particularly during the second half of the century. Textiles and engineering played the central role in the future economic development of the town. Two major companies came into existence at this time, which continued as major employers into the twentieth century in the form of the Hammersen weaving mill, established in 1869, and the metallurgical firm *Osnabrücker Kupfer- und Drahtwerk*, founded in 1873. As the population increased and the town began to develop the structures of a modern urban settlement, employment in building and construction became important. In 1855 the first railway arrived as part of a stretch that joined the town with

Löhne in Westfalia. In the following year Osnabrück developed a connection with Emden, followed by further lines which joined it with Cologne in 1871 and Hamburg in 1874. The new railway station was opened in 1895. The second half of the nineteenth century also witnessed the development of many of the most important schools, the arrival of electricity and the development of a modern sanitation system. As a result of these transformations Osnabrück had an employment structure characteristic of an industrialized German town by the outbreak of the First World War, as indicated in Table 1.1.[64]

By the twentieth century political administration in Osnabrück operated at a series of levels, which continued into the Weimar and Nazi period. At the top lay the *Reich*. Below that came the individual states which went to form the newly unified German territory, in this case Prussia. However, Prussia consisted of areas previously taken over during its expansion from the seventeenth century, in our case consisting of Hanover. Below, this level came the *Regierungsberzirk*, or regional government, which played a large role in the implementation of legislation originating further up. Even lower came the *Kreis*. Osnabrück city government operated at this level, with its own democratically elected officials and town council before and after the Nazis, as well as a Mayor, subservient to the *Regierungspräsident* (perhaps regional president, although literally government president). At the higher levels the Nazis introduced the *Gau*, with Osnabrück falling into Weser Ems. Lower down the Nazis operated through the implementation of various police organizations, while the British occupation also introduced changes. In keeping with German political development between 1871 and 1949, government of the town worked from the top down so that the *Regierungspräsident* essentially acted as a representative of the regional and national government, through whom instruction from further up filtered.

One of the most significant political changes during the nineteenth century, reflecting the national picture, consisted of the rise of the SPD in the town, which took place as a result of industrialization and the consequent growth of a working class in Osnabrück.[65] By 1890 the SPD had become the largest party in Osnabrück, with 37.8 per cent of the vote in the *Reichstag* poll of that year, reflecting the breakthrough at the national level. Trade union and strike activity intensified by 1914.[66]

The First World War meant Osnabrück experienced economic problems faced throughout Germany, with the introduction of rationing in 1914 and deterioration in the quality and supply of food due to the Allied blockade and the harsh winter of 1917.[67] This background and the defeat of 1918 led to the November Revolution of that year. A workers and soldiers council came into existence on 8 November but by the beginning of 1919 the signs of the upheaval disappeared, as Weimar democracy became established.[68] Osnabrück, like the rest of Germany, suffered during the early Weimar economic crisis, particularly as a result of the rising inflation, although this situation changed following the currency stabilization of 1923.[69] But the number of unemployed had reached 2,000 in November 1923, while those working part time also increased. However, as the 1920s progressed the figures fell as the German economy and industrial production increased.[70]

Table 1.2: The Employment Structure of Osnabrück in 1925

Employment Sector	Number of Osnabrückers Involved	Percentage of Osnabrück's Population Involved
Craft and Industry	18,938	56.80
Trade and Commerce	12,818	38.40
Theatre, Music, Acting and Teaching	321	0.96
Health Care	1,143	3.43
Other	125	0.37
Total	33,345	100.00

Source: Walter Kolkmeyer, *Die Wirtschaftliche Verflechtung der Stadt Osnabrück* (Hanover, 1931), p. 31.

By 1925 Osnabrück counted 89,076 people, of whom 46,292 consisted of women, while men totalled 42,787, with the former constituting 52 per cent of the population. A total of 11,887 women worked in the town. They played a particularly significant role in the textile, food processing and paper industries. In all 33,345 people found themselves employed in Osnabrück in 1925, concentrated overwhelmingly in craft, industry and commercial occupations, as indicated in Table 1.2. The largest industrial occupations continued as those which had developed during the nineteenth century, so that 6,725 worked in metal production, 3,236 in clothing, 2,473 in construction and 1,349 in textiles.[71] The growth of a welfare state under the Weimar Republic meant that the city authorities helped nearly 14,000 people in 1928, which included pensioners, war victims and school meal recipients.[72]

Religion was important in Osnabrück, especially as it was the seat of an Archbishop, with a diocese spreading to the North and Baltic Seas. But while the Roman Catholic Cathedral may represent the grandest building in the *Altstadt*, this part of the town is also littered by a number of impressive Evangelical churches, especially *Katherinenkirche* and the *Marienkirche*. The late Weimar years actually saw significant religious building including the completion of the *Paulskirche* in Schinkel in 1929. Equally, the Roman Catholic Church also oversaw construction, including the completion of a new children's home on 18 April 1931.[73] The dominant personality in Roman Catholic life in Osnabrück consisted of Archbishop Wilhem Berning, who held his post from 1914-55. During the Third Reich religion represented the main alternative social milieu to Nazi indoctrination and repression in Osnabrück. Berning, on the Roman Catholic side, and the oppositional evangelical pastor, Richard Karwehl, who had responsibility for a parish in the working class area of Schinkel, acted as central figures in the religious resistance which occurred.

Largely independently of the Churches, both the working and middle classes of the town had developed a rich cultural life by the end of the 1920s. Sporting clubs covering football, handball, swimming and athletics had emerged from the end of the nineteenth century, which meant that public swimming baths and sporting fields had developed throughout Osnabrück. Much of this activity was connected with the SPD milieu.[74] For middle class cultural activity the opening of the city theatre in 1909 represented an important landmark.[75] The town also had a rich orchestral life and its own city museum from 1890, together with a public library opened in 1902.[76]

The main political development in the history of Osnabrück during the Weimar Republic consisted of the end of the period of office of Dr Julius Rißmüller as mayor: he finally resigned in 1927 after 26 years in office. A professional civil servant, without any apparent party allegiance, he had assumed the position in 1901 and gained the nickname of 'Kompromißmüller', because of his ability to survive the dramatic political changes of his term of office. His period had seen significant improvement in the life of Osnabrück including the arrival of electricity and trams. In his place in 1927 came Dr Erich Gaertner, chosen by an electoral commission, who would hold his position until 1945. Like his predecessor, he was a professional civil servant, but had also received the Iron Cross for service as a frontline officer during the Great War. His period of office would witness even more dramatic changes than that of Rißmüller.[77]

At a party political level the SPD remained the most significant grouping during the Weimar Republic, counting most deputies in the town chamber. Its membership had declined from 1,730 in 1919 to 1,200 by 1927.[78] For most of the 1920s the second largest grouping consisted of the Catholic Centre Party, reflecting the denominational make up of the city, followed by the more right wing *Deutschnationale Volkspartei* and the *Deutsche Volkspartei*.[79] At the other end of the political spectrum the KPD remained a small party in Osnabrück during the 1920s, counting a few hundred members and mustering just a small percentage of votes in elections.[80]

Meanwhile, the NSDAP in Osnabrück seems to have emerged in 1924 from a group called the *Bund Fredericus Rex*, which, in turn, grew from the Osnabrück *Freikorps*. The dentist Otto Marxer became the leading figure in the newly formed Osnabrück NSDAP. A visit by Goebbels in November 1925 attracted an audience of 400. Adolf Hitler paid his first visit to the town in June 1926, but this appears to have caused little stir at a time when the fortunes of the Nazis stood at a low ebb. By this time the Osnabrück SA counted 35 members. A local branch of the Hitler Youth also existed, together with a propaganda 'cell'. In Prussian elections on 20 May 1928 the Nazis obtained just 3.6 per cent of the vote in Osnabrück, exceeding the Prussian average of 2.6 per cent.[81] Therefore, on the eve of our period the Nazis remained in Osnabrück, as in the country as a whole, a marginal party. The events of 1929 would have the same impact on the local as on the national scale, as the city became a whirlpool of activity involving all sections of the political spectrum.

At the end of the Weimar Republic Osnabrück may be seen as a reflection of medium sized German towns throughout the Reich in terms of its population and ethnic constitution. However, it had is own unique history and characteristics, which, as we shall see, influenced the actions of those who resided in the town as much as the dictates of the regime under which they lived and the economic circumstances which they experienced. But what were the unique characteristics, which helped to distinguish Osnabrück from other medium sized German towns? First, geographical location. Its position in north Germany is clearly not unusual, but its relative isolation, fifty miles from Bielefeld and Münster and 60 miles from Bremen and Dortmund, the closest cities, is. This meant, for instance, that the post-War hunger crisis did not impact upon the town in the same way that it did upon contiguous urban conurbations. The political history of Osnabrück is not especially unusual, although it did have a small KPD. In religious terms, the division between Roman Catholics and Protestants does make it different in the north German setting. Religious allegiance played a significant role in determining attitudes towards the NSDAP (see Chapters 3 and 4). Roman Catholics tended to distance themselves from the Third Reich, both because of the existence of the Catholic Centre Party, and, after 1933, the alternative allegiance which their religion offered, especially under the local leadership of Archbishop Berning. However, as we shall see, the picture was complicated, partially, in the evangelical case, because of the influence of Richard Karwehl. Economically, Osnabrück expanded through textile, clothing and metallurgical production from the end of the nineteenth century, together with construction. Local firms such as Hammersen and the OKD had emerged, but Osnabrück also acted as home to branches of larger companies such as the automobile makers Adler. Socially, the structure of the town reflects other similar German locations, with an employment concentration in industry, commerce and trade. A large working class, living in its own quarters, was distinguished from the middle classes. Over the years 1929-49 Osnabrück and its inhabitants would face a series of profound changes.

The Historical Memory of the Years 1929-1949

An examination of the historiography of the town before, during and after the Nazis reveals that local enthusiasts have studied virtually all aspects of its development. Scholars and students at the University, above all those working with the Professor of Modern History, Klaus J. Bade, have involved themselves in this process. Thus, we already have much published information on the history of the town between 1929 and 1949.

In fact, we need to go back to the Second World War to trace the beginning of the historiography of the town in our period, as the study of the consequences of the Third Reich upon it actually began while the regime still existed. In 1939 the local authorities began to put together a chronicle of Osnabrück's experiences during the War and produced a manuscript in seven parts, together with appendices, all now held in the city archive.[82] In fact, this *Kriegs-Chronik* survived into peacetime and became the *Stadt-Chronik* (or city chronicle), also held in manuscript form in the NSO.[83] This source provides much information on all aspects of everyday life in the town during the years it covers.

The first major published studies of the period covering the Third Reich appeared in the 1960s, when Karl Kühling wrote two books on the subject, dealing with the years 1925-45. Kühling was one of the leading journalists in the town under the Nazis, but survived denazification unscathed. He based his two books on newspaper articles he had previously written. These cover all aspects of the history of Osnabrück in the years under consideration, and are solid scholarly accounts, which educated Osnabrückers would have read.[84] More recently, another local historian, Wido Spratte, has published two volumes focusing upon the social history of the town, more specifically the consequences of bombing and the situation of Osnabrück during the post-War dislocation, focusing upon the local population as victims.[85] Subsequently, a study of the post-War refugees who moved to the town has appeared, edited from the *Institut für*

Migrationsforschung und Interkulturelle Studien at the University, an altogether more scholarly exercise.[86]

Examining the Nazi period specifically, a wide range of publications have emerged in recent years, often small in scale. Thus we can point to three volumes which detail the events of the period through the position of the generally accepted victims of the Third Reich. These essentially aim to retrace the years 1933-45 by examining particular aspects of the history of the period in detail.[87] One of these volumes is published by an organization which has issued a series of other pamphlets which have focused upon specific aspects of the Third Reich and provide important background information on the years 1933-1945 in the form of the *Antifaschistischer Arbeitskreis Osnabrück*. The pamphlets from the 1980s covered resistance, the SPD and foreign workers, produced by a variety of authors.[88] These highly critical accounts, some of them unbound, would have appealed to a few politically motivated anti-fascists. They contrast with the works of Kühling and Spratte, issued by Wenner, the local publisher.

The historiography of Osnabrück during our period has increasingly focused upon specific subject areas and groups. This partly results from the efforts of the local historical journal, the *Osnabrücker Mitteilungen*, edited by the director of the archive, which has published focused scholarly articles on the Nazi period and its aftermath for several decades. It has, for instance, produced several essays on the position of the Churches under the Third Reich.[89] Those on the Roman Catholic Church have now been superseded by a monumental work on Bishop Berning under the Nazis.[90] Separately from this, the local pastor Richard Karwehl has also received much attention because of his opposition to the evangelical establishment under the Third Reich.[91] Meanwhile, as previously mentioned, Gerd Steinwascher has published one of the most important volumes on the town and the surrounding administrative district during the Third Reich, containing reports of the local *Gestapo* between 1933 and 1936.[92] At the same time Eva Berger has tackled sterilization and euthanasia under the Nazis, although this forms one aspect of more general histories she has written on medicine in the town over a longer period.[93] This illustrates how open and detailed knowledge of Nazism has become even on a local level.

All of the leading political parties in Osnabrück have received attention from local scholars, a process which predated the focus upon the social history of the town, although some of the studies are not even published. The main study on the rise of the Nazis surfaced in 1975, as an unpublished manuscript[94] but no major book exists on the Nazis in Osnabrück, although the work of Kühling covers this theme. Other right wing parties have also received attention,[95] especially the antisemitic *Stadtwächter*. A manuscript exists on this movement,[96] but it also attracted attention from Jeremy Noakes.[97] As part of the memorialization process for the victims of the Third Reich, a volume on the SPD was published on the one hundredth anniversary of the foundation of this organization,[98] as well as pamphlet focusing specifically upon the Nazi years.[99] Similarly, trade unions[100] and the KPD[101] during our period have not been ignored. But while the book on the former is a solid and scholarly account, that on the latter is a sketchy unpublished manuscript.

Ethnic minorities in the town have also received attention, above all the Jews. Together with several minor studies of the Osnabrück Jews, two major ones have also appeared. The first, by Karl Kühling, originally published in 1969, traced the history of this minority from its medieval origins to 'The Great Death', which occurred under the Nazis.[102] In 1989 there followed a remarkable book by Peter Junk and Martina Sellmeyer, which focused upon the consequences of the Third Reich for the Jewish population and traced the history of virtually every Jew who lived in the town in 1933, an excellent example of micro history produced by two local historians in a professional way.[103] Attention has also focused upon the most famous Jewish resident of Osnabrück, the artist Felix Nussbaum.[104]

The focus upon Jews reflects the more general level of attention received by this community under the Nazis on a national level, which meant that local historians turned to them fairly soon after the end of the War. More recently, foreign workers have begun to receive attention. A useful pamphlet appeared in 1982, under the auspices of the *Antifaschistischer Arbeitskreis*.[105] By the end of the 1990s, coinciding with the move for the compensation of former Nazi labourers, this group began to receive much attention. One local schoolteacher of Dutch origin, Volker Issmer, published two books focusing on his compatriots who found themselves working for the Nazis in the town during the Second World War, one of which dealt with the camp in Ohrbeck, just outside Osnabrück.[106] In addition, two scholars working at the University, Michael Gander and Ute Weinmann, embarked upon a research project which involved travelling to Belorussia and the Ukraine to interview people who had formerly worked in the town.[107] The publicising of their work in the *Neue Osnabrücker Zeitung* brought the plight of the foreign workers to the attention of Osnabrückers.

Nevertheless, amongst all of the research which has focused upon both ethnic majorities and minorities in Osnabrück between 1929 and 1949, local historians have not paid attention to one group in the form of the Romanies.[108] This, however, has not meant that the city administration has ignored them. In post-War Germany the memory of the Holocaust has become central in national consciousness on both a national and civic level. Therefore, the town square now has two plaques, which commemorate the victims of the Nazis. One of these lists the Jews deported from the town while the other contains the names of the Romanies who suffered the same fate. In this aspect of the civic memory the latter therefore carry the same weight as the former.

In fact, we can see the focus on the period 1929-49 in Osnabrück as part of the remembering process which has taken place for the victims of the Nazis on a national scale since the end of the War. Liberal German nationalism since 1945 essentially revolves around the idea of recreating a new form of identification in which remembering the crimes of the Nazis forms a central plank.[109] In Osnabrück this has involved local historians producing books on all aspects of the consequences of the Nazi regime, often published by the leading civic institutions involved in the process of remembering in the form of the city museum and the city archive, and has also involved the civic authorities erecting plaques for the victims of Nazism.

Nevertheless, not all of those who write about the years 1929-49 have the memory of the crimes of the Nazis as their main concern. The volumes of Spratte, for instance, focus upon the problems which the ethnic majority experienced. At its most basic and banal level in Osnabrück, history has been popularised by Edgar Schroeder, who, interestingly, has not produced a volume on the Third Reich but has focused upon the positive aspects of the history of the town.[110]

Spratte and Schroeder are not the only writers to have concentrated upon the ethnic majority in our period. Several other historians have examined the situation of ethnic Germans at the end of the War.[111] It is tempting to see them as part of a mainstream of local amateur historians who have little concern with Nazism and its victims but choose, instead, to focus either upon the positive development of Osnabrück, in the case of Schroeder, or the local ethnic Germans as victims of the Allies, particularly in the case of Spratte. In the foreword to his book on the air war over Osnabrück, Spratte writes: 'This relentless war against children, women and old people often exceeded the suffering and distress on the front'.

The development of Osnabrück in our period therefore appears to have received full coverage from a variety of scholars interested in all aspects of the town's history. Virtually no ethnic group or section of the population appears to have escaped the attention of historians. Majorities and minorities all have their own narratives, written by a variety of professional and amateur historians. The works of Schroeder and Spratte are available in all of the Osnabrück bookshops, as is the study of Junk and Sellmeyer on the fate of the Jews, indicating that the local popular memory encompasses both majorities and minorities. While the work of Schroeder is superficial, much of the rest of the local literature can, at worst, be described as solid and informed, and, at best in the case of Junk and Sellmeyer, outstanding local studies.

This therefore leads us to ask, as we did at the beginning, whether we need a new study with Osnabrück as its focus. The answer remains yes because of the *Alltagsgeschichte* approach taken by the present volume (although the books of Spratte and the one edited by Bade, Meier and Parisius would fit into this tradition) and because of its uniqueness in examining the experiences of all ethnic groups in one location, as well as its time frame. Such an approach allows us to focus upon the two key themes of change and continuity, through the different regimes which controlled Osnabrück between 1929 and 1949, and inter-ethnic relations.

2

THE ECONOMIC CRISIS
AND THE RISE OF THE NAZIS

The Late Weimar Crisis

In the classic historiographical divisions of twentieth century Germany, the late Weimar Republic represents a compact period, characterized by two overwhelming realities, which impacted upon all geographical areas, all ethnic groups and most individuals. These realities consisted of the economic crisis, sparked off by the Wall Street Crash in 1929, and the rise of the Nazis from a marginal party to the largest political grouping, seizing power at the start of 1933. The Wall Street Crash immediately impacted upon the economic and political situation, which had never proved particularly stable at any time under the Weimar Republic. The years 1929-32 simply represented the death throes of this unpopular regime.

The economic crisis resulted in a rise in unemployment and the collapse of businesses in Osnabrück. Local unemployment statistics mirrored those at the national level. Much information survives upon the political collapse, upheaval and violence in Osnabrück during these years. The Nazis had become the largest party here by 1933. Their rise had involved an increase in political violence, typical of that described by scholars of other parts of Germany.[1] The period 1929-33 represented one of intense political activity, with regular elections at all levels of government from municipal to Presidential, as dictated by the Weimar constitution. The constant failure of coalition government, the electoral system based upon proportional representation, the use of Presidential power by Hindenburg and the scheming of politicians from a wide range of political parties to reach the top of the greasy pole made stable government impossible.[2]

The late Weimar period meant the intensification of political activity in every urban location in Germany, including Osnabrück, where political meetings seemed to occur on a daily basis as messiahs vied with each other for the purpose of attracting converts. These political ideologues came from all parts of the political spectrum and included Nazis and Communists, as well as representatives of the more central political parties such as the SPD, the DVP and the DNVP.

Osnabrück had a rather quirky development because of the emergence of an extremist political party, the *Stadtwächter*, essentially a one man show under the leadership of Dr Heinrich Schierbaum, which made a breakthrough in 1929 and helped to radicalise politics in the town. Partly concerned with what it saw as local political corruption, this party of the middle classes also peddled antisemitism in its eponymous newspaper, which matched that which the Nazis circulated. The survival of copies of this publication and the absence of similar local Nazi material suggests that the *Stadwächter* played more of a role in the rise of antisemitism in Osnabrück before 1933 than the NSDAP.

The economic and political events of 1929-32 resulted in traumatic changes for individuals. The rise in unemployment meant personal hardship for thousands of people in the town, as did the increase in short term working. The political upheaval may not have had an impact upon such a large percentage of the population, but only the most apathetic of individuals could have failed to notice the rise in political activity. Thousands attended these meetings, many in desperation because of their own economic circumstances, or out of fear of what would happen if the other side seized power.

Economic Collapse

Although some growth occurred during the Weimar Republic, most historians have seen the whole period as one of economic stagnation. Some phases of the Weimar economy saw more productivity and lower inflation than others. Thus the period 1919-24 was characterized by post-War stagnation followed by booming inflation, while, during the years 1924-9, after the implementation of the Dawes Plan to ease German reparations payments, as well as an upswing in the world economy, the situation 'was not quite as bad' as 'the periods immediately before and after'.[3] While growth occurred between 1924 and 1929, it remained slower than that in other industrial states.[4] Peukert wrote that: 'Structural mass unemployment and poor economic growth are the two most visible symptoms of Weimar's "sick economy"'.[5] He placed much stress on global economic factors as responsible for stagnation, but also pointed to internal problems. 'It was often argued at the time that the relatively high share of the economy taken by wages acted as a check on growth', a hotly debated subject by economic historians, although Peukert argues that secure growth could have solved problems between employers and workers.[6] Other factors also held back the Weimar economy, including reparations, again a controversial issue amongst experts,[7] as well as the fact that the German economy was so dependant upon US loans.

This last fact meant that Germany suffered particularly as a result of the Wall Street Crash because American banks called in their loans and refused to offer any new ones.[8] All economic indicators after 1929 illustrate the extent to which the economy ground to a halt. Production and investment fell. Bank collapses occurred in 1931, triggered by the closure of the Austrian *Creditanstalt* in May of that year.[9] Wages fell, as profits declined, although deflationary pressures meant that workers did not experience the fall to the same extent that they could have done.[10]

Mass unemployment 'was by far the most conspicuous feature of the crisis' and the one that impacted most upon 'ordinary' Germans. Short-time working and the fall of wages also had negative consequences. The 8.5 per cent unemployment rate in 1929 had risen to 14 per cent in 1930, 21.9 per cent in 1931 and a staggering 29.9 per cent in 1932.[11] Peukert pointed out that blue and white collar workers suffered most. 'Among them, in turn, workers in the building industry and in heavy industry fared worst. As a whole, collieries and plants were shut down, industrial communities often lost their sole source of employment'. Both men and women suffered. 'By 1933 many people could look back on five years without work.' As in all cases of unemployment, the crisis did not simply result in a fall in living standards, but also in psychological scars due to the lack of a structured working day and a loss of prestige.[12]

The Economic Crisis in Osnabrück

The economic meltdown which occurred on a national and global scale after 1929 affected locations throughout Germany, including Osnabrück, where business failed, unemployment rose and increasing numbers of people received welfare payments. While the second and third of these manifestations left traces in archives and newspapers, it proves more difficult to reconstruct the collapse of the Osnabrück economy from 1929.

The year before the coming of the crisis did not seem to suggest what would follow. In the late 1920s the local authorities had financed the construction of 970 homes.[13] Projects begun at the end of the 1920s continued into the 1930s, including the completion of a housing estate on the Sonnenhügel, as well as the building of the employment office, which ironically opened in the first summer of the economic crisis, 1930.[14] But the number of homes built with public funds had fallen to just 263 in 1930.[15] Other indicators from the end of the 1920s did not suggest a coming crisis. At the end of 1929 one in three Osnabrückers had an account with the city savings bank, containing an average of RM720.[16] One of the biggest employers in the town, the engineering firm of *Osnabrücker Kupfer- und Drahtwerk*, managed to pay a dividend of 6 per cent on a capital stock of RM9,600,000 in 1927-8.[17]

But the years 1929-33 were characterized by a constant decline in orders for Osnabrück firms and by severe domestic and international competition. This resulted in a dramatic cutback in operations, which meant that serious struggles over wages occurred.[18] At the 1932 annual meeting of the steel making firm Klöckner, the business year 1931-2 was described as 'the most catastrophic...for half a century', with a loss of RM10 million.[19] One of the most obvious consequences of the downturn in the metallurgical sector consisted in the rise of unemployment, as well as a halt in salary increases and pay cuts. In 1931 the Osnabrück *Stahlwerk* cut its salaries by ten per cent. The number of people employed in the metal industry declined from 11,076 to 7,512 between September 1923 and September 1930. In fact, during the latter year one in four of the unemployed in Osnabrück consisted of metal workers.[20] The textile sector in the town underwent a similar crisis. The biggest firm, Hammersen, introduced part-time working in January 1929, meaning reduced wages.[21]

Unemployment rose in Osnabrück as in the rest of the country as indicated in Table 2.1, peaking at 10,579 in January 1933. The employment office in Osnabrück gave details of the sectors affected in the *Regierungsbezirk* on 15 January 1930. The 7,657 people counted consisted of 6,575 men and 1,082 women. The areas most directly affected included the metal industry counting 1,074 men and 27 women out of work, construction (1,739 men), labouring of various types (1,666 men and 125 women), while 314 male and 141 female professionals also experienced joblessness.[22]

What did these statistics mean in human terms? Information from the health office in Osnabrück actually indicates that the number of children who died before they reached their first year, fell from 1,242 in 1931 to 1,126 in 1932 but then rose to 1,573 the year after. The figure peaked at 2,271 in 1935.[23] The overall death rate actually decreased between 1929 and 1932, falling from 12.06 per thousand in 1929 to 8.52 in 1932. This slight fall in death rates would suggest that the rise in unemployment had no impact upon the health of the local population although the 1932 annual report of the Osnabrück health office, which produced the death rate statistics, also pointed out that: 'The nutritional condition of wide sections of the population has clearly deteriorated in comparison with the previous year' and that 'women and mothers who give everything to their children...are suffering especially'.

The same report mentioned the existence of welfare support for women and mothers in Osnabrück.[24] In fact, while the provision of welfare may not have prevented people falling into poverty, it did, in what remained an advanced industrial state, mean that people would not starve, even though some individuals received no support at all, especially following the austerity package introduced by Chancellor Brüning in 1931. Although much of the assistance came from private sources, the Weimar Republic provided for large numbers of groups requiring assistance, including war veterans, pensioners, mothers and the unemployed. While the national state 'created the legal framework for the public welfare system in the Weimar Republic, local governments assumed the major responsibility for welfare activities'.[25] This system may have worked during the years of relative stability, but it came under extreme strain after 1929.[26] As the unemployment insurance scheme faced increasing pressure, crisis welfare payments became the norm. The increase in the number of people out of work also resulted in a decrease in the level of benefits. These latter developments also occurred as a result of the deflationary policies pursued by the Brüning and von Papen governments.[27]

Osnabrück during the early 1930s reveals an increase in the number of people receiving welfare payments of various types from both the local state (see Table 2.1) and charities, together with a decrease in the amount of money which they obtained. In 1929 the town spent around RM100,000 on the support of the unemployed and needy.[28] By February 1930 the city had to pay for those individuals who had not gathered enough national insurance contributions. The employment office found itself providing a total of RM11,660 in this month to 3,401 people (2,961 from unemployment benefit and 440 from crisis payments), which went towards the cost of food, rent, coal, clothes, lighting and medical care.[29]

A meeting of the Osnabrück welfare committee in October 1930 revealed the way in which the crisis caused by unemployment had deepened. The head of this body, Senator Schulte, declared that: 'The coming winter will probably be the most difficult of the last decade.' The levels of people out of work did not simply mean an increase in the number of those who needed support, but also meant a loss in taxation contributions, creating a financial crisis for the civic authorities. Schulte believed that one in nine of the population of Osnabrück obtained some sort of assistance from the town authorities, a total of about 2,200 people. In order to meet its obligations it needed to raise an extra RM700,000 in revenue.[30]

By September 1931 a total of 6,043 Osnabrückers received either unemployment benefit or crisis payments. By this time communal kitchens had come into existence to provide food for those in need. As a consequence of the rise in unemployment, the fall in revenues, and the general crisis, the town had overspent by RM600,000 in 1931 in its attempt to maintain welfare support.[31] The city authorities did not simply supply financial support. At the end of 1931 mothers of children affected by the crisis could obtain vouchers from the city children's office, which entitled them to half a litre of milk per day for each of their children below the age of seven. In 1930 this body had distributed around 140,000 litres of milk.[32] Not surprisingly, the financial situation in the town continued to deteriorate as a result of the downturn in economic activity. The budget for the year 1932 worked on the basis of an income of RM20,400,000 and on outgoings of RM22,180,000 despite measures to cut down expenditure.[33]

Table 2.1: Total Number of Unemployed in Osnabrück, 1929-33

Date	Number of People Unemployed	Number of People Receiving Benefit
9 January 1929	3,500	2,899
17 April 1929	2,478	1,899
17 July 1929	2,066	1,454
9 October 1929	2,065	1,464
15 January 1930	3,630	2,780
30 April 1930	3,482	2,770
31 July 1930	3,740	2,410
31 October 1930	4,204	2,677
31 January 1931	6,106	3,868
20 April 1931	6,233	3,599
20 July 1931	5,962	3,263
12 October 1931	6,706	4,134
31 January 1932	8,335	5,522
30 April 1932	8,396	4,862
31 July 1932	7,688	3,904
31 October 1932	7,890	2,955
31 January 1933	10,579	4,893

Source: NSO Rep 430-101-7-43-331, Volumes 6-9, 'Politische Wochenberichte über die wirtschaftliche und politische Lage in der Stadt Osnabrück u.a. an die Polizeidirektion Bremen, 1929-33'.

The financial problems faced by the city council meant that it could not afford to offer funding to all of those affected by the unemployment crisis. On a national scale there may have been 'over a million people capable of work who were without either a job or any form of support' during the winter of 1932-3.[34] In Osnabrück the *Winterhilfe* united six charities representing different sections of Osnabrück society. Its activities included collections, as happened in December 1930.[35] Similarly, the Evangelical Church in Osnabrück made efforts to assist the unemployed and their families, distinct from those which it undertook in association with the *Winterhilfe* using a group called the *Osnabrücker Verein für Innere Mission* (Osnabrück Association for Domestic Misions). The wide range of its activities included sending 12 mothers and forty children for breaks in Ostfriesland during the summer of 1931, as well as attempting to find agricultural work for young women.[36] An article in a periodical issued by one of the evangelical churches in Osnabrück also tackled the issue of what to do if beggars came to the door, suggesting that readers should give such people vouchers issued by the *Evangelische Wohlfahrtdienst*.[37]

The local state and charities tried to assist the unemployed to find some sort of work, using the principle of 'work relief' which would 'preserve welfare clients' commitment to industrial discipline and their intellectual and physical abilities to resume wage labour when the opportunity arose. Local authorities attempted to get the unemployed within their administrative boundaries to undertake what was essentially voluntary work, particularly in public works,[38] a precursor of developments in the Third Reich.

From the end of 1929 the Osnabrück employment office used those seeking work in all sorts of public works projects, particularly housing. In 1929 it utilised a total of 35,070 days work from unemployed people in various schemes, up from a figure of 16,474 in 1928. The employment in 1928 focused upon canal building, the erection of the old castle wall, housing construction and work on green spaces. A meeting of the city council in June 1930 demanded that 'Everything must be done to create work'. The programmes included the building of fifty small houses, the improvement of several streets, squares and bridges and refurbishing the city theatre. In June 1931 the city employed 710 people in such schemes. In February 1932 the unemployed found themselves involved in the construction of allotments in Wüste and a sporting club in Schinkel. Similarly, 200 young people volunteered to help in the building of sporting facilities for the OKD, suggesting the exploitation of the unemployment crisis by the larger companies for their own ends. By this time the Osnabrück employment office had reached agreement with the local professional schools to provide courses for people involved in a wide range of employment including electricians, mechanics and tailors.[39]

The local authorities displayed particular concern about young people in order to prevent them from falling into depression consequent upon a period of long unemployment after their apprenticeships. 'Hopelessness and self doubt' would otherwise become the normal everyday thoughts of these groups. The, city authorities, the churches and the trade unions organized educational activities. Between November 1930 and April 1931 two hundred young people between the ages of 17 and 21 attended weekly classes, which focused upon both academic and more practical subjects. In January 1930 ninety young girls attended classes in cooking, housework and the occupations in which they had already worked. For the purpose of the 'bodily and spiritual' welfare of young people, financial support from the Children's Office of the city allowed trade union and ecclesiastical bodies to run courses with lectures, sport and walking. In addition the city authorities, as a precursor to the Nazis, established work camps in Esterwegen on the outskirts of Osnabrück.[40]

The Political Crisis:
Electioneering, Violence and the Rise of the Nazis

While unemployment provided the background to the rise of the Nazis,[41] it does not explain their success, as those without jobs did not tend to vote for the NSDAP, as demonstrated especially by Jürgen Falter. His statistical analysis reveals that the NSDAP tended to do much worse than the KPD in areas with unemployment rates of over 25 per cent.[42] But the Nazis linked the despair which befell Germans at the beginning of the 1930s with the imposition of an 'alien' Weimar Republic in 1919. This reflected the central ideological concepts of Nazism, revolving around race and nation. Many Germans ignored the threat to democracy which the NSDAP displayed in the hope that they could experience prosperity again and have a restored sense of national pride. The Nazis attempted to appeal to more than just one interest group. They moved away from the class based politics which had characterized German history since 1870, especially with the emergence of the SPD, and attempted to offer solutions to the economic problems of all sections of German society.[43]

While early Weimar politics may have witnessed some acts of violence, especially the years 1919-24, with attempted left wing revolutions, political murder and failed right wing coups, a period of comparative political tranquillity followed during the years of relative economic prosperity between 1924 and 1929. The collapse of the economy and the rejuvenation of the Nazis brought German politics to a frenzy as people sought a way out of their despair. The NSDAP may have got in through the ballot box with a substantial percentage of the vote, but it turned the last years of Weimar democracy into a period in which spectacle and violence, together with campaigning for elections of any significance, became central in everyday life. Other parties played a role in the intensification of political

activity, including the most desperate opponents of the Nazis, the SPD and
KPD. But it was the Nazis who perfected electioneering techniques at the
end of the Weimar Republic,[44] allowing them to put forward radical
solutions to complicated problems and to sell them in a revolutionary way,
which has given rise to the concept of the group as a political religion.[45]
Thus, in national terms, the Nazis managed to seduce a significant
percentage of the German population into voting for them.

Osnabrück mirrors the national picture but has one unusual feature in
the existence of the *Stadtwächter*, which put forward many of the same
policies as the NSDAP (although in a less sophisticated way) above all
antisemitism. While the two groups worked together in the town, the Nazis
would have succeeded in Osnabrück without the *Stadtwächter*. But the
existence of this organization made the task of Hitler's followers somewhat
easier. In some ways we might see the *Stadtwächter* as a Nazi party on a local
scale. While the Nazis succeeded, the *Stadwächter*'s history consisted almost
of farce, another possible scenario for the NSDAP under different
circumstances.

Like Hitler, the leader of the *Stadtwächter* consisted of a failure who
turned to politics filled with deep resentment and bitterness. Dr Heinrich
Schierbaum was born in Voxtrup, a suburb of Osnabrück, in 1883, the son
of a farmer and eventually set himself up in alternative medicine, having
developed a 'serious rheumatic illness'. His bitterness came from the fact
that the medical establishment ignored him. As did the local press, which
would not print his advertisements, one of the reasons why he established
his own newspapers. In 1928, Schierbaum had to pay a fine of RM2,000 for
libelling a local medical dignitary, Dr Dietz,[46] the first of numerous similar
cases taken out against him.

The main way in which the party publicised itself consisted of the
successive newspapers which Schierbaum established. The first and longest
lived of these consisted of the eponymous *Stadtwächter*, launched on 28
April 1929 and lasting for exactly two years. There then followed the
Reichs=Wächter, which counted a few editions at the end of 1931, and finally
OD=AL, during the second half of 1932. These organs published articles
on all aspects of Osnabrück life as seen through the eyes of Schierbaum
and his followers, from local finances and medicine to the position of the
theatre and the supposed power of the Jews. The *Stadtwächter* appears to
have reached a circulation of 20,000, suggesting that a substantial
proportion of the local population read it.[47]

Schierbaum's party gained seats in elections for the city council on 17
November 1929 when Osnabrückers not only had the option of the
mainstream national political parties, but also organizations such the
Tenants Protection Organization, the Evangelical Non-Political Party and

the People's Health Party. The results illustrate the volatility of politics at this time in Germany. The SPD obtained 9,475 votes with 12 seats and the Catholic Centre gained 8,022 and 10 seats, while the *Stadwächter* came third, with 5,447 and a representation of seven, even though it had only put five candidates forward.[48]

The *Stadtwächter* focused upon a series of issues, which appealed primarily to the lower middle classes. The front page of the first edition of the eponymous newspaper points to two of it obsessions, with the title of 'What We Want! The Osnabrück Theatre Conflict. Alternative Medicine Against State Medicine.'[49] Schierbaum devoted considerable attention to the former issue. Much of the run of the newspaper focused upon the various legal actions taken out against Schierbaum and his defence against them. Antisemitism represented a core theme in the propaganda of the group.[50]

The *Stadtwächter* newspaper devoted much attention to itself because it faced dozens of legal cases, resulting in fines and even imprisonment of its staff. This was because of its journalistic style, which pulled no punches in the language it used and in the directness with which it attacked individuals and institutions ranging from other local newspapers to the mayor of Osnabrück, Dr Gaertner. At a trial in April 1930 the newspaper had to pay a fine of RM1,500, while in the following month Schierbaum received a prison sentence of 3 months, although he actually payed a fine instead. Nevertheless, the editor Jursch does seem to have gone to prison in September 1930. The newspaper also criticized many court decisions including the ruling against Jursch, linking Jewish businesses with the judges who reached this decision.[51]

The trials of the *Stadtwächter* only served to fuel the fire of its persecution complex, which meant that it attacked all of those in authority, usually linking them with Jews. Jeremy Noakes listed the major concerns of the paper as exposing the alleged secrecy of government, 'putting forward a populist hostility against the establishment' and attacking individual targets which did not tie in with the interests of the lower middle classes such as department stores, health insurance offices and the extravagance of the administration, as well as international capital and the Jews.[52]

The party therefore pursued ideas and policies which linked it directly to the emerging NSDAP, with which it had some connections and for whom it offered support. The *Stadtwächter* remained an amateurish organization which made little impact outside Osnabrück.[53] While it poisoned public opinion through the pages of its journal it does not seem to have used its deputies in the local council to any great extent and certainly did not have the same impact on the streets as the Nazis. The party also held meetings in some of the prominent political venues in Osnabrück, such as the *Stadthalle* on 23 August 1930, which began with a long speech by Schierbaum tracing his ancestry and discussing the contemporary political situation, although the main concern of the evening consisted of the latest fine which he had received.[54]

Because of its local focus and its lack of organizational ability, the *Stadtwächter* did not put up any candidates at elections at a higher level than the city council. Instead the newspaper suggested to its readers that they should vote for Hitler.[55] An analysis of the election results of 17 November 1929 by Paul-Josef Heuer confirmed that the group obtained its votes from middle class districts in the city centre rather than the working class areas of Sutthauser Strasse, Eversburg or Schinkel.[56] At this stage the *Stadtwächter* gained more votes than the Nazis, but we can assume that most of the party's supporters would subsequently have switched their allegiances to the NSADP in regional and national elections.

The demise of the *Stadtwächter* in 1931 did not quite mean the disappearance of Schierbaum, who reincarnated himself in several new guises until the Nazi takeover in 1933 and his death one year later. At the end of 1931 he published a newspaper entitled *Reichswächter*. The front page of the opening issue carried the title of: 'What We Want', followed by a list of ten demands. By this time it seems that Schierbaum had become converted to the racial ideology more typical of the Nazis, as he put forward blood and soil concepts. He further demanded a taxation system which favoured local producers, and a new constitution. Point eight called for 'the abolition of the Jewish gold standard', while the last demanded military service and the right to work for all individuals.[57]

Not completely defeated, Schierbaum's movement went through a final incarnation in the form of the *Weiße Wehr*, again with one more short lived newspaper carrying the title of *OD-AL*. This small group existed from the second half of 1932 and into 1933 focusing upon issues of landownership, race and the constitution. It also devoted much attention to the world economic crisis and discussed the way out of it for the Germans. The real end for Schierbaum came with the Nazi seizure of power as the new regime eliminated this political party in the same way as it did all others, as illegal. Schierbaum found himself in prison between the summer of 1933 and the summer of 1934 and died shortly afterwards.[58]

Thus came to an end a unique and bizarre aspect of the political history of Osnabrück during the interwar years. Ultimately, the presence of the quack doctor in the town made little difference to its long term political development. Dr Schierbaum paved the way for the Nazis in Osnabrück, but they simply marched over him and forgot any support which he may have offered. In the new Germany after 1933 only one party could exist. All opposition would face either assimilation, or, more commonly, elimination, the fate which befell Schierbaum's dying movement.

Table 2.2: Percentage of Votes Gained in *Reichstag* Elections in Osnabrück, 1924-1932, with National Figures in Brackets

Party	7 Dec. 1924	20 May 1928	14 Sept. 1930	31 July 1932	6 Nov. 1932	5 March 1933
SPD	30.5 (26.0)	33.3 (29.8)	26.2 (24.5)	27.0 (21.6)	23.7 (20.4)	21.5 (18.3)
KPD	3.7 (9.0)	3.9 (10.6)	4.6 (13.1)	6.0 (14.3)	9.9 (16.9)	6.7 (12.3)
Catholic Centre	21.6 (13.6)	21.6 (12.1)	19.9 (11.8)	21.0 (12.5)	20.5 (11.9)	19.5 (11.3)
DVP	20.4 (10.1)	15.1 (8.7)	8.0 (4.5)	1.8 (1.2)	3.3 (1.9)	2.2 (1.1)
DNVP	11.5 (20.5)	8.2 (14.2)	3.6 (7.0)	5.4 (5.9)	7.4 (8.3)	7.0 (8.0)
NSDAP	—— (3.0)	3.7 (2.6)	27.6 (18.3)	35.0 (37.3)	32.9 (33.1)	41.7 (43.9)
Others	12.3 (17.8)	15.2 (17.1)	10.1 (17.0)	3.8 (6.2)	2.3 (6.5)	1.4 (4.3)

Sources: Anja Carl, 'Der Landesverband Osnabrück der Deutschnationalen Volkspartei (DNVP) von 1919 bis zum Ende der Weimarer Republik: Geschichte, Organization, Politik', unpublished MA dissertation, University of Osnabrück, 1995, pp. VI-XII; Richard F. Hamilton, *Who Voted for Hitler* (Princeton, 1982), p. 476.

The rise of the NSDAP in Osnabrück reflected its success elsewhere in the country. In the *Reichstag* election of 20 May 1928 the party managed to attract just 2.6 per cent of the vote on a national scale, and 3.6 per cent in Osnabrück, below the average for the Gau Weser-Ems of 5.2 per cent. The symbolic breakthrough came in the *Reichstag* election of 14 September 1930 when the party rocketed to 18.3 per cent, although, in between, provincial votes had pointed to its rising success. The NSDAP actually did considerably better in Osnabrück, securing 27.6 per cent, while Hitler's share of the vote in the town at the first ballot of the Presidential election of 1932, 30.2 per cent, mirrored the national figure of 30.1 per cent. This shadowing continued in the final three *Reichstag* elections of 1932 and 1933 as Table 2.2 indicates.

While slight variations may exist in the relative fortunes of the parties, electoral patterns remain similar on both the national and the local scale. An important reason for the differences lies in the strength of the Catholic Centre Party, where the average variation between the local and national picture in all of the elections stands at between 7.5 and 10 per cent. The success of this grouping here would also help to explain why right wing 'evangelically orientated' parties such the DVP and DNVP did worse than they did in the country as a whole, i.e. because they had a lower percentage of the electorate which would gravitate towards them.[59] Clearly, underlying the strength of the *Zentrum* stands the large Roman Catholic minority within the city, about half of whom would appear to have voted for it throughout the early 1930s. This would probably also account for the relative weakness of the KPD.

The statistics in Table 2.2 only present part of the picture because *Reichstag* elections formed just one level of electioneering in Osnabrück. The Presidential vote of 1932 led to the biggest explosion of interest with Hitler coming from nowhere to finish second. In addition, we have also pointed to the town council poll of November 1929 when the *Stadtwächter* made its first appearance. Furthermore, elections also took place for the Prussian National Assembly on 24 April 1932 and 5 March 1933, which again confirmed the Nazis as the largest political party. In addition, a referendum took place about the Young Plan on 22 December 1929, while another vote occurred on 9 August 1931 about dissolving the Prussian National Assembly. Therefore, between the end of 1929 and the start of 1933, Osnabrück experienced at least 11 different polls at various levels of representation from civic to Presidential.[60]

Behind this list of elections lay a frenzy of political activity including disorder on the streets and in venues throughout the town. We can focus our narrative particularly upon the activities of the Nazis under the two themes of electioneering and violence, which allows us to flesh out the everyday realities of political life in one German location during the last years of the Weimar Republic. The NSDAP did not create the level of political activity by itself because part of the reason for the frenzy lay in the fact that the opponents of the Nazis desperately sought to keep them out.

As Table 2.2 illustrates, those who went to the polls in Osnabrück during the early 1930s had a series of major choices open to them covering all parts of the political spectrum. On the extreme left stood the KPD, which, after 1930, fared badly, even in comparison to its performance on the national scale. The communists essentially consisted of a revolutionary socialist body which continued the original ideological traditions of the

SPD. The KPD appealed mainly to the working classes, although, by the end of the Weimar Republic, it turned its attention to the unemployed.[61] But as the electoral figures suggest, the Osnabrück KPD made relatively little headway despite the numbers of people out of work and intensive efforts to attract them to the cause. The local branch had begun campaigning amongst the unemployed from the end of 1928 and held meetings for them as well as issuing pamphlets appealing to them. The KPD also worked in factories and with trade unions. In September 1930 its membership totalled 700. Its main support during elections came from the working class districts of Sutthauserstraße and Sonnenhügel. Nevertheless, it counted just one member of the city council after the elections of November 1929.[62]

The main working class grouping remained the SPD, which did better in Osnabrück than it did in the country as a whole, probably due to the presence of a large proletariat working especially in textile, metallurgical and engineering factories. By our period Wilhelm Wiltmann had become the local SPD leader. The grouping had the same aims as the national organization and similar objectives to the KPD in looking after the interests of the working class population within its domain. It had also, again mirroring the national picture, developed a whole range of sub-groups with concerns such as women and youth.[63]

The Osnabrück party with the largest divergence from the national norms consisted of the *Zentrum*, explained by the large Roman Catholic minority in the town. The group had always appealed to a constituency which cut across social boundaries.[64] Moving further to the right we can see that the DVP and the DNVP performed worse in Osnabrück than in the country as a whole, almost certainly explained by the strength of the Catholic Centre. According to the local historian of the DNVP the party attracted a variety of supporters from professionals and civil servants to the working classes, although figures from the early 1920s point to an under-representation of the urban working classes, certainly outside the town, where agricultural workers were the main basis of support. It did not simply consist of an elitist grouping but also had connections with the right-wing *Stahlhelm*. In 1932 the DNVP in the *Regierungsbezirk* counted 2,000 members out of a nationwide figure of 70,000, suggesting overrepresentation.[65]

Table 2.2 would seem to suggest that the DVP, slightly to the left of the DNVP on the political spectrum, had its constituency undermined by the Nazis, especially if the analysis is taken back to 1924, when the party obtained 20.4 per cent of the vote. While the DNVP lost votes between 1924 and 1928, it held its own, and even increased its share of the vote after 1930, suggesting that it also obtained support from the DVP, which collapsed on both a national and local scale.[66] This would not necessarily contradict the view of one Osnabrück study which claims that the membership of the DNVP did not shift to the NSDAP.[67] Nevertheless, Falter has asserted that over a third of DVP and DNVP votes switched their allegiance to the Nazis between 1930 and 1932.[68]

As Table 2.2 indicates, support for the NSDAP in Osnabrück mirrors the national picture in electoral terms, particularly in the Reichstag elections of 1932 and 1933 when the difference between the local and the national picture stands at less then 2.5 per cent. The development of the party organization in the town follows the picture elsewhere in Lower Saxony and Germany as the Nazis became a truly national grouping during these years. In terms of membership this increased, on a national scale, from 108,717 in 1928 to over one million by 1932.[69] The Osnabrück branch of the NSDAP had begun to expand during 1929 when it split into four sub groups covering different parts of the town, again reflecting developments on the regional and the national scale, as reorganization of the *Gaue* took place in Lower Saxony. From 1928 the party hierarchy decided that an individual branch could count just 15 members. By September 1930 Osnabrück had ten separate Nazi groupings, each with their own Führer covering the areas East, South, West, North, Middle, Eversburg, Schinkel, Haste, Nahne and Voxtrup. On a national scale the number of local branches grew from 1,378 in 1928 to 11,845 in 1932.[70]

Osnabrück lay in the Gau Weser-Ems, a region which had an electoral pattern, which, like the town itself, mirrored the country as a whole, according to statistics for the Reichstag election of July 1932. The Nazis obtained the highest share of their votes in the Protestant north and east of the country, while the lowest came in the Roman Catholic west and south, pointing to the strength of the Centre Party in these areas. In addition, the Nazis did better in rural than urban areas, where the left wing SPD and KPD retained much of their traditional support. The NSDAP also tended to obtain higher percentages of the vote in border areas, notably in the Roman Catholic Palatinate, as well as areas next to Poland. In terms of party membership, middle class groupings were over represented while the working classes were under represented. Thus, at the start of 1933, workers made up 29.7 per cent of the party but 46.3 per cent of society as a whole. The figures for white collar employees stood at 18.6 and 12 per cent respectively, for, the self-employed at 19.8 and 9.6 per cent and for civil servants at 15.2 and 4.8 per cent.[71]

Unfortunately, no statistics have survived on the social make up of members or voters of the NSDAP in Osnabrück during the early 1930s, although newspaper commentaries and official files do give some indication of the Nazi constituency. A membership list from 1925 details 78 people consisting of: 19 businessmen, 11 civil servants, 7 white collar workers, 10 artisans, 5 self-employed, 3 engineers and two workers. By the end of 1929 the local branch had an SA cell with sixty members. By July 1931 an SA Hostel existed in Möserstraße, providing meals for local members. In 1932 the party established a *Berufsbeamtenring*, a sub-grouping for professional employees.[72]

The Nazi rise to power was not a smooth path, despite the rapidity with which the party moved from a group representing outcasts and the disaffected to the largest political party in Germany from 1929 to 1932. The process involved massive organization, investment and electioneering, together with a readiness to use violence. A chronicling of the political developments of these years will help us to live the realities of the rise of the Nazis on the local scale.

An Osnabrück police report from August 1929 described a local group with '650 signed up members…gripped by a period of constant growth'. The leadership consisted of a 'Führer' in the form of Dr Marxer, his deputy, the businessman Karl Friedrichs, a press officer, a cashier, a leader of the SA, also Marxer, his deputy and the representative of the Hitler Youth, Siegfried Wagner. According to the report the SA had forty members at this time.[73]

Nazi activity increased, especially the use of propaganda, from the end of 1928, focusing upon rich Jews in the town.[74] On 18 January 1929 the party held a meeting in the *Festsaal* attended by 300 people. By April the Hitler Youth had 25 members between the ages of 14 and 18. By the autumn of 1929 the Nazis had increased their level of appeal. A meeting held in the *Stadthalle* on 28 September attracted '600-700 people from all classes…addressed by…*Gauleiter* Röver'. By November the SA and the propaganda department devoted all of their efforts to publicity, using bicycles and motorbikes to aid their efforts. Over 3,000 leaflets publicised a meeting which took place in the *Stadthalle* on 8 December, advertised in the main railway station as well as in various parts of the town.

The year 1929 therefore counts as one in which the Nazis increased the level of their political activity and began to compete with other local groupings in attracting attention. Certainly, by the end of the year, they had become a powerful force. The local secret police devoted more attention to this group than to any other political party. By the time of the Wall Street Crash, the Nazis had laid the groundwork and established their local infrastructure, ready to make use of the opportunities which presented themselves as a result of the economic crisis.

Although the DVP and the DNVP carried on their activities apace, these seem unimpressive in scale and intensity compared with the rising Nazis. A meeting of the DNVP held in the *Festsaal* on 18 February 1929 attracted an audience of 300 to hear speeches about the economic and financial situation of the *Reich*. More information survives on the left wing groupings, especially the KPD, viewed in the secret police reports, like the Nazis, as a threat. At the start of 1929 these police reports spoke of the KPD remaining fairly mute. The highpoint of left wing activities took place on the traditional workers May Day when a procession of 150 people took place, far less supporters than the Nazis attracted.[75]

The year 1930 saw increasing activity and the national breakthrough for the NSDAP which occurred at the *Reichstag* election of September. While political campaigning by both the Nazis and their opponents peaked in the late summer and autumn, much prepatory activity went into the success of September. As early as January the NSDAP held a public meeting in the *Stadthalle* which attracted an audience of 700. The speakers focused on the central Nazi concerns of slavery to foreign bankers and the influence of the Jews. The audience contained KPD hecklers, a characteristic which would become increasingly common. In the same month a KPD meeting on the fate of the unemployed in the Schröder pub attracted 200 people.[76] By early February the Nazis pursued 'an intense advertising and propaganda campaign in the whole of the working class district of Osnabrück, so that they are holding public meetings and lecture evenings in the most diverse locations where they can distribute a mass of propaganda material.'[77] As the spring and summer progressed the activities of both NSDAP and KPD, as well as other political groupings, continued apace.[78] It reached its highpoint in September before the *Reichstag* election. One of the largest gatherings occurred in the *Stadthalle*, again organized by the Nazis and, on this occasion, attracting 1,800 people. Outside stood 300 people, including communists. One of the most notable events during the campaign consisted of a DNVP meeting addressed by the leader of the party Alfred Hugenberg. Only the SPD attracted the same audience as the Nazis. A meeting it held in the *Stadthalle* on 2 September also had 1,800 spectators.[79] Needless to say the Nazis and their opponents did not cease their activities after the September poll.[80]

If 1930 represented the year of the first major breakthrough for the NSDAP, 1931 became one of consolidation and continued growth. No let up occurred in campaigning. In January meetings took place almost on a daily basis. Thus, on Sunday the 5th the Nazis organized a morning celebration in the Capitol cinema followed by an orchestral concert and speeches to celebrate the New Year. On the following day in the Steinhage pub, a Nazi public meeting attracted 300 people. On the 23rd 600 people attended another NSDAP meeting in the Klushügel Restaurant. On the evening of 29 January the Nazis actually held two meetings, one in the *Stadthalle* and the other in the *Festhalle*.[81] The KPD continued to send hecklers and protestors against these gatherings as well as paying particular attention to the unemployed. Again, like the Nazis, the KPD seemed to organise daily meetings and marches during early January, although these continued to attract less support and attention than those of their right wing opponents. The events of January set the pattern for the rest of the year. Although the regularity of meetings did not manage to maintain the same pace for the whole of 1931, there were some highpoints. For instance, on 20 June the NSDAP organized a celebration of summer attended by 600 people.[82] Unemployment remained a major concern for all of the political parties. On 18 September the SPD held a meeting on the subject in the *Festsaal*, which was 'more than overflowing'.[83] By this time the SA had become something of a force in Osnabrück, despite the ban which existed on the wearing of uniforms. Its activities included assisting the unemployed. Its home in Möserstraße, of '60 square metres' included a kitchen, which provided about 130 meals a day.[84]

The highest frenzy of political activity arrived in 1932 as a result of two *Reichstag* polls, in July and November, and the Presidential challenge of Hitler against Hindenburg in March and April. Elections to the Prussian *Landtag* also occurred in April, meaning particularly intense activity in the spring. By early 1932 the NSDAP had clearly become a highly organized professional mass party, so that the propaganda activity and leaflet distribution which had begun to take off in 1929 and 1930, as well as the mass meetings, which had grown in 1930, had, by the beginning of 1932, become part of the everyday life of Osnabrück. In the first week of January, for instance, the party distributed leaflets, moved offices to 24 Spindelstraße, and held a meeting attended by about 700 people in the *Stadthalle*.[85] Campaigning for the first Presidential ballot on 13 March meant:

> ...organized election meetings on almost a daily basis, which were generally well attended...The NSDAP carried out campaigning with all its strength...On the night of the 3rd to the 4th of the month the SA of the NSDAP fixed political posters (vote for Hitler) in red and other oil colours throughout the whole town, on the pavements, shop windows and other locations.

In contrast, the KPD 'held some public election meetings, but was generally very discreet'.[86]

Campaigning continued into the second Presidential ballot and the Prussian *Landtag* of April. Election fever reached another high point in July as a result of the *Reichstag* poll held on the 31st of that month. The SPD engaged in at least as much activity as the Nazis. On 11 July the front page of the *Freie Presse* declared that 'over 5,000 people marched under the banner of the Iron Front'. Another Iron Front rally in the palace courtyard on 22 July attracted 3,000 people. Speakers focused upon the threat of the Nazis, the policies of the government and the hunger crisis. As many as 5,000 people apparently attended the final Iron Front rally on 28 July.[87]

The NSDAP participated in similar intense activity. A local police report from early July stated:

> The National Socialist propaganda activity was fully focused on the coming election in the reporting week. As well as a public gathering there were several cell meetings. The public meeting took place on Saturday 9/7/32 in the *Festsaal*...
>
> During the reporting week the SS, SA and HJ came to the attention of the public with various propaganda marches. On Sunday, 10/7/32, about 400 Osnabrück SA people participated in a Gau parade in Bremen.[88]

The highlight of this election campaign consisted of a rally at the *Sporstplatz Klushügel* addressed by Adolf Hitler on 24 July and perhaps attended by 25,000 people.[89] His plane arrived at 9pm and he appeared 15 minutes later to speak for just half an hour on the need for victory and the issue of reparations.[90]

The Nazis and their opponents continued to campaign throughout the late summer and into the autumn, reaching another peak of activity for the final major election of 1932 which occurred on 6 November, although some apathy had descended by this time, as meetings did not attract quite the same amount of attention from either press or the local population. But Nazi rallies did result in crowds of 2,000 on 24 October and 7,000 on 31 October. Earlier, on 20 October, a crowd of 7,000 had gathered on Pottgrabenplatz, where the speakers included Goebbels.[91] The decline in support for the Nazis at the November 1932 elections actually meant Hitler became Chancellor in January 1933 after negotiating with the conservative parties.[92]

Electioneering became part of the fabric of society between 1929 and 1932. The local Nazi party changed from a loosely organized band of political outsiders and non-entities, to the largest party in Osnabrück during 1929-30. Before this time the local organization had simply held meetings attended by a few hardcore extreme nationalists. But by 1930 the rallies of the Nazis had become large scale events attracting thousands of people. Osnabrück remained something of a provincial backwater, which meant the national hierarchy made few appearances, with Hitler and Goebbels making one visit each. But the sophisticated national propaganda machine which had developed around the Nazis on a national scale also functioned in this small town. As the police reports demonstrate, the local grouping publicised its events extremely well through the distribution of leaflets and the use of posters.[93]

The level of Nazi electioneering contrasted with some of the other leading parties in Osnabrück, which did not have such a sophisticated propaganda machine. The KPD remained a rag-bag group, with limited funding, little support and a poor propaganda machine compared with the Nazis, although on a national level the Communists had a sophisticated organization with its own milieu, covering social life, youth, trade union activity and politics. Propaganda focused upon the 'power of the word' through newspapers, education and lectures.[94] These activities remained less dynamic than those of the Nazis and appealed to a focused working class constituency. While the 1932 election meetings organized by the Nazis in Osnabrück could attract thousands of people, those of the KPD could barely muster a few hundred. But the communists often turned up and interrupted Nazi meetings. In addition, they also involved themselves in street fighting with the SA on a regular basis after 1929. But they resembled matchsticks standing in the way of the Nazi steamroller.

The only party which could compare with the NSDAP consisted of the SPD, which, during 1932, did hold meetings which brought together an audience size which matched that of the Nazi gatherings. Similarly, as in the case of the KPD, some of their activists participated in heckling of and street fighting with Nazis. But the SPD did not have the broader based appeal of the NSDAP, which meant that it could not stand firm against the oncoming tide.

While the Nazis ultimately based their seizure of power on the legitimacy of the ballot box, behind this development lay a catalogue of violence. On the one hand we can see the disorder as a reaction against the economic and political crisis of the years after the Wall Street Crash.[95] But discussion of street fighting needs contextualization against the background of German history in the first half of the twentieth century and more specifically the centrality of war during these years, which made violence a central part of political culture. The events of 1929-32 remained mild compared with the carnage of the First World War and, even more so, the Second, when killing became a fact of everyday life both upon German soil and upon the areas invaded by German armies.[96] A significant percentage of those who became involved in disorder by joining paramilitary groups during the inter-war years had experience of military service between 1914 and 1918.[97]

The disorder of 1929-32 also needs contextualization against the background of the realities of political discourse in the interwar years. While the type of campaigning outlined above may have represented one side of the coin, political violence became just as much a part of the everyday life of Germany from the revolutions of 1918 and their suppression through force, the Kapp Putsch, the murder of Walter Rathenau, and the Munich Beer Hall Putsch. The events of 1929-32 simply follow on from these major acts of political violence, which aimed at overthrowing the state. In fact, we might argue that the violence at the end of the Weimar Republic remained mild compared with what happened during the early years of this regime.[98] In his study of disorder during the Weimar years Dirk Schumann stressed the impact and legacy of the failed revolution of 1918, although he recognized that political violence had occurred before the First World War. He argued that after the 'civil war phase' of the German revolution and its aftermath (1918-21), violence took on `another more controlled, but more long lasting form, in which rival political camps were involved in a struggle for the control of the public sphere'.[99] Schumann stressed the need to look at the Weimar Republic as a whole. The crisis of the early 1930s simply intensified the violence.[100]

We can also contextualize the disorder of 1929-32 within Nazi ideology. Emerging from the First World War, the Nazis glorified the cult of fighting and the cult of the soldier, while opposing what they viewed as the intellectual Weimar Republic. In *Mein Kampf* Hitler outlined the centrality of physical training for all members of German society, which would culminate in a period of military service for males once they left school. Nazi orators regularly made speeches about violence and political expansion. The disorder also formed part of the camaraderie which kept the paramilitary SA together.[101]

In the early 1930s the Nazi storm troopers concentrated their violent attention above all on their left wing opponents and, to a lesser extent, certainly in the case of Osnabrück, upon Jews. The regular street brawls involving KPD, SPD and SA resulted in serious injuries or even deaths. The KPD, made up overwhelmingly of members of the working classes and, as ideological communists, not committed to the liberal Weimar Republic, represented the losers, as much as the extreme right did, in the new order established in 1919. The new regime tried to stamp out any of the remaining revolutionary activity, which had helped to bring it to power. Osnabrück Communists shared considerable responsibility for the disorder which broke out in the final years of the Weimar Republic, as they sought to prevent the rise of their most hated political opponents by any means possible, including violence, which the KPD would have regarded as legitimate, just as the Nazis did, indicated by the paramilitary groups which the KPD established.[102] The SPD represented the main winners in the settlement of 1919 and therefore the Weimar Republic symbolized its success. While members of this group did not indulge in the kind of almost gratuitous violence which KPD and NSDAP supporters regarded as legitimate, they certainly came under attack from the Nazis and naturally fought back, especially through the *Reichsbanner*, originally established as a propaganda group.[103]

We can chronologically analyse the most violent incidents in Osnabrück, which peaked in 1932. On 22 May 1930 the *Osnabrücker Zeitung* carried the following report:

> There was a serious outbreak of violence in Wegmann's assembly rooms at the final tram stop in Iburgerstrasse on Tuesday night. The National Socialist German Workers Party held a recruiting meeting there attended by about 200 people. Most of them were National Socialists but the Communists also had a notable contingent. The speaker was a Berlin National Socialist. The Communist Ludwig Landwehr made himself heard and climbed on to a table in order to speak. The communist speaker mentioned the last Berlin disturbances which had resulted in fatalities. The statements of the speaker faced strong opposition which eventually degenerated into violence. A terrible tumult followed. Mr Landwehr hid underneath the table as all sorts of missiles whistled through the hall. The opponents hit each other with sticks, beer glasses and chairs while a large part of the audience hastily made its way to the exits. A large number of window panes were smashed to pieces as a result of the fighting.

Three months later, on 27 August 1930, a struggle took place between communists and Nazis outside the employment office involving about twenty people and resulting in the arrest of two of the former and four of the latter.[104]

The rest of 1930 appears to have resulted in relatively little violence, perhaps because of the absence of any further electioneering after the *Reichstag* poll of 14 September. But this explanation for the decline of political terror would not hold good for 1931 because the available evidence suggests that violence increased during a year without any significant elections. Alternative explanations would include a continuing deterioration caused by the absence of any end in sight to the economic crisis. Furthermore, violence probably bred violence against the background of the economic situation. Newspaper articles and police files allow us to reconstruct several of the major events of 1931 in considerable detail. On 17 May disorder involving Communists and Nazis occurred in Johannisstraße. On the 30th a more significant disturbance occurred during an SA march beginning in Haarmanbrunnen and involving 'about 40-50 communists...divided up into several gangs and standing on the street corners in Möserplatz' opposed by 'about 130 SA people gathered together'.[105]

By the time these events had taken place the state had introduced measures to observe and control violence. A Presidential decree of 28 March 1931 demanded that all political demonstrations needed registration with local police authorities, in case 'public security and order are endangered'. In the latter case, the local authorities could ban demonstrations.[106] This had followed another decree from as early 5 July 1930 which forbade the wearing of National Socialist uniforms.[107] But such measures had a limited impact, as violence continued, with Brownshirts simply continuing their activity in white shirts.[108]

One of the most serious disturbances in Osnabrück occurred on 8 August 1931. While the local police may have banned several marches during the course of the summer, they decided to allow the one of 8 August to go ahead on condition that the participants did not wear uniforms. But 'out of 300 participants about 160 to 170 turned up in brown trousers and gaiters as well as white shirts; apart from these there were 7 people with brown shirts, white metal buttons and also with green mirrors present. Apart from that the SA also appeared with a flag containing a swastika'. As a result of the waving of the banner and the wearing of the uniforms the procession was declared to be dissolved. But another gathering had reformed, which was, however, broken up, partly with the help of truncheons. There were further attempts to reform the procession in several other streets, which the police again hindered with the help of violence. 'The number of the onlookers considerably surpassed the number of demonstrators in numerical terms.'[109]

The local police did not authorise any open air meetings of the NSDAP or the SA for the rest of August.[110] In early November a few minor skirmishes occurred between Nazis and Communists[111] while on Saturday 5 December the *Osnabrücker Zeitung* carried the story of a 'Bloody Political Act on Arndplatz', referring to an assault on a local SA leader. The attempts to control violence seem to have had relative success as there followed several months free of any significant disturbances in Osnabrück. The culmination of these measures came with the ban on the SA of 13 April 1932, which dealt 'an effective blow to the Nazi Party'.[112] On 16 March 1932 the local criminal police closed down the 'Brown House', the headquarters of the SA in Osnabrück, following several incidents of violence on the 12th and 13th of that month revolving around the Presidential election.[113] No significant disorder occurred again until midsummer's day when fights between Communists and Nazis, leading to various injuries, broke out throughout Osnabrück.[114] In a communication sent to the *Osnabücker Zeitung* the local NSDAP also claimed that organized attacks by the KPD occurred on the following day.[115]

In late June and July the SPD supporting *Freie Presse* reported various incidents in which Nazis attacked the Iron Front. At the end of the following month it mentioned attacks in Sonnehugel carried out by members of the SA.[116] On 19 August 1932 the *Osnabrücker Zeitung* received a communication that on '17/8/32, somewhere around 20.00 hours, a national socialist passing by the trade union house in Kollegienwall was abused by three loafing youths...When the National Socialist refused to tolerate the molesters with calm words, the red highway robbers assaulted him, shoved him on to the pavement and trampled on him'. This incident actually escalated further and involved between 60 and 70 people outside the trade union house. Shortly after this, on 1 September, three members of the SA attacked a member of the *Reichsbanner*, 'in broad daylight'.[117]

Fighting between communists, socialists and Nazis became regular in Osnabrück during the early 1930s, reflecting events elsewhere in Germany. Only a small number of incidents in Osnabrück involved more than a few people. The most substantial of these occurred on 8 August 1931. In essence, the police lost control on this evening, which largely explains why the violence escalated. But it did not really represent a full scale riot compared with incidents elsewhere in Germany at this time.[118] Communists and Nazis in Berlin were attacking each other on a daily basis by the end of 1931, while 17 people were killed on a nationwide basis as a result of political violence on 10 July 1932.[119] The 29 arrests in Osnabrück on 8 August 1931, by comparison, hardly suggests a major public order incident. Few serious injuries appear to have occurred on this evening, or on any other evening in the history of Osnabrück between 1929 and 1932, although many of the attackers from both sides of the political spectrum had this aim in mind. Property damage remained largely absent becasue the targets consisted of political opponents in the struggle for control of the streets. Ultimately, the events in Osnabrück may best merit the description of small town violence. Some brutalisation may have taken place, but, in the context of the events of the years 1933-45, the incidents of 1929-32 remain just a prelude to the violence which would follow. The small size of the KPD helps to explain the relatively low level of violence which took place in this provincial backwater. This differs greatly from the tribal conflict which occurred in one of the biggest centres of Communist support, Berlin.[120]

Individuals living in either Osnabrück or any other part of Germany would, nevertheless, have experienced vast changes during the period 1929-32, but we should not isolate these years either in economic or political terms. The Weimar Republic experienced economic crises throughout its existence. While the one which struck from 1929 may have had the deepest and most widespread personal consequences, the citizens of Osnabrück had already experienced the economic collapse and insecurity of the post-War dislocation. Similarly, the violence which gripped Germany in the early 1930s had its origins in the First World War and its immediate aftermath, even in Osnabrück, where a mutiny occurred on 8 November 1918 followed by the establishment of a soldiers' and workers' council on the following day.[121] The rise of the Nazis, while dramatic, also needs contextualization within the fast moving political changes which had occurred in Germany since 1918 and, even, since the foundation of the nation state in 1871.

Yet the early 1930s did have unique characteristics. The intensity of the depression, its personal effects, as well as its impact upon the local political scene, meant individuals could not have failed to have noticed and experienced the dramatic changes taking place in their midst. The most obvious manifestation of these changes would arrive in the early months of 1933, especially for those who had opposed the rising NSDAP and who now faced incarceration.

PART II

ETHNIC MAJORITIES

3

THE ESTABLISHMENT OF A NEW SOCIETY 1933-39: SOCIAL AND ECONOMIC TRANSFORMATION, PROPAGANDA AND REPRESSION

The election victory of 1933 gave the Nazis the chance to deliver on the promises which they had made in the election campaigns of the early 1930s and provided them with an opportunity to achieve their ideological goals.[1] The economic changes which would occur during peacetime affected the lives of all Germans, mostly for the better. However, whatever carrots the Nazis may have offered, came with even larger sticks. The new regime worked in three ways. In the first place, it implemented significant economic and social transformations, which improved the lives of most ethnic Germans before 1933. Together with this process, the Third Reich used an all embracing campaign of persuasion, which encompassed propaganda, culture and education. Those to whom neither economic benefits nor persuasion would appeal faced repression, a fate which befell both the political enemies of the Nazis and those regarded as racial or social outsiders in the new order.

The Anatomy of the Osnabrück NSDAP

The Nazi seizure of power resulted in the implementation of *Gleichschaltung* at the national, regional and local level. This process involved a suspension of institutions and a change of personnel in all areas of public life. Democracy disappeared, replaced by a new top down authoritarian structure in which elected representatives in the city council, the regional parliament and Reichstag lost their power. In their place came new structures, as Osnabrück illustrates. The *Gauleiter* acted as the regional representative of the central government under the new Gau system. Carl Röver held this position in the *Gau* Weser-Ems, within which Osnabrück lay, from 1929-42, when Paul Wegener succeeded him. Below the *Gauleiter* stood the *Regierungspräsident*. On 27 March Bernhard Eggers took this position over from Adolf Sonnenschein, who had held office from 1922. Eggers died in 1937 and was replaced by Wilhelm Rodenberg. Below the *Regierungspräsident* Dr Gaertner retained his position as Mayor of Osnabrück until 1945. A series of individuals became Osnabrück *Kreisleiter* including the dentist Dr Fritz Hoffmann, from 1933 until 1935, and the businessman Wilhelm Münzer, one of the first National Socialists in Osnabrück, until 1940. Münzer was followed by *Gau* inspector Wehmeier.

Gleichschaltung did not simply mean the replacement of government officials and the implementation of a new system of local government. It also resulted in the purging of a variety of people from their positions, especially after the passage of the Law for the Restoration of the Professional Civil Service on 7 April 1933. Those who lost their jobs included heads of schools, the magistrate Senator Schulte, and the leader of the press and information office, Dr Richard Hugle.

As for the instruments of control in Osnabrück, Brigade 64 of the SA was under the leadership of Otto Marxer until the beginning of 1933, followed by Ernst Bischoff, Ferdinand Esser and a Mr Reichert until the end of 1938, after which the group lessened in importance. Similarly, the police at the Osnabrück *Regierungsbezirk* level had a series of leaders including Marxer, Hans Aderhold, Paul Kanstein, Alexander Landgraf, Walter Schlette, Otto Weiß-Bollandt and Ernst Bach. At the town level the longest serving and most important head of police consisted of Alfred Jung, who held the position from 1937-45. The Osnabürck *Gestapo*, organized at the *Regierungsbezirk* level, divided into three sections: I, responsible for 'Administration'; II, 'Politics'; and III, 'Defence'.[2]

It is also worth noting one final figure in the Osnabrück Nazi establishment, Erwin Kolkmeyer, who, while he may not have held particularly high office, remained on the scene throughout our period. This watchmaker had joined the NSDAP in 1929 and held the position of leader of the *Altstadt* section (where his shop stood and still stands) of the Osnabrück *Kreis*.[3] As we shall see, he played major role during *Kristallnacht* and was remembered by several interviewees. He probably did more than any other local Nazi official to poison the political climate of Osnabrück.

Social and Economic Transformation

When the Nazis came to power in 1933 they focused upon two main social and economic tasks in the form of solving unemployment and implementing social transformations according to ideology. They achieved the former through a combination of public works schemes and rearmament, the glorification of work and the introduction of labour conscription. These methods ensured that unemployment had disappeared by the end of the 1930s, although economic conditions improved marginally. The Nazis also focused upon transforming the position of women and the family in their attempts to increase fertility, which meant the attempted removal of women from the workplace. By 1939 the economic chaos of the early 1930s seemed a distant memory while limited success had occurred in increasing fertility. In economic terms Osnabrück, like other German towns, contained a majority of people who found themselves better off in 1939 than during the final years of the Weimar Republic.

The most significant economic transformation which took place in the first six years of Nazi rule consisted of the decline in unemployment. In early 1933, the number of registered unemployed in Germany peaked at over six million. By 1939 it had fallen back to 104,200.[4] The figures for Osnabrück mirror the national ones. The January 1933 figure of 10,579 had fallen to 8,030 by June of the same year and 4,045 by March 1934.[5] By 1938 a situation of full employment existed in the town, as businesses faced labour shortages. In November of that year the labour office of the Osnabrück region had 1,693 jobs on offer, of which 769 still remained vacant at the end of the month.[6]

Unemployment in Germany decreased as a result of a series of policies. The implementation of public works programmes in the middle of the 1930s combined with the introduction of labour conscription continued policies pursued by the Weimar Republic. Road building and cars played a major role in this process, while labour conscription particularly involved drafting people into agriculture. Subsequently, from about 1936, under the leadership of Hermann Göring, rearmament became the driving force of the economy as part of the Four Year Plan preparing the country for war in 1940, which meant that towns such as Osnabrück, with large engineering and metallurgical bases, prospered, as did the companies within them. These developments fitted in with Nazi ideology, which had a contempt for idleness. The labour shortages which existed by the end of the 1930s meant the working classes laboured longer hours than they had done at any time since the First World War. Big business benefited more than the workers from the economic upswing, especially if we consider that the latter lost their own independent representatives immediately after the Nazis seized power.[7]

The economic development of Osnabrück illustrates these changes. A 1934 document produced by Kolkmeyer showed that the number of people employed had fallen from 46,000 to 42,000 between 1925 and 1933. About seventy per cent of the population made a living from industry, trade and transport. Kolkmeyer stated that the late Weimar crisis had affected nearly all sectors of the local economy and resulted in the closure of 866 concerns. Industrial and craft production had suffered epsecially, but so had other sectors of the economy. The self-employed percentage of the population stood at 18 per cent, compared with 48 per cent for workers and 30 per cent for white collar workers. Kolkmeyer listed 2,141 small businesses in the town in January 1934 employing 1,424 journeymen and 1,372 apprentices. These concerns included 106 bakers, 171 hairdressers, 218 painters and decorators, 212 tailors, 222 cobblers and 157 carpenters.[8]

Under the leadership of Gaertner, economic policy focused upon solving unemployment,[9] using a blaze of publicity in the local press. On 13 August 1933 the *Osnabrücker Zeitung* announced 'Osnabrück Creates Work' as a result of schemes introduced by the city authorities. The article listed eleven programmes, which involved improvements to roads, railways, trams and public buildings. Between 500 and 600 people obtained work for between six to eight months. A press release from the city administration in November 1933 outlined the implementation of a plan, under the leadership of the city construction office, to provide work for 1,000 men for five months covering the course of the winter costing 'not less than 2.7 million marks', involving the restoration of public buildings, the improvement and construction of housing and further improvements in transportation including roads, bridges and canals.[10]

Another blaze of publicity greeted the launch of further work creation programmes in March 1934 The city authorities had secured RM731,050 from both central government and local banks which would provide 59,940 days of work and further hoped to obtain another RM1.5 million which would mean the creation of another 100,000 days of employment. The finance obtained went towards improvements in transportation, housing and public buildings.[11] In May the city authorities secured funding to improve the theatre,[12] while a winter work creation programme announced in October 1934 meant further transportation improvements.[13] In June 1935 the city government put forward a plan to spend RM584,648 to continue further building, followed by RM1,112,400 for 1936, which would provide thousands of days of employment. The finance came mostly as a result of the upswing of the local economy.[14]

Who benefited from these developments? We might argue that the entire population did. In the first place the public works schemes provided employment, albeit of a fairly menial nature in most cases. Local morale received a boost as the population saw the improvement of buildings and streets. The changes also brought a cash injection into the local economy which would have benefited most concerns of any size in the town. In addition, the building programme also meant the construction of new housing, mostly for the working classes.[15]

One of the areas where home building occurred was the working class district of Schinkel. In the autumn of 1936 a total of 101 houses were being constructed here.[16] In 1938 the city saw the construction of 780 new homes, although only 193 of these used public funds. The figure of 780 meant the building of 8 new homes for every 1,000 inhabitants in the city.[17] But these developments simply continued the work of the Weimar Republic. In addition, we need to remember that the majority of funding came from bank loans and housing associations.[18]

In view of the menial nature of the labour involved in construction, the Nazis made sure that they found enough people to carry it out, formalized in early 1935 with the introduction of labour passes. As the *Osnabrücker Zeitung* declared of the 31,600 issued in the town, 'The creation of labour passes will guarantee that the mobilized labourers will work in the right employment.' Propaganda campaigns also attempted to make manual labour attractive through the use of phrases such as 'soldier of labour' and 'The Battle of Labour'.[19]

Incentives and propaganda went together with a heavy stick because refusal to work could mean incarceration.[20] From 1933 unemployed men under 25 no longer received benefits. In September 1933 those obtaining support had to work at least 24 hours per week. In 1938 all those under 65 receiving benefits had to carry out four hours of labour per day.[21] In May 1938 eleven faced transfer to a concentration camp in Berlin.[22]

An examination of businesses in Osnabrück, particularly those involved in engineering, during the 1930s reveals that they certainly benefited from the economic upturn. The number of concerns began to grow by the middle of the 1930s. The 1934 annual report of the Osnabrück Industrial Inspection Board stated that the number of businesses in the *Regierungsbezirk* had increased to 3,236 from 2,692 in 1932. However, the report pointed to continuing difficulties in textile production, particularly cotton, where working hours had gone down to 36. Growth had taken place especially in the engineering sector.[23]

Engineering and metallurgical companies such as Karmann, Klöckner, and the OKD benefited most from the economic upturn caused by rearmament.[24] The OKD, which manufactured a variety of light metals, including copper and aluminium, employed 1,244 people in January 1933, 300 of them part time. By 1936 the number had gone up to 2,500 and by the outbreak of War it reached 3,500. By this time the OKD employed people on Sundays. The turnover for the business year 1938-9 had reached a record of RM60 million. The growth of these years also allowed the renovation of the existing buildings and the construction of new ones.[25] The Klöckner-Werke also witnessed a considerable increase in production, requiring longer hours from its workers. As early as 1936 the company began asking the local industrial inspectorate for permission to employ people on Sunday, as well as on Good Friday and Easter Monday in order to 'complete urgent state contracts'.[26] Following orders from Brazil, Sweden, Italy and Lithuania, the firm obtained permission in January 1939 to employ 135 people over 18 for up to ten hours per day over a period of 3 months. On Good Friday 1939 a total of 530 people worked for Klöckner.[27] We can see a similar picture for the automobile factory, Karmann, as car production in Germany increased from 82,000 in 1933 to 223,000 in 1938. During this period Karmann made the bodies for several different firms including Adler and Ford, two of the big five motor companies in Germany. In April 1938 it employed 150 people for up to ten hours per day.[28]

The expansion of metallurgy and engineering in Osnabrück points to the fact that big business benefited more than the workers needed to man the increases in production. Those finding themselves employed on public holidays and night shifts spent time away from families and social activities which they may have preferred carrying out, although they would also have earned overtime pay.[29]

Economic growth did not benefit artisans in quite the same way as industrial workers or big business, despite Nazi propaganda, which regarded artisans as central in the *Volksgemeinschaft*. The regime introduced a raft of measures in an attempt to protect this group, with limited success.[30] This went together with propaganda campaigns to proclaim the value of the artisan. For instance, in October 1933 Osnabrück held a 'Day for Osnabrücker Craftsmen', as part of a week long celebration of 'The German Craftsman'.[31] In the autumn of the same year a 'Brown Congress' took place in Osnabrück in which concerns of all sizes, including the smallest ones, could advertise themselves and their products.[32] But the number of businesses in Osnabrück remained steady during the 1930s, falling by just one from 1,420 in 1933 to 1,419 in 1939.[33] The number of apprentices declined by a quarter between 1927 and 1938, although most of this fall had occurred during the late Weimar economic crisis.[34]

The general improvement in economic conditions partly came about as a result of the glorification of labour. During the 1930s this formed part of the propaganda campaign to get people back into employment.[35] The first May Day celebrations in Osnabrück under the Nazis, described as 'The National Day of Work in Germany', involved '34,000 Germans Marching to Honour Work'.[36] Similarly, four years later the *Osnabrücker Tageblatt* declared 'Germany's New Ennoblement: Work!'[37]

The glorification of labour went together with the establishment of all manner of organizations attempting to improve working conditions. These partly came into existence to replace the free trade unions which the Nazis had abolished upon coming to power. Thus the most important body consisted of the DAF, part official trade union with the aim of controlling the working classes, part propaganda machine for the purpose of worker motivation, and part working men's society which provided social activities both within and outside work. The DAF came into existence on 10 May 1933 and would have twenty million members as well as a bureaucracy of 40,000. The organization worked together with a series of other bodies for controlling labour, including the NSBO (Trustees of Labour), involved in labour organization and representation, and Strength Through Joy and Beauty of Labour concerned with improving working conditions and social facilities.[38]

Osnabrück during the 1930s illustrates the activities of the DAF and its sister organizations. The local DAF devoted much attention to educational provision for workers. In June 1934 it took over a training school in Vehrte from the city authorities with the aim of training economic and political leaders together with workers' councillors in order to prevent any negative ideas affecting their worldview.[39] Two years later, in the summer of 1936, the DAF in Osnabrück offered a wide range of courses and lectures. The practical ones included textiles and clothing, carpentry, painting, building, mechanical work, engineering, paper work, commerce, languages and home economics. More political subjects included 'The Struggle for the Preservation of German Blood', 'Jewry' and 'German Space'.[40] In the summer and winter semesters of 1938-9 a total of 8,000 people participated in such courses.[41] The DAF also played a role in Nazi propaganda as illustrated by a march which the organization held in July 1933, culminating in a rally in the stadium of the town's football club, attracting an audience of 50,000, according to *the Osnabrücker Zeitung*, raising 84 Nazi flags and publicising its activities.[42]

The DAF carried out much social activity through the Strength Through Joy Movement. For instance, in December 1934 the organization sent out letters to factory directors informing them of a programme established by the Imperial Office for Travel, Walking and Holidays to help 'work colleagues, who until now have never had the opportunity to have a holiday journey allowing them to get to know their homeland outside the immediate vicinity of their home'. As part of a Christmas present workers could purchase travel vouchers costing between RM5 and RM20.[43] The organization further played a large role in sporting activity in the town. In the spring of 1936, for instance, it held weekly courses in general keep fit activities and table tennis.[44]

Strength Through Joy claimed that it facilitated the growth of social life in Osnabrück during the 1930s. In 1935 it arranged twelve performances at the theatre, while a further 161 were attended by members of the Strength Through Joy Movement. In all, the organization rather dubiously took credit for the evening activities of 140,000 'work colleagues' in 1935. In

1937 Strength Through Joy also claimed that it assisted 9,000 Osnabrückers per year to go on holiday either within Germany or to another part of Europe. The sister organization of Strength Through Joy, which aimed at improving the situation of factories, Beauty of Labour, claimed to have instituted changes in twenty factories in 1935.[45]

But much factory improvement and social life continued either with minimal support from Nazi quangos or completely independent from them. The DAF would have approved of the establishment of a workers' reading room by the OKD in 1938 and played a role in the opening ceremony of the new sports fields of Hammersen in 1936. Similarly, the Nazi party participated in the 'Day of the Gymnasts', held in September 1934, attended by many local functionaries, including Gaertner.[46] These local events reflected national sports festivals, which predated the Nazis but continued under the Third Reich in Nuremberg in 1934 and Breslau in 1938.[47]

Some sporting activity took place independently of the local state. The Osnabrück branch of the German Alpine Society appears to have continued as normal, with its membership increasing from 179 in 1933 to 242 by 1938.[48] On the other hand the Nazis closed down the *Sportverein Eversburg* because they considered it a socialist organization,[49] as part of the clampdown upon all youth and socialist organizations.[50] Other sporting groups, including the *Osnabrücker Sportclub* and the *Osnabrücker Turnverein*, came under the Nazi wing.[51] Much sporting activity, which had evolved during the course of the nineteenth century in Osnabrück, therefore carried on under Nazi control. Local traditions may have continued, but not independently.

The improvement in the position of the working classes formed part of the overall social policy of the Third Reich which fitted into the aim of creating a healthy *Volksgemeinschaft* which would produce increasing numbers of fit Aryans. In order to achieve such aims Nazi policy placed much effort into improving the health of those it deemed necessary of saving, as well as eliminating those with incurable hereditary conditions. An increase in the population of ethnic Germans meant that those who produced more than the norm would receive financial incentives as well as honours from the regime. Women took pride of place in the propaganda of this new society, which viewed single people and childless couples negatively.[52]

In order to construct the new social order the Nazis established a whole series of organizations, which aimed at improving the 'biological health' of those deemed worthy of support. The most senior body consisted of the NSV, the second largest party organization after the DAF, counting 12.5 million members by 1939. Its activities included the collection and distribution of charity as well as propagandising Nazi social welfare ideas. The NSV formed part of the Head Office for People's Welfare and worked together with the *Winterhilfswerk* (WHW) and the *Ernährungshilfswerk*.[53]

Osnabrück illustrates the activities of these organizations, especially the NSV. By the autumn of 1934 it placed much effort into assisting mothers and children through its subsidiary body *Hilfswerk Mutter und Kind*. It had, for instance, established a nursery. Furthermore, a kitchen offered food to those no longer entitled to assistance from the WHW. In addition, the NSV provided milk for schoolchildren.[54] By May 1936 the NSV had established nine homes which looked after 600 children on a daily basis.[55] In 1937 it spent RM78,555 on children's homes and nurseries in Osnabrück, financed 260 recovery courses for mothers, and sent 1,613 children to the countryside for holidays.[56]

The NSV represented just one organ of the Nazi welfare state. Above it stood the Office for People's Health which carried out other activities. Families could receive particularly generous benefits from this department, including home helps. A Mrs Hülsmann, who 'gave birth to her 4th child' in March 1939 obtained assistance 'from 13/3 – 18/3/1939 and received RM10'.[57] Meanwhile, 55 families living in the housing estate in Bremer Strasse received a settling in allowance of RM300 to RM750.[58]

Propaganda went together with the attempts to help the local population, linking health with race. In the winter of 1936, 'the Office for People's Health' ran a series of lectures 'concerning the most important health questions' including 'hereditary diseases, tuberculosis, cancer, dental health, sporting injuries, the care of mothers and children, the care of tubercular patients and care of the disabled'[59] The local press raised awareness about the fight against cancer, the activities of the WHW and assistance for war victims.[60] The fight against cancer became central in National Socialist health policy, encompassing an attempt to change eating habits and a campaign against tobacco.[61]

How successful were the Nazis in improving the health and social welfare of the local population? Little change occurred in the death rates of either children or adults between the late 1920s and the late 1930s, reflecting the position of Germany as an advanced industrial state with good welfare provision under both Weimar and the Third Reich. While the number of deaths at birth in Osnabrück went from 55 in 1928 to 39 ten years later, the overall death rate per 1,000 inhabitants went from 8.7 in 1928 to 10.3 in 1938 and 6.8 in 1939. The mortality rate of children less than one year old stood at 7.5 per thousand in both 1928 and 1938.[62] The main causes of death remained those which we would expect to find in an advanced state. In 1937, 203 people died of cancer, 164 of respiratory diseases, 199 from heart disease and 37 from tuberculosis.[63] An interesting indication of the consequences of Nazi policy may be an examination of the suicide rate in Osnabrück before the War, which went from 21 per 100,000 in 1932 to 26.4 in the following year, the peak year in the 1930s, and stood at 20.4 in 1939.[64]

Crime statistics may also help to reveal the success of Nazi economic and social policy, as they should demonstrate a decrease. In addition to the fact that we would expect a more law abiding society at a time of increasing economic prosperity, we also need to bear in mind a decrease in the sort of street violence which had characterized the end of the Weimar Republic and which surfaced only at the very beginning of the Third Reich, with the elimination of Communists, and on 9 November 1938. We are essentially concerned with everyday crime in assessing the success of Nazi social and economic policies, otherwise we enter a complex ethical discussion about the rights and wrongs of any regime.[65]

Table 3.1: Crime in Osnabrück, 1933-7

Type of Crime	Number in 1933	Number in 1936	Number in 1937
Murder	1	1	3
Robbery	3	14	11
Theft	1,522	1,256	1,314

Source: NSO Rep-430-201-16B-65-58, Kriminalstatistik, 1936, 1937; NSO Rep-430-201-16B-65-129, Kriminalstatistik 1933.

Figures produced by the Osnabrück police suggest that non-political crime did decrease under the Nazis before the outbreak of the War, as Table 3.1 demonstrates. The decline is most dramatic in the area of theft, while robbery increases marginally, as do the number of murders, although both rises are so small that we cannot really read anything into them. In contrast, the decline in the number of thefts suggests that Nazi policy made a difference. This may have had as much to do with the fear of the consequences of committing such crime, which could now result in severer penalties,[66] as it did with a reaction to a significant rise in living standards.

Women would play a central role in the new national community. While the ideology of the regime aimed at getting men back to work, it wanted to remove women, partly in order to make space for male labourers, but also because of the function of women in the new order as producers of increasing numbers of Aryans. Although the regime had limited success both in removing women from the workplace and increasing the birth rate, it completely succeeded in a third aim of eliminating women from political life. The regime established all manner of organizations involved in women's lives, including the NSV and *Hilfswerk Mutter und Kind*.

In trying to change the position of women, the Nazis worked in a state where women had seen some improvement in their position. Claudia Koonz claimed that the First World War had '"emancipated" millions of young women by giving them the status and autonomy women's rights advocates had demanded for decades'.[67] They carried out new jobs vacated by males fighting on the German fronts. Progress continued into the Weimar Republic. Between 1919 and 1932, 112 women were elected to the Reichstag and by 1929 Germany counted 2,500 female physicians, 300 lawyers and several dozen judges and professors. By 1925, 1.7 million more women worked than had done in 1907. In addition, some measure of sexual liberation had taken place as witnessed by the existence of groupings which publicised women's sexual needs.[68]

The Nazis viewed such advances negatively because of the ideological role which they assigned to women as baby producers. During the 1920s women had played a small role in the rise of the NSDAP, counting just 7,625 members in September 1920, or six per cent of the total. While the Nazis had worked with women's organizations during this decade, the first significant grouping set up by the party consisted of the *NS-Frauenschaft*, established in July 1931. During the Third Reich two major women's organizations existed in the form of the NSF, the more political of the groupings, concerned with organizing women, and the *Deutsches Frauenwerk*, more interested in organizing the social life of women in the interests of the nation.[69]

Intervention in women's lives commenced at childhood in the *Jung Mädchen* and the BDM. While women who had reached adolescence by the early 1930s could look back to a time before the Nazis, those born in the late 1920s would have gone through the beginnings of the life cycle of indoctrination, although the defeat of the Third Reich in 1945 meant that they never experienced the end of this process. While the Hitler Youth existed from 1926 the BDM surfaced in 1930.[70] The youth groups aimed at girls between the ages of 10 and 21. At the end of their schooling women would, following the passage of the Law for Work Service in 1935, along with their brothers, undertake a compulsory year's labour, which could encompass all manner of employment from factory work to land tillage to commercial occupations. Following this experience women might join the NSF, although in 1938 the organization counted just 2,294,677 members, while the DFW had 1,783,335.[71]

Osnabrück women born between 1920 and 1923 recalled their experiences with the BDM. Agnes Adel, who attended St Ursula during the 1930s remembered: 'We did not have a bad time in the BDM and the JM.' She regularly participated in BDM activities until the end of the War and gained a position of authority, responsible for girls up to the age of fourteen.[72] Similarly, Aneliese Diehl, from a working class protestant background recalled her time in the BDM as 'nice and romantic'.[73] In contrast, the middle class Maria Grün had been a member of a Roman Catholic youth organization dissolved by the Nazis and never joined the BDM.[74] Inge Walter had the most negative memories:

We girls had to join the JM, Young Girls. In our family it was like this. We were poor people. My father was a weaver and earned very little and I had no uniform. That had to be a blue skirt, a white blouse and this neckerchief with leather knots. We had to meet in the afternoons. That was undertaken by the JM, and I always ran at the end because I always came with a dress. Somehow the leader was too stupid and I got a brown waistcoat, with a swastika sign on the sleeves. My father said: `This brown shit is not coming into the house any more'. The waistcoat was therefore kept somewhere else. When I went out I had to collect it from my neighbour. That was very bad for children. But in general childhood was inspired by this organization. I did not have to go into the BDM, *Bund Deutscher Mädchen*, that was for fourteen and fifteen year olds, because my mother was dead and I had to work at the steelwork and look after the house.[75]

The interviews would suggest that Protestant girls and, by implication, their parents, viewed the BDM positively. The most negative reactions came from the Roman Catholic Maria Grün and the father of the Roman Catholic working class SPD supporting Inge Walter.

As in all aspects of the life of Osnabrück during the 1930s, propaganda tried to persuade local women about their role in the Third Reich, particularly their service as mothers. This went together with benefits awarded to those mothers and families regarded as *Kinderreich* (literally rich with children). The local press played a leading role in the praise of the German mother. A piece in the *Neue Volksblätter* of 21 May 1939, entitled 'To German Mothers', accompanied by several pictures of women with children, began: 'Throughout time the greatest joy in the life of a woman has been to give birth to children and to bring them up under the protection of a good marriage and a proper family life.'

'In everyday life the cult of motherhood found expression in the increasing popularity of Mother's Day',[76] as reported by the *Osnabrucker*

Tageblatt on 22 May 1939. 'Can a mother's day have been more filled with rays of sunshine, more joyous and more beautiful than this one. It was as if the spring had expressly adorned our city on this festive day of honour'. This particular Mother's Day combined the conventional celebrations with the distribution of the German Mother's Cross, introduced in 1938 for those women who had more than three children. To musical accompaniment and statements by members of the Hitler Youth, 1,971 mothers received the cross, 586 of whom had more than eight children in gold, 572 with six or seven children in silver and 813 with four or five children in bronze.[77] Some women even received their crosses posthumously.[78]

Giving birth to large numbers of children also meant financial benefits. For instance, those women with three children under ten received Honour Cards, which entitled them to preferential treatment while shopping.[79] On 20 August 1935 the *Bund der Kinderreichen* in Osnabrück wrote to the Mayor asking him to follow the example of other German cities by introducing a series of measures for families with over three children. These included grants for every child after the third, reduced rent, gas, water and public transport.[80] In May 1938 the city finance office made a grant of RM10,150, divided between 18 families, who received between RM550 and RM750 each to assist them to move into a housing estate for *Kinderreich* families.[81]

Despite the incentives introduced by the Nazis, which, however, continued policies adopted by the Weimar Republic towards the *Kinderreichen*,[82] the NSDAP had limited success in increasing the birth rate. It had fallen from 3.6 per cent in 1900 to 1.47 by 1933. The prevention of abortion for those deemed genetically sound and the abolition of contraceptives meant a slight increase to 1.97 per cent by 1938.[83] In Osnabrück the number of births grew from 1,428 in 1928 to 1,762 in 1938.[84] The six years of Nazi rule up to 1939 may have resulted in some increase in the birth rate, but this remained comparable to the other leading western states.[85]

As well as assisting healthy mothers the Nazi women's organizations impacted on Osnabrück in other ways. Advice centres offered help on biological health and the rearing of children.[86] The *Hilfswerk Mutter und Kind* had begun to run courses in Osnabrück in November 1934 covering housework, the bringing up of children, sewing and nursing.[87] A new home for mothers also opened in Osnabrück in 1937.[88]

Economic growth prevented the new regime from removing women from the workplace.[89] Between 1933 and 1935 the percentage of women in the workforce did decline from 37.1 to 31.6 as unemployed males came back into the labour force. But while 900,000 women may have returned home, an equal number replaced them. In 1936 over eleven million women remained in the German labour force with 4.65 million in agriculture, 2.7 million in industry and crafts, 1.9 million in trade and transport, 1.3 million in domestic service, and 500,000 in public service.[90] The introduction of labour service, which came into operation in Osnabrück at the end of 1934 also ensured that women continued to work.[91] As the War approached Osnabrück women found themselves working unsociable hours in engineering factories. For instance, Klöckner employed 130 women on three shifts in the autumn of 1938,[92] while in the following year it employed women on Good Friday.[93]

For significant sections of the population, the economic changes instituted by the Nazis had resulted in much improvement before 1939. The elimination of unemployment as a result of public works building programmes and rearmament, which meant the creation of new jobs by the private sector, as well as forced labour, represented the biggest difference. The desperation of the late Weimar period no longer existed. The various schemes introduced by the Nazis to make workers feel good about themselves also had an impact. The attempts to change the position of women had some success, but hardly fulfilled the ideological goals of the Nazis. However, in many cases the NSDAP simply continued policies introduced by Weimar, including support for families and work creation programmes. One of the most fundamental changes consisted of the readiness to use force.

Persuading Adults in Peacetime

While the Third Reich implemented significant economic and social changes before 1939, these transformations were backed up by a policy of persuasion which encompassed all aspects of the lives of the residents of German towns. Propaganda aimed at selling both the regime and its ideology of the Aryan *Volksgemeinschaft*. The Third Reich used various methods of persuasion, which operated on different levels. In the first place it utilized fairly crude propaganda techniques of the type which it had employed before the seizure of power. Mass meetings and street parades, for instance, continued. But the Nazis now had the chance to have a more profound impact upon Germans. The methods of persuasion impacted upon every aspect of life, perhaps most profoundly upon the calendar, which determined the dates of festivities in the new state, revolving around the central events in the Nazi rise to power and, just as importantly, around Hitler.[94] More obviously the NSDAP took control of the broadcasting media in the form of cinema and radio. It further controlled high culture including theatre, opera and museum exhibitions, which increasingly focused upon core Nazi themes such as race or military expansion.

The Nazis established methods to directly control propaganda and culture immediately after they came to power. The Ministry for Popular Enlightenment and Propaganda began work on 12 March 1933. A Law of September 1933 set up the Reich Chamber of Culture, which had responsibility for literature, theatre, music, radio, film, fine arts, and the press. Through these bodies Goebbels, as Minister of Propaganda, had ultimate control over the media and artistic life in the Third Reich.[95]

The NSDAP implemented root and branch changes in the everyday ritual of ordinary Germans. People found themselves celebrating new holidays and saw the introduction of events such as 'Stew Sundays', which involved collective eating for the purpose of bringing the national community closer together. Furthermore, Germans discovered that street names had changed and, perhaps most dramatically of all, that they would have to greet each other in a new way.

In Osnabrück some of the major streets changed their names. Most notably, Neumarkt became Adolf Hitler Platz on 30 March 1933, while Friedrich Ebert Allee became Horst Wessel Allee.[96] On 13 July 1933 the Reich Interior Minister, Wilhelm Frick, issued a directive informing all public employees to use the 'German Greeting', 'Heil Hitler', while everybody would have to hold up their right arm when singing the national anthem or the Horst Wessel song.[97]

The central days of the Nazi rise to power were celebrated with mass festivity. For instance, 30 January. In 1935, 'Hitler flags fluttered in every street, while the machines stood still in many businesses and factories: as in the rest of Germany, Osnabrück commemorated the day of the victorious uprising of 30 January with numerous factory gatherings'.[98] In 1937 swastikas decorated streets throughout the town while all of the local Nazi groupings held meetings in the evening,[99] events repeated in 1938.[100]

Similar proceedings commemorated 9 November, the date of the failed Munich Beer Hall Putsch. The events of 1934, publicised in advance in the local press, began at 7.30 in the morning, with the arrival of SA men to lay a wreath, and concluded with the coming together of various groups of marchers, including representatives of the SA and the Hitler Youth in Pottgraben at 8pm. The memorialization of those who died for the movement represented the theme of this day. In 1937 commemorators included 'representatives of the party and state', from the NSF, schools, factories, local authorities and the army. A notice in the *Osnabrücker Tageblatt* told people to hang out flags on 9 November.[101]

While 9 November became a day of commemoration, 20 April, Hitler's birthday, developed into a day of celebration. It both formed a central day in the new calendar and a focal point in the creation and manifestation of the 'Hitler Myth'.[102] Reporting of the movements and speeches of Hitler in the Osnabrück press indicates the level of fanaticism, which surrounded the *Führer*. The celebration of his birthday simply represented the pinnacle of this process. Other actions by Hitler received much attention in the local press. In November 1933 the *Osnabrücker Zeitung* carried a report about a radio speech which he made under the headline of: 'Osnabrück Hears the *Führer*! The Whole of Osnabrück Gathered Around the Loudspeaker',[103] pointing to the importance which the Nazis placed upon radio.[104] Advanced notices actually appeared in the press urging the population to listen to such broadcasts by Hitler.[105] Eulogization reached a peak in March 1938 when Hitler made his third visit to Osnabrück, simply passing through on a journey from Hamburg to Cologne. But the front page of the *Osnabrücker Tageblatt* of 31 March carried a series of sycophantic statements in bold headlines including: 'A Frenzy of Enthusiasm Over the *Führer's* Special Train – Nine Minutes: An Unforgettable Experience – A Cry of Jubilation from the Thousands on Platform 1'. The front page story continued with mini headlines such as '14.02 – 14.11', and 'Platform 1 Experiences Its Greatest Day'. A picture accompanied the story. Not all of those present at this event reacted so positively. Werner Funk recalled:

I, for instance, first despised Hitler when I saw him on the platform in Osnabrück. The train travelled very slowly and then stopped. And then I saw our honourable *Führer* with a face plastered with make up. He was probably very pale and was therefore fabulously made up. Because he travelled by so slowly, I think: he made himself up like a tart, that is our *Führer*.[106]

While radio broadcasts and visits to Osnabrück may have represented special treats for Hitler fanatics, the staple date in the calendar consisted of the Führer's birthday, culminating in the 50th birthday celebrations of 1939, the last before the outbreak of the War. The events of 1933 already went 'far beyond any "normal" honouring of a Head of Government. The streets and squares of practically every German town and village were festooned with the outward signs of adulation and public acclamation of the "People's Chancellor"'.[107] In Osnabrück German and Nazi flags fluttered throughout the town, while church bells and services also celebrated the event.[108] But the events of this year, and their reporting, remained fairly low key in comparison with the years just before the outbreak of War.[109]

The peak of fanatical festivities arrived with Hitler's fiftieth birthday in 1939, publicised days in advance. On 16 April the *Neue Volksblätter* indicated the 'Progression of the Day', in several paragraphs addressed 'To All Osnabrückers.' The article continued: 'The 50th birthday of the *Führer* will be celebrated as the festive day of the nation in Osnabrück in the fullest sense of the word'. It would begin with singing in various places throughout the town. Between 11 and 12 the Army would parade through the town. Celebrations involving all sections of the Hitler Youth and the BDM would proceed during the afternoon. In the evening there would follow a parade of Nazi officials after which an SA march would occur. Dancing and music would also take place in the evening. On 20 April 1939 the *Neue Volksblätter* printed a copy of a birthday card from the town, as well as recalling the three occasions when Hitler came to Osnabrück complete with photographs. On 21 April both the *Neue Volksblätter* and the *Osnabrücker Tageblatt* carried pictures of the previous day's festivities.

Hitler remained at the centre of Nazism. The celebration of his birthday represented the highpoint of the 'Hitler Myth'. The festivities for both his birthday and other days in the Nazi calendar allowed a focus upon the successes which the party had achieved. The NSDAP also cemented its place in the everyday lives of Germans by impacting upon their consciousness by the commemoration of national days. The celebration of German nationalism became synonymous with the Nazis and, in turn, Adolf Hitler.

The NSDAP also adapted other more traditional days to reflect their ideology. For instance, the Osnabrück *Volks and Schützenfest*, an annual event which took place every summer tied up with pride in the distinctiveness of the locality, involving a parade and the election of a King and attended by some of the leading local Nazis, including Münzer in 1934 and Gaertner in 1937.[110] Similarly, the Party continued to make much of mid-summer day, as they had done before 1933.[111] Most importantly, celebrations of the traditional worker's day, 1 May, continued.[112] It now became 'The National Holiday of the German People'[113] and 'The Holiday of the German People's Community'.[114] The programme for 1934 involved about 30,000 men participating in marches.[115] This had increased to 40,000 in 1936, who all, according to the *Osnabrücker Zeitung* of 3 May 1936, 'paid homage to the *Führer* on Klushügel'.[116]

The celebration of national days simply became one aspect of the spectacle of Nazism. Public displays, and the urging of local people to participate in them took place on a daily basis. 'Stew Sundays' involved members of all classes sitting together with the aim of solidifying the people's community, as explained by the *Osnabrücker Zeitung* of 7 November 1935: 'On Sunday a communal meal of stew will be served in 14 rooms in Osnabrück. Rich and poor sit at the same table. Comrades, who live next to each other in their everyday lives, can get to know each other; one can hear the problems and needs of the other'. The party issued 3,000 tickets for sale at RM1.10. Apart from attempting to create a feeling of solidarity amongst the local population, Stew Sundays also had the aim of raising money for the WHW. As well as the serving of this dish in public, housewives were urged to prepare it and to give leftovers to the WHW. The organization of the event, which tended to occur in winter, functioned at all levels, involving anything from one Nazi subgroup, to the whole of Osnabrück, to the entire country.[117]

Stew Sundays remained a relatively subtle way of indoctrination. The public political meetings which had accompanied the Nazi rise to power continued with the same regularity after 1933 and formed a core part of local newspaper reporting. Some of the largest rallies occurred when senior Nazi figures spoke in Osnabrück. Thus 20,000 people attended a meeting addressed by Hans Frank, *Reichsminister* without portfolio, in March 1936.[118] A large crowd also greeted a speech by Baldur von Schirach, the Hitler Youth leader, two years later.[119]

After 1933 the SA marched and met at will,[120] as did the SS. At the start of February 1933, for instance, the Osnabrück SA held a 'German Evening' led by a speech from Dr Marxer.[121] The SA organized a commemorative evening every year to remember the death of Horst Wessel, killed by communists in 1930.[122] SA marching, meanwhile, remained part of the everyday life of Osnabrück, particularly during the major commemorative days. The SS also held their own evenings.[123]

As well as the jackboot politics of the paramilitary wings of Nazi party, more sedate political meetings, essentially academic lectures, characterized Osnabrück in the 1930s. For instance, the Osnabrück 'propaganda cell' organized a series of gatherings to take place on 21 January 1937 on the theme of 'World Enemy No.1, Peace with Moscow???'[124] Meetings on racial themes occurred regularly. On 25 March 1935 the *Altstadt* branch of the Osnabrück NSDAP held lectures about 'Race as Fate.'[125] In March 1937 a larger meeting in the *Stadthalle* included speeches by Erwin Kolkmeyer and Dr Warning, leader of the Gau Racial and Political Office on 'The Biological Fate of Germany.'[126]

Public lectures reached a fairly limited audience running into hundreds or thousands, although newspaper reporting meant the message could reach the entire population of Osnabrück. More importantly, by the 1930s, mass media had arrived in Germany, more specifically, radio,[127] which really took off in that decade, and cinema, established since the early decades of the twentieth century. The Nazis made good use of both media throughout the 1930s. By 1937 the *Reichskulturkammer* had a branch in Osnabrück.[128]

Cinema spread all aspects of Nazi ideology, above all race, where Goebbels took a personal interest in standardising contents and eliminating any opposition.[129] In Osnabrück all of the cinemas were rebuilt either just before the Nazis came to power or during the course of the 1930s. As well as indoctrination through the films, Swastikas also greeted audiences within the theatres. Cinemas took part in the various Nazi celebration days, as they showed films about the Nazi rise to power. In addition, they also helped to indoctrinate children.[130] The biggest events in Osnabrück cinema during the course of the 1930s arrived in August 1938 when up to ten thousand people attended a series of open air propaganda films held on Klushügel.[131] But most of the films shown in Osnabrück had no overt propaganda message. In July 1937 the screenings at the Universum consisted of 'The Glass Bullet', a detective story, and 'Intermezzo', about 'the exciting life of a great female artist'.[132] In fact, throughout the 1930s, less than thirty per cent of films shown at German cinemas had a political theme.[133]

Nazi ideology also influenced high culture, although racial views did not first appear with the Nazi seizure of power, having a tradition dating back to Wagner and before.[134] Nevertheless, as Edward Bahr has argued, the propagation of racial ideas now became central to Nazi cultural policy.[135] Part of the process of *Gleichschaltung* in music[136] involved eradicating Jewish composers, especially Mendelssohn, Meyerbeer, Offenbach, Schoenberg and Mahler, none of whom appeared on the programme of the Osnabrück Symphony Orchestra after 1933.[137] During the 1938-39 season the works of non-Jewish German and Austrian composers dominated the programmes of the Osnabrück City Orchestra, with pieces by Beethoven, Brahms, Bruckner, Hermann Grabner, Armin Knab, Max Reger, Helmut Riethsmüller, Karl Schäfer, Schumann, Richard Strauss and Max Trapp.[138]

Theatre in Osnabrück also became integrated into National Socialist ideals, stemming from the Theatre Department of the Propaganda Ministry, which 'oversaw all personnel, subsidy and programme policy'.[139] In April 1933 the Jewish director of the Osnabrück City Theatre, Fritz Berend, was sacked and replaced by Walter Storz as the name of the building changed to the German National Theatre.[140] The programme remained predominantly German. In the 1938-9 season the only non-German play consisted of *Hamlet*, although the ten opera performances in that year included works by Verdi, Tchaikovsky and Ponchielli.[141] But many of the programmes carried statements by leading Nazis. For instance, a programme for a performance of Verdi's *Don Carlos* on 25 April 1937 included a message from Goebbels on 'German Theatre Culture'.[142] Yet we should not overestimate the changes which occurred in German theatrical performances under the Third Reich. Certainly, new plays with Nazi themes appeared, but much of the repertoire remained the same with foreign works continuing to feature.[143]

Museum exhibitions also spread Nazi ideology, as the content of some of those in Osnabrück during the 1930s demonstrates. As with other aspects of high culture, the propagation of racial and militaristic views through such events did not represent a new development in German life.

The German Hygiene Museum had organized travelling exhibitions throughout the early decades of the twentieth century.[144] In this context a wandering display on 'Heritage and Race Amongst the German People' reached Osnabrück in February 1935.[145] In 1939 the city museum opened a section looking at Osnabrück's military history and glorifying the soldiers stationed there.[146] Earlier, in April 1934, an exhibition had taken place commemorating 'the struggle of the SA and the NSDAP in Osnabrück'.[147]

Perhaps the most important artistic exhibition in the town during the course of the 1930s consisted of the Osnabrücker Art Show, which occurred in 1935, organized by the *Dürerbund*, a member of the *Reichskammer* for Visual Arts, but excluding anything from the most famous Osnabrück artist of this time, Felix Nussbaum.[148] Such selective exhibitions occurred against the background of an artistic policy directed by the ideological underpinnings of the Third Reich and controlled by the Reich Chamber of Visual Arts.[149]

Persuading Children in Peacetime

While those who had reached adulthood by the beginning of the 1930s may have needed new forms of persuasion to win them over to the new racial Germany, the transformation of the minds of children began at an earlier age. As with other aspects of life in Germany during the 1930s the Nazis attempted to take total control, not simply within the schools, with new syllabi and new teachers, but also in the social life of pupils through the influence of the Hitler Youth, which, by World War Two, had touched the minds of most German children and adolescents outside school time by offering them a combination of play and indoctrination. This did not usually succeed in the case of those with parents opposed to the regime, particularly if they came from socialist or devout Roman Catholic backgrounds.

Education faced reconstruction from top to bottom, with the establishment of a new ministry and the introduction of legislation to change the curriculum. The measures passed did not simply wish to change the education of children, but also to control those who instructed them. They aimed at influencing all levels of the education of children and adolescents from elementary until high school and beyond.

At the top of the educational administrative tree the Nazis established the Ministry for Science, Education and People's Training in May 1934.[150] But educational policy under the Third Reich had more overtly political aims including the implementation of racial consciousness. State education would not aim primarily at intellectual development, but at the production of healthy human beings, as well as at the building of character, with the ultimate aim of serving in the army. The adults produced should not consist of theoretical but political people, 'men of action'. Girls should essentially have a preparation for motherhood, in order to produce racially pure Aryan Germans. These aims looked forward to future German warring and expansion, especially in eastern Europe.[151]

Nazi aims meant both changes in the organization of schools and, more importantly, the transformation of the syllabus to reflect them, with the introduction of lessons on racial biology and military awareness. A new professional organization for teachers, the NSLB, existed from 1926. Under the Third Reich membership became compulsory so that by 1936, 97 per cent of all teachers had joined the group, 32 per cent of whom also had NSDAP membership cards.[152] The Osnabrück branch of the NSLB held fairly regular meetings, including one on 27 May 1936 to greet the election of a new local leader, Herr Lilienthal, with cries of 'Sieg Heil'. An earlier meeting of 4 December 1935 had listened to a lecture on the *Führer* principle.[153] This reflects the overall aim of Nazi education of teachers which wanted a 'teaching personality – rooted in the National Socialist worldview – which guaranteed an education of indoctrination'.[154]

The regime implemented new measures at the different levels of schooling aimed at the injection of Nazi ideology. At the elementary level one of the most important pieces of legislation consisted of the 'Decree for the Introduction of the Guiding Principles for the First Years in Elementary Schools', which declared that 'elementary schools, had, together with other types of schools and in conjunction with the Party, labour service, and the army, the highest task of educating German youth for the Führer and the nation for entry into the people's community'. Similar measures came into operation at the higher levels of school education.[155]

A series of sources allow the reconstruction of schooling in Osnabrück between 1933 and 1939. In 1933 the state did not control all education, as some fee paying schools existed, including St Ursula. Gradually, this school came under Nazi control, a process completed at the outbreak of War.[156] The last confessional elementary schools, essentially Roman Catholic, also lost their independence by 1939, having previously controlled the education of about half the pupils in Osnabrück with this religious background.[157]

Some Osnabrück teachers did not have Nazi leanings despite the fact that the overwhelming majority of them had become members of the NSLB. The *Realgymnasium* counted twelve full party members out of a total teaching personnel of 36 in 1935. By the end of 1938 the former had increased to 21.[158] Elsewhere, educational cleansing occurred. At the *Ratsgymnasium* ten new teachers secured positions in 1933-4 at the expense of others.[159] The Roman Catholic *Gymnasium Carolinium* boys school counted 22 teachers in 1933, all Catholics, thirteen of whom had served in the First World War, just one of whom had joined the NSDAP up to that time.[160]

In the case of St Ursula, a mixture of allegiances existed, predominantly to God, because many of the teachers consisted of nuns, as remembered by pupils. Margret Friedrich stated that, in addition to the nuns 'we had a whole series of young teachers…who had no interest and nothing to do with any Nazis.'[161] When asked if she had noticed any changes in the school as a result of Nazi influence, Josefa Herz replied:

No, the sisters were very anxious, I still know that. The crosses – the cross always hung behind the desk – always had to be under Hitler to the left or the right and the picture of Hitler over the desk, and the sisters had to greet us with Heil Hitler. And when there were holidays we all had to gather together in the inner courtyard and stand there in rows and files, and then the flags were raised up high with a swastika and the German flag, and then we had to sing 'Deutschland, Deutschland über alles'. And then 'Die Fahne Hoch, die Reihen Festgeschlossen', the Nazi song. The sisters had to participate, and they did, because they were scared, one could see that.[162]

In the school syllabus the amount of time devoted to physical exercise, biology, history and geography grew, while that devoted to mathematics and foreign languages declined.[163] In the academic year 1933-4 Osnabrück high schools taught fairly traditional subjects. History teaching, for instance, ranged from the German Empire to 'England in the Period of Absolutism'.[164] Table 3.2 indicates the changes in time devoted to different subjects during the course of the 1920s and 1930s as reflected in one Osnabrück secondary school, the *Gymnasium*.[165] While exercise clearly played a role in building up fit children, biology, history and geography provided knowledge of various aspects of the German environment, in contrast with the now less important foreign languages.

But, as Table 3.2 indicates, physical exercise clearly increased. In 1934 the new Ministry of Science, Education and People's Training brought in a 'third exercise hour', which followed the reintroduction of boxing into senior boys' schools. In 1937 the weekly hours devoted to exercise had risen to five for boys. Competition between schools played a large role in physical exercise. On 22 June 1934, for instance, Osnabrück children participated in the German Youth Festival, which involved a variety of sporting competitions. In order to oversee the implementation of physical exercise a new government office for physical education came into existence in 1934.[166]

The increase in physical exercise during the 1930s reflected other educational preparations for war. For instance, the building of model aircraft became part of woodwork lessons in boys' schools as a result of a ministerial decree from 17 November 1934. In the following year an exhibition on air travel in the town included models produced by Osnabrück schoolboys. A competition in the academic year 1937-8 resulted in the construction of 658 model aircraft in schools in the town. The school activities complemented the flying corps of the Hitler Youth and the *Jungvolk* in the town.[167]

Table 3.2 Timetable of the *Gymnasium*, Osnabrück, 1924 and 1938.

Year	1924	1938
Physical Exercise	24	40
German	31	33
History	19	22
Geography	12	16
Art	14	12
Music	14	14
Biology	7	16
Chemistry	2	4
Mathematics	33	27
Latin	53	35
Greek	36	30
English	15	12
Religion	18	12
Total	287	279

Source: NSO Dep-58b-1, 'Strukturwandel in Aufgaben und Ausgaben 1932 bis jetzt', 1938.

Instruction in biology took off as part of the process of racial indoctrination. By 1936 pupils at the *Ratsgymnasium* learnt about death rates and their implications for 'the senescence of the German people'.

Philosophical instruction in the same year had also become racialized, with teaching under the title of 'Culture and Race'. This meant that 'the importance of the Nordic races for culture and racial unity as a condition for culturally productive periods shall be demonstrated'.[168] Meanwhile, as early as the 1933/4 school year the compulsory elements of citizenship studies at the *Reformsgymnasium* consisted of instruction on 'People, State and Personality', which included consideration of 'the fundamentals of race.'[169]

By 1939 essays written by students at the *Gymansium Carolinum* carried copious references to the works of Hitler and other senior National Socialist figures.[170] The study of geography had also become infused with racial ideas. In primary schools: 'Geographical education has, to a large extent, the task of realizing the aims of National Socialist education policy. At the centre stands the German people with its hundred million and its living space.' Instruction would focus upon the dependency of Germans and other people upon living space.[171]

By the outbreak of War the Nazis had transformed the education of schoolchildren. While the changes may have built upon developments from the nineteenth century, the new curriculum increasingly focused upon ideas which had previously received limited attention, including racial hygiene. The introduction of more physical training and aircraft building brought to the attention of schoolchildren the possibility of Germany fighting a war in the near future.

School instruction formed just one aspect of the education of children. The first Nazi boys grouping came into existence at the founding meeting of the NSDAP on 13 May 1922. The Hitler Youth was actually established in 1926. An important turning point in its history came with the appointment of Baldur Von Schirach as Imperial Youth Leader on 30 October 1931. Membership of the organization had reached 107,956 by the beginning of 1933 and 3,577,565 by the end of 1934, including members of the BDM. Growth did not occur at quite the rate which the party hierarchy had hoped for during the 1930s, despite the fact that the Hitler Youth gradually devoured all other confessional and political groups for young people. Membership only became compulsory in March 1939. The 7,728,259 members at the start of 1939 constituted 87.1 per cent of all youths between the ages of 10 and 18. The Hitler Youth as a whole divided into sub-groups according to gender and age. Full membership only occurred in the ages 14-18. Between 10-14 children joined the *Jungvolk*.

The activities of the Hitler Youth infleueced all aspects of the everyday lives of young Germans, with the aim of instilling belief in the party and the *Führer*, as well as instigating military values, so that young men underwent a lengthy preparation for national service. As well as weekly activities, children spent time with their peers away from home. Members of the Hitler Youth also played a central role in the Nazi celebrations of the 1930s. The organization further became involved in school activities so that many teachers were members.[172]

The Hitler Youth grew gradually in Osnabrück during the course of the 1930s. The ten members of April 1929 had increased to 8,850 males and 7,000 females by 1939. As the membership grew so did the number of Osnabrück sub-branches and Hitler Youth homes. By 1931 three different groups existed. Initially, the organization met in lofts, pubs, cellars and empty houses. After 1933 school rooms also came into use. At the end of 1937 the Osnabrück Hitler Youth decided to build twelve homes from scratch so that each sub-group within the town would have its own, beginning with Eversburg and Schinkel.[173]

The Osnabrück Hitler Youth participated in a range of activities. They played a central role in the Nazi commemorative days, as well as in other events organized by the local NSDAP. The Hitler Youth, like the rest of the Nazi movement, did a lot of marching in Osnabrück during the 1930s. For instance, they participated in 'propaganda marches' over the Whitsun weekend in 1933. On 6 July 1938, 818 members of the Osnabrück Hitler Youth gathered together in front of the town hall to begin 'a march to the border'.[174]

Members of the group also participated in political meetings, which involved leading figures in the local or national establishment. The biggest day in the history of the Osnabrück Hitler Youth occurred on 26 March 1938 when Baldur von Schirach visited the town, made a speech and inspected members of the local organization. Thousands of marchers greeted him, as he spoke from the balcony of the town hall.[175] Similarly, on 6 June 1937 the entire membership of all branches of the Hitler Youth turned up to hear speeches by Münzer and Gaertner.[176] Münzer spoke at the annual gathering to celebrate the entry of each particular year's youth into the *Jungvolk*, accompanied by Nazi ceremonial and aimed at giving newcomers a sense of their own value within the party.[177]

Hitler Youth members participated in activities away from home, such as the winter camp for leaders which took place in the Osnabrück Youth Hostel from 24 January to 5 February 1937 and from where the *Neue Volksblätter* subsequently published extracts from daily reports written by participants, such as that from 3 February:

> After the usual morning formalities, washing, bed making, flag hoisting and eating, the local leader Hafner made a short speech about topography. We then marched towards Westerberg in order to put into practice observing, describing, and examining the land, as

well as sharpening the senses and practising camouflage. At the same time we had a good overview of the city of Osnabrück. We were divided and each of us could see that he had learnt something. As a leader one must have more ability and be able to achieve more than his comrades.[178]

Like members of the BDM, males recalling their days in the Hitler Youth often did so fondly. Hugo Weiss, born in 1927, recalled that: 'At the age of ten I became a youth leader, the superior for twelve boys, which naturally enormously impressed me. At the age of twelve I was a youth column leader and thus had command over thirty boys'.[179] Günther Adam, meanwhile, born in 1921, had a less positive experience. He had joined a grouping called the *Bund Deutsche Jungmännern* (League of German Young Men), a type of Scout Movement, at the age of eleven. This became part of the *Jungvolk*. 'But everything then took on a more military character. Then one had to stand still and stand to attention and that was not for me'.[180] More organized resistance to the Hitler Youth also surfaced in Osnabrück.[181]

Before 1939 the Third Reich used a wide range of methods to influence public opinion, attempting to persuade people of the rightness of the Nazi path from the cradle to the grave, from dusk to dawn, in the streets and in the home. Consequently, the regime did convince much of the population about the rightness of its cause, although many others simply kept their heads down, as they would do under any political regime. Nazi rule allowed the developments of the early 1930s to reach a higher level of sophistication, as the party had control of the instruments of the state. They influenced not only political discourse, but also had an impact on culture at all levels. More importantly, the changing educational curriculum, as well as the growth of the Nazi youth organizations, meant that the NSDAP began to mould the minds of children, potentially creating a tactile population for the foreseeable future.

The Elimination of Political Opponents

As a non-democratic regime which aimed at creating a new society, the Third Reich did not simply implement creative measures but also used destructive policies. The Nazis initially focused upon eradicating those regarded as threatening in the form of members of the SPD and the KPD, using concentration camps and emergency legislation. Attention then turned to those who threatened the new racial order in the form of the hereditary sick. The state also constantly kept an eye on any other potential opposition ranging from the Churches to anybody who uttered a word out of place, which the surveillance system which operated helped it to do.

The ease with which political opposition faced elimination suggests that neither organized nor spontaneous resistance could have done very much after 1933, other than survive, waiting for the regime to weaken. The SPD and KPD lived either in exile, moving around Europe as the Nazis took over different states,[182] or worked underground within Germany, as Peukert has demonstrated with regard to the Ruhr where one of the largest left wing power bases before 1933 continued to operate, despite surveillance and threat of arrest.[183] If one of the strongest and most organized socialist groups in Europe declined to participating in scattered meetings in secrecy, what chance did either the Churches or the hereditary sick stand against the Nazi juggernaut? The answer remains little, certainly in terms of overthrowing the regime. Nevertheless, the Churches took a moral stand against the Third Reich, although they did not challenge it.

Two central themes therefore present themselves when dealing with the elimination of opposition. First, what measures did the Nazis take to deal with enemies. And, second, what sort of possibilities existed for resistance. The NSDAP used a combination of legality, or quasi-legality, and force, backed up by surveillance. The elimination of the biggest threat, the Left, took place after the election of January 1933, when the Nazis introduced a series of emergency measures which lessened the freedom of the press and resulted in the arrest of political opponents and the suspension of parliament. The *Reichstag* election victory of 1933 allowed the full rage of the beast to sound, so that all potential left wing opponents faced arrest and incarceration in camps. Perhaps the most important measure in the entire twelve years of Nazi rule consisted of the Enabling Act of 23 March 1933, which essentially allowed the party to do anything it wished including closing down the *Reichstag*. In the following few months all other political parties became illegal, resulting in the establishment of a one party state.[184] Having laid the legal basis for the elimination of its political opponents, the new regime then moved on to tackle the racial threat, dealing first with Jews, who did not disappear until the War, and then with the hereditary sick, in which the crucial measure consisted of the passage of the Law for the Prevention of Hereditary Diseased Offspring of 14 July 1933. In addition, new measures attempted to bring both the Protestant and Roman Catholic Churches under control.

Abolishing the parties of its political opponents demonstrated that the NSDAP had a willingness to use force. It relied on two instruments in the form of the paramilitary forces and the concentration camp. Initially, the SA played the major role in the arrest, beating up and incarceration of left-wing opponents. This organization reared its head again on *Kristallnacht*, when its members burnt down synagogues and Jewish shops.[185] During the

1930s, the *Gestapo* also came into its own, keeping tabs on any potential resistance through a system of surveillance which relied upon informers.[186]

The *Gestapo* maintained order with help of the SS, which played the leading role in running the camp system. The introduction of places of incarceration for the purposes of 'protective custody' took place immediately after the Nazi seizure of power. Dachau proved the model camp, existing from March 1933 until 1945, but others followed throughout the country. They declined in importance after 1933, but took off again following the arrests of *Kristallnacht*, truly coming into their own after 1939, as the Nazis established all manner of death and concentration camps throughout the European continent.[187]

Incarceration in concentration camps required the cooperation of the legal profession as most of the arrests which occurred did so in a quasi legal way. The courts played a major role in the elimination of the KPD and SPD, as they tried those arrested during the early years of the regime under measures introduced to extend offences of high treason. As early as March 1933 special courts came into operation, which would function for the next twelve years to deal with any actions which threatened the regime.[188]

The new regime initially eliminated all forms of potential political opposition from the Left, which meant arrest and incarceration of active members of the SPD and KPD in towns throughout Germany, as well as the suspension of local democracy, developments which have received attention in local studies of towns throughout the Reich.[189] The Nazis came out as the leading party in Osnabrück following the *Reichstag* election of 1933, securing nearly 42 per cent of the vote, compared with 21.5 per cent for the second placed SPD.[190]

Although the NSDAP gained power at the end of January 1933 and introduced emergency measures, campaigning by the opposition SPD and KPD continued into February. Meetings took place in the *Stadthalle*, together with street fights between Communists and Nazis. On 2 March 1933, following the passage of the Decree for the Protection of People and State as a result of the *Reichstag* Fire of the previous day, the local police arrested three members of the local KPD and confiscated 15,000 leaflets, as well as taking some leading SPD functionaries into custody. By this time the local state had started to prevent the publication of newspapers, most notably the SPD's *Freie Presse* from 23 February. The *Osnabrücker Volkszeitung*, which supported the *Zentrum*, suffered the same fate in the following month.

After the election victory of 5 March Nazis celebrated on the streets of Osnabrück. Just as the new regime eliminated opposition on a national level, it also did so at the communal level. During the spring all political parties, other than the NSDAP, became illegal, as did free trade unions.

March and April witnessed the arrest of 10,000 communists and socialists throughout the country. In Osnabrück, local elections were due to take place on 12 March, one week after the *Reichstag* poll. However, on 11 March the symbolic killing of political opposition in the town occurred when the SS occupied the Trade Union House in Osnabrück and placed a placard over the entrance declaring 'SS Home'. All employees faced expulsion from the building as members of the SS threw paper out of the window and smashed the doors and desks. This action followed the outlawing of the SPD, KPD and trade unions on 7 March. The NSDAP inevitably won the elections of the following day.[191]

The following months witnessed purges from Osnabrück political life of both leading figures in the establishment and communists, socialists and trade unionists. In addition, the works of writers such as Stefan and Arnold Zweig, Thomas and Heinrich Mann, Erich Maria Remarque (born in Osnabrück) and Bertolt Brecht faced removal from bookshops and public burning on 10 May, a pattern repeated throughout the country. Some of the leading local officials from the Weimar period found themselves facing periods of extended leave including Adolf Sonnenschein, the *Regierungspräsident* and Johannes Drees, a *Zentrum* member of the *Reichstag*.[192]

By the end of March ten Osnabrück Communists faced detention including Ludwig Landwehr. Seven arrests took place on 18 March and by the end of the month thirteen people were in custody in Osnabrück. A newspaper report of 29 March alluded to the trial of leading communists in the town, who faced prison terms of two and three months. The number of people in custody did not decline until the end of the year, standing at three at the end of December and four by the following June, all held in a camp in Papenberg.[193] A total of 120 Osnabrückers faced incarceration under the Third Reich for political reasons, made up of 88 members of the KPD, 25 from the SPD, 5 from the DDP/DNVP, 1 from the *Zentrum* and 1 from the SAPD. The Communists August Arndt and Ludwig Landwehr spent eight and six years respectively in Sachsenhausen, where Emil Jagusch also found himself interned. All three survived to tell the tale. But six communists and seven members of the SPD from Osnabrück died in detention, mostly during the War, far away from the town, some of them having faced arrest on several occasions.[194]

The SPD and KPD represented a way of life for many sections of the German working classes.[195] But in Osnabrück virtually all traces of any sort of left wing activity had disappeared by the middle of 1935, following a concerted campaign by the local police authorities to mop up any remnants of resistance. The Higher Regional Court in Hamm in the Ruhr held responsibility for trying those accused of high treason over a vast area stretching northward to Osnabrück and beyond. Its decisions reveal that even the most innocuous activity was crushed.

The trial and elimination of Osnabrück Communists and Socialists took place in a series of stages, with some court proceedings receiving newspaper coverage. The first to face trial in Hamm included those arrested in the general round up of left wingers in the spring of 1933. For instance, in late July six Osnabrück Communists received prison sentences of between one and two years for high treason because they had remained members of the KPD until March 1933.[196] On 7 November two Osnabrück Communists faced sentences of one year and fifteen months for possessing communist leaflets and a gun, allegedly for the purpose of high treason.[197]

Johann Stump, the leader of the Osnabrück KPD had faced arrest in the spring of 1933. A search of his home on 28 February found a large quantity of leaflets including 15,000 copies of 'Ernst Thälmann to the Unemployed' and 500 copies of 'The Struggle to Smash the Fascist Regime, Hitler, Papen, Hugenberg'. He received a prison sentence of eighteen months. Seven of the other leading Osnabrück Communists were also arrested at the beginning of March for arranging a meeting.[198]

A few weeks later, the police seized more people in Osnabrück for trying to distribute leaflets about a demonstration to take place on 1 May, following a meeting in nearby Altenbögge.[199] Arrests continued into the summer. August Schnell, for instance, had attempted to build a so-called 'Red SA', belonged to 'Red Sport' and had met with other people with the aim of spreading communist propaganda, for which he faced two years in prison.[200]

In the spring of 1934 four arrests of people accused of trying to establish a KPD cell in Osnabrück took place after a tip off to the police by a witness, who claimed that one of the accused, had tried to persuade a passenger he had got to know on the tram to distribute leaflets. The four people arrested were given prison sentences of just over six months.[201]

After the spring of 1934 little organized left wing political activity took place in Osnabrück, although local police reports pick up anything which did happen, usually on a minor scale. In August, for instance, we learn that copies of a KPD publication fell through letterboxes in Osnabrück while the same report claimed that a KPD headquarters in Gelsenkirchen sought to establish a cell in Osnabrück.[202] At Christmas of the same year the police seized several copies of leaflets with the title of 'War Cry' and 'The KPD Lives'.[203] The local *Gestapo* became concerned about an increase in left wing activity in January 1935 which led to the arrest of the former leader of the SPD in Osnabrück, Wihlelm Wiltmann.[204]

Traces of organized left wing activity certainly survive into 1935, particularly the distribution of leaflets,[205] but it simply posed no threat because of a combination of surveillance, policing and judicial power. Such actions simply demonstrate that a few brave souls still lived in German towns prepared to face arrest and imprisonment for their cause. They remained very much a minority, unable to achieve anything in a state apparatus with the sort of power which the Nazis had established.

Osnabrück differed from some of the major urban centres, especially the Ruhr, where left wing activity continued. The town's relative isolation would largely explain the lack of such activity. But some resistance did continue in Osnabrück. An SS report singled out listening to illegal radio from Moscow on a regular basis at '246a Mellerstraße. Between 20 and 25 people are to be found there'.[206] The *Gestapo* in Osnabrück reported that sixteen different forbidden publications circulated in the town during November 1934. They ranged from exile newspapers such as *Der Deutsche Weg*, produced in Holland, to leaflets of an overtly communist nature with titles such as `Fight United for Thälmann's Freedom'.[207]

The range of political 'crimes' which the Nazis had introduced meant that disobedience became an everyday occurrence. Those people carrying out acts of defiance would, in many cases, hardly have considered themselves to have acted in a political way. Showing disrespect for Hitler could land an individual in trouble with the *Gestapo*, as could acts which did not display enough allegiance to the party. Informers played a large role in this process. The case of Otto Bohl represents a fairly typical case. He faced arrest in the summer of 1934 for distributing Communist leaflets, after a woman with whom he had lived for six months had informed on him. She told the police about his Communist friends and publications and the fact that he refused to use the Hitler greeting. As a result of his various misdemeanours, Bohl faced a prison sentence of two years.[208]

Such activity did not threaten the regime. Individuals alone or in groups may have carried out their own defiant actions, but the KPD and SPD remained powerless against the legal measures, the surveillance activity and the concentration camp system. This applied especially in small town Osnabrück, geographically isolated from the major area of working class activity of the Ruhr, over fifty miles away to the south.

Church and State Before 1939

Much of the research on Nazi attitudes toward the Churches suggests that it opposed religion because of its power over the minds of the population. The party wanted to bring the Churches, like all other organizations in the country, under its control. Some clerics stood up to the regime, which did not crush the established Churches in the way that it did the left wing groupings, so that individual ministers could make statements from the pulpit, often leading to denunciation to the *Gestapo*. Only Jehova's Witnesses, who pursued an unstinting opposition to the Nazis, faced constant persecution and elimination.[209]

The Nazis gave legitimacy to a revolutionary evangelical group, the German Christians, which brought politics firmly into religion and counted about 600,000 followers. The German Christians rejected the Old Testament, ejected 'non-Aryans' from their congregations and denied the Jewish ancestry of Jesus.[210] This group remained distinct from the mainstream German Evagelical Church, even though the latter had come under Nazi control following the election of Ludwig Müller, an admirer of Hitler, as Reich Bishop. This went together with an 'Aryan Paragraph' forbidding the clergy from taking a stance on political issues. Against the conformity of the Protestant hierarchy, there came into existence in September 1933 the Pastors Emergency League. It counted 7,000 members by the beginning of 1934. The Protestant Church during the 1930s therefore had three major divisions. Ideological Nazis did not look upon any of them favourably.[211]

Osnabrück illustrates the above divisions. The German Christians came into existence here following a meeting held in the town on 27 June 1933, although this body had relatively little success, largely due to a strong group of confessing Christians, who had opposed the Nazis even before they seized power.[212] According to the *Gestapo* the German Christians originally counted five from thirteen of the Lutheran pastors in Osnabrück amongst their members but this figure had declined to just two by the autumn of 1934, although meetings continued.[213]

Vigorous opponents of Hitlerism in Osnabrück predated the German Christians. They centred around the figure of Richard Karwehl, who took over the working class parish of Schinkel at the end of the First World War. During the early 1930s Karwehl participated in the activities of a group which opposed the rising Nazis, the Young Evangelical Conference, giving lectures on subjects such as 'National Socialism and the Church'.[214] In 1931 he published an article entitled 'Political Messianism: The Confrontation Between Church and National Socialism', which criticised the NSDAP on both political and religious grounds. He quoted the 24th point of the early twenty five point Nazi plan which accepted religious freedom as long as it did not threaten the state or undermine the morality of the German races. Karwehl contrasted the ideals of the Nazis with the spirituality and values of Christianity and concluded that 'a people does not live by ideology but by God's word'.[215]

Around the figure of Karwehl the Evangelical Church in Osnabrück developed a branch of the Confessing Church, established on a nationwide basis in May 1934 in opposition to the official leadership of Müller. The Barmen Declaration of that month stated: 'We reject the false doctrine that the State, over and above its special commission, should and could become the single and totalitarian order of human life, thus fulfilling the Church's vocation as well'. J.S. Conway has pointed out that the Confessing Church simply pursued a path of religious rather than political resistance, desiring to uphold Christian values and remain distinct from the state.[216] The 'Osnabrück Circle', as the group around Karwehl became known, attracted up to thirty supporters amongst local clerics, and broke from the Confessing Church in 1935 because it believed that the latter had moved too close to Nazi ideology following the appointment by Hitler of Hans Karl in that year as commissioner for Church affairs with the aim of bringing religion under tighter control. The Osnabrück Circle established itself as the Hanoverian Pastors Brotherhood in 1939. Throughout the 1930s an ideological struggle continued in Osnabrück, encompassing not simply developments at the national level, but also those at the state level of Hanover. Karwehl continued to speak out and write against Nazi ideology but did not make an impact on the national scale.[217]

Did the ideological questioning lead to any concrete opposition to the racial and social policies of the Nazis in Osnabrück? Did local pastors face persecution for their beliefs? How did the evangelical population react to the new regime? On a national level some opposition to the racial and social policies of the regime took place, especially the euthanasia programme during the War.[218] Evidence indicates that pastors had difficulty with the local *Gestapo* in Osnabrück. For instance, in 1937 Pastor Saalbach received a telephone call asking him to proceed to *Gestapo* headquarters. Having refused, an officer confronted him on the street and accused him of insulting Berhnard Eggers, the recently deceased *Regierungspräsident*. In August 1938 two *Gestapo* officials waited for Saalbach in his office, following a visit to his parish, and accused him of participating in anti-Nazi activities by distributing the leaflets of an independent youth organization. Nevertheless, other than a warning, nothing seems to have befallen Saalbach.[219]

While the Osnabrück Circle may have stood up to the regime because it threatened its control of the minds of the local population, it does not appear to have opposed antisemitism or sterilization. Furthermore, before the War the local state does not seem to have regarded any of the factions of the Evangelical Church as threatening. As to the attitudes of the local Evangelical population towards the NSDAP, little evidence survives of any groundswell of opinion against the party. The only occurrences which would suggest otherwise consist of the meetings held during the middle of the 1930s by the Osnabrück Circle, discussing doctrine and attitudes towards the Nazis, which could attract audiences of as many as 1,000, as happened on 31 March 1935.[220]

The Roman Catholic Church had a relationship with the Third Reich as complex and ambivalent as that of the Evangelical Church at both a national (or, perhaps more accurately, international) level and in Osnabrück, the seat of one of the most outspoken and controversial German Bishops of the first half of the twentieth century, Wilhelm Berning. As with the Evangelical Church, the main concern of both the hierarchy and the ordinary parish priest consisted of the protection of the position of the Roman Catholic Church and its doctrinal power. Only when this came under threat did this organization awake from its complacency.

The role of the Church under the Third Reich has come under intense scrutiny. At the international level, John Cornwell has produced a strong critique of Pope Pius XII, *Hitler's Pope*, focusing especially upon both his relationship with the Nazis and his antisemitism, continuing the long tradition of negative scrutiny which this figure has faced.[221] At the German level, the Roman Catholic Church has also received much attention,[222] especially around the figure of Bishop von Galen of Münster,[223] although many scholars have also focused upon the persecution which it faced[224] and the resistance which it offered,[225] especially as, like the SPD and KPD, it offered an alternative milieu in its areas of strength.[226] One source has listed the fate which individual priests faced throughout Germany.[227] At a local, or perhaps regional, level Wilhelm Berning, Bishop of Osnabrück from 1914-55, has attracted much attention through a series of articles,[228] crowned with a monumental biography about his relationship with the Third Reich.[229]

Much of the controversy about the Roman Catholic Church revolves around the Concordat, signed by Pius XII in the summer of 1933, which meant that the Church maintained considerable autonomy from the state. The German Bishop's Conference had already broadly welcomed the new regime in a statement issued at the end of March. However, by 1935 relations had broken down as the Nazis attempted to take over all aspects of the lives of its citizens, which, by the outbreak of the War, meant the closure of numerous Roman Catholic organizations, the banning of processions and the removal of roadside crosses, as well as the launching of immorality trials against individual priests, which caused much bitterness amongst congregations and clergy.[230]

Osnabrück demonstrates these contradictions. On New Year's Eve 1934 Berning delivered a remarkably positive sermon about the new order, beginning as follows: 'We Catholics happily recognize the *Führer* principle. In the Church we have the Pope, the representative of Christ, as the absolute leader, who is answerable to nobody except God and his conscience'. But four years later the same Bishop criticized the Nazi suppression of Catholic journals and newspapers.[231] Berning initially welcomed the Nazis and played a role in Church negotiations with them, but subsequently stood up to them by visiting the Concentration Camp in Emsland, as well as opposing educational policy and the attempts to control Roman Catholic ceremonial.[232] On 6 April 1936 the *Kirchliches Amtsblatt für die Diöseze Osnabrück* carried a front page article opposing a campaign to persuade parents to allow their children to enter the *Jungvolk* because, if they did so, they would have to answer to God for turning away from Christianity. As we have seen, many Roman Catholic families in Osnabrück viewed the Hitler Youth with suspicion, preferring, instead, to keep their children in Roman Catholic organizations until they faced closure.[233] These included the *Kolpingfamilie*, a missionary society, which provided accommodation for apprentices, as well as offering them education. The DAF viewed the group negatively because it threatened its monopoly over labour, leading to confrontation and the closing down of regional and local branches throughout the course of the 1930s,[234] as Osnabrück illustrates. The city branch faced dissolution in 1937 when a Winter Festival went ahead in its hostel on 17 October attended by 500 people, despite the fact that the *Gestapo* had forbidden it. The police intervened, called the meeting to a halt, and subsequently closed the branch and confiscated all of its property.[235]

For much of the 1930s the local Catholic establishment had fought an ultimately losing battle for the continuing survival of its schools, which also resulted in a major attack on the educational policy of the Nazis delivered by Berning on 5 December 1937.[236] The fact that the schools did not face dissolution until the outbreak of War[237] meant six years of children went through an alternative education system which produced citizens more capable of questioning the Nazis, the entire reason why they faced closure.

As well as interfering in Roman Catholic life the regime persecuted adherents of this religion in Osnabrück. This may partly have its origins in the events of 14 August 1932 when the verger of *Johanniskriche* kept out SA men on the grounds that 'entry into God's House of non-Catholic organizations in closed formation is forbidden'.[238] In September 1933 the *Gestapo* made one of its first interventions in local Church affairs when it confiscated printing machinery for the publication of a local newsletter.[239] In September 1937 the secret police visited and interrogated Pastor Franz Gartmann from the Cathedral because he had collected money for loud speakers for the Church. Wilhelm Kessler of St John's faced trial for participating in a forbidden meeting of the *Kolpingfamilie* in the summer of 1937. During the course of the 1930s and, more especially, into the War, the Nazis arrested and eliminated local priests. For instance, Theodor

Biedendieck of the *Heiliges Kreuz Kirche* in Schinkel had to retire in 1939 after allegedly disrupting a torch lit procession on 30 April 1938.[240]

For much of the 1930s the Roman Catholic Church represented the main alternative to Hitler loyalty in Germany.[241] The fact that it controlled almost every aspect of the lives of its adherents profoundly irritated the NSDAP. *Gestapo* reports from Osnabrück, which devote much attention to the Catholic Church, provide details of both the range of its activities and the annoyance of local Nazi officials. A typical commentary from March 1935 stated: `The Catholic campaign is proceeding forward unhindered. It is trying with great intensity to bring in all Catholic organizational activity. Above all from the side of the Catholic clergy there are constant attempts to establish new organizations and to increase membership of existing organizations.'[242] The local Nazi establishment also disliked Roman Catholic processions as well as its women's organizations and sporting bodies, which it viewed as political because they did not owe allegiance to the NSDAP.[243]

We can see the struggle between Catholicism and state as a continuation of the *Kulturkampf* of the late nineteenth century.[244] By the end of the 1930s the Roman Catholic Church lost out because of the dissolution of many of its organizations and the persecution of its clergy. Like dissenting Protestants its main concern consisted of saving its own neck and maintaining its authority. Nevertheless, it offered a dissenting tradition and the main alternative social milieu to Hitler worship in Osnabrück. Unlike the SPD and KPD opposition, which had largely disappeared by the middle of the 1930s, the Roman Catholic Church held its own, even though it came under scrutiny and faced persecution from the *Gestapo*.

The Nazis had less trouble in dealing with smaller Christian groups, which had few members in Osnabrück. Jehova's Witnesses, for instance, had a tiny presence,[245] and did not have the same impact as they did in the smaller town of Osterode.[246] One family which did live in Osnabrück, the Lavermanns, faced several visits and searches by the *Gestapo*, as recalled by the daughter, a child at the time.[247] The Nazis persecuted this group to elimination, particularly because of its pacifism and partly because, like the Roman Catholic Church, they were an international organization.[248]

Sterilization

The centrality of race and the breeding of healthy Aryans in Nazi ideology meant the implementation of a policy to eliminate the unhealthy by the use of sterilization before 1939, which became euthanasia during the War. As a result of the passage of the Law for the Prevention of Hereditary Diseased Offspring in 1933 sterilization became central in medical practice under the

Third Reich, performed on 320,000 people, or 0.5 per cent of the population between 1 January 1934 and the outbreak of war.[249]

This figure points to the acceptance of sterilization amongst the medical profession, which had discussed this policy and used it before 1933. Gisela Bock has demonstrated that such ideas emerged with Social Darwinism after 1850.[250] Hans-Walter Schmuhl, meanwhile, has focused upon the evolution of the concept of 'racial hygiene' during the course of the nineteenth and early twentieth centuries, which ultimately resulted not simply in sterilization but also euthanasia. Racial hygiene meant concern both with individual human beings and with the health of an entire population or 'race'. If a whole nation had the status of one body, eliminating the unhealthy sections, either by preventing them from breeding or by murdering them, would improve the health of the body politic as a whole. This paradigm led to the development of concepts of unworthy lives suitable for elimination.[251]

The eradication of unhealthy genes became central in this process, and had moved beyond the theoretical before the Nazis seized power. Sterilization had actually taken place from the end of the nineteenth century and into the Weimar Republic. Marriage clinics during the 1920s had advised those deemed not to possess 'hereditary fitness' to remain childless.[252] Burleigh and Wippermann have pointed out that by July 1932 'the Prussian government had formulated the Reich Sterilization Law, which it forwarded to the Reich government that winter. By the time it arrived, the Reich government was in the hands of Adolf Hitler.'[253]

Nazi rule allowed a party with radical policies to finally implement concepts which had circulated from the nineteenth century. The NSDAP's racial hygiene ideas continued those of other eugenicists such as Alfred Grotjahan.[254] As outlined clearly in *Mein Kampf*, while healthy 'Nordic types' should procreate in order to protect the 'purity of the racial strain', the state 'must see to it that only those who are healthy shall beget children'. The state 'must proclaim as unfit for procreation all those who are inflicted with some visible hereditary disease or are the carriers of it; and practical measures must be adopted to have such people rendered sterile.'[255] The NSDAP made racial hygiene, including sterilization, part of its programme during the election campaign of the early 1930s with the support of leading eugenecists.[256]

Medicine under the Nazis, with the help of doctors, therefore became central in the evolution of the racial state. Caring became secondary in the desire to create a fit population. Under the new ethics, those with the right genes would receive medical care and encouragement to breed, while those with the wrong ones would face sterilization, carried out in hospitals throughout the country. Doctors became 'heroic biological soldiers of their people' who carried out their 'eugenic task'. The issue of resistance seems to have played little role in the medical profession as 45 per cent of all doctors had NSDAP membership, while 85 per cent joined at least one Nazi organization.[257] In order to perpetuate Nazi medical ideas, the training of doctors changed during the course of the 1930s.[258] Not all practitioners participated in eugenics as sterilization tended to take place in specific institutions. In Osnabrück Dr Üthmöler, a gynaecologist, refused to carry out operations in his clinic in 1934.[259] He remained an exception, however. 'Few doctors would oppose the Nazis on political, ideological (including religious), or medicoethic grounds'.[260]

The implementation of racial hygiene policies needed legislative backing resulting in the passage of a series of laws. The most important of these consisted of the Law for the Prevention of Hereditary Diseased Offspring of 14 July 1933. This established Hereditary Health Courts, which would use medical experts to decide upon those who would face sterilization. The starting point, however, consisted of physicians and those in charge of hospitals and asylums. People with the following diseases could face sterilization: 'congenital feeble-mindedness'; schizophrenia; manic depression; hereditary epilepsy; huntington's chorea; hereditary blindness or deafness; serious physical deformities. In addition, chronic alcoholics could face the operation. While individuals or their families could appeal against the decision of a court, the operation could take place against their will. An amendment to the law from 1935 allowed the termination of pregnancies of women with the above diseases.[261]

Documents in the NSO allow the reconstruction of the everyday realities of sterilization in the Third Reich as well as pointing to its frequency and centrality in hospital life. The majority of operations in Osnabrück occurred in the *Osnabrücker Heil- und Pflegeanstalt*, the largest hospital in the town. While Osnabrück had possessed a marriage clinic from 1925, the local health office also established an Advice Centre for Hereditary and Racial Care on 1 January 1936, which would hold up to 10,000 cards with information on individual family trees, detecting genetic defects. The Hereditary Health Court in Osnabrück counted six members, 3 doctors and 3 officials, the latter of which also included a doctor in 1936. Referral of cases did not simply take place from individual doctors but also from the local health office. The examination of people for hereditary defects became part of medical pratice. In 1935 an investigation took place to detect the genetic diseases of the 250 pupils who attended the two schools for backward children in the town, revealing that 67 per cent of them had hereditary defects and, presumably, faced future sterilization.[262]

Between the passage of the Law for the Prevention of Hereditary Diseased Offspring and 31 March 1936, 205 people faced sterilization in the *Osnabrücker Heil- und Pflegeanstalt*, made up of 79 women and 129 men, questioning the concept of sterilization under the Nazis as an antifeminine project.[263] The years of birth varied from 1894 to 1917 in the case of the women and 1871 to 1917 in the case of men, with numerous cases of males born before 1890 undergoing the operation.[264] The 1937, 1938 and 1939 annual reports of the local health office provide detailed statistics about the occurrence of sterilization in the town as a whole, together with justifications for the operation. The total number actually went down from 152 in 1937 to 126 in 1938 and 119 in 1939. By far the most common reason for performing the operation consisted of schizophrenia. The directors of hospitals initiated most of the sterilizations.[265]

A couple of the numerous personal files in the NSO illustrate the process involved. First, the case of Wilhelm,[266] born in Duisburg in 1875 and living in Osnabrück. This is a straightforward example of an alcoholic, whom the Hereditary Health Court decided needed sterilizing. Its report pointed out that: 'Wilhelm did not have any particular illnesses during his childhood' but was subsequently released from the Navy 'because of problems with his cardiac muscles and cardiectasis. His first marriage ended in divorce and he is now married for the second time.' He faced criminal charges due to his alchololism for the first time in 1922. In 1936, he went to court for the 23rd time and received a jail sentence of 1 year because of fraud. Unfortunately, Wilhelm had also spent time in the *Osnabrücker Heil- und Pflegeanstalt* on several occasions where doctors decided that they 'were dealing with a severe alcoholic, for whom alcoholism had become constitutional, i.e. it had developed on the grounds of a psychopathic state of mind' and had not been controlled by several courses of treatment. 'The Hereditary Health Court...is dealing...with a hardened drinker ...Wilhelm has never done anything in his whole life, as stated by a neighbour...These are exactly the sort of people who can be seized by the Law for the Prev. Here. *(sic)* so that this hereditary disposition cannot be passed further.' The court decided on sterilization on 24 August 1938.[267]

Patients and their families did not always accept the decisions of the Health Courts, especially as they often had to pay for the operation.[268] In the case of Frida, born in 1918, the court decided on 26 February 1936 that she should face sterilization because of 'congenital feeble-mindedness'. Her father appealed to the Higher Health Court in Celle and sent a letter to the Chancellery in Berlin stating 'that his family was free from hereditary diseases'. This led a local health official to declare: 'he clearly does not know what hereditary diseases are'. This official continued:

The fact that the son Wilhelm was released from the fourth year of the junior school, that Frida herself only made it to the second year of the school for backward children, that the son Klaus similarly only reached the second year of the school for backward children and that the daughter Kirstin[269] also attended the school for backward children, makes it obvious that feeble-mindedness in this family is not only congenital but also positively hereditary.

This is the case of a real backward school family. The fertility of this family is well known and not, as the father claims, desirable but highly undesirable. The National Socialist state does not simply want lots of children, but lots of children of healthy stock, and the fertility of the family with feeble-mindedness causes the regime considerable problems. It is my conviction, that the Law for the Prevention of Hereditary Diseased Offspring should target precisely such families.

After pointing out that Frida had failed an intelligence test set for her, the official concluded, with even more conviction, as well as anger: 'When the father writes, that one has not told him on what grounds the proceedings against his child have been taken, this is also not correct. The father has not looked for me a single time in order to ask what it is all about'.[270] This particular case raises two contradictory issues. First, the extent to which some individuals went to protect their children, even writing to Hitler's office in Berlin. On the other hand, the file indicates the equally strong passion of the health official carrying out a policy in which he believed. The latter seems to have seen his desire come to fruition as the sterilization of Frida appears to have occurred after the intervention of the Ministry of the Interior.[271]

With such officials, it seems difficult to imagine how any individual could save his child. In fact, sterilization, persecution of the church and the incarceration of political opponents represented just three aspects of the Nazi eliminationist policies during the 1930s. The new government developed a whole concept of asocials, which encompassed the workshy, beggars and Romanies, who could find themselves in concentration camps, especially in the larger cities following campaigns to round them up.[272] Furthermore, the Nazis carried out a sustained campaign against homosexuals.[273]

Change and Continuity, 1933-9

The population of Osnabrück experienced dramatic transformations in the first six peacetime years of Nazi rule. Economically, the ethnic majority would have witnessed an improvement in their position, although not to the extent that it would change health and mortality, which had evened out by this stage in the demographic history of Germany. But unemployment had disappeared by the middle of the 1930s. Large companies, especially those engaged in armaments, did particularly well. Full-time employment often came at the cost of a loss of liberty because of the implementation of forced labour programmes. The various forms of Nazi propaganda attempted to persuade Germans that the improvement of their economic position was worth the loss of freedom. It also attempted to spread an ideology in which racial values stood at the centre. Those who would not accept these ideas could offer various forms of resistance,[274] but this could result in arrest or incarceration, whether the basis of opposition consisted of politics, religion or simply the desire to protect a relative threatened by racial policy.

Nevertheless, while the NSDAP may have Nazified and racialized a significant percentage of the population, evidence from Osnabrück suggests that alternative social milieus survived, especially those revolving around the churches, if not the socialist organizations, whose isolation meant that they received relatively little help from the bastion of protest in the Ruhr. In contrast, Osnabrück remained a centre of Roman Catholicism in north Germany, with traditions stretching back over a thousand years.

4

WORLD WAR TWO
AND THE CONSEQUENCES
OF ALLIED BOMBING

What Difference Did the War Make?

World War Two forms a caesura in the history of both twentieth century Germany and Europe, as well as the development of Nazi Germany. In the penultimate volume of his social history of Germany, covering the years 1914-49, Hans-Ulrich Wehler has written that the conflict allowed 'the full unveiling of the true nature of national socialism and the aims of its charismatic *Fuhrer*'.[1] While this statement especially applies to the consequences of racial expansionist policies in eastern Europe, it also has relevance for the German populations which remained at home, most notably for those deemed outside the national community as well as for anybody who carried out acts perceived as disloyal, as the Nazi state crushed its opponents with even more force than it had done before 1939. The cover of War allowed the regime to implement a series of final solutions.

The conflict also meant a change in economic policy, which, in turn, influenced the social development of the Reich. While rearmament had begun to drive the economy forward from 1936, after 1939, and, more especially, after 1942, when Albert Speer became Armaments Minister, it dominated the economic and social life of Germany because of the manpower needs it created, changing the ethnic composition of German towns and transforming working patterns. At the same time, the needs of the *Wehrmacht* also changed the gender and age balance of German towns.

However, for most Germans who remained on the home front the central memory, and the one which had the most profound impact upon their lives, consisted of the Air War, which, especially after the intensification of bombing in 1943, completely transformed the nature of German towns and cities. This was largely because of the physical destruction caused by Allied bombs as both private and public buildings collapsed. By 1945 millions of homes had disappeared.

The War can therefore be said to have had a series of dramatic consequences for Germans. First, it led to increasing intolerance. Second, it caused massive physical damage. And third, it dramatically changed the nature of economy and society because of the necessity to gear up for Total War. By 1945, when Allied armies arrived from all directions, Nazi dreams lay in complete ruins as Germany reached the lowest point in its history as a nation state.[2]

The Centrality of the Air War

In the collective memory of Osnabrück during the Second World War, the Allied bombing campaign remains vivid. Virtually every individual interviewed for this project had a personal story to tell. At the same time, Wido Spratte has produced a detailed account of the consequences of the bombing, while both the *Kriegs-Chronik* and Karl Kühling's history of the town during the Third Reich provide much detail about the Air War.[3] The Osnabrück city museum has also issued a publication focused upon the massive attack of 13 September 1944, which destroyed much of the city centre.[4]

Table 4.1: The Consequences of the Air War on Osnabrück.

Year	Number of Attacks	Deaths	Injuries	Homeless
1940	8	10	66	561
1941	3	0	7	0
1942	7	173	418	5,658
1943	1	11	10	60
1944	36	952	866	59,799
1945	23	277	328	21,783
Total	78	1,433	1,695	87,861

Source: Wido Spratte, *Im Anflug auf Osnabrück: Die Bombenangriffe, 1940-1945* (Osnabrück, 1985), pp. 156-7.[9]

There are two major explanations for the remembering of the Air War in Osnabrück. First, the sheer weight of information which has survived, both in the newspapers, which reported most of the attacks, and in the archive, where numerous files make mention of the consequences of the bombing, above all the *Kriegs-Chronik* and the documents of the air raid police, which have survived in perfect condition. These allow a detailed recreation of every attack which occurred. These documents point to the second reason for the centrality of the Air War in the collective memory of Osnabrückers: the damage it inflicted. The consequences of eighteen months of intense bombing from the air, and more sporadic attack over the entire course of the War, meant that large sections of Osnabrück, above all the town centre, became ruins. The regularity of attack and the possibility of death also meant that those living in Osnabrück could not forget their experiences. In all, the town faced 78 raids, summarised in table 4.1. Over 650,000 bombs of various sorts fell on the town, causing 4,386 fires of different sizes and destroying 7,158 homes, seven churches and thirteen schools.[5] The heaviest attacks in 1944 and 1945 saw the dropping of tens of thousands of bombs, the creation of tens of thousands of homeless people, and tens of millions of *Reichmarks* worth of damage.

The vast majority of the attacks (59) occurred in the last two years of the war, as did most deaths, injuries and homelessness. The number of people who found themselves without a roof over their heads totalled 88 per cent of the town's population, if we accept that Osnabrück housed 99,173 people in March 1939.[6] But the figure needs clarification because some people lost their homes more than once, moving from one form of temporary accommodation to another. While more than four fifths of the housing in the city centre faced destruction, the figure fell to below fifty per cent elsewhere and to five and four per cent in the suburbs of Eversburg and Haste respectively.[7] The death rate, using the figures in Table 4.1, is less than 1.5 per hundred of the population, twenty five per cent of whom consisted of foreign workers.[8]

Although Allied bombers killed *just* 1,433 people in Osnabrück during the War, this represents a significant loss of life. But Osnabrückers did not stress their suffering in the interviews carried out, as they recalled their experiences in a matter of fact way. This even applied to the Adels, whose home experienced a direct hit. The one significant exception consisted of Hugo Weiss, who claimed that the bombing increased the resistance to the Allies,[10] but, as Neil Gregor has demonstrated, this simply represented a perception fed by Nazi propaganda.[11] The clearest memories of most interviewees focused on *Kristallnacht* and the consequences of Allied bombing. The literature on the history of Osnabrück during the War and the Nazi years overall reflects this pattern. While Spratte may have chosen to focus upon Osnabrückers as victims in his books on the Air War and the social conditions of the immediate post-War years, the *Stadt Chronik* and Kühling's history of the Nazi period have taken a broad sweep which examines all aspects of the town's history during the War. We might even suggest that the memory of the bombing in Osnabrück has been underplayed. While plaques to Jews and Romanies killed by the Nazis exist in the town square, a similar memorial to those killed by bombing is absent. Ultimately, the experience of the destruction caused by the Allies remains fixed as one of the central events in the modern history of Osnabrück.

National and international attention on the Air War over Germany has until recently tended to ignore the experience of the German civilian on the ground largely because he is regarded as having had some responsibility for the fate he suffered and also because his experience did not approach that of ethnic minorities.[12] Those studies that have appeared on the Air War fall into various categories. First, and perhaps most authoritatively, both the RAF and the US Air force produced surveys of their work shortly after the end of the War.[13] In this guise several semi-official accounts also appeared, including one by Bomber Harris.[14] The second major category of books on the Air War consists of 'boys-own' style accounts written by admirers of the work of the Royal Air Force, often former pilots or other military personnel, paying scant attention to the consequences of bombing upon the German civilian population below.[15] Such works stress the courage of the men of the RAF, as the destruction of Germany resulted in the loss of 55,000 members of Bomber Command, although it 'killed over half a million German civilians' and 'destroyed 3.37 million houses'.[16] Serious, balanced and objective studies by academics have also dealt with the Air War, written by English and American scholars,[17] as well as by German ones.[18] Some works, particularly in recent decades, have also dealt with the ethics of the destruction of German cities.[19] Until recently, relatively little serious academic research focused upon the experience below the bombs, particularly in the English language.[20] German scholars have dealt with this theme in more detail, usually attempting to achieve this task in a non-judgemental manner and often focusing upon one aspect of the Air War.[21] The concern with the experience on the ground has intensified since the publication of Jörg Friedrich's *Der Brand*.[22] Local studies of the consequences of bombing, which go into extreme detail about experiences under the bombs, tend to point the finger at the Allies.[23]

Stephen A. Garrett tackled the central ethical and military issues involved in the bombing of German cities by the RAF. He questioned the necessity of the intensity of the bombing in the defeat of the Nazis, particularly the move from precision to area bombing in the spring of 1942, following the appointment of Arthur Harris to the position of Head of Bomber Command on 20 February, with the aim of undermining civilian morale. Garrett doubts whether this happened although the Osnabrück interviewees suggest he came to the wrong conclusion, as does the research of Gregor.[24]

Two further issues present themselves here. First, the consequences of bombing for arms production, as one of the central aims of the Air War was to destroy factories. While, according to the official British report published after the conflict, production peaked in the summer of 1944, it declined to 1942 standards by the spring of 1945.[25] As the narrative on Osnabrück will demonstrate, municipal authorities used an army of labourers for the purpose of repairing the damage caused by bombing, a task which they achieved within days. Nevertheless, by the spring of 1945, and especially from the autumn of 1944, when raids intensified, the level of repair needed meant that the available labour simply could not keep pace, especially as the city centre lay in complete ruins.

This affected morale, despite the official British view that 'there is no indication that' the German civilian's 'morale reached breaking point as a result of air attacks'.[26] Although people tried to continue their lives as far as they could, while faced with constant bombing as buildings collapsed around them, they became resigned to defeat by the spring of 1945. Earl R. Beck, referring to the final winter of the War, has written: 'A deep sense of gloom lay across the country. No longer was there any relief from the hardships of overly strenuous work, the fear of the next bombing raid, the struggle to keep outworn clothing wearable, the worries about the steadily approaching forces from the east and the west'.[27]

Allied bombing divided into a series of phases. The winter of 1939-40 did not result in any sorties, other than for the purposes of distributing leaflets. On the night of 13/14 May 1940, the first attack occurred in the Ruhr against oil installations and marshalling yards. Most of the early targets consisted of power supplies and airfields. From July 1941 attention shifted to railways, with area bombing taking over in February 1942. Following the Casablanca Conference of January 1943 Churchill and Roosevelt decided to coordinate their bombing and focused upon a range of targets with the aim of 'the progressive destruction and dislocation of the German military, industrial and economic system and the undermining of the morale of the German people to a point where their capacity for resistance is fatally weakened'.[28] This phase of the War witnessed the first major attacks upon urban targets, beginning with Lübeck on 28-9 March 1942, when fires destroyed sixty per cent of the town. Other significant landmarks included the attack on Cologne on the night of 30 May causing 2,500 fires, and Hamburg in July 1943, resulting in the dropping of 10,000 tons of bombs and 40,000 deaths. In the meantime raids also focused upon Berlin during 1943 and 1944 at a high cost in loss of aircraft.[29] The final phase of the Air War occurred in the winter of 1944-5 as German defences weakened and British and American bombers increasingly picked off their targets at will. Smaller and less important locations such as Osnabrück now faced the full wrath of the Allies.

The progress of the Air War naturally meant an increase in the number of aeroplanes in use as well as a growth in the availability of weapons which became ever more sophisticated as the British and US economies geared up fully for Total War. This allowed the development of better navigational equipment, as well as the emergence of more effective bombs and larger aircraft which could fly over longer distances.[30] At the end of 1939 Bomber

Command 'consisted of 23 squadrons, amounting to only 280 aircraft and trained crews.'[31] Hundreds of aircraft took part in the largest attacks on individual cities from 1943 to 1945.[32] Clearly, the intervention of the United States significantly changed the War to the advantage of the Allies. The 515 aircraft available to Bomber Command in September 1939 had increased to 5,277 by May 1945.[33] In the entire duration of the War 1.35 million tons of bombs fell upon German soil, increasing from 10,000 tons in 1940 to 120,000 in 1943 and peaking at 650,000 in 1944, with a further half a million tons in the final few months of the war in 1945. Nearly half of these, 46 per cent, fell on cities, fifteen percent on industrial targets and 39 per cent elsewhere. The 3.6 million homes destroyed meant that 7.5 million people had no shelter over their heads.[34]

The Reality of Bombing on the Ground

Our central concern lies with the everyday experience of one German town under the bombs. Osnabrück did not experience serious Allied attacks until the latter stages of the War, with the tonnage which fell upon it increasing together with that which landed upon Germany as a whole.[35] The percentage of homes destroyed in the town compares with that of some of the most heavily damaged locations, at 55 per cent.[36] The number of people who died, on the other hand, remained fairly low, in comparison with the estimated 50,000 people killed in the attacks on Hamburg in 1943 and the 35,000 murdered in Dresden in 1945, even if we take into account the far larger populations of these cities.[37] The explanation for the relatively low death rate in Osnabrück may lie at least partly in the preparations which the town had made against air attack even before 1939. These included the education of the population for the reality of an Air War,[38] the development of a warning service, especially an air raid police, the construction of bunkers, both public and at places of work, and the building of anti-aircraft units.[39]

Osnabrück had its first head of air raid police from 1935 in the form of Alfred Jung. The number of men employed during the War peaked in September 1939 at 195, including 77 police reservists. The figures fell back to 151 at the beginning of 1945, including 89 police reservists.[40] The air raid wardens alerted the population to the danger of air attack by securing the blackout and looking after sirens. They received assistance from thousands of personnel in clearing up after air raids. Thus the 160 police of May 1942 had a back up force of 644, which increased to 173 and 704 respectively by May 1944, meaning the availability of 877 men.[41]

Osnabrück developed an extremely thorough system of air raid shelters, which could house a large proportion of the population and which must provide the main explanation for the low death rate in the town. By January

1942 capacity existed for 48,370 people out of a total in the town of 91,587, over fifty per cent. By July 1944 bunkers existed for 102,983 people from an estimated population of 105,860 meaning over 97 per cent.[42] As Spratte has pointed out, this meant a provision of more than 100 per cent, as the real population of the town stood at less than 100,000.[43] The regularity with which air raid warnings sounded meant that people should have had enough time to make their way to the bunkers. In August 1944 air raid warnings went off 102 times, including 6 on 27 August alone.[44] The shelters came in all shapes and sizes owned by a combination of the local state and local government institutions, businesses and individual households.[45]

The shelters played an essential role in keeping the population of Osnabrück alive, particularly when we consider the limited strength of the air raid defence personnel and equipment in the town as the conflict progressed. Before the outbreak of the War some anti-aircraft stations existed in the highest parts of Osnabrück, especially around Westerberg, which subsequently increased in number. As males of military age disappeared, civilians, as well as youths, came to assist in this role. By the summer of 1942 over 100 school teachers had registered both as flak helpers and guards in schools warning of the outbreak of fire.[46] Despite concerns about interruptions in the education of youths, the local state, following instructions from higher up, began using children as helpers in 1943.[47] Alfred Müller joined one anti-aircraft unit on 15 February 1943 together with others born in 1927 and 1928, some of whom remained in their position for as long as a year. He served in a unit of 4 in Kalkhugel.[48] 'At the end of the War, the personnel of the Osnabrück anti-aircraft batteries consisted, in almost equal proportions, of old frontline soldiers, Russian prisoners of war and young helpers.'[49]

But what was the reality of the Allied bombing for civilians on the ground? Although sufficient archival material exists to reconstruct every raid which took place on Osnabrück, we can focus upon some of the deadliest and best documented attacks, using both German and British sources. Relatively little activity occurred over Osnabrück's skies until 1944, although some large raids took place in 1942. With no strategic or symbolic significance, the intensification which occurred in 1943, focusing upon Lübeck, Hamburg, Cologne and Berlin, did not affect Osnabrück. But from 11 January 1944 until 25 March 1945 Allied aeroplanes bombed the town 58 times, reducing its centre to ruins. As RAF records reveal, these raids did not always concern themselves specifically with the town, but it faced attack as part of more general missions, focusing particularly upon the Ruhr to the south as well as Hanover and Berlin to the east.

The first raid occurred on 23 June 1940, as part of a general attack on targets in north Germany, Belgium and Holland.[50] Twelve bombs weighing about 300 kilograms in total hit the Klöckner-Werke, as well as houses in Lüstringer Strasse and land in Dodesheide. One person working in the Klöckner-Werke died as a result of shrapnel and four others were injured.[51] The events of 23 June caused much uneasiness amongst the population.[52] The rest of 1940 resulted in seven further attacks upon Osnabrück of a similar scale, involving a small numbers of deaths and injuries. The most serious, in terms of loss of life, occurred on the afternoon of 3 July, killing 4 people and injuring 30 others. All of the dead worked in the Klöckner-Werke. A local police report noted that the attacks had caused nervousness and anxiety amongst the population, and that the nightly air raid warnings had particularly affected children.[53] The only other significant attack of 1940 occurred on the night of 18 September, when thirteen bombs which fell on the town meant the evacuation of 645 people as well as two deaths.[54]

Following the pattern elsewhere in Germany, and reflecting the War in Europe as a year of consolidation for the Nazis, 1941 resulted in little activity over the skies of Osnabrück, with just three sorties.[55] The most serious of these, and the last, occurred on the morning of 8 August. About 200 incendiary bombs fell on the town, together with six larger devices, injuring seven people in total. The attack concentrated on the central part of the city where both the railway and Klöckner lay, but 37 bombs fell on homes.[56]

Although only seven attacks occurred on Osnabrück in 1942, they were of a different magnitude from those before. A total of 173 people lost their lives while a further 5,658 found themselves without shelter. The worst raids occurred on 10 August and 6 October. A police report of 14 August provides the details of the attack of that month.

About 35 enemy aeroplanes, which flew as low as 200 metres, attacked, over the course of 1 hour and twenty minutes, the centre of the city, the closed southerly localities and the south western part of the town as well as the installations of the harbour and the goods station. 180 high explosive bombs, five blockbusters, 1,000 phosphorous bombs and 19,000 incendiary devices were dropped. Regretfully 60 people died, of whom 29 were in the shelters; 23 people are seriously and 69 lightly injured. 70 houses are completely destroyed, 150 are severely damaged and 480 lightly damaged. The damaged buildings included the following large structures: a hospital (*Städt. Frauenklinik*) almost completely destroyed, the main laboratory of the city hospital almost completely destroyed, 3 schools damaged, including the *Staatl. Oberschule für Jungen* almost completely destroyed, the main post office (above all the telephone operations) severely damaged, a tower burnt in the Herz-Jesu Church, St Paul's church roof and glass damaged, two children's homes severely damaged, one cinema (Universum) severely damaged, the advice centre of the Osnabrück *Landkreis* (annex) completely destroyed, one hotel and coffee house (Germania) completely destroyed, a further hotel partly destroyed, customs office severely damaged, a grocery warehouse severely damaged, a clothes factory as well as a warehouse totally damaged, a cigar factory completely burnt to the ground, the city savings bank, court buildings and city car park lightly damaged.

Some of the leading armaments factories also suffered damage including Karman and Klöckner. The air raid police dealt with the fires caused by the incendiary bombs. About 130 men helped to isolate the affected areas, while 800 helped to clear up the rubble, including members of the *Wehrmacht*.[57] The reports by the air raid police on the attack of 10 August gave more statistical details. A total of 4,035 buildings suffered some sort of damage, including 205 completely destroyed at a cost of RM75 million. The city authorities purchased thousands of pieces of crockery and cutlery in order to look after the needs of those left homeless by the attack. They also employed 969 labourers to help repair the damage.[58]

No sooner had they repaired the damage caused on 10 August than another destructive raid occurred eight days later resulting in further deaths and devastation to buildings.[59] On 6 October there followed an even worse attack than that of 10 August, specifically targeting Osnabrück and involving 237 aircraft.[60] This raid caused 79 deaths and RM100 million worth of damage, while 2,029 people lost their homes.[61] In order to repair the damage caused both by this air raid and those earlier in the summer the city authorities employed

> ...a whole army of labourers from outside the town: 520 painters and glaziers, 589 joiners, 282 carpenters, 881 builders and building assistants, 299 roofers, 113 plumbers, 81 electricians, 50 stucco workers, making 2,815 men in total. In addition, there were 562 French prisoners of war, in the form of 2 working battalions with 235 men, as well as 152 glaziers and 75 roofers; furthermore 215 Russian prisoners of war and 250 men from an SS Brigade-Building Company.[62]

Life returned to something resembling normality for Osnabrückers during 1943, as the town did not suffer any attacks for more than a year, with a gap from 6 November 1942 until 22 December 1943. This represented the calm before the storm because the latter raid signalled the beginning of unrelenting attacks which continued until the spring of 1945. Again, we can concentrate on some of the most destructive raids of 1944 and their aftermath, before concluding with details of the final and most devastating attack of Palm Sunday 1945.

Although raids resembling those of 1942 took place in the first few months of 1944, a series of three devastating attacks in May brought the level of destruction to a new scale. The town was bombed on the 7th, 8th and 13th of that month, while two further raids, again causing much death and damage, occurred 31 May and 6 June, followed by a pause until September.[63] After the first of these incidents on the morning of 7 May the Air Raid police listed 126 people, including 38 foreign workers, who had lost their lives as a result of the dropping of over 1,000 bombs.[64] The following evening 159 bombs caused the death of a further 34 people.[65]

But these attacks remained the foretaste to what would follow on the afternoon of 13 May. On this day separate air raids occurred against targets in 'eastern Poland and Germany', including Osnabrück, upon which 466 tons of bombs fell. The RAF report on the attack upon Osnabrück spoke of 'good results' with designated targets successfully hit including the marshalling yard and Klöckner.[66] The Osnabrück air raid police recorded that '290 buildings were completely destroyed', while a further 3,507 were damaged to varying degrees. The working class area of Schinkel, next to the Klöckner factory and the railway station, bore the brunt of the attack. The buildings hit included the *Marienhospital,* the gasworks, the waterworks and the post office, which meant that the population went without gas, water and post for several weeks. A total of 239 people lost their lives (including 67 foreigners), while a further 6,000 had to find new accommodation.[67] In order to deal with water supply the local state brought in 14 'drinking water lorries'. Sixty men cleared the streets of debris. Thousands of others, including convicted criminals, soldiers and foreigners repaired the damage over the next few weeks.[68]

September 1944 meant further devastation, particularly as a result of raids on the 13th and 26th. The former, along with the final attack of 25 March 1945, was the most destructive of the whole War. Between 18:26 and 18:40 over 13,000 bombs fell upon Osnabrück resulting in 141 deaths (including 15 prisoners of war and 21 foreign workers) and damage to nearly 10,000 buildings, including the complete destruction of 1,500, and the igniting of 830 fires. Public buildings destroyed included the town hall and the justice buildings together with hospitals, schools and cinemas. Railway travel suffered in all directions.[69] Four days later 5,377 men found themselves involved in the clearing up operation.[70] The *Kriegs-Chronik* described the situation in Osnabrück on 14 September:

The whole town was in bewilderment, countless places of employment were left empty, as many people who had suffered loss had something more important to do than to fulfil their daily duties; here there were people involved in putting out fires, there they were endeavouring to secure furniture from their homes and items stored in their cellars; at many locations in the town rescued household objects were piled up waiting for an opportunity to be evacuated...

All available workers, whether military or civilian, started working from daybreak onwards, in order to rescue, to bury, to at least temporarily clear up the blocked up main roads again.[71]

By this time, with anti-aircraft cover disappearing, British and American aeroplanes bombed German towns and cities at will. The regularity and severity of the attacks in the final few months of the war meant that repairing the damage sustained on 13 September and in raids which followed became impossible until well into the second half of the 1940s. Although the local state made efforts to look after those losing their homes, the most successful method of dealing with this problem, on the part of those bombed out, consisted of moving to relatives in the countryside, as indicated by the case of the Adels. Their shop and house in Hasestraße faced a direct hit on 13 September as they hid in a bunker nearby and consequently spent the remainder of the War and its immediate aftermath with relatives in the nearby settlement of Bohmte.[72] The flight of people away from Osnabrück and other towns throughout the Reich symbolized the collapse of morale and the fear installed by constant bombing as towns increasingly became devoid of buildings and people.[73]

September 1944 resulted in three further attacks on Osnabrück, the most severe on the 26th, following two smaller ones on the 19th and 23rd.[74] October 1944 saw three more attacks, the most serious of which occurred on the 12th killing 43 people and leaving 10,000 without a roof over their heads.[75] The worst of the seven raids of November took place just after midday on the 21st when 60 aeroplanes dropped over 5,000 bombs. Some of these fell on already destroyed ground, an increasing reality as the town became rubble. But this raid resulted in one of the most tragic incidents in the War in Osnabrück as an orphanage suffered a direct hit, which killed fifty children.[76] From now on the bombs rained down on the town with increasing regularity. Seven raids followed in December.[77] By this stage of the War the season of good will no longer had any influence as Osnabrück faced attack on 24 and 31 December and 1 January.[78]

The Allies began the New Year as they meant to carry on. In the first three months of 1945 Osnabrück experienced 22 further raids, more than a quarter of the raids which occurred during the whole War. Some remained fairly minor, but others were massive, especially the final one on 25 March, as well as those which occurred on 16 and 19 February and 14 March.[79] The *Kriegs-Chronik* reported on the situation on the ground immediately after the Palm Sunday attack of 25 March when 200,000 bombs rained on the town from about 300 aeroplanes between 9:48 and 10:15 in the morning, leading to 170 deaths, damage to nearly 3,000 buildings and the outbreak of more than 600 fires which left 15,000 people homeless.[80]

The masses, which streamed out of the bunkers, were greeted with a horrible sight: just as on 13 September, a large part of the city centre was today enveloped in grey, black or brownish clouds of smoke, with a particular intensity over the OKD; the previously clear blue sky had darkened, the air was full of the smell of burning. Every individual now rushed to his house; those who found it undamaged were clearly happy, but how about the many thousands in low spirits, through whose homes the burning heat had roared, and who because of the amazing scope of the fires covering entire parts of the town, could not reach them. Despite this as soon as they could gain access they made their way to their houses to secure the remains. Thus during the afternoon the well known but still heart-wrenching pictures of human suffering unfolded themselves: crying women, despairing men, who pull out beds, clothes etc from the possessions surviving in the house remains and load them on to handcarts; entire bands of people bombed out of their houses march through the streets, and know not, where to; in front of the palace walls and many other places lie countless pieces of furniture, whose guards protect them from thieving hands and endeavour to find a wagon to secure their removal.[81]

Such were the pictures of desolation and the situation facing Germans in Osnabrück and throughout the rump of their country in the spring and summer of 1945. The Allies completely disrupted the normalities of everyday urban life. The city authorities struggled to keep up water, gas and electricity supplies as reservoirs, gas holders and power stations faced direct hits in the carpet bombing of 1944 and 1945.[82] The attacks, which devastated the whole of Osnabrück city centre consequently destroyed some of its most important buildings, despite futile efforts to protect them.[83] Seven churches faced destruction during the course of the conflict, concentrated in the town centre and the areas surrounding it. The Roman Catholic Cathedral experienced several hits leading to fires. The Herz Jesu Church, which lay in Schinkel, the site of much arms production, suffered damage as a result of attacks on 10 and 18 August 1942, forcing parishioners to attend services elsewhere. The massive raid of 13 September 1944 finished it off and burnt out the towers and roof of the Cathedral. Attacks in February 1945 resulted in serious damage to the *Johanniskirche* and the *Rosenkranzkirche*.[84] Air raids had also damaged and destroyed several protestant churches, particularly in the later stages of the War.[85]

Nazi Reactions to the Bombing

The realities of the destruction occurring around the heads of Osnabrückers meant that those in authority at both a national and local level, could not hide the consequences of the Air War, but, instead, had to make efforts to assist those who lost their homes. One method consisted of making financial payments, at least in the early stages of the conflict. For instance, 'Master carpenter Franz Landwehr', whose house suffered 'complete damage on 18/8/42' and who lived with his wife and five children 'in a shed erected on their own land' received RM150.[86]

As the war progressed and the bombing intensified financial compensation and the building of sheds proved insufficient solutions to the problem of weekly saturation bombing. Evacuation to the countryside increasingly became the solution, initially for children, but then for much of the population.[87] This meant the abandonment of plans for the billeting of those bombed out on to people with surviving houses and the construction of temporary accommodation within Osnabrück approved in 1942 and 1943.[88] In August 1943 the Mayor compiled a list of places of temporary accommodation for those bombed out, which consisted of hotels, churches and schools.[89] By the end of 1943 the local authorities also began considering the consequences of the War on the supply of food and other essentials (already rationed) because of the destruction of shops and made arrangements for itinerant traders.[90]

As well as offering material assistance to the population, the local state made efforts to keep up morale and support for the War, essential in view of what Osnabrückers could see happening around them. Again this proved easier in the earlier stages of the conflict when bombing remained sporadic, than its final winter. The policy encompassed various strategies. In the first place, the *Neue Volklsblätter* published regular articles asserting, in an increasingly unconvincing way, as the rain of bombs became heavier, that the actions of the Allies would only make Germans more determined, creating a 'blitz spirit' in reverse. Such articles normally followed air raids.[91]

The local state, together with the local press, also placed much effort into commemorating those killed by Allied bombing. From 1942 the largest stories in the newspapers consisted of articles memorialising those who had lost their lives as a result of air attacks, as death on a massive scale became part of everyday reality. The supreme irony of the War for the Nazis lies in the fact that the main form of public spectacle no longer consisted of the marches of the party, but the commemorations which took place for the dead after every air raid, with dozens or even hundreds of coffins laid out in public.

The memorialization thus had two aspects to it, in which the press and the local state played their roles. In the first place the newspapers carried a list of all those who had died in an air raid shortly after it happened. Thus on 14 August 1942, in an oft repeated episode, the *Neue Volksblätter* published a text box, preceded by an iron cross, listing the seventy people who had died in the first large scale attack of 10 August. Before the list came the following statement: 'As victims of the surprise British bombing attack on the night of 10 August on the city of Osnabrück and its immediate surroundings the following gave their lives for Germany'. The box concluded with a statement from the *Gauleiter* which read:

> The population of the city and region of Osnabrück stands grief stricken in front of the coffins of these victims. They also fell in the struggle for Germany's freedom and future and will remain unforgotten. Our thoughts particularly go out to the dependants of the dead, whose heavy loss we will help to bear. The legacy of the dead will inspire us to come closer together in an unbreakable will to carry out our duty in the struggle for existence of our people and therefore make our contribution to the victory and future of the Great German *Reich*.

The party used every propaganda opportunity, out of necessity as the coffins piled up, to keep up morale. Every attack, no matter how small, resulted in the publication of a similar text box in the *Neue Volkslblätter*. As the death toll increased, so the list of names commemorated grew larger. Thus the names following the raid which cost the most lives, on 13 May 1944, took up almost a page of the newspaper. By this time the *Gauleiter* had cut his gratitude to just a few sentences, beginning: 'As victims of the enemy bombing attack on the city of Osnabrück the following laid down their lives'. He concluded: 'They also fell for the freedom of our people and the future of the *Reich*. We bow down in respect for the victims and what they gave us. Our deepest sympathies go to the dependants.'[92]

The NSDAP also organized collective funerals laying out the coffins of those who had died in air raids. If the scenes of carnage following attacks had not been horrific enough, the sight of rows of coffins would have moved anybody. While sympathy for the Nazis may have worn thin as the war progressed and while representatives of the party may have again used these mass funerals to score propaganda points, they indicate sensitivity to the feelings of those who had lost their relatives. But this is the least one would have expected from a party which praised the virtues of the German population, which was now dying for it. These mass funerals therefore became the main form of Nazi spectacle in Osnabrück during the War. While the marches of the years before 1939 may have symbolized the readiness of the party to take over Europe, the piles of coffins, especially in the final years of the conflict, symbolized its death throes.

The first mass funeral in Osnabrück appears to have occurred on 25 June 1942 to commemorate the 10 people who died during the attack of 20 June. On this occasion the coffins were laid out in the courtyard of the palace. This essentially constituted a funeral with full military honours as representatives from the army, the NSDAP and the police participated. *Kreisamtsleiter* Stratenwerth declared that the deaths which had taken place would make the people of Osnabrück more determined to fight on and avenge the losses.[93] On 15 August a commemoration took place for the seventy people killed five days previously:

> During the fourth hour of Friday afternoon the victims of the latest British attack were laid to rest following an organized communal ceremony in the front court of the crematorium.
>
> The coffins stood in five rows covered with a swastika flag and adorned with flowers in front of the main hall, with each side of each coffin flanked by six pallbearers from the SS, SA, political leaders, members of the remaining formations, Army, SHD, postal service, and factory groups amongst other services.
>
> On the large lawn behind the entrance the relatives of the dead, the representatives and delegates of the party, state and army and organizations had taken their positions, on the side in front of the building stood the flags and banners. An honorary company of the Army was represented with a band and music and the funeral march from *Eroica* opened the commemoration. [94]

May 1944 proved a particularly traumatic month with 478 people dying as a result of four attacks, the highest monthly total. On 11 May a ceremony in the crematorium had, laid out before it, 127 coffins, each with a swastika covering it. Eight days later more coffins bedecked with a swastika awaited burial following the attack of 13 May, which had cost 241 lives.[95] The mass burials continued, but the ceremonial declined as the authorities struggled to keep the basics of life going.

The Collapse of the New Society

By 1945 the Allied bombs had destroyed the new society which the Nazis had created during the course of the 1930s as German towns lay in ruins. While the intensification of bombing during the second half of the War guaranteed the end of Nazi dreams, the decision to embark upon expansion began to undermine the pre-War economic and social successes even before the bombs began to fall. Military mobilization tore families apart and often resulted in the loss of menfolk forever. Economic mobilization with its focus upon armaments production, especially in the latter stages of the conflict, meant that consumer goods and, increasingly, the basics of everyday life, including food and clothing, disappeared. By the spring of 1945 Germans throughout the Reich found themselves homeless, jobless and hungry, as the state in which they lived collapsed due to total defeat at the end of Total War.[96]

In purely economic terms the focus on public works of the early 1930s had already turned to rearmament by 1936. With the outbreak of War urban locations throughout the country witnessed a heavier concentration on engineering and metallurgy, particularly towns such as Osnabrück, which had already developed as a result of these industries. With fronts throughout Europe the Nazis needed massive reserves of manpower because of the numbers of soldiers required to protect them. This meant that with the passage of time, and despite the presence of foreign workers, women and children increasingly manned factories, which, in turn, meant that the Nazi position on women as mothers needed modification. The welfare state, which developed during the 1930s, came under increasing strain with the growing focus on arms production against the background of Allied bombing. The economic gains which had occurred before 1939 came under threat even before the Air War began to take its toll precisely because production focused upon armaments at the expense of all else.[97]

While growing military production in Osnabrück required increasing manpower, so did the armed forces, which meant a decline in the supply of readily available men to work in the factories. The number of Osnabrückers who perished totalled over 5,000 consisting of 3,075 officially reported as dead and 2,242 as missing.[98] The knowledge of relatives fighting on the various fronts which the Nazis had created meant constant worry for those left behind, as recalled by several interviewees, most poignantly Werner Funk:

There was a strict Catholic family near us in the neighbourhood in Bohmter Strasse...They had two sons, and I know that the mother went to the *Herz Jesu* Church everyday, so pious was she...She had lost her first son. Hans was now a soldier in Russia. By chance I had leave and so did he. He was determined not to go back to the front. He had to return. However, he had already exceeded his stay by three days. I said: 'Hans, you have to go. They'll shoot you and take your parents to a camp'. He said: 'No, then I can also die here'. He did not want to go back there. I could not help anymore. The woman then brought the chaplain from the *Herz Jesu* Church, who then spoke to him. He finally went and she received, a week later I believe, the news that the son had fallen for 'people, Führer and Fatherland'. The mother was now a 'heroic mother' – but she was beyond consolation.[99]

Perhaps even worse was the experience of the Adel family, whose house suffered a direct hit by a bomb on 13 September 1944. As Agnes recalled: 'On the day that we were bombed, we immediately received the news that our Hein is missing – on the same day, on the same morning'.[100]

As these extracts suggest, military call up of men meant that the population of Osnabrück became more feminine and younger, as revealed in Table 4.2. The largest change occurred between 1942 and 1943 when the proportion of men over 16 fell from 36 per cent to 34 per cent. From 1944 evacuation meant a decline in the overall number of people living in the town.

Table 4.2: Changing Composition of Osnabrück's Population, 1939-45.

Date	Males over 16	Males under 16	Females over 16	Females under 16
March 1939	35,401	10,287	43,005	9,940
March 1940	36,015	10,656	43,456	10,296
March 1941	36,953	10,677	45,174	10,324
March 1942	37,314	10,627	45,730	10,274
March 1943	32,822	10,324	44,035	9,980
March 1944	33,192	10,275	44,630	9,934
March 1945	24,397	6,382	25,794	7,485

Source: NSO Dep-3c-335, Angaben zur Bevölkerungsstatistik.

The fall in male numbers occurred precisely at the time when increased arms production required more labour power following the appointment of Albert Speer as Armaments Minister in 1942, which resulted in a reorganization of the economy to focus more specifically upon war production. However, as Richard Overy has demonstrated, the percentage of industrial workers labouring for the arms industry had already increased from 21.9 per cent in 1939 to 50.2 per cent by 1940, reaching 61 per cent by 1943. This meant that other sectors of the economy suffered. Overy has also pointed to the fact that efficiency and productivity increased dramatically between 1942 and 1944, following Speer's appointment, although from 1944 the bombing took its toll. The increases of 1942-4 occurred because of automation and better use of factory space, which allowed the use of unskilled labour, especially foreigners. But Germans had to make up some of the shortfall, which resulted in significantly increased working hours.[101] In the case of Osnabrück the employment office complained in June 1942 that it had 6,533 vacant positions compared with 4,658 at the end of December 1941. This was despite the fact that, in the intervening six months, 10,286 people, including 4,841 women, had entered the labour market.[102]

The development of several Osnabrück firms during the War illustrates the increasing importance of armaments production in the town and the working conditions faced. The OKD employed about 3,500 people who not only faced the constant fear of bombing, but also excessive working hours. In February 1944, the 3,292 industrial workers consisted of 2,183 Germans and 1,109 foreign workers and prisoners of war. The German figure included 1,551 adult males, 493 women and 139 youths under 18. The factory made semi finished products from copper, aluminium, bronze, brass and special alloys. This clearly meant heavy work involving exposure to heat and dust. By this time workers faced shifts of twelve hours, with just two breaks of 15 and 45 minutes. In all 740,964 working hours should have been carried out per week, although illness, family circumstances and absenteeism meant that this figure was not achieved.[103]

Klöckner, meanwhile, employed 3,875 people by 1944. Working flat out, both Germans and foreigners involved in the hardest tasks received extra food rations to keep up their strength.[104] Expansion in the size of the workforce had taken place from the early stages of the war. In January 1940 the firm needed an immediate increase of 160 men, which would grow to 1,000 by the end of the year. This meant recruiting people from both the *Regierungsbezirk* and from further away, as well as making use of prisoners.[105]

Karmann changed from an automobile factory to a plant which built parts for aircraft, reflecting the fate of car manufacturers throughout the Reich.[106] 'In the first days of October 1939, virtually the entire automobile programme came to a halt at Karmann'. Because of its strategic importance in armaments terms Karmann's plants faced regular attack from the air, starting in September 1940.[107] As well as dodging the bombs, overtime for those working in the factories had become a way of life. As early as March 1940 weekly hours had increased to 47½.[108] A report by the industrial inspectorate from May 1944 gave details of the working conditions in the

Karmann plant in Martinistrasse, involved in the production of aircraft parts and 'army tools'. The factory employed 111 clerical personnel and 1,109 workers, of whom 543 consisted of Germans, made up of 451 adult males, 40 women and 52 youths under 18. Foreigners and prisoners of war accounted for the other 566 labourers. About 30 per cent of the Germans consisted of specialists not called up because of their age. By this time working hours on weekdays had increased to almost twelve from 7am until 6.45pm, with two breaks of just 15 and 45 minutes, and to seven hours, from 7am until 2pm, including a 45 minute lunch break, on Saturdays. In addition, a night shift had also come into operation, which involved about 20 per cent of personnel.[109]

At least in the early stages of the War Germans employed in factories still had some leisure time. Propaganda glorifying labour continued, as evidenced by the handing out of war service crosses for the most productive workers. On 6 May 1941 a celebratory event occurred to present 21 of these to employees in Klöckner and the Teuto-Metallwerk.[110] In the summers of 1941 and 1942 the *Deutsches Berufserziehungswerk*, allied to the DAF, organized education and training in Osnabrück, continuing similar events run by the DAF during the 1930s. The programme for 1941 and 1942 concentrated upon chemistry, physics, mathematics, iron and metal work, engineering and building. While some space remained for foreign languages, humanities subjects had generally disappeared, as had instruction in racial ideology.[111]

The NSDAP continued to emphasise the importance of sport throughout the war.[112] In October 1941 the KDF arranged an evening in the *Stadthalle* celebrating the importance of sport.[113] The DAF and KDF also encouraged sport in factories. A letter from the KDF sent out to all factory leaders asked them to provide time for physical exercise.[114] At least until 1942 the OKD also supported spare time activities in its factories. On 14 September 1940 its annual summer sports day occurred in its own sporting grounds. Two years later the OKD, together with other factories, participated in a sporting day organized by the SA.[115]

War production had consequences for smaller firms. An article in the *Neue Volksblätter* of 1 October 1940 stated that the first problem for artisans lay in the call up to the armed forces, which meant that many small enterprises had closed. Furthermore, the concentration on armaments production meant that 'it is self explanatory that aeroplanes can only be built in aeroplane factories and not in the workshops of artisans'. Armaments factories also made efforts to secure available raw materials, which again impacted upon artisans. The Artisans Chamber of Commerce disappeared. Measures to control labour supplies implemented in 1943 forced the transfer of employees to places of work regarded as having

importance for the war effort.[116] On 25 February 1943, for instance, the
regional Chamber of Commerce for Weser-Ems based in Bremen, which
now had control of trade in Osnabrück, sent a letter to the firm of
Friedrich Zinn, informing the owners that, under the Decree for the
Release of Labour Supplies for Employment of Military Importance, it
faced closure. The enterprise had three days to send the names of its
workers to the local employment office.[117] Bakers, butchers and millers
played a crucial role in feeding local populations, while facing labour
shortages. Builders, carpenters, roofers, smiths and mechanics found
themselves working round the clock as the bombing campaign
intensified.[118]

Standards of living increasingly suffered as the War progressed, not
simply because of the bombing, but also because of rationing, which, in the
case of some articles, notably butter, had begun before September 1939.
This policy came into operation for several reasons. First, the experience of
the First World War, as German collapse had largely occurred because of
the Allied Blockade and the consequent lack of food and raw materials.
Second, the shortage of labour, which impacted upon both agricultural and
industrial production. At the same time, the armed forces and armaments
production took priority when it came to the allocation of all goods,
whether metals, textiles or food. As the war progressed and the focus upon
armaments increased, consumer goods became increasingly scarce. Dietary
habits changed, the availability and quality of food lessened and prices
consequently increased. Before the bombs came down, the availability of
food and consumer goods played the largest role in determining the public
mood.[119]

Rationing in Osnabrück came into operation on 27 August 1939.[120] With
the passage of time, the items rationed and the quantities available changed.
By the end of 1940 shops opened until 7pm because people did not have
enough time to purchase the goods they required. Vegetables had become
increasingly difficult to obtain, with the exception of cabbages and turnips.
The only 'fruits' consisted of lemons.[121] By 1944 the situation had severely
deteriorated. At the height of summer all types of berries failed to reach the
market in sufficient qualities. The same applied to cauliflower. While new
potatoes sufficed, shopkeepers decided not to sell them on Saturday
because of the throng of people trying to buy them.[122] By this time those
working in armaments production faced a shortage of clothing and
shoes.[123] The following extract from the *Kriegs-Chronik* gives an indication
of the situation in January 1945, when the full effects of the Air War
manifested themselves:

One of the most important provisions, milk, has become increasingly scarce for the population of Osnabrück, because milk traders who come from outside regularly stay away. Many families obtain just half a litre of skimmed milk for a whole week, and not even one drop of milk sometimes comes to the house. Equally, the provision of coal has taken on increasingly nasty forms: people place themselves in endless queues in front of the gasworks and next to the harbour and are greatly relieved if they get hold of a hundred-weight of bad burning briquettes, which is used very quickly.[124]

As reported by the Osnabrück press, various initiatives attempted to solve the problem of rationing and shortages. In the first place, particularly at the start of the War, the local state offered advice on making full use of the available foodstuffs. An article in the *Osnabrücker Tageblatt* of 1 October 1941 told housewives how to save on both heating materials and food by employing 'tower cooking', i.e. placing saucepans on top of each other. In the following spring the same newspaper reported on a cooking course run by the NSF.[125] Some people grew food in their back gardens, while others cultivated allotments. The local press encouraged this activity, in an almost absurd way in some instances. An article in the *Neue Volksblätter* of 3 July 1940 carried the headline of 'Fighting the Enemy in the Allotment'. Meanwhile, in June 1940 land in the city became available for cultivation, for which individual Nazi cells within the town took responsibility.[126]

The War had dramatic consequences for the social policies launched during the 1930s,[127] which in turn impacted upon the health of the local population. Above all, Nazi ideological aims for women faced serious revision because of labour shortages. In the early years of the conflict some semblance of normality continued. A report covering 1940-1 indicated that adults could receive grants of up to RM36 per month, while couples could obtain RM54 and children RM11. Those given such allowances included widows with young children who could not manage in the War, especially as a result of inflation.[128] Meanwhile, in November 1940 the Mayor of Osnabrück authorized the granting of one off payments to poor people from other locations, pensioners, war invalids and dependants. Those who had children would receive RM3 for each one. In October 1941 a total of 1,092 individuals received support, costing RM5,220.[129] The state only played one part in the care of the needy during the War. The semi-official WHW also contributed. In March 1942 it organized a concert for the purpose of raising money for schools.[130] The Churches also looked after those in need. For instance, during the 1944-5 winter of bombs the Roman Catholic Church cared for children as their schools collapsed.[131]

The War meant a rise in the death rate, a fall in the birth rate and an increase in the incidence of disease. Peter Marschalck has estimated that the German population lost seven million people as a result of these developments, although Günter Steinberg, taking a longer term perspective, has viewed the War as the basis for the demographic development of Germany for the rest of the twentieth century. His study of the conflict laid much emphasis upon the consequences of the immigration of German refugees from eastern Europe from 1945.[132] In Osnabrück the death rate reached its height in 1944 at 13.8 per thousand as deaths exceeded births in that year. The number of people dying from tuberculosis reached its peak in 1945. In August 1943 the *Stadtkrankenhaus* had 50 beds for those with the disease. Suicide rates, however, remained fairly stable, at least in the first three years of the war.[133]

The position of women offered one of the best tests of the success of Nazi ideology during the War. The wish to increase the number of children born to those with the right genes became increasingly difficult in a situation in which partners became separated and feared producing offspring which the husband might never see or which might die in an Allied bombing raid. Similarly, the decline in the number of men and the increasing need for labour power made it more and more difficult to keep women out of factories, despite the continuing desires of some members of the Nazi hierarchy to do so. Foreign workers could not fill all the gaps, and also represented a sexual threat to the German family.[134]

The glorification of motherhood continued as did the Nazi women's organizations, at least in the early stages of the War.[135] In October 1939, for instance, with the regime and German society essentially still in peace time mode, gatherings took place throughout the Reich for the purpose of handing out mother's crosses to *Kinderreich* women. These had now become 'honorary symbols of the home front'. A ceremony in Osnabrück also occurred on Mother's Day 1940.[136] In the following March a meeting occurred in the Goldbeck restaurant in Osnabrück attended by mothers and fathers of *Kinderreich* families. The leading speaker declared that all male and female comrades should produce four healthy children as 'we must become an expanding people, in order to maintain living space throughout time and fill it with German blood'.[137] As late as September 1944 Gertrud Scholtz-Klink spoke to a gathering of women in Osnabrück, 'in the middle of a town bloodied by bomb terror', declaring that German women are remaining true to the *Führer*.[138]

In the early stages of the conflict at least, the various organizations established for women continued to function. December 1939 saw the opening of a new headquarters for the NSF in Osnabrück. In the same month the Schinkel-Central NSDAP opened a *Hilfswerk Mutter und Kind*.[139]

On the tenth anniversary of the establishment of this body in Osnabrück, in February 1943, the *Neue Volksblätter* carried a feature which examined its work in the *Regierungsbezirk*, stressing help offered for children both before and after 1939.[140]

Employment increasingly impacted upon women as the conflict progressed. Even before the War the majority of German women worked, with some of them labouring long hours, another development which increasingly became the norm. Overy, unlike other analysts of women's employment in wartime Nazi Germany, which assert that the state 'failed to take advantage of a large reservoir of unused female labour', in contrast to the UK, USSR and USA, points out that the proportion of women employed in Germany always exceeded that in the UK and the USA. Whereas the German figure went from 41.4 per cent to 51 per cent from May 1940 to May 1944, the corresponding rises in the UK and the USA went from 29.8 to 37.9 and 25.8 to 35.7 respectively.[141] Part of the historiographical disagreement may lie in the fact that the number of women in employment actually fell from 14.6 million to 14.1 million between 1939 and 1941, although it rose again to 14.9 million by 1944.[142] This points to a reluctance to mobilise women in the early stages of the war, not, according to Tim Mason, because of the ideological opposition of Hitler, but because such a measure would prove too unpopular.[143] Although the Nazis had taken steps to redirect labour towards the armaments industries in the early stages of the War, it was only after the impact of Stalingrad, in January 1943, that they introduced a measure to mobilize 3 million women between 17 and 45. This failed because only about 1 million extra women actually joined the workforce, the majority on a part time basis.[144]

The majority of women in Osnabrück worked long hours during the War, as revealed by a variety of sources. At the start of the conflict the press piled on the pressure by publishing articles resembling those aimed at men during the 1930s In May 1940 the *Neue Volksblätter* published a piece with the title of 'Women at the Work Bench: They Stand Together with their Men in Osnabrück Enterprises'. The article concluded:

> One can do everything if one wants! *Kinderreich* mothers manage it, young women with small children work around it, and so many older women, who were in many cases already there during the First World War have come back again with a calm acceptance and have sat at the work bench…as they did 26 years ago to do their duty.[145]

The leading Osnabrück engineering companies employed women from the early stages of the War, increasing their hours, along with men and foreign workers, as the conflict progressed. In the spring of 1944 the OKD employed 410 women on a full time basis and 60 who worked part time, mostly engaged in lighter tasks. The former seemed to have carried out similarly longer hours to their male colleagues.[146] Anneliese Berger worked in the accounts department at the OKD and recounted that she had to carry the heavy calculators with her into the bunker when the air raid warning sounded.[147]

This experience represents just one of the many employment stories of women in Osnabrück. Shop work was common as revealed by Aneliese Diehl, who worked in a grocery store at the start of the conflict.[148] Lora Kraft worked in her father's shop which sold textiles and fabrics until a bomb destroyed it in 1943, after which time the family continued storing goods in various houses in Osnabrück and nearby Bramsche.[149] Anna Allewelt had a varied experience during the War:

> On 1 September 1939 my husband was called up and our business – upholstery and decorations, Osnabrück Johanisstrasse 23 – closed. I subsequently went to the Röscher works as a clerk where I was employed until the birth of my daughter in 1941. We lived from the remainder of the income after that.[150]

The Adel sisters had contrasting experiences. While Agnes found herself employed mostly outside Osnabrück in a variety of tasks, Anni remained to work in her father's hardware shop until a bomb destroyed it.[151] Lilo Meyer had her working life in Osnabrück disrupted on several occasions by the Air War:

> I began an apprenticeship as a commercial clerk in the office of a hat wholesaler in Goethestrasse. This building was completely destroyed and the business transferred to Bohmter Strasse. Then we had to go into the bunker in Bohmter Strasse. But the business was also destroyed there, the firm moved out of Osnabrück and I went to a firm called Weitkamp, where I was employed as a commercial clerk.

Inge Walter remembered the war as an extremely difficult time, as her mother died in 1940 when she was only fifteen years of age:

> I had to be at Klöckner at half past seven, and when I returned at seven I had to shop with ration coupons, cook for my father, repair my father's blue overalls, as they always had holes in the pockets from the tools he carried in them. Then there was a repair, then there was a hole on the repair, and then came the repair underneath again and a

new pocket followed, then the sewing needle broke and one did not have any. And then one had to go into the bunker at night. I hardly got any sleep. My father had to be at Hammersen at 6 o'clock in the morning. I had to get up at half six at the latest...Every six weeks we had to wash our clothes. We lived upstairs under the roof. The washroom was in the courtyard. I had to go to the washroom at 3 o'clock in the night, heat the boiler, and had to be at the steelworks by 8.[152]

Such stories point to the collapse of German society and economy during the War as a result of economic mobilization and bombing. Although the worst effects of the conflict did not bite until after 1942, the situation which existed in German towns at the end of the War, in the form of round the clock bombing, resulting in destruction, and constant working, meant that the *Volksgemeinschaft* increasingly lost its illusions about the benefits which the Nazis could bestow. The constant working of the years after 1942, the Allied bombing and, ultimately, the rubble of 1945 point to the failure of Nazi economic and social policy. While most people may have seen an improvement in their living conditions by 1939, the desperation of the final years of the conflict meant that they found themselves facing the worst conditions which any Germans would experience during the twentieth century.

Persuading Adults in Wartime

Against this background propaganda had a major role to play.[153] But War meant that the urban goose steppers of the 1930s no longer paraded through German towns as they now fought real enemies in Soviet snows or Saharan sands. As the bombs fell education became increasingly difficult as school buildings collapsed. The propaganda mechanisms of newspapers and film broadcasts became less effective because of the manpower shortages and economic mobilization which had taken place. As the regime collapsed, stark reality, untainted by Nazi public relations, stared people in the face in the form of destroyed and desolate buildings. Although the 'Hitler Myth' actually reached its zenith following the early German victories in 1940, it collapsed as a result of the defeats and bombing which followed.[154] In these circumstances the mass produced cinema played a large role in informing public opinion and raising morale.[155]

Wartime public spectacle made less of an impact in Osnabrück even before the bombs came down, although it never completely disappeared. The celebration of the central days of the Nazi calendar continued on a reduced scale. The memorialization of the Nazi seizure of power even occurred on 30 January 1945, which the *Neue Volksblätter* reported under the heading of 'Our Victory Will Come from Faith and Fighting Strength'. Unlike the pre-War period the events of this day took place in the National Theatre on a Sunday afternoon, attended, according to the report, by representatives of all of the major Nazi bodies and 'a great number of party comrades', presumably the most diehard of believers. In a desperate speech, admitting 'the great winter slaughter' in the east of the *Reich*, 'Gau speaker Bruns' concluded that: 'Germany will never die, if we ourselves do not want that'.[156] Similarly, the last celebration of 9 November occurred in 1944 throughout the country, when the commemorations concentrated on the establishment of the *Volkssturm*, the home guard consisting of young and old, to defend the Fatherland in the spirit of 9 November.[157]

Hitler's birthday celebrations became a pale shadow of their former glory, even though the press reported them with the same sycophantic language as before. In 1941 the *Neue Volksblätter* wrote that on 20 April Osnabrück gave 'the greatest German of all time its love, gratitude and honour', even though the festivities just involved meetings in the National Theatre and the Capitol Cinema. By 1943 and 1944 the celebrations consisted of a gathering in the National Theatre with music and speeches.[158]

The NSDAP mass meetings which characterised the pre-War period became much smaller in scale and focused mainly on the necessity for military victory. One of the biggest events occurred in the week after 9 November 1940, under the theme of 'We Will Be Victorious With the *Führer*' and included speeches, rallies and films.[159] On 18 March 1941 Osnabrück participated in one of its biggest days of memorialization and public spectacle of the War, which did involve marches, called to remember those who had died during the conflict.[160] Those gatherings taking place at the end of the War had become increasingly desperate, simply focusing upon the need to continue fighting. At a large rally in September 1944 the deputy *Gauleiter*, Joel, claimed that the experience of 1918 would not be repeated and that, despite the Air War, Germany would still win under the leadership of the Nazis. One of the last gatherings occurred at the end of January 1945 when Gauleiter Paul Wegener almost admitted defeat by pointing to the critical situation, but claimed that the Nazis, under the leadership of Hitler, would remain unshakeable.[161]

The SA continued some of its public spectacles, at least in the early stages of the War. In April 1940 it held a march with members of the armed forces which culminated in a rally in the Ledenhof. A similar series of events occurred in the following year aimed at raising morale, awareness of the War and the role of local troops.[162] Stew Sundays lessened in frequency, although one did take place in March 1941 organized by the Osnabrück city centre branch of the NSDAP.[163]

Lectures became less regular, but did occur. In April 1942 a doctor from Bremen asked: 'Are the White Races Dying Out'.[164] Public lectures in the early winter of 1943 covered a wide range of subjects and involved experts from around the country. Those on 'history and geopolitics' included 'Professor Dr Scheel, Kiel and Copenhagen ("Germany and the North")', and 'Professor Dr Suchenwirth ("The East in German History")'. Other academics gave lectures on Asian subjects including Japanese culture.[165]

The cinema remained a constant, linking the period before and after 1939. Attendance increased during the War, even though the number of German feature films produced declined drastically as the conflict progressed. The staple diet consisted of a mixture of escapist films, political features and newsreels.[166] One study has divided the films on show in Osnabrück cinemas during the War into various categories including: 'premiers'; foreign films, including some Hollywood exports such as *Laurel and Hardy* and *Mickey Mouse*; propaganda, which included *Jud Süß*, shown in October 1940, followed by *The Eternal Jew* in December, and the pro-euthanasia feature film *Ich Klage an* the following year, about a doctor who eventually decided that his wife, who had contracted multiple sclerosis, should die; films for youths and children; cultural and documentary films; and features about historical figures who ranged from Johann Strauß to Frederick the Great. Cinema in wartime therefore aimed both at focusing people's minds on the struggle which they faced, as well as attempting to help them to escape from it.[167] As long as the theatres remained standing because, like all other buildings, they faced destruction as a result of the Air War. For instance, the cinema in Alte Münze in Osnabrück was damaged following an attack in September 1942. It reopened at the end of 1943 but only survived until September 1944.[168]

High culture continued as before during the early stages of the conflict but died as the war progressed, the bombs fell, black outs ruled the nights and armaments production increasingly took away free time and artists.[169] In addition, militaristic themes became increasingly important, particularly in museum exhibitions. An article in the *Neue Volksblätter* of October 1940 pointed out that those events which did occur would end by 9.30.[170]

Theatre and musical performances which the regime saw 'a wartime instrument for the strengthening of moral',[171] continued into 1943 in Osnabrück. A publication giving details of performances in the National Theatre in the 1940-1 season carried an article from Dr Gaertner, which ended: 'Theatre is not a luxury, theatre is essential'.[172] By this time the programmes came with evacuation plans in the event of an air raid warning.[173] In the winter of 1941-2 a total of 106 performances of fifteen works took place. By now much of the audience consisted of members of the *Wehrmacht*.[174] In the summer of 1944, as bombs rained down and foreign troops approached German soil from all directions, the theatre closed. Actors and male singers had to serve in the army after 20 August following a directive from Goebbels, while their female colleagues found themselves in factories.[175] Music had also continued apace in the early stages of the War. The winter season of 1940-1 consisted of 53 performances in Osnabrück ranging from instrumental recitals to puppet theatre performances.[176] The total excluded opera, which in this season witnessed the performances of ten different works including Wagner and Puccini, and operetta, which counted seven different works.[177]

Some musical and theatrical activity continued into 1944. People still attended concerts, plays and films in order to 'flee from the all too grey reality of everyday life into the world of illusions', which the authorities realized and therefore made every effort to keep such activity going until physical destruction made it impossible.[178] Musical performances planned for the winter of 1943-4 included performances of Bruckner's fifth symphony, Beethoven's ninth, and Bach's St Matthew Passion.[179] On 22-30 May 1943 the 'Gau Cultural Days' had witnessed two performances of Beethoven's ninth, together with chamber music and Lieder evenings.[180] A similar event occurred in the following May and included a musical performance by the Hitler Youth Orchestra of Osnabrück encompassing works by Telemann, Gluck and Mozart.[181]

War became a major theme in Osnabrück exhibitions. In October 1940 the armed forces demonstrated their hardware in locations throughout the town including the Stadthalle and its gardens, as well as in several streets. The same month witnessed the opening of a 'museum' in the town hall commemorating the Peace of Westphalia. In January 1941 the museum hosted an exhibition of about 150 drawings by Wilhelm Petersen, who had served with the Waffen SS in Holland, Belgium and France. In March 1942 up to 25,000 people may have participated in 'The Day of the Wehrmacht', when the army organized a series of events and showed off its hardware.[182]

These military spectacles formed part of the propaganda campaign and satisfied the curiosity of the Osnabrück population about the War. Exhibitions brought some military reality to the home front, albeit in a sanitised manner. The Allied bombs represented the real truth of war for Osnabrückers, as did the loss of relatives. But some escapism did survive in exhibitions. One which took place at Christmas 1943 involved the display of paintings on the festive theme.[183] One of the largest cultural events in Osnabrück during the War consisted of an exhibition of contemporary Dutch art which took place in the palace in October 1941.[184]

Persuading Children in Wartime

The War and the Allied bombing campaign had a deep impact upon both popular and high culture in Osnabrück, particularly towards its conclusion. Similarly, the salad days of the Hitler Youth came to an end with the outbreak of War, so that its members increasingly came to play a role in military operations on the home front as grown males disappeared. As British and American bombs achieved their aims, schooling became increasingly difficult, and in the latter stages of the conflict, children faced evacuation to the south of the Reich.[185]

The War had various consequences for German schools. In the first place, many teachers disappeared as a result of military call up. By the end of 1939 a total of 62 from Osnabrück served in the armed forces.[186] Those teachers who had fought in the First World War faced an early call up. The disappearance of so many staff meant that schools had to resort to desperate measures, including calling people out of retirement,[187] as well as cutting down teaching hours.

Schools found that their children vanished for a variety of reasons so that traditionally structured school days had become a thing of the past, particularly as bombing raids intensified and, more regularly, sirens sounded. Older boys faced military service.[188] Schools which lost pupils at the front naturally commemorated them. The May 1944 edition of the journal published by the *Gymnasium Carolinium* carried the front page headline of 'They Died for Germany', followed by a list of 24 names.[189]

The death of pupils did not represent a major reason for their disappearance from schools. More importantly, the state used them on the home front. Pupils from the *Staatliche Oberschule* worked on harvesting in September and October 1939 and subsequently unloaded ships in the harbour, piled up wood and delivered Christmas cards.[190] Similar events occurred at the *Ratsgymnasium*, particularly as the school became a gathering station for the mobilization of troops between 30 August and 12 September, which meant that soldiers slept on the floor while horses stood in the courtyard. During this period, and in the months which followed, pupils worked in the port and helped with the harvest.[191] Because of manpower shortages during the War, the use of children became normality, particularly in agriculture.[192] From 1943 teenage boys also worked as flak helpers, as both Johannes Hesse and Karl Mosse recalled. Hesse remembers employment on three shifts per week from 10pm until 6am. Mosse stated that those who took part were 'not responsible for the guns, that's why soldiers were there, but ammunition had to be moved, one had to pay attention, one had to observe, the machinery which was set up according to specific instructions had to be checked.'[193]

Children also disappeared from schools as a result of evacuation, particularly in the later stages of the War as part of a nationwide relocation of as many as 5 million individuals, which meant an eastward and southward moving urban to rural migration. While some of those affected felt the wrench from their parents, others recognized the safety the move provided as they found themselves in relatively peaceful new surroundings, despite usually having to live in camps.[194] The 350 Osnabrück children who went to the Sudetenland in April 1940 returned six months later.[195] By the summer of 1944 over 300 Osnabrück children had faced evacuation, mostly to camps in the south.[196]

The bombing and the air raid warnings also severely disrupted education. The diary entries of Dirk Siegel in his final school year, 1940-1, indicate that sirens had an impact even before the bombs started to fall.[197] Those schools destroyed by bomb damage included the *Gymnasium Carolinium* in 1943, which meant that its pupils had to attend school in nearby Bersenbrück, Melle or Kloster Oesede. Karl Mosse went to the last of these for the final two years of the War: 'I had to travel either by bicycle or with the train, when the trains did not run, when the trains were not shot at or when they could not run because of sirens.'[198] On 13 September St Ursula was destroyed in one of the biggest raids of the War, which killed four of the nuns who taught there.[199]

Regular attendance, lessons and syllabi no longer existed, although central government introduced measures to control the syllabus.[200] In Osnabrück, the regime continued to display concern about the amount of time devoted to physical exercise, which stood at 1½ hours in October 1944, assuming that bombing, work or any other interruptions did not intervene.[201] The number of pupils attending school declined drastically, as did the number of educational establishments as the bombs began to take their toll. One solution consisted of shortening the time periods for lessons from fifty to thirty minutes. By the end of the War education had become almost impossible. Not only did older children find themselves forced to work in all sorts of occupations as their schools disintegrated, they also found that those lessons which did progress did so under the supervision of 'sick, older or war disabled teachers', who tried to keep order in the chaos.[202] As if the various interruptions did not disrupt and decimate education enough, pupils also found that they had to participate in the collection of all sorts of material which might prove of use to the War effort, from metals to paper and bones.[203]

The collapse of education meant a decline in youth discipline, despite attempts to prevent this. The Hitler Youth, for instance, continued its activities, especially at the start of the War, although, as the conflict progressed, its members found themselves more directly drawn into it.[204]

The annual ceremony to celebrate the accession of a particular year's children to the movement continued until 1944, although with much less ceremonial than had occurred before 1939.[205] The pre-War activities of playing at soldiers, participating in sport and spending time in camps with other youths still took place,[206] although the necessity for labour on the home front meant that such events declined.

The Hitler Youth played a more direct role in the control of young people during the War under police regulations passed in 1940. Members of the organization worked with the NSV and the police to patrol 'dance halls, restaurants, cinemas and the public areas, streets and squares'. Youths found smoking in public would initially receive a warning followed by heavier penalties for persistent offenders. A police report from 12 August 1940 pointed to the fact that '46 female and 22 male youths' had faced arrest. 'From these 28 female and 11 male youths under 18 were brought to the attention of the police because of participation at a public dance without supervision from qualified educators or from an adult person authorised by them'. They each received a fine of RM1. But the same report noted an overall decline in youth criminality. Two months later, however, the police published details about young people arrested for venturing out after dark, participating in dances and going to a pub. Most seriously, four members of the Hitler Youth faced arrest and prosecution after being found involved in 'sodomy' in a public washroom. Other young people continued to face arrest for dancing, stealing or venturing out after dark.[207] Such activity may have constituted resistance, or at least nonconformity, to Detlev Peukert, but we might simply see it as youths carrying out normal activity criminalized by a regime obsessed by controlling everyone in its domain.[208] Volker Issmer has pointed to the existence of Edelweiß Pirates, a youth resistance group, in Osnabrück and its environs.[209]

The peacetime methods of persuading both youths and adults became increasingly difficult during the course of the War. While some semblance of normality survived until the middle of the conflict, the demands of wartime labour and the toll taken by the bombing changed this situation. 'Total War' and constant blackouts left little time for festivities, which had characterized the 1930s. Goose-stepping ceased: it had always represented a preparation for War, which became reality after 1939. Touring museum exhibitions tried to bring this reality to the home front in a sanitized way, but British and American bombers did so much more directly. Germans could now see the consequences of Nazism, untainted by public relations. The new education system of the 1930s simply collapsed because of a lack of teachers and bombing from the air.

The propaganda of the peacetime years partly served the function of preparing Germans for War. When conflict broke out, time for further indoctrination declined and perhaps became less necessary as the struggle completely engaged minds and bodies, although the Nazis recognized the need to maintain continuities in cultural activities, for instance, by their desire to keep cinema and theatre going. As the War turned and, more importantly, the bombs fell, people could increasingly recognize the true meaning of Nazism.

Everyday Repression and Resistance in Wartime

The fighting allowed the regime to become more intolerant towards all of its real and perceived enemies in a situation in which its survival increasingly became a central issue, especially after the bombs began to rain down. Even before the Allied campaign reached its height, justice against those carrying out acts of criminality, whether of a political nature or not, had become increasingly draconian and arbitrary. Special courts established in 1933 and headed by judges with NSDAP membership cards really came into their own during the War, having grown in number from a national figure of 26 in 1933 to 74 by 1942. The one responsible for Osnabrück sat in Hanover.[210] The courts made particular use of the 1934 Law for Protection Against Treacherous Attacks on the State and Party and for the Protection of Party Uniformities, as well as the Decree Against People's Vermin passed on 5 September 1939. Crimes under the last of these included looting, the exploitation of wartime conditions for one's own benefit, theft from metal collections, listening to foreign radio stations, misuse of ration cards and relationships with foreign workers. As a result of wartime developments, the rights of defendants were essentially reduced to zero.[211] These developments occurred against the background of the expansion of the power of the SS during the course of the War.[212]

Two overwhelming and contradictory realities stare out at anyone considering the issues of repression in wartime Germany. First, the regularity with which people faced arrest for all manner of crime. And, secondly, despite the penalties which individuals could receive, in the form of imprisonment, hard labour or death, most people carried out some act which could lead to prosecution, often on a regular basis. These developments took place in a society where informers played a major role, which meant that ordinary Germans usually had an idea of whom to trust. Oral, court and *Gestapo* records in Osnabrück allow a reconstruction of the realities, regularity and consequences of wartime resistance, or, perhaps more accurately, criminality.

Surveys carried out by the US Army in Marburg, Hersfeld and Eschwege at the end of the War revealed that 51 per cent of the 666 people questioned claimed to have listened to foreign radio broadcasts during the Nazi period.[213] Osnabrück sources would confirm this picture. Interviewees certainly admitted to this act during the War, as well as to keeping it secret from those who could potentially report them. The Adel sisters, for instance, remembered a salesman from Hanover who came to their father's shop and listened to radio broadcasts from all over Europe with him.[214] Similary Elisabeth and Heinrich Wand regularly heard such broadcasts, a fact which they shared only with their closest acquaintances.[215]

Listening to radio remained a relatively mild 'crime' compared with that committed by Werner Lorenz in 1944. After joining the army he marched to an airfield near Münster to fly to Frankfurt an der Oder to take part in an offensive against the Red Army. On the way he concluded: 'No I am not going'. He threw away his weapons and turned back, walking forty kilometres: 'I had to watch out, to avoid being seized…Whoever was seized, was hung. – I made it, I am still alive.' He lived the last nine months of the war in the countryside with the support of a farmer, part of an SPD underground support group. Lorenz pointed out that he weighed up the options and, influenced by the death rate on the Russian front, and the possibility of surviving underground in the Osnabrück countryside, he 'made it'.[216]

The Adels, Wands, and Lorenzes all had an awareness of the danger of the 'crimes' which they committed and all spoke to narrow circles, which they knew they could trust. This argument suggests that resistance could occur as long as people kept quiet about it and did not allow individuals close to the regime or informers to find out about it. Criminal proceedings against Osnabrückers during the War provide numerous examples of those who spoke to the wrong people and therefore faced prison sentences as Robert Gellately previously illustrated using *Gestapo* case files in Würzburg and Düsseldorf.[217]

In some Osnabrück cases, imprisonment seemed almost inevitable because of the blatancy of anti-Nazi behaviour. The best example consists of the housekeeper Berta Eva. 'She is unloved by acquaintances and neighbours, because she has a very loose tongue', which meant that several women had little hesitation in reporting her. Between 17 May and 24 August 1940, she worked for a laundry with a Mrs Haß, who reported that Eva regularly made statements hostile to the state such as: 'Göring and Goebbels have married whores, who were employed in the theatre. Adolf Hitler is not capable of procreating and can therefore not marry…Hitler must be placed against the wall and shot.' She made these accusations in front of customers, for which she faced dismissal. She then worked in another laundry and made further statements regarded as treasonable and also spoke unwisely in her neighbourhood. The six women who testified against her pointed to her unpopularity. She faced 3 years in jail because of 'offences against the treason law'.[218]

Other careless people who faced prosecution included Heinrich Hack, a bricklayer who worked at the OKD and who uttered inadvisable comments to several of his colleagues. He told one of them that he listened to foreign radio broadcasts and also made statements against senior Nazi figures. He faced three years in prison.[219] August Stahl made pro-British statements to the wrong people including, following an air raid: 'I personally have a high estimation of the English'.[220] The teacher Bernhard Last received a prison sentence of six months for simply having stated to someone, who reported him, in the town square on 2 April 1944 that `we have already half lost the war'.[221]

Many of those facing prosecution did so for theft, as well as other activities considered as 'parasitic'. Osnabrück criminal statistics from the second quarter of 1944 reveal 72 serious thefts.[222] In July 1942 three youths received prison sentences of between three and a half and four years for carrying out a series of thefts involving ham, bacon and bicycles.[223] Maria Thiemeier was described as people's vermin and received a three year prison sentence, following a trial at the special court in Hanover, for stealing money from two handbags in an air raid shelter.[224] Cases involving breaking the regulations introduced to control food supply and the economy during the war occurred regularly, particularly the misuse of ration coupons. Luise Grun faced a prison sentence of six months and a fine of RM300 for stealing coupons from the Food Office while employed there.[225]

Little political persecution occurred in Osnabrück during the course of the War because the organized parties had disappeared by then, although, as Werner Lorenz suggests, some clandestine, but effective, organization survived. The only overt act of persecution carried out against the Left occurred following the almost successful assassination attempt on Hitler of 20 July 1944, which unified a series of groups across the political spectrum. The round up which followed resulted in the arrest of between 5,000 and 6,000 people in the Reich.[226] The people seized in Osnabrück faced internment in the work camp at Ohrbeck just outside the town. Heinrich Niedergesäß, Heinrich Groß, Fritz Szalinski and Wilhelm Mentrup then went to the Neuengamme concentration camp near Hamburg.[227] Inge Walter remembered:

> My father was arrested again after the attempt on Adolf Hitler in 1944, he was taken to Ohrbeck, this work camp for six weeks. It was a long time before we found out where he was. I had a step sister, who worked for the police and she found out all the people who were

initially held in the cellar of the palace – there were hundreds of people, they arrested them in the night. There were then only twenty who remained who were then taken to Ohrbeck. Six weeks later my father came home. He was the last one who was released from there. The others ended up in concentration camps, Neuengamme and so on.[228]

The Churches in Wartime

Although most of the battles between the churches and the state had occurred before the outbreak of the War, further persecution and opposition took place during its duration, particularly with regard to the Roman Catholic Church. In Osnabrück, little evidence exists of either persecution of or resistance by Protestants between 1939 and 1945, although their religion would still have represented an important aspect of their alternative social milieu. On a nationwide basis, the majority of evangelical pastors found themselves serving in the armed forces, often as ordinary soldiers, reflecting the support of the hierarchy for the war once it started. Individual ministers stood up to Nazi eugenics and official opposition to euthanasia occurred: 35 had to endure incarceration in Dachau for various forms of opposition. But the Jews disappeared with little intervention from any branch of the Evangelical church.[229] In Osnabrück, charitable work by the church occurred.[230]

At the end of the War the headquarters of the Hanoverian protestant Church sent out questionnaires to all ministers within its domain, encompassing 43 issues, from relationships with the NSDAP, damage to church buildings, and the size of the congregation. Most of the answers indicate a slight decline in attendance at services and participation in the various activities of the Church. Thus, in St Michael the number of visitors declined from 6,498 in 1940 to 3,247 in 1944. Communicants fell from 433 in 1939 to 325 in 1945, while the number of confirmed children dropped from 68 in 1940 to 37 in 1945. These patterns mirror those in other Osnabrück churches, displaying a fairly small decline in attendance, largely explained by bombing, full time employment and movement away from the town. The number of people who left St Michael totalled 171 between 1936 and 1944 out of a congregation of about 5,000. The *Katherinenkirche*, on the other hand, lost about 2,000 of its members, out of a congregation of around 19,000, although most had left in the middle of the 1930s. Nevertheless, the Church still played an important role for a significant percentage of the Protestant population during the War, providing an alternative to Hitler worship. Many of the respondents to the survey denied having participated in any of the Nazi days of celebration. The pastor of *Katherinenkirche*, for instance, emphatically wrote: 'Services on national holidays were not held by me!' Most of the questionnaires claimed to have had some trouble with the regime, either before or during the War. The minister of *Katherinenkirche* had visits from the *Gestapo* in 1941 and 1942, the second after someone in his congregation had denounced him for allegedly making utterings against the Waffen SS.[231]

The Roman Catholic Church continued its *Kulturkampf* during the War although, like the Evangelical establishment, it did little to prevent the fulfilment of the main ideological aims of the Nazis, even though individual priests stood up to euthanasia and antisemitism.[232] The 'final struggle' in the new *Kulturkampf* occurred in 1941 'as the Nazis launched what was to prove their final all-out offensive against the institutions, traditions and values' of the Catholic Community, which Kershaw asserted caused antagonism both in the Church hierarchy and amongst the Catholic population. The closure of monasteries caused particular consternation.[233]

The opening month of the War saw the progression of services as normal in the Osnabrück diocese which stretched far beyond the town[234] but by its end 70 priests and 57 laymen had faced prosecution.[235] These included Wilhelm Paul, vicar of St Joseph, who had to pay a fine for making statements against the regime. Joseph Schroeer, meanwhile, rector at the *Marienhospital*, spent over a month in custody during the autumn of 1941 for printing and sending out religious material to members of the *Wehrmacht* and for distributing the anti-euthanasia speech made by Bishop Galen of Münster. Similarly Stephan Vosse, who worked in the Cathedral, and was described as a 'hated opponent' of National Socialism, faced prosecution for sending religious publications to politicians.[236]

Matters came to a head in Roman Catholic life in the Osnabrück diocese during the summer 1941 when the *Gestapo* intervened and confiscated property and buildings belonging to the Church. Seven of these buildings lay in the *Regierungsbezirk* and two in the town in the form of the convents of St. Angela and St. Ursula.[237] On 2 August officers of the *Gestapo* went to both convents and told the nuns that they had until midday of the 6th to vacate their rooms. On 5 and 6 August the authorities informed the nuns from both institutions that some of them would have to work for the army in a military hospital established at St Angela.[238]

Euthanasia

The cover of the War allowed the Nazis to pursue various final solutions including one against those regarded as unworthy of life. Sterilizations actually fell fairly dramatically in Osnabrück from an annual average of over 100 before the War to 33 in 1940, 56 in 1941, 20 in 1942 and 17 in 1943,[239] after which time the impact of Allied bombing on both hospital buildings and the bodies of Osnabrück citizens meant that sterilization became something of a luxury medical practice.[240]

More importantly, the War allowed the implementation of euthanasia, the real indication of an attempted final solution. This caused consternation amongst religious circles, most famously in the sermon by Bishop Galen of Münster on 3 August 1941,[241] as well as other sections of the population, including the relatives of those who would die, particularly parents.[242] The policy evolved from the pre-War sterilization programme. The action taken after 1939 had a long history, at least in its gestation, dating back to the end of the nineteenth century.[243] The accession of the Nazis to power meant a preparation for the actions taken at the start of the War, both through the circulation of the concept of euthanasia as well as the use of new inhumane methods of dealing with physically and mentally handicapped people. The action initially began against children as the War broke out and subsequently included adults in the so-called T4 action. Some disabled people died in concentration camps while others perished in hospitals located away from major population centres, specially designed for carrying out euthanasia. The killing continued well into 1945, intensifying as Allied troops penetrated German soil.[244]

Euthanasia did not actually take place in Osnabrück, but psychiatric patients from here faced transfer to hospitals elsewhere in order to die. As Eva Berger has demonstrated, psychiatric treatment in the town during the course of the 1930s and 1940s adopted new methods of treatment including electric shock therapy.[245] The main deportation of patients from Osnabrück occurred from the *Landes Heil- und Pflegeanstalt* in April 1941 as part of a round up continuing the T4 actions launched in the previous year, which occurred in the major medical establishments in Lower Saxony. A total of 180 patients made the journey, all of whom probably died, although death certificates only exist for 45. A further major deportation appears to have occurred in February 1943 involving 25 'unsettled sick people' to an institution in Mersiritz Oberwalde, all of whom seem to have died.[246]

Trials of those accused of directing and participating in the euthanasia action occurred in Hanover in 1948 and 1949. The proceedings provided a list of 77 patients who left the *Landes Heil- und Pflegeanstalt* during the course of the conflict, although it does not seem to include people deported as part of the actions of April 1941 and February 1943. The list provided details of 'type of transferred patient'; who fell into three main groups. The first actually consisted of foreign workers sent back to their homeland, primarily Poland. A smaller category of criminals counted just three persons. The overwhelming majority, 58, were described as 'mental patient'. This group included one person described as Jewish and another as a foreigner. The reasons for transfer included 'lack of places' in the case of the third group, as well as the wishes of relatives. While the foreigners went back to their country of origin, the Germans went to institutions in Münster, Bielefeld, Lüneberg and Hildesheim. The table does not make clear the ultimate fate of the people who faced transfer, but it appears that it did not always mean death.[247]

The relatives of some of those deported on the two major transportations subsequently gave evidence at the trial. Grete Kuhl recalled the story of her brother, Johannes Laken, who first became ill in 1927 and was looked after in the *Landes Heil- und Pflegeanstalt* in Osanabrück. At the end of 1940 he faced transfer to a similar institution in Hademar in Hesse. In June 1941 the family received information from there about the death of Laken as a result of angina, but Mrs Kuhl did not even know that her brother suffered from this illness. Walter Gluh whose sister Berta died in 1941 told a similar story.[248]

The trials of the late 1940s focused upon those regarded as responsible for the deportations of the mentally ill from the province of Hanover, which included Osnabrück. These proceedings did not focus upon those who carried out the transportations at the ground level but, rather, those responsible at the provincial level, from where we can extract information about developments in Osnabrück. The major suspects included Ludwig Gessner, Georg Andreae and Paul Fröhlich, senior civil servants at the provincial level, all of whom were acquitted in September 1950, following an investigation lasting two years.[249]

Several people working in the *Landes Heil- und Pflegeanstalt* in Osnabrück gave testimony during the trial. The main figure to come under investigation in the town consisted of Dr Albert Kracke, the director of the *Landes Heil- und Pflegeanstalt*. Kracke, with the help of contemporary documentation from 1942 and 1943, simply claimed that those people deported in 1942 and 1943 left because of the destruction of the hospital by bombing, which made the local population uneasy about the prospect of having potentially dangerous people wandering freely in their midst. But a document from 1952 asserted that both Kracke and another doctor in the hospital, Bernhard Jutz, had knowledge of the fate of the 180 people taken away from the *Anstalt* in April 1941, as revealed in a questionnaire, which they completed. However, no further legal action occurred against them. Both Kracke and Jutz denied knowledge of the consequences of their actions, as did other employees at the hospital, hiding behind the fact that the actions of April 1941 were 'secret'. All denied having received instruction about what would happen to the deportees and the employees of the institute collectively remained silent under investigation.[250]

Despite the denials and the wall of silence, we can assume that the employees at the hospital had a fairly good idea of the fate of the deportees.

Many of those questioned admitted to having heard whispers in the town about their deaths. Simply claiming that they did not know the ultimate fate of the patients seems remarkable, even if no concrete written evidence has survived. If the population knew and protested about the T4 programme, little doubt exists about the culpability of the employees of the *Landes Heil- und Pflegeanstalt.*

The Difference the War Made

By the end of the War Osnabrück society, reflecting the physical landscape of the town, had faced a dramatic transformation as a result of the events of 1939-45. In this short period of time the town witnessed some of the most dramatic changes of its recent history. The peaceful economic recovery which had occurred after 1933, albeit as a result of the preparation for War from 1936, lay in ruins by 1945. Any advances which may have occurred in living conditions simply disappeared either because of the increase in working hours or, more seriously, the consequences of allied bombing, even though not all areas of the town endured the same experience of destruction. At the same time levels of nutrition fell, as did birth rates, while death rates increased. Separation of families due to mobilization and evacuation became a fact of life.

As these harsh realities stared Germans in the face, the propaganda machine still attempted to persuade them of the rightness of the Nazi cause. This proved easier in some media, such as cinema, than others because the manpower shortages and Allied bombing made some propaganda impossible. At the same time, schooling became extremely difficult, due to the labour requirements of the War economy, stretched because of the need to fight throughout Europe and, once again, because of the consequences of bombing.

Against this background all those regarded as threatening, criminal or undesirable faced intense persecution. Legislation broadened the range of crimes which could result in incarceration as the SS and the concentration camp system came into its own throughout Europe. Interviewees for this project, as well as others, have demonstrated that 'resistance' was possible, especially if one kept safe company.

But in 1945 the centre of Osnabrück, reflecting the situation in towns throughout the remaining sections of the *Reich,* lay in ruins. Any progress which may have occurred in the years 1933-9, was eradicated, to the extent that Germany reached the lowest point in its modern history in the middle of 1945. The years which followed could only result in an improvement in the everyday lives of those Germans who had survived the destruction caused by nearly six years of Total War.

5

DEFEAT AND RECOVERY, 1945-9

Introduction

Whatever else the march of the Allied armies into Germany may have meant, it signified the end of the bombing nightmare. The arrival of British and American troops represented liberation for most of those living in western towns, except the most ardent of Nazis. Unlike the Soviet troops in the east, British and American forces did not take the same sort of revenge for the acts committed against them. The new masters of Germany faced a series of political, economic, social and cultural tasks, most of which they had largely fulfilled, with the cooperation of the local population, by the establishment of the Federal Republic in 1949.

In the first place, the Allies faced a series of political challenges. The immediate one consisted of flushing out Nazis. In addition, they had to restore order, in view of the criminality which had become rife amongst both natives and foreigners. Once order had returned, the new rulers turned to the task of nurturing the democratic traditions which had existed before 1933. While Germans played the leading role in this process, the Allies sat in the background and assisted in the elimination of Nazi ideas using a combination of denazification and re-education. The dormant seeds of democratic politics germinated after the Allies arrived. The SPD quickly re-emerged while the old centre and right wing parties reconstructed themselves, especially in the form of the CDU.

The bombing had serious consequences for the economic infrastructure of Germany. Factories, houses, railway stations and all forms of transport lay in ruins. In the spring of 1945 production of any sort had come to a virtual standstill, not simply because of the level of destruction caused, but also because of the continuing focus upon armaments, which had meant the neglect of other sectors of the economy, which now resulted in shortages of basic goods and black marketeering. Manpower problems developed in the early stages of peace as foreign workers left and German soldiers had not yet returned. This proved short lived because millions of German refugees from the east filled any labour supply gaps. Unemployment, which the Nazis had solved, therefore returned. But the German economy recovered quickly, symbolized by the introduction of the *Deutschmark* in June 1948.

The Allied bombs destroyed Nazi racial and social reconstruction. The welfare state lay in complete ruins. Many people wanted handouts while others went back to basics, to which they had become accustomed during the War, by growing food in their back gardens. Housing remained a problem for much of the population, which consequently found itself living in makeshift accommodation or sharing the homes of complete strangers, who resented them. Schooling remained patchy in the complete chaos of the first post-war years, as teachers had died and the bombs had destroyed school buildings. Against this background criminality, particularly black marketeering, became rife, while health suffered.

The latter years of the War had meant that traces of a normal social life had disappeared as constant bombing led to both destruction and black outs, while round the clock armaments production meant little time for any social activity. The sporting and high cultural activities of the early Nazi years had disappeared. In the post-War period the rebirth of culture symbolized the return to normality.

By 1949 German towns had made great strides on the road to recovery. Individuals and institutions increasingly forgot the nightmare of the War. The reintroduction of democracy, the changing landscape, from one of desolation to one of reconstruction, the growth in employment opportunities and the increase in food supplies, facilitated the process of forgetting. The bleak desolation of the spring of 1945 disappeared. By 1949 Germans could practice democratic rights, fill their stomachs, escape from the fear of death, and pursue a social life. The German 'economic miracle' had begun. The democratic structures which would turn the Federal Republic into one of the stalwarts of western liberalism, were established. During the course of four years despair gave way to optimism.

The Arrival of the British: Inter-Ethnic Relations, Denazification and the Establishment of Democracy

The foundation of the Federal Republic in 1949 represented the culmination of a process, which had begun in the spring of 1945 as the western armies had marched into Hitler's *Reich* and eradicated the overt traces of Nazi power through a combination of coercion and denazification of local elites. The invaders used a limited amount of force, while the re-education and eradication of the old order did not actually mean that former Nazis disappeared. Instead, they continued to remain part of the life of German towns, although they faded into the background.

While the official surrender of Germany occurred with VE Day on 8 May 1945, for locations throughout the country defeat became a reality earlier in the year, as Allied troops moved into the *Reich*.[1] The demoralization of the population caused by bombing and the absence of any substantial military force meant that little resistance existed in many towns. War 'officially' ended in Osnabrück on 4 April with the arrival of the 8th corps of the Second British Army, on their way to Berlin, an event which encountered little resistance. The Commander in Chief, Sir Bernard Law Montgomery, wrote 'Osnabrück was cleared'.[2]

Over the next few weeks the occupying forces took control of the town and set up the structures and personnel to control it in the immediate future. At the top of the new administrative tree stood the governor of Osnabrück, Colonel Geoffrey Herbert Day, who remained in post until the end of 1947. The British military government promoted Johannes Petermann, the deputy mayor of Osnabrück from 1926-38, who had never held Nazi party membership, to the position of Mayor, and then, from October 1945, to the position of *Regierungspräsident*. Gaertner, meanwhile, found himself in a camp in Brussels, after trying to flee. While ultimate executive authority lay in the hands of the military authorities, the evolution of local and regional democratic structures after 1945 meant that Germans increasingly played a role in their own destiny, particularly as political parties came back to life again.[3]

But how did the population of Osnabrück react to the new occupying Army and how did relationships between British forces and the Germans run over the next four years?[4] The Osnabrücker Maria Grün probably summed up the feeling of many western German citizens upon the arrival of British or American troops.

And we reckoned there would be revenge, that they would use us for terrible things...we were all at least partly guilty for these terrible miseries, we invaded Holland, we destroyed Belgium and France, and so many English and Americans had to risk their lives in order to free us from this terrible Hitler and we were filled with gratitude.[5]

Other Osnabrückers claimed that they did not fear the prospect of British troops arriving in the town towards the end of the War, despite the bombing. Heinrich and Elizabeth Wand claimed that they were not afraid of the approaching British, despite the devastation the RAF had caused.[6] When Lora Kraft was asked whether she had hoped that the Nazis would lose the war, she simply replied: 'It was all the same to us whether we won or lost. The main thing was that it was over. The main thing was that Adolf was not there any more.'[7]

The British authorities initially forbade fraternization but 'within a short time the policy collapsed under the pressure of humanity and common sense'.[8] Germans and Britons had a range of relationships during the late 1940s, which varied from the positive extreme of love to the other extreme of violence. While rape did not take place on any significant scale in the western zones of invaded Germany,[9] 'the borderline between rape and prostitution was often a fluid one: many American and British soldiers paid for their pleasures in cigarettes, chocolate and bread. Both young girls and married women had liaisons with members of the occupying forces'.[10] The Osnabrück *Stadt-Chronik* spoke of women obtaining chocolate, cigarettes and food by flirting. It also mentioned, in disapproving terms, German girls who visited the quarters of British soldiers: 'At dances, which the English organize in their accommodation, and where German musicians also have to play, Osnabrück girls swing to the clang of jazz music in the arms of foreign soldiers'.[11] In some cases liaisons between English soldiers and German women led to permanent relationships, as the example of Dick Roberts and Waltraud Klein in Osnabrück indicates: in this case they met because Roberts found himself living in the house of Waltraud Klein's father.[12]

After the lifting of the non-fraternization ban natives and Britons certainly mixed, as recalled by Lora Kraft: 'My sister and my brother-in-law could speak very good English. They developed friendships with English soldiers…The English…were friendly, amicable so to say. I had no negative experiences'.[13] Several interviewees, who had some previous knowledge of English, worked for the British as translators, including Werner Funk, Heinz Frank and Josefa Herz. All had to improve their English and all had positive experiences with the occupiers. The last of these remembered her spell as a translator in a barracks as the best working experience of her life. She described one officer as 'very distant, but very polite. I liked the fact that they were so distant. They were really all like that, the officers, they treated me very politely.'[14]

Although the majority of Osnabrückers remembered the British invaders positively, almost fondly, relations between the two groups did not always progress so smoothly, as fights sometimes took place between local youth and invaders. A British report from July 1946 stated:

There has been a marked deterioration in the conduct of British troops in Osnabrück town. It is shown by a considerable increase in attacks and assaults on German civilians. 13 cases have been reported and a further 9 have been brought officially to the notice of public safety. This compares to an average of 1 or 2 cases for the previous six months. The attitude of the German population is definitely less friendly towards us. The main grounds of complaint are food and requisitioning accommodation.[15]

Violence between British soldiers and Germans also occurred during the late summer and autumn of 1948. On 21 August a crowd of forty locals watched a fight between two English soldiers and a group of natives, in Hegertorwall. On 14 October, a similar incident took place nearby, outside the Walhalla guesthouse, when two drunken English soldiers attacked two German civilians.[16] These events probably resulted from underlying tensions between locals and Britons but the fighting may have represented a growing self-confidence amongst the Germans, who had emerged from the pit of desperation in which they lay immediately after the war ended.

Nazi sympathisers, or those suspected of having any connections with the party, faced the worst experiences with the occupying authorities, as part of the policy of denazifaction. The Nuremberg trials represented the national and international aspects of this process,[17] but similar events occurred on a local scale.[18] The attempted eradication of Nazism had several aspects to it, of which trying those accused of war crimes formed one. 'In the three western zones a total of 5,035 people were accused of war crimes or crimes against humanity' of whom 486 faced the death penalty.[19]

Those accused of such actions in Osnabrück did not receive such stern sentences. Instead, the local *Kreisleiter* simply faced short prison terms. When the sentences ended, the individuals accused, such as Erwin Kolkmeyer, simply returned to their normal lives, as if the Third Reich had never existed. Kolkmeyer actually received an initial prison sentence of two years following a trial which took place in June 1948, although he subsequently faced a further sentence of ten months for his part in the *Kristallnacht* pogrom. He had fled to southern Germany immediately after the end of the War and spent two years in hiding before facing capture and spending time in a camp in Recklinghausen. The reporting of the June 1948 trial described him as 'one of the wildest men' in Osnabrück during the Nazi period. Although he protested his innocence, sixteen witnesses testified against him pointing to his role in the incarceration of people in camps, his activities following Hitler's seizure of power and his part in the persecution of the Jews.[20] Two months after the trial of Kolkmeyer, Karl Waschmann, former leader of the Economic Office in Osnabrück, found himself in court, charged with crimes against humanity. He received a three month prison sentence because he had appeared at a pub in Hasetor in SS uniform in November 1937 and had taken out a guest and beaten him to the ground with a stick because he replied to Waschmann's 'Heil Hitler' greeting with 'good evening'.[21]

Few other Osnabrückers were tried. Instead, many faced arrest, internment, or interview by denazification panels, which aimed at eradicating Nazis from government and important economic positions. At one point 545 of these panels existed in the American zone of occupation alone. About 64,000 people in the British zone had faced automatic arrest by the end of 1946. The legal basis of these developments consisted of directives passed by the Allied Control Council. In December 1945 it issued Control Council Law No. 10 which specified Punishment of People Guilty of War Crimes, and Crimes Against Peace and Against Humanity. By this time all those having anything to do with the military authorities had to fill out questionnaires. Control Council Directive No. 38 from 12 October 1946 divided Germans into five groups consisting of: 'major offenders'; 'offenders'; 'lesser offenders'; 'followers'; and 'persons exonerated'. Such measures aimed at going through the population with a toothcomb, as much of the process of internment and arrest had already taken place by the autumn of 1946. In fact, by November 1947, 2,144,022 people had questionnaires evaluated in the British zone, out of a total population of 22 million. None of these fitted into groups I or II, while the largest proportion, 58.4 per cent, came under category V. A further 29.4 per cent had proceedings against them suspended, while only 1.3 per cent fell into group III.[22]

Osnabrück provides an example of this process on a local scale. The work of the denazification committee in the town began in October 1946 and examined a total of 46,000 people over the next six years.[23] The majority of those who filled out the necessary forms came under the fifth category devised by the Allied Control Council in the form of 'persons exonerated' and therefore had no further action taken against them. The same fate applied to those who fell into the fourth category of 'followers', essentially party members. Those in the third grouping could have their bank accounts frozen and lose their jobs, while anyone in category one or two faced internment. The military authorities in Osnabrück had already dismissed 123 employees from the city administration by the middle of August 1945.[24]

According to contemporary police accounts, the activities of the denazification committee caused unease amongst the local population. By December 1947 Osnabrückers simply wanted the whole process to come to an end as they felt that the most active Nazis had been identified.[25] Interestingly, local exonerated prominent Germans manned the occupational denazification committees. Karl Kühling, for instance, played a role.[26] In June 1946 the Osnabrück political parties suggested their own people for the committees.[27]

Surviving, but uncatalogued, documents in the NSO allow us to look in some detail at the activities of the local committees. A random list of 61 people, for instance, reveals that those examined fell into a total of 43 different occupational categories, suggesting that the committees left no stone unturned. They ranged from businessmen to railway employees.[28] The form which individuals filled out contained questions covering physical appearance, education and occupation. Most importantly, it listed dozens of Nazi organizations and asked individuals whether and when they had belonged to them.[29]

As most of those who filled out the form fell into the category established by the Allies, they faced no further action. The following represent typical examples. A male teacher born in 1894, who had held membership in the NSV between 1936 and 1944.[30] A female teacher born in 1913 had joined the National Socialist German Students Federation from 1935-8, the NSF from 1933-45, the NSV from 1943-5, the NSLB from 1940-5 and the *Deutsche Studentschaft* (German Students) from 1934-8. Despite this, the committee felt that they needed to take no further action, even though membership was not compulsory in any of these organizations.[31]

Some cases required a thorough investigation, which included the questioning of witnesses, as the example of a businessman born in 1897 indicates. The denazification committee considered his case on 14 October 1947. He claimed to have joined the NSDAP in 1933 at the suggestion of his business partner. He also admitted to having a picture of Göring and a photograph of himself in SA uniform in his factory. Fourteen witnesses attended his hearing including former employees, acquaintances and fellow Nazis, each confirming the businessman's Nazi connections. One woman who worked for him claimed that he 'was more than a National Socialist in name only. In a factory meeting which took place in 1936 or 1937, he explained, "Every member of this factory must become a member of the NSV"'. The committee decided that the accused fell into the category of 'lesser offender', which meant he lost his position with his firm and could not play a leading role in a public or business organization.[32]

Numerous other individuals lost their jobs or had their bank accounts frozen. For example, a bookkeeper with the municipal authorities, born in 1894, who held Nazi party membership from July 1933 to September 1934 and 1942-5, when he became a *Blockleiter*. He had also joined the *Reichsbund der Deutschen Beamten* and the NSV from 1934 but did not hold office. He claimed that he only wore a uniform on special occasions and had not wanted to become a *Blockleiter*.[33] Those falling into category 3 of offenders not only faced exclusion from public employment and confiscation of their assets, but often had to regularly report to the local police station. Thus we have the case of a master electrician born in 1891. He lost his job and could not take up employment in any leading firms or in any occupations where he would have significant contact with the public. He also had his property and bank account frozen and had to report to the police every two weeks.

This punishment would essentially have ruined the individual concerned, as it stopped his livelihood, at least in the short term. He made an appearance at the local police station on eight occasions between November 1947 and January 1949.[34] Alternative careers for those who lost their jobs did not always prove easy to find. Thus we learn of one individual sacked from government employment following his encounter with the denazification panel, who faced prosecution in 1947 for selling cigarettes on the black market.[35]

The eradication of the NSDAP allowed the re-emergence of democratic parties. The SPD and KPD came back to life again, while the parties of the centre right reconstituted themselves. These developments took place under the watchful eye of the British occupying authorities.[36] In Osnabrück the military authorities allowed the rebuilding of political parties, under official licence, from September 1945,[37] but a police report from September 1946 described the population as 'very cautious' towards those which had come into existence again, stating that the meetings which took place attracted people more as a result of curiosity than political interest.[38] Nevertheless, political activity had already begun before the military authorities had even authorized it. The Free German Unions in Osnabrück held a meeting to officially reconstitute themselves on 13 August 1945.[39] They held their first annual general meeting in March of the following year.[40] On 25 November a public demonstration involving both SPD and KPD took place, where the speakers included the returned Ludwig Landwehr.[41] During the course of 1946 a CDU grouping also came into existence in Osnabrück. Konrad Adenauer addressed a public meeting in front of the Cathedral on 28 July 1946.[42]

Significant dates for the re-establishment of democratic politics came in the autumn of 1946, as elections took place at the parish level on 15 September and the city level on 13 October.[43] As a result of the latter elections the SPD came out as the largest party, followed by the CDU, although during the course of the next few years the latter became dominant. Leading local personalities during these years included of Adolf Kreft, CDU Mayor from 1945-6 and 1948-9 and Heinrich Herlitzer of the SPD, who held the position from 1946-8 and 1949-51.[44]

Democratic life therefore re-established itself in Osnabrück fairly quickly. Thousands of people in the town underwent the denazification process, which found a small group of minor perpetrators. Most of those who fell into categories 1-3 received a punishment commensurate to the crimes they had committed which meant they could return to their normal lives in a short spell of time, perhaps justifiably so in the case of some of the lesser offenders. On the other hand, should the leading Nazis, such as Kolkmeyer, have disappeared from the town forever? Or did the few years in prison suffice for the crimes he had carried out? He may not have had direct responsibility for the deaths of people in Osnabrück, but, as a leading member of the SA and a *Kreisleiter*, he played a central role in creating the atmosphere which allowed the murder of Jews and Romanies. The major perpetrators at the national level faced execution, while thousands of minor local ones endured several years of ostracization. Perhaps for the purposes of reconciliation such people needed to return to their normal lives after they had faced punishment.

Economic Reconstruction

During the summer of 1945 industry reached a stasis, not only because of bombing but also as it moved away from armaments production to peacetime manufacturing. The War had destroyed much of the transport system both between and within towns and cities. The concentration on armaments had further meant a neglect of agriculture, which resulted in food shortages. Furthermore, the population structure had changed. Although the War had killed around 7 million Germans, the political settlement of Central and Eastern Europe had resulted in the westward migration of over ten million Germans. In addition, those people who had fled to the countryside as the bombing had intensified began to return during the summer of 1945. The Allied occupation and the division of the country into four zones, together with an, at least initial, desire to keep the German economy down for political reasons, also halted production.

Despite these facts, the German economy got back on its feet rapidly. Economic historians have pointed out that Germany still had some advantages after 1945 and that the bombing had left much intact. The arrival of millions of Germans from eastern Europe may have acted as an increasing drain on scarce resources, but it also provided a cheap source of labour, essential for the reconstruction of German towns and cities. Furthermore, despite the intensity of bombing, the Nazis protected some of their factories, which meant, for instance, that West Germany had only lost 6.5 per cent of its machine tools. In addition, some sectors, such as coal and the iron and steel industries, suffered light damage. Finally, between 1948 and 1950 the West German economy received over 2 billion dollars in relief and reconstruction funds.

Most historians have pointed to the introduction of the *Deutschmark* in June 1948 as the turning point in German economic recovery. The new currency provided a foundation for stable prices and wages. It wiped out over RM400 billion of debt accumulated during the War. Until this time production had increased only gradually. In 1947 most industrial production stood at a much lower level than it did in 1936. In the six months after the introduction of the new currency industrial output had increased by 50 per cent and the average working week had also grown significantly. By 1948 building reconstruction was well under way and unemployment had reduced significantly, although the scars of bombing would not completely disappear for decades, while unemployment still stood at over 1.5 million in 1950.[45]

An examination of the above developments in Osnabrück illustrates both the bleak economic realities of 1945-7 and the increasing speed of recovery from 1948. The beginnings of peace meant that Osnabrückers experienced modern life without its basic essentials as reported in the *Daily Mail* of 2 July 1945, referring to the situation in early April:

> Water, gas, sewerage and telephone services had ceased, and the town was full of thousands of uncontrolled foreign workers and prisoners of war.
>
> Out of the 1,820 vehicles in the town service, 870 had been destroyed by bombing or fire, 780 had been stripped of batteries or tyres, and most of the remaining 170 had been driven off either by the retreating *Wehrmacht* or foreign workers.
>
> Six doctors remained out of the peace time medical service of 121.

Another account points out that: 'Osnabrück had the highest level of destruction in the province of Hanover and the fourth highest in the British zone'.[46]

In order for recovery to take place, the town first of all needed to get its population back.[47] The *Stadt-Chronik* claimed that 61,399 people lived in Osnabrück, both natives and foreigners, at the end of April 1945, which increased to 81,859 natives by the end of the year.[48] By June 1946 the total had risen to 96,118, which, however, represented a 10.7 per cent decrease from the 107,081 counted in May 1939.[49] Only a slight increase would take place over the next few years, so that 99,211 people lived in the town in 1948.[50]

The growth in population occurred due to a combination of factors including a post-War baby boom, the return of people to their homes from the countryside, the arrival of prisoners of war, and the coming of refugees from eastern Europe. Against this, Osnabrück had a fairly high death rate. In 1947 the 848 deaths exceeded the 802 births.[51] The migration which took place into the town occurred against the background of the departing foreign workers and prisoners of war. Like the rest of Germany Osnabrück therefore experienced the greatest migratory moves in its history during the immediate post-War years,[52] meaning that the ethnic mix of the war years disappeared.

The return of prisoners of war became one of the most important factors in changing the mood of women who had waited for their sons or husbands. The continued separation from menfolk still in the Soviet Union proved one of the most depressing aspects of the post-War experience for women and children awaiting return, although when this actually happened problems arose with reintegration into the family as well as local society and economy.[53] Heinz Frank recalled his happy arrival in Osnabrück from Russia in November 1945:

I returned home early in the morning – with slippers, wearing no shoes. I knocked on the door and then explained everything. My grandfather was asleep downstairs, my parents were asleep upstairs and then my mother came down and said: 'Heinz are you here again', and touched me, felt my whole body to see if I still had all of my arms and legs and then shook me.[54]

Frank reached Osnabrück fairly early, as the return of prisoners of war from the Soviet Union continued until Konrad Adenauer visited Moscow in 1955 and secured the release of the final 10,000.[55] Until the end of 1949 as many as thirty former prisoners of war returned to Osnabrück every month, although 1,444 were still missing.[56] On 16 March 1948 the Red Cross opened a reception room on platform one of the railway station to greet and re-orientate returning prisoners.[57]

Although husbands continued to return to Osnabrück as late as 1955,[58] some women had lost their men forever.[59] In 1947 Osnabrück counted 5,300 war widows.[60] One report from that year claimed that the population of Osnabrück, which totalled 91,264, consisted of 49,574 women and 41,699 men, a difference of 7,884. The shortfalls were particularly noticeable in the 21-40 age groups.[61] In 1949 the employment office claimed that nearly 30,000 women in the *Regierungsbezirk* supported themselves. One woman described her experience to the *Neues Tageblatt*:

I was married. But only for three days. Then my husband had to return to the front and I never saw him again. Did I become old? Oh, I cried a lot. The howling did not help. My parents died prematurely. The remaining savings account has been used up. I had to work to stay alive.[62]

While this may represent normality, the late 1940s also witnessed an increase in the number of marriages which took place in Osnabrück, as well as in the whole of post-War Europe, as people had waited for the conflict to end before tying the knot.[63] The number of marriages in the town rose from 718 in 1945 to 1,144 by 1948.[64] On the other hand, the early post-War years also witnessed an increase in the number of divorces, paternity suits and marriage dissolutions from 158 in 1935 to 1,091 in 1948 (presumably for the *Regierungsbezirk*). The *Niederdeutscher Kurier* of 4 November 1949, which reported this increase, gave a variety of explanations:

> The quick marriages during the war, the marriages by proxy, the sending of letters to unknown soldiers, which in one case happened in Osnabrück so that the marriage was consummated without the partners seeing each other. Similarly the housing shortage, which has resulted in people constantly being on top of each other in a single tiny room has completely changed people and in extremes has made them bad tempered, has often led to divorces.

While the demographic return to normality therefore had positive consequences for those who resumed their pre-War lives, as well as for the economy which needed manpower, it also created new problems for those who lost their husbands or decided they could not live with them any more.[65]

The introduction of the *Deutschmark* in 1948 symbolized the beginning of economic growth. The new notes arrived in the middle of June and on the 20th, 'X-Day', every Osnabrücker obtained DM40 from designated points. While, on the one hand, the *Deutschmark* wiped out debts, on the other, it diminished the value of savings. One year after the introduction of the new currency the *Neues Tageblatt* asked a series of people whether the *Deutschmark* had improved their economic situation, including a metal worker, an artist, a shopkeeper, a businessman and a pensioner, all of whom answered positively. The interviewees spoke of increasing confidence, shops containing goods, secure profits and the ability to save.[66]

Rebuilding represented the most important symbol of the return to normality. Just as the arrival of the *Deutschmark* may have given people financial confidence, the reconstruction of buildings would have confirmed the end of the Nazi period and the War to their own eyes. Nothing could have reminded them more of the catastrophe they had just lived through than the sight of ruined buildings greeting them every morning. The reconstruction focused upon both municipal buildings and housing.[67]

Before construction could take place, the local residents had to clear rubble. Dick Roberts, 'engineer officer of Osnabrück', pointed out that 'there was rubble everywhere' and witnessed people moving it,[68] a process which continued for several years. During 1945 the British authorities ensured that clearing up occurred, targeting 300 people in September and closing down 'several small factories' in December when the necessary manpower did not come forward.[69] In 1947 the city council decided that 5 per cent of the population should take part in such work, for which they would receive extra rations. A type of conscription came into operation involving individuals from all sections of Osnabrück society. Firms would give their workers leave of absence to assist in this process. The reconstruction of both public buildings and housing necessitated the development of a series of building plans in the early post-War years. Homes only appeared slowly: 903 by the end of 1946 and 2,520 by the end of 1947. Locally produced building materials, which were in short supply for much of the period, played a large role in this process.[70]

Some people received grants to help in the reconstruction of their homes. For instance, Walter Spitzbarth obtained RM37,000 for the purpose in 1947-8, while Franz Sommer got over RM9,000.[71] Others who rebuilt their homes faced bureaucratic hurdles in their attempt to obtain the scarce building materials, as remembered by Agnes Adel: 'I went to the city authorities and every morning, yes every morning, called into the Mayor's office in order to get a permit for lime and cement…And every morning I sat outside the mayor's for hours on end.' Eventually her family obtained enough building material to rebuild their house.[72] Others also had difficulty in obtaining other types of permits. On 31 March 1949 the Osnabrück housing department had 9,734 uncompleted applications for the reconstruction of homes, including 800 special cases. It received 220 new applications between 14 and 31 March, but only completed 153.[73]

The city authorities also reconstructed the major municipal buildings, most symbolically the town hall, in preparation for the three hundredth anniversary of the signing of the Treaty of Westphalia, which had occurred in the building in 1648. An article in the *Neues Tageblatt* of 7 October 1948 glorified 'The Men Who Are Building the Town Hall', including refugees and men who lived in Osnabrück during the week but returned home to the countryside during the weekend. Another piece from the *Niederdeutscher Rundschau* of 20 August 1949, entitled 'Immortal Osnabrück' joyously reported the reconstruction of traditional buildings in the city centre destroyed in the final few months of the war. While the rebuilding programme continued into the 1950s and 1960s,[74] the positive nature of the press reporting by 1948 indicated the recovery and growing confidence of the town.

At the same time as private and public buildings reappeared, the infrastructure of Osnabrück came back to life. The bombing meant the reconstruction of gasworks, water pumping stations, electricity generators, pipes and cables from scratch. In 1946 electricity supply had reached its highest level ever, although water remained below its peak of 1943, while gas stood at just a quarter of the level of 1939.[75] The bombing had destroyed all aspects of the transport system in Osnabrück. The number of motor vehicles had declined, for instance.[76] Similarly, the port of Osnabrück had faced destruction due to a combination of bombing and vandalism by foreign workers after the war, although the city authorities had largely repaired this damage by the end of 1946.[77] The bombing had severely disrupted public transportation, which, in the immediate aftermath of the war, made movement almost impossible, both to and from Osnabrück and within it. The British also imposed restrictions upon the distance which people could travel, initially to just a few miles, and from 11 July 1945 up to 100 kilometres. In the opening months of peace this proved difficult in any case because bombing had destroyed so many railway lines and bridges, as well as the railway station, which had faced attack on numerous occasions. But by July 1945 a total of 22 trains operated in and out of the main station in Osnabrück, mostly to carry freight. This figure increased gradually to 100 by August 1946 and 200 by May 1949. By the end of that year the railway system in and around Osnabrück, including the main station, returned to near normality.[78]

Travel within Osnabrück also proved difficult because the tram and bus system had almost disappeared. In March 1945 the *Wehrmacht* had confiscated six of the twelve buses in the town while the occupying authorities subsequently took over the rest. The trams initially had difficulty travelling because of the damage caused to electricity supply and rails as well as the presence of rubble. They ran again by July 1945 and repairs to wagons, engines, track and pylons occurred during the course of the late 1940s. By February 1948 about 70,000 people used Osnabrück buses and trams on a daily basis.[79] Freedom of movement must have symbolized the escape from the traumas of War.

Economic activity in the first few months of peace came to a virtual standstill, which meant unemployment became a significant problem even though the employment office reopened as early as 12 April. A report by the military authorities of 26 April pointed to a series of problems including 'A large exodus of people from Osnabrück owing to bombing' and 'General disinclination to work'.[80] By September a total of 30,295 employable people lived in Osnabrück, with 26,851 in employment and 3,444 without a job, giving an unemployment rate of 12.8 per cent.[81]

During the summer of 1945 many people found themselves either working in clearing up or in the service of the British.[82] Industrial production had risen by August as some factories had repaired damage sustained during the war and reached capacity resembling the 1930s. The 'tannery, CA Weitkamp, Osnabrück, is making progress towards normal conditions, from the extensive damage sustained during the war. The buildings are well on their way to complete repair'.[83] The OKD had begun production by the end of August, moving away from war goods towards the making of wire.[84] In fact, by September 1945 a total of thirty concerns in Osnabrück employed over fifty people. The largest included Karmann, with 431, and Hammersen, with 229.[85]

The return to full production and full employment took some time, especially with the arrival of thousands of refugees from eastern Europe. In the summer of 1946, 532 concerns employed more than five people, but the number of people involved totalled 17,334 compared with 22,422 in 1937-8. Some of the biggest falls in employment had occurred in firms involved with metal production and therefore directly connected to the war, while others, such as transportation, had seen an increase in the numbers they employed.[86]

The most striking fact about the post-War Osnabrück economy lies in the speed of the recovery. As early as 1947 a total of 13,500 businesses of all sizes existed in the *Regierungsbezirk*, 90 per cent of the 1939 figure.[87] The larger metallurgical and engineering firms made a recovery even if they did not return to the glory which the Nazi rearmament had given to them. For instance, the military authorities confiscated a third of the destroyed OKD, which employed 850 people in the autumn of 1945. Although this total increased to 1,800 by the company's 75th anniversary in 1948, it lay below the 3,500 achieved in the Nazi years.[88] Karmann, meanwhile, returned to peacetime production fairly quickly, which meant constructing bodies for a variety of automobiles including the Volkswagen Beetle.[89]

Everyday Problems and Realities

The speed of political and economic reconstruction found reflection in the social conditions of Osnabrückers, although they initially had to face a series of problems. The fundamentals of life, which many lacked, consisted of food, although not on the scale of other parts of the country, and shelter, which meant that many people had to live in makeshift accommodation. At the same time children faced disruption to their lives because of the lack of school buildings. These three fundamental problems led to an increase in crime, especially black market activity, and to some health problems. As in the case of economic activity in Osnabrück, the introduction of the *Deutschmark* in June 1948 heralded significant improvements as food and other materials became readily available, which meant that crime decreased.

In 1948 Osnabrück officially counted 12,600 'war victims', including 5,300 widows.[90] The following represent typical examples:

Mrs Krey was bombed out of her house twice, first in Stahlwerksweg and then Rudolfstraße. She obtains the means for her survival and that of her 17 year-old son, who is at the Wittekind Middle School, by sewing. As she has been suffering due to her sensitive eyes for several weeks and is being treated by Dr Mayweg, she cannot earn enough to support herself.[91]

Even more desperate is the case of Mrs Kifler, who wrote to Bishop Berning: 'I have two little children, one of four years old and another of eight months. As both of my children were very ill two weeks ago, I have been in the cold church for two weeks with nothing to burn'.[92]

These stories point to the shortages which existed, particularly food and fuel. In fact, Germans found themselves consuming less after 1945 than they did during the War. The British set a daily calorie target of 1,150. In some areas, such as the Ruhr, people received an official ration of just 700-800 calories per day in early 1947. A series of factors caused these food shortages. The 1945 the harvest remained lower than usual because in the final months of fighting agriculture did not have sufficient resources or manpower directed towards it. The 1946 harvest barely surpassed it while the cold winter of 1946-7 made things even worse. Underlying these statistics lay bureaucratic chaos involving the British and American administrations. The situation improved in 1948 due largely to a better American harvest and a general global nutritional improvement, together with the establishment of Bizonia, which meant cooperation between the British and US regimes. The introduction of the *Deutschmark*, perceived by many on the ground in Osnabrück as the turning point, symbolized the improvement in nutritional conditions. By July of 1948 people living in Bizonia received a near normal daily ration of 2,000 calories, compared with a level closer to 1,000 during 1946 and 1947.[93]

Osnabrück illustrates the food shortages on the ground, as well as pointing to the solutions which people found to overcome them. In the immediate aftermath of Nazi defeat Osnabrückers helped themselves to supplies of corn, sugar, butter and other products which lay in the harbour and in depots run by the *Wehrmacht*, which meant that families temporarily found themselves eating more than they had done for several years. But by the end of April 1945 problems with transportation meant that people had difficulties obtaining butter, milk and potatoes. By the end of May the military authorities had issued 77,569 ration cards.[94] In August 1945, when the daily ration stood at 1,100 calories it proved difficult to reach even this target due to the problems with securing enough produce from the surrounding countryside.[95] During the winter Osnabrückers had problems obtaining all manner of foodstuffs including basics such as flour, cabbages and potatoes.[96]

The situation remained dire during 1946. In February the monthly ration of meat had fallen to 450 grams, although marmalade increased to 500 grams. Children saw a growth in the amount of milk they received at the expense of their bread quota. The situation came to something of a crisis in the summer of 1946 when the fat and fish ration declined.[97] Several doctors signed a declaration at this time which stated that 'the German people are at the door of starvation in the eighth year of the rationing of foodstuffs'.[98] Similarly, the city council wrote a letter to the occupying authorities on 6 August, by which time the daily calories were about to decline to 900, declaring that:

> Two years after the conclusion of military operations the distribution of foodstuffs is reaching its lowest point ...
> The council and the population of Osnabrück are prepared with the best will to work with the military government and have demonstrated this willingness again and again, but how will further work be possible, when the ghost of hunger threatens to cripple each individual willing to work?[99]

Conditions further deteriorated because of the 1946-7 winter when temperatures dipped to as low as minus thirty degrees centigrade. In March 1947 Osnabrückers received 1,383 calories per day instead of the 1,550 promised on their ration cards. Shortages continued for much of the year so that between May and July individuals received an average of just 1,000 calories.[100] In December the city council again complained to the military authorities, on this occasion because of a reduction in the amount of bread received, although improvement had occurred by this time.[101]

Nevertheless, problems did continue into 1948. As late as May people still spoke about food shortages on an almost obsessive basis.[102] The introduction of the *Deutschmark* represented the real breakthrough in food supply in Osnabrück. A police report from 21 July commented on the change of mood amongst the working classes. 'Amazingly goods arrived overnight to be set up in the shops and display windows opened for view'.[103] While rationing may have continued after the introduction of the *Deutschmark*, the hunger years had ended.

But even during the immediate post-War period few Osnabrückers starved. Helmut Segschneider and Wido Spratte have written about the lengths to which people in the town went to avoid hunger. Segschneider included 'hunting', 'agricultural activity', stealing, begging, hoarding and black market activity.[104] The location of Osnabrück as a town surrounded by countryside meant that food supply problems never reached the depths which they did elsewhere in Germany.[105] People could visit their relatives in the countryside or cultivate their gardens.

We can look at some of the solutions pursued both by individuals and by groups collectively, as Michael Wildt did for Hamburg, examining hunger, protest, the black market and 'self-help'.[106] In Osnabrück strikes against hunger took place in May 1948 involving factories throughout the *Regierungsbezirk*. The trade unions protested against the reduction in the bread and meat rations over a period of two days. The strike, which brought a large part of Osnabrück to a standstill, culminated in a protest in front of the Cathedral.[107]

The local state made efforts to assist the population by handing out meals and bread, in a scenario reminiscent of the final years of the Weimar Republic. In September 1945 the mayor of Osnabrück authorized the establishment of between 5 and 8 communal kitchens for the purpose of supplying food to around 10,000 people during the winter. These kitchens existed until at least 1947. In March of this year they catered for an average of 1,600 people, an increase from the normal figure of 1,200.[108]

Some people made use of their contacts outside Osnabrück, either in the surrounding countryside or even abroad. Werner Funk claimed that he could get potatoes, eggs and ham from farmers just outside the town. While he sometimes virtually starved, on other occasions he found himself bloated.[109] Others received packages from their relatives abroad, especially in the USA.[110] As during the War those people who had gardens exploited them. Renate Schlosser remembered: 'We had a huge poultry yard with chickens, ducks, turkeys and pigeons which always provided us with something to eat'.[111] Aware of the value of gardens, the local state instituted plans to confiscate the largest of them,[112] which infuriated the local gardener's society.[113]

Food did not represent the only commodity in short supply at the end of the War. Clothing also proved hard to come by, which meant that as late as December 1947 some Osnabrück children stayed away from school because they had no shoes.[114] But, after food, the lack of coal caused the most discontent because of the cold winters of 1945-6 and, more especially, 1946-7. In December 1946 Osnabrückers only obtained twenty per cent of what they normally needed. Under such circumstances people resorted to desperate measures in an attempt to secure enough heating material to remain warm. People even died trying to obtain coal from railway lines.[115]

Lack of food, clothing and heating material went hand in hand with the shortage of housing which Allied bombing had caused. The arrival of German refugees as well as the policies of the British Army in confiscating homes for its own use aggravated existing problems. The military government had taken over 71 homes by July 1946, which meant that 500 people had to find somewhere else to live.[116] In January 1948 Osnabrück had a population of 90,000 people, but homes available totalled just one third of the pre-War figure.[117] A report in the *Neues Tageblatt* of 26 March 1949 stated that the town still needed 15,000 new homes.

For much of the late 1940s Osnabrückers, reflecting the plight of all Germans, therefore had to find alternative accommodation while they rebuilt their homes.[118] The most common solution consisted of sharing with other families.[119] In the immediate aftermath of the war the family of Gerhard Strauss lived in a house with his grandparents and aunt.[120] Police reports commented that placing several families, often unrelated, together, in shared accommodation, could lead to quarrels.[121] Unlike the food situation, which the introduction of the *Deutschmark* largely solved, the housing shortage continued into the 1950s.

What effects did lack of food, housing shortages, cold and the other post-War dislocation problems have upon Osnabrückers? Clearly, Germans had to live in smaller homes, albeit temporarily, and also suffered nutritional problems. But did these shortages coalesce with the cold to cause deterioration in the health of Osnabrückers, perhaps leading to an increase in infant and adult mortality rates? The economic crisis of the late Weimar period had not had this effect, while health had generally improved under the Nazis until the consequences of War began to bite. At the same time did the shortages of the post-War period lead to an increase in crime rates?

On a national scale evidence points to a deterioration in the health of Germans after 1945 as well as an increase in mortality rates. In the summer of 1945, for instance, Berlin had an infant mortality rate of 60 per thousand, compared with the norm in industrial societies at the end of the twentieth century of around ten. Hundreds of thousands of people died as a result of the winters of 1946 and 1947. The accommodation and food crises represented the main contributing factors to the spread of tuberculosis, typhus, influenza and scabies.[122]

Does Osnabrück reflect this picture? Before answering this question we need to recognize that, in addition to the food and housing crisis which existed in the town, Osnabrück also suffered a hospital bed shortage as a result of the bombing. Furthermore, shortages of medicines and doctors existed, the latter partly due to the fact that those involved in Nazi medical practices now had to pay the penalty for their actions. These problems became particularly acute in the immediate aftermath of the War, but improved, in the case of bed supply, by 1946.

A letter from the Osnabrück health office of July 1945 stated that no medicines existed for the treatment of contagious diseases, while other indispensable drugs were not available in the town. A report from the following year described the medical supply situation as 'catastrophic'.[123] One of the victims of the drug shortage in Osnabrück immediately after the arrival of the British in the town was the sister of Cilly Stein, as the latter recalled:

> She had diphtheria and as soon as the doctor established that, she would have got the medicine for diphtheria, but he didn't come until the next day…She travelled through the whole town on her bicycle but found no doctor. On the other side of the canal in Haste, she also knew one, we used to live in that area, and this doctor had dealt with her before. He gave her the medicine, and on the following day he could not remain in peace, he came over the canal with the barge and made sure she went into hospital. Everything went very well initially, but she then had a relapse, and she was gone within three days.[124]

The city authorities put much effort into the recruitment and training of doctors and nurses.[125] Although some doctors had lost their jobs as a result of denazification, their number in Osnabrück increased from 94 in 1945 to 120 in 1947. In this period the number of doctors imprisoned had decreased from 10 to 3, although eight others found themselves without work in 1949. Meanwhile, the number of dentists had grown from 41 to 58 in the same period, although this still stood below the 1943 figure of 69.[126]

The number of hospital beds remained fairly constant in the early post-War period, although some hospital rebuilding also took place. Thus we find that both the *Städtische Krankenanstalt* and the *Landes Heil und Pflegeanstalt* had the same number of beds in 1946 and 1947 at 984 and 507 respectively.[127] A British investigation into the latter in May 1949 claimed that the 700 beds which it counted remained insufficient. While the men's wards 'show at present a vacancy of 41 beds…the women's wards are grossly overcrowded'.[128]

Despite this particular statement the majority of evidence points to sufficient hospitals, beds and medical cover in Osnabrück after the War, but a lack of medicines, which ties in with the shortage of food and other commodities in Germany before the introduction of the *Deutschmark* in 1948. A short term increase in the death rate and the rise in disease resulted from these shortages, combined with the cold and the housing situation, as recognized by local doctors who issued a 'Resolution Against Hunger, Cold and Housing Shortages' in August 1946.[129] One other major problem consisted of a blood shortage, caused by a lack of people healthy enough to undergo transfusions.[130]

Statistics point to a deterioration in health at the end of the War compared with the situation before 1939. As Table 5.1 demonstrates, 1,574 people died in 1945, which exceeds the 1938 figure. Nevertheless, the years after that show a significant decline year by year so that the 1946 figure fell below that of 1938. Medical reports point to the changing health situation. One from 1948 commented:

> As a result of the improvement in nutrition since the currency reform the overall nutritional and physical situation of the average person has somewhat improved...
>
> In particular the health and nutritional situation of babies in their first six months can be described as good.[131]

The health report of the following year stated that most people had witnessed an increase in weight which meant that they approached their ideal.[132]

Table 5.1: Death Rates in Osnabrück 1938-48.

Year	Number of Deaths
1938	1,415
1942	1,994
1945	1,574
1946	1,326
1947	1,154
1948	1,010

Source: NSO Typescript, Fol. 2184, 'Verwaltungsbericht der Stadt Osnabrück, 1948'.

Post-war health problems caused by food shortages, poor housing and cold therefore remained temporary, peaking in 1945 and declining after that time, certainly if measured by mortality rates. While people in other parts of Germany may have had worse experiences, deaths in Osnabrück between 1938 and 1948 never went above 2,000 per year and never fell below 1,000. The highest mortality rates occurred as a direct result of the consequences of the War. In the case of Osnabrück, while hunger may have existed, few people starved to death.

However, this hunger, combined with post-War anarchy, resulted in widespread criminality, particularly amongst those who did not have gardens or access to extra food beyond the official rationing. Stealing and the buying and selling of goods on the black market became part of everyday reality in German towns between 1945 and 1948. The restrictions imposed upon food transformed it into a valuable commodity.[133]

Stealing took off in the summer of 1945. While food became especially precious, so did coal during the winters of 1946 and 1947. In the week ending 16 August 1945 the Osnabrück police reported 33 burglaries, 24 robberies, 38 thefts and 38 bicycle thefts. Burglars took '3 pigs, 2 geese, 10 hens, 11 rabbits, machines, tools, clothing and groceries'.[134] By the end of the year the theft of coal also took off. On 21 November police arrested three people with about four hundred weight of coal which they had stolen from the railway station.[135] In January 1947 the police carried out a raid on 'coal thieves' in Eversburg. The weekly number of burglaries in the spring of 1947 still stood at thirty.[136]

The press particularly focused upon criminal gangs in Osnabrück. One of these, organised by Nikolaus Schöll, in his mid-thirties from Duren, together with Willi-Heinz Dieckmann, in his mid-twenties, carried out 'butter thefts' as their 'speciality', stealing at least 22 hundredweight during 1945 and 1946.[137] In March 1947 the police arrested Bruno Kleusser who organized the theft of a variety of products including food and electrical equipment.[138]

It seems difficult to place the above cases purely at the door of hunger as the goods stolen did not simply consist of food, which would not, in any case, have been consumed by the thieves but subsequently sold on to those who wanted something more than what they obtained from rationing. This desire to supplement the few grams of meat, bread and vegetables provided the main explanation for the growth of the black market which took off from 1945. The next few years witnessed a constant battle between the police and the traders. Evidence points to the involvement of an extraordinary number of people.

The police regularly seized goods from black market traders. In December 1945, for instance, confiscated products included over 662 pounds of meat, 198 pounds of ham, 85 pounds of butter, 225 pounds 'of sausages of all types', 54 'pieces' of poultry, 97 eggs, 42 pounds of sugar and 1,625 grams of tobacco.[139] Similarly, in May 1947 the police seized 38 live piglets, 1 live sheep, 32 pounds of butter, 97.5 pounds of ham, 86 pounds of fresh meat, 12 sausages, 50 hundredweight of potatoes and 2,755 eggs.[140]

The attempted control of the black market represented one of the main drains on police manpower in Osnabrück during the immediate post-War years, although, in view of the numbers of people who bought and sold such goods, it proved difficult for the authorities to make any sort of impact. In September 1947, for instance, the police dealt with 736 people, although this represents something of high point. Table 5.2 points to the more typical scale of detection between 1946 and 1948, although we can assume that this represents the tip of the iceberg. The table indicates that activity remained fairly constant throughout these years and would not decline until after the introduction of the *Deutschmark*.

Police attempts to control black market activity focused upon raids and street controls. The former could often result in numerous arrests and could involve large numbers of officers. In June 1946 the police carried out 228 raids.[141] The largest raid in the late 1940s occurred on 6 April 1948 and involved 60 police officers. Four hundred people, 261 men and 139 women, were transferred to the criminal police in the town hall. This event not only indicates the level of police resources which went towards the attempted control of the black market, but also, once again, the number of people involved.[142] Police searches did not usually result in the same level of instant success as this raid on Augustenburgerplatz. In April 1946 the police instituted 7 'street controls' and 26 'railway controls', increasing to 12 and 24 respectively two months later, a level maintained for much of 1946 and 1947.[143]

Table 5.2: Black Market Activity Detected
by the Osnabrück Police, 1946-8

Date	Number of Cases	Value of Goods Seized in RM	Number of People Involved
September 1946	108	3,100	105
November 1946	69	1,000	69
December 1946	57	812	57
February 1947	70	1,420	70
June 1947	50	1,000	50
August 1947	55	8,500	55
December 1947	50	800	55
January 1948	16	400	16
February 1948	55	925	55

Source: NSO Rep-430-201-16B-65-83.

Police reports reveal that black market activity was not organized.[144] Those caught simply faced fines,[145] which offers one explanation as to why the black market proved so difficult to stamp out. In more serious cases defendants could face prison as indicated by the prosecution of two people who sold goods which they obtained from the store room of a pub, which also counted as theft. They received prison sentences of 2 years and eighteen months, while their accomplices faced six months and one year.[146]

The arrival of the *Deutschmark* meant goods became affordable and easy to obtain as black market activity essentially disappeared. A police report of

October 1948 asserted that, 'In the area covered by the town the black market is no longer to be seen in public', although it did mention the arrest of 17 people.[147] An article in the *Niedersächsischer Kurier* of 11 March 1949 gave details of the number of goods seized in the previous few years which included 1,054 animals, 19,864 kilograms of meat and sausages, 73,300 kilograms of potatoes and 195 kilograms of coal. The level of black market activity between 1945 and 1948 points to the fact that few people starved in Osnabrück as a result of food shortages. While official rations remained low, the vast majority of the population had access to foodstuffs through a variety of avenues. If they chose not to participate in illegal activity, they could grow food for themselves or obtain fresh produce from relatives in the surrounding countryside.

The Rebirth of Education and Culture

The propaganda, education and culture which had formed a core part of Nazi policy during the 1930s came to a virtual standstill because of Allied bombing. In the field of education and culture 1945 became a turning point. Schooling faced a series of catastrophic problems, most obviously the lack of buildings because of the bombing.[148] As the British Army marched into Osnabrück it found that it had destroyed most of the schools in the town. Fifteen had faced total destruction, 11 'heavy' and 29 'medium' damage.[149]

Evacuated children returned during the summer of 1945. A group of 400 initially remained stranded, which led one mother to make a seven day bicycle journey to Salzburg in June 1945.[150] Virtually no education occurred between the end of March 1945 and Monday 3 September. The *Ratsoberschule* took in its three highest classes on 15 October, which simply received instruction in German, mathematics and religion.[151] Johannes Hesse did not resume his schooling at the *Carolinium* until January 1946.[152] The number of pupils in Osnabrück increased gradually during the late 1940s. For instance, the total of elementary schoolchildren grew from 8,031 in 1946 to 10,700 in 1949.[153]

Reconstruction occurred fairly rapidly, although some children still found themselves without proper school buildings at the end of the 1940s. Fifty elementary school classrooms came back into use between 1945 and 1947, although this small number meant that instruction had to take place between 8am and 6pm.[154] Alexander Dicke remembered returning to the *Staatliche Oberschule für Knaben* in October 1945, where instruction occurred in a small number of rooms. 'The walls were still blackened with smoke, the assembly hall was gutted and the gym also demonstrated considerable damage'.[155] St Ursula offered instruction to twenty classes consisting of 600 schoolchildren in all by 1946, although this took place in the St Angela nunnery. Permission for the reconstruction of the original St Ursula did not arrive until December 1946 and schoolchildren did not return there until 1951.[156] Students from the *Schola Carolina* initially found themselves studying in nearby Nahne, before moving back to use some rooms in the school in March 1946, even though the building still lay in ruins, which meant instruction sometimes took place in the cold with rain falling in through the roof.[157] As late as 1949 the 225 elementary school classes in the town only had access to 100 rooms. Meanwhile, a report in the *Niedersächsischer Kurier* claimed that 135 children had to share one classroom in Schinkel.[158]

Pupils in Osnabrück also suffered from shortages of teachers and books. Some teachers had died but the military authorities also checked the background of those who survived for Nazi connections. When school began again in the autumn of 1945 a total of 4,138 infant school pupils had to share 68 teachers. In 1947 128 teachers had to cope with 8,743 junior school pupils. The *Ratsgymnasium* had a more respectable staff-student ratio. Although the British authorities had only accepted 6 of its teachers by the autumn of 1945, by Easter 1948 a total of 22 staff taught 558 pupils. [159]

A combination of wartime losses and, more importantly, British re-education policy also meant a shortage of textbooks. The production of new ones in the British zone proceeded at the rate of 9,940,000 between 1945 and 1947, meaning 2.25 books per child. Children at the *Ratsoberschule* found that they had virtually no schoolbooks upon their return because of the British ban on anything with Nazi content. This meant that early lessons concentrated upon mathematics and science. [160]

The local state and charities provided children with nutrition of various types. For instance, in October 1946 the German Red Cross distributed 'milk soup' from its headquarters in Osnabrück.[161] Similarly, a Roman Catholic organization, the *Annastift*, provided lunches for seventy children in February 1947, some of whom were orphans.[162] More importantly, the military authorities had decided at the start of 1946 that children in the whole of the Weser-Ems region between the ages of 6 and 18 should receive a meal at school, upon payment, which would contain about 300 calories. From May 1946 some children could receive free school meals including those whose parents depended upon social security, those from large families and those from poor families.[163] By July 1948 a total of 15,000 Osnabrück children received meals at school, 2,700 free.[164] But a report from the *Niedersächsischer Kurier* of 8 September 1948 pointed out that 'our children still suffer from bitter hunger'. A letter written by the chief school doctor in February 1948 claimed that a sample of 1,648 children in Osnabrück had revealed that 75.6 per cent were underweight while 24.4 per cent were overweight. On the other hand, the same sample demonstrated that 78 per cent were taller than average, while 22 per cent were below average height.[165]

An Osnabrück child in the immediate post-War years therefore lacked the basic comforts which children in the town would experience later in the century, above all an education. Schooling dramatically improved by the end of the 1940s, although pristine school buildings would not become the norm until the 1950s. Children suffered as a result of food shortages to the same extent as the adult population. While the military authorities and charities tried to provide food for them, they still hungered.

The newly established educational system could also go some way towards eradicating the ideological injections which had occurred under the Third Reich for those who returned to school, now exposed to Nazi-free textbooks and, in theory at least, non-Nazi teachers. The rest of the population had to experience re-education in other ways. The weeding out of former Nazis from state employment represented one aspect of the denazification process. In addition, a new media, culture and sport came into existence with the help of the military government, but usually at the initiative of Germans, which tried to eliminate traces of the recent past.[166]

Part of the process of forgetting about Nazism involved the remembrance of its victims and the period before the party came to power.[167] On 19 September 1948 a memorial service occurred in the *Blumenhalle* for the purpose of commemorating all the victims of National Socialism, attended by representatives from the military government and the leading political parties.[168] This event took place just before the large scale commemorations of the 300th anniversary of the signing of the Treaty of Westfalia. The religious, cultural and sporting events peaked in October shortly after the introduction of the *Deutschmark* and emphased the arrival of peace and recovery.[169]

Rebirth in the cultural sphere had begun immediately after the British entered Osnabrück against the background of a cultural policy which supported the reconstruction and security objectives of the invaders.[170] The last edition of the *Neue Volksblätter* had appeared on 1 April 1945, three days before the British entered Osnabrück. Thereafter the military authorities licensed German newspapers. Although some regional publications reached Osnabrück shortly after the British invasion, the first city newspaper consisted of the *Osnabrücker Rundschau*, established by a British captain and edited by a team of both Englishmen and Germans. It began in the spring of 1946 and lasted until September of that year. Several other similar newspapers licensed by the British followed during the second half of the 1940s, including the *Neues Tageblatt*. In November 1949 the *Osnabrücker Tageblatt* appeared again.[171]

High cultural activity in the form of theatre and classical music took off in the summer of 1945, having disappeared during the final stages of the War. Theatre began with variety shows put on in a British barracks from 8 August. The first 'serious' performance of a play occurred in what remained of the town theatre on 1 December in the form of Max Mell's *Apostelspiel*. Fifteen further performances of various plays occurred in 1946, while, in the following year, the staple classics of the German stage had returned. The total number of performances in Osnabrück increased from 158 in the 1945-6 season to 265 in 1947-8, while the number of theatregoers had grown from 75,331 to 206,251.[172]

Classical music began as soon as the British lifted their ban upon public gatherings. In the middle of July 1945 an event took place in the *Blumenhalle*, which included opera and operetta arias. The reconstituted Osnabrück Symphony Orchestra with 44 players gave 93 performances in the 1945-6 season. Chamber music evenings also quickly took off, as did opera and operetta.[173] More popular forms of music took longer to recover. For instance, a local song society, the *Neue Liedertafel*, did not reconstitute itself until April 1946, holding a Schubert concert on 7 June. Heating shortages prevented similar events from taking place during winter evenings. Once again 1948 represents the turning point in the history of the *Neue Liedertafel*.[174] In this year the OKD male choir also reconstituted itself.[175]

Classical music represented a relatively neutral art form. While the Nazis focused upon some composers more than others, this particular cultural activity had limited potential as an ideological tool compared, for instance, with cinema, whose contents changed in the immediate post-War years, as propaganda films glorifying war and racism disappeared. Replacements included *Welt im Film* 'a newsreel produced jointly by the British and American occupying powers for compulsory screening in the cinemas licensed to operate in their respective zones and sectors of Germany and Berlin'.[176] The first cinema to reopen in Osnabrück after the War consisted of the Lichtburg in Bohmter Strasse, which carried a film with the title of *Die Zaubergeige*. Others followed during the next few years as cinema once again became the main form of mass entertainment.[177]

The visual arts also quickly recovered and shed their Nazi skin. As early as 20 April 1945 the British authorities in Osnabrück allowed the writer and educator Ludwig Bäte to take responsibility for cultural activity in the town. The first museum exhibition took place in October 1945, subsequently going from strength to strength after two years of rebuilding. The city museum reopened in September 1948. Exhibitions included the works of artists banned under the Nazis, such as Erwin Weiß, a pupil of Oskar Kokoschka, which took place in October 1945.[178]

Sport, which had formed a central plank of Nazi policy, had also largely disappeared in the final days of the war, but, once again, its rebirth occurred fairly rapidly. The military authorities first of all had to purge the committees of some of the largest sporting organizations of Nazis. In addition, they also closed down some sporting clubs, including, in swimming, the *Osnabrücker Schwimverein* and SC Neptun. While some clubs with Nazi associations faced dissolution, others suppressed by the Third Reich came back to life, including the *Sportsverein Eversburg*, closed in 1933 because of SPD connections. Initial problems for sport in Osnabrück included the damage caused by the bombing which had destroyed playing fields, swimming pools and gyms. But competitive football matches had begun by the autumn of 1945, with the rebirth of the town championship.[179]

The churches also returned to normality after the War. As we have seen, they actually represented one social milieu which survived during the conflict, even if ministers in the town had faced arrest and even if participation in services had declined.[180] In this sense the Churches provided relative continuity from the end of the Weimar Republic to the birth of the Federal Republic. Return to normality for the Churches after the War essentially meant the reconstruction of buildings destroyed during the bombing, freedom to preach, and the return of congregations to their pre-War size. In the short-term services had to take place in make-shift locations. For instance, those of the *Marienkirche* occurred in the museum for a spell.[181]

The Return to 'Normality'

The immediate post-War years in Osnabrück therefore meant a period of initial difficulty, followed by the return to 'normality'. Compared with the plight of ethnic minorities and post-War refugees, as well as with the situation which existed under Allied bombs in 1944 and 1945, those ethnic Germans who emerged from the rubble of the spring of 1945 faced a relatively bright future. Certainly, some had lost their closest relatives. Admittedly, they had to endure housing and food shortages but no evidence exists in Osnabrück to suggest that starvation occurred. Many people lived in bad housing, a situation which, for some, did not improve until the 1950s. Furthermore, they also had to endure the cold winters of 1945-6 and 1946-7.

But at least they had survived both the Nazis and the Allies. They were alive, although some Germans may have wished they were dead between 1945 and 1948. However, if one compares the situation after 1945 with that during the War, the latter period clearly represents one of gradual recovery. Buildings did not collapse: they came back to life. While the rubble which existed everywhere may have caused despair, the cranes would have led to hope. People could now come out of their homes at night, rather than living underground, hiding from an enemy trying to kill them from the skies. They could also partake in the normal activities of urban life such as religion, the cinema, music and sport. They could speak to strangers without fear of the *Gestapo*. Not only were people alive, they were free from the NSDAP. This proved no consolation for former Nazis, but even they did not have a particularly bad time of it. Losing their jobs and facing disqualification from public employment probably represented a fair punishment for minor offenders.

Even if the first few years of the peace brought social and economic difficulties for native ethnic Germans who had survived the war, the years after 1948 meant a permanent improvement in the quality of their lives. The food shortages, lack of housing and cold winters represented temporary hiccoughs. After the introduction of the *Deutschmark* in July 1948 the German economy and standards of living began the upward climb which would not significantly slow down until the last decades of the twentieth century. For those who had managed to survive the Nazis and the Allies, the post-War period represented a happy ending, if not immediately, then certainly in the longer term.

6

GERMAN REFUGEES

Realities and Histories

At the end of the War the western Allies participated in one of the most dramatic population displacements in history, which meant the movement of over ten million Germans into the rump of their country, truncated by the desire of the Soviet Union to move its border westward, which had resulted in Poland and the USSR taking over territory which belonged to Germany in 1937. At the same time the newly liberated (at least from Nazism) eastern European states, particularly Poland, Czechoslovakia and Hungary, decided to expel their ethnic German populations from their borders because of their real or supposed connections with the Third Reich, even though Germans had lived in eastern Europe for centuries, in some cases predating the majority populations. In addition, millions of Germans simply fled west in order to escape the invading Soviet Armies, bent on revenge for the brutal actions which the Nazis had pursued in the USSR.[1]

While the Soviet Union held the major responsibility for this population transfer, the western Allies did not stand up for the Germans of eastern Europe. They, along with the USSR, dealt with the consequences of the expulsion, as the Germans from the East found themselves living in the rump state controlled by the four Allies. In May 1946 a total of nine million refugees lived in the four zones.[2] By the start of 1949 the largest proportion, 37.2 per cent, lived in the Soviet zone because of its proximity to the regions which had lost population. The British zone held 32.8 per cent, while the American one contained 28.2 per cent and the French 1.8 per cent.[3]

These bare, but shocking statistics, hide millions of tales of personal hardship. The harrowing stories behind the figures began in the homes of those who would eventually find themselves in western locations. The iconic image in early post-War Germany consists of people moving westward with a cart carrying whatever possessions they could load on to it. These carts sometimes travelled hundreds of miles westwards with their owners who would never again see the homes which they had left. In other cases, Germans fled with virtually nothing, ending up in a location devastated by bombing, where they had to try and begin their lives anew.

As Robert G. Moeller has demonstrated, the refugees quickly attracted the attention of leading German historians, who turned to *Zeitgeschichte*, especially Theodor Schieder, who edited a series of documentary volumes on the expulsion. The attention received by this group lasted for decades, unlike Jews and Romanies, and quickly became one of the central concerns of contemporary German historians, although not Anglo-American ones, who ignored the refugees until recently.[4]

We now have studies covering all areas of origins and settlement, overwhelmingly in German. The historiography reveals that many refugees became 'hut people' for years to come, living in temporary accommodation in the form of prefabricated barracks. Others faced billeting upon those families which still had a home standing. Although much resettlement occurred in smaller locations which had not suffered massive bomb damage, medium sized towns such as Osnabrück found themselves having to take thousands of newcomers in addition to the natives who returned when the War ended. This exacerbated the housing crisis caused by bombing.

As well as the problems with accommodation, the new German residents of Osnabrück found themselves facing the other hardships endured by natives, often on a magnified scale because they were foreign to the town and therefore did not have the same networks as people who knew their surroundings. Refugees generally took longer to find work and had a higher unemployment rate than natives well into the history of the Federal Republic. Similarly, they had greater difficulty in solving their dietary needs in the hunger years as they could not generally grow food in their back gardens (which they did not possess, unless they lived in the home of another family) and had no relatives in the surrounding countryside to bring them produce grown on farms.

While much of the population of Germany in the late 1940s may have faced a traumatic experience trying to rebuild their lives, the refugees from eastern Europe endured some of the most difficult psychological problems precisely because they were refugees who had left all their possessions and surroundings behind and now found themselves in a devastated and unwelcoming landscape, at least in its appearance. Although the refugees certainly did not suffer the same fate as Jews or Romanies, they endured a worse one than those Germans who at least lived in the place of their birth and therefore had familiarity with and knowledge of their, admittedly, changed surroundings. Ultimately, the refugees, unlike the murdered Jews or Romanies, would rebuild their lives, but they would often take longer than natives and would in some cases never regain the social status which they had enjoyed in the East.[5]

Origins and Journeys

Individuals and families travelled hundreds of miles from their homes before reaching their final destination.[6] Osnabrück provides instances of such journeys, as well as containing examples of the different types of groups who moved to the town at the end of the War. We can divide these into three: adults and families, who originated overwhelmingly from territories east of the new German border on the Oder-Neisse Line; 'Clobber Soldiers', with origins in states in east and south east Europe, which had expelled their Germans, and who now found themselves discharged in Osnabrück; and orphans, who had lost their parents as a result of the War and ended up in the town.

Table 6.1: Origins of Refugees in Osnabrück in June 1949.

Place of Residence before 8 May 1945	Number
RB Köslin (Pomerania)	657
RB Stettin (Pomerania)	548
RB Grenzmark Posen West Prussia (Pomerania)	582
RB Franakfurt (Mark Bradenburg) east of the Oder	258
RB Liegnitz (Lower Silesia) east of the Görlitzer Neiße	433
RB Breslau (Lower Silesia) east of the Görlitzer Neiße	1,258
RB Oppeln and Kattowitz (Upper Silesia)	607
East Prussia	1,608
Austria	133
Hungary	---
Czechoslovakia	374
Yugoslavia	15
Rumania	12
Deported and expelled Germans from other regions	2,523
Total	9,008

Source: NSO Dep-3c-983, Monatlicher Nachweis der Bevölkerungsvorgänge, Osnabrück Stadt, 1 Juni 1949.

About eighty per cent of refugees in Lower Saxony originated in areas east of the Oder-Neisse Line, half of whom came from Silesia, of which, in turn, half originated in the *Regierungsbezirk* of Breslau.[7] The statistics gathered by the refugee office in Osnabrück confirm the Prussian origins of the majority of expellees in the town. In June 1949 the 9,008 refugees made up 8.6 per cent of the total population of 104,460, a significant proportion according to any comparison and reflecting the national average.[8]

Table 6.2: Growth in the Refugee Population of Osnabrück, September 1946 to June 1949.

Date	Number of Refugees	Total Population	Percentage of Refugees Amongst Total Population
September 1946	3,222	95,089	3.4
March 1947	4,687	97,617	5.0
September 1947	6,516	98,646	6.6
March 1948	7,491	99,528	7.5
September 1948	8,239	100,785	8.2
June 1949	9,008	104,460	8.6

Source: NSO Dep-3c-983, Monatlicher Nachweis der Bevölkerungsvorgänge, Osnabrück Stadt, 1 September 1946, 1 März 1947, 1 September 1947, 1 März 1948, 1 September 1948, 1 Juni 1949.

As Table 6.2 indicates, the increase in the total number and percentage of refugees had occurred gradually, indicating that most of them did not make their way to the town directly from their place of origin, but arrived slowly, particularly from the Soviet zone. Thus, out of the 959 refugees who moved to Osnabrück between 28 October and 21 November 1945 a total of 271 had come from the Soviet zone, although the 568 who arrived directly from provinces East of the Oder in this period exceeded this figure.[9] The main streams of refugees in the town came directly from Prussia or other parts of Europe via transit camps in Friedland (near Göttingen), in the case of those from the south east, and Helmstedt, Vorsfelde and Uelzen in the case of those from the east.[10]

Osnabrück refugees have recalled their experiences, reflecting the importance of the expulsion in German national memory since the end of the War.[11] From the recollections of these new Osnabrückers, we obtain an idea of origins, journey, choice of Osnabrück (to the extent that it existed) and arrival. Liselotte Burchardt, who lived in Alt-Christburg in East Prussia, left her home with her children on 22 January 1945 as the Red Army advanced. They had seven wagons and fled with a Polish family who worked for them, although the latter only travelled as far as Danzig, where the Burchardts remained for three weeks. The Burchardts then moved further but 'the Russian' stopped them in Stelin in Pommerania and all seventeen members of her group went into accommodation for refugees. Several smaller moves and unsatisfactory places of accommodation followed over the next three months, during which time Poles and Russian soldiers stole many of the possessions which the Burchardts tried to bring out of East Prussia. In November 1945 Mrs Burchardt went with her children, by this time carrying only what they could on their backs and with their hands, to a relative in the Soviet sector of Berlin. During the journey Poles stole these items as well. She arrived in Berlin on 22 November. In the city she received a card stating that the US army held her husband as a prisoner of war. She also learnt that her mother and sister now lived in Osnabrück and decided to make her way there, arriving on 5 December 1945.[12]

Liselotte Burchardt made it to Osnabrück as part of a family, in contrast to orphaned children and prisoners of war. 'Action Clobber' looked after soldiers released in Osnabrück. These newcomers went into an 'isolation house' and registered with the Department for the Care of Refugees. They then contacted the employment and housing offices. About 400 'Clobber Soldiers' had arrived in Osnabrück at the start of 1946. The city authorities wanted to use their labour power for the reconstruction of the town but many either registered sick or left Osnabrück, sometimes in a vain desire to return home.[13] The local state had established a camp at the end of 1946, run by the Red Cross and the *Caritasverband*, to house newly arrived prisoners of war released in Osnabrück. The camp provided them with accommodation and food until their release. Most of those housed here came from England.[14]

Orphans arriving in Osnabrück had perhaps the most harrowing experiences of all. On 19 October 1945 the Mayor of Osnabrück wrote the following letter to the *Caritasverband*:

> Sixty thousand children must be taken from border camps into the *Bezirks* of Osnabrück, Aurich and Oldenburg in order to be found a new home. One knows nothing about their parents! Several thousand

of these children shall remain in our town. Our orphanages are
destroyed, however.

It is now important to find families who will accept them, care for
them and rescue them from misery.[15]

Some of the newly arrived children found accommodation in public
buildings.[16] On 5 May 1948 the *Neues Tageblatt* appealed for clothing for
fifty children held in a Protestant orphanage, using life stories in its
advertising campaign, which gave details of the journeys of children to the
town. For instance, the case of seven year old Peter.

> Peter is the boy who was picked up at the traveller's aid society in
> Osnabrück. In his company was an aunt, who was fifteen years old.
> Both came from Tilsit and hiked through Saxony to Hamburg in
> order to find their collective great aunt there. The people of Hamburg
> said: 'Not here', and put a card for Osnabrück in their hands. Peter
> came to the orphanage in Schölerberg in this way.

The case of 'little Karl' is even more heart wrenching. He arrived from
Litzmannstadt.

> Little Karl has absolutely no idea where that is...He was two years
> old when his mother was expelled with him and Richard. They
> reached the British zone via Chemnitz. On the way they had more
> daily experiences than one can imagine. On one occasion the mother
> crossed over the border in order to collect knitting machines. By
> doing so she wanted to build a new existence for herself. On a station
> somewhere the mother found out by accident that the father still
> lived in a prisoner of war camp somewhere in the East.

Reception and Resettlement

Upon arriving in a devastated Osnabrück, refugees first of all needed
somewhere to live, at least on a temporary basis until the town itself got
back on its feet and allowed them to establish their own lives. In the
meantime, as refugees, they had to rely on official help provided by the
British authorities, the local state and charities. They began arriving
immediately upon the cessation of hostilities, before any organization had
come into existence to assist them. By the end of 1945 a total of 1,500 lived
in the town.[17]

A refugee office did not come into existence, under the overall control
of the welfare department, until October 1945. Its first task simply
consisted of registering the newcomers. A publicity campaign involving

cars with loud speakers and placards called upon all refugees in the town to register on Saturday 11 November. The new office discovered that they moved in and out of Osnabrück in large numbers at this stage. In January 1946 the refugee office became a self-standing body. Its employees consisted almost equally of natives and refugees.[18] The tasks of the newly autonomous Osnabrück refugee office quickly increased beyond registration to include further purely bureaucratic tasks such as the writing of weekly and monthly reports[19] and the compilation of precise statistics. The more concrete measures included helping with the search for and provision of accommodation, supplying clothing, giving out ration cards and assisting with medical needs.[20]

While the local state gradually took control of the care of refugees in Osnabrück, the major charities also played a role in looking after them. The Red Cross, for instance, established an office at the railway station, which aimed at assisting all of those moving into Osnabrück at the end of the War.[21] The *Caritasverband* also established a mission at the railway station. The following provides an example of the help it offered to individuals who arrived in Osnabrück:

A mother, a refugee from the eastern zone, comes with both children – Willi, 13 years old, and Hilde, 15 years old – to the Travellers Aid Society. The woman has been on the move with her children for half a year; she has been sent from one camp to another because they have been overflowing with inmates, deadened because of all her needs, she asked us for advice and accommodation in her hour of need. Following the death of her husband the woman, who was not in a position to fight for the means of subsistence for herself and her growing children due to the suffering, left her Silesian home.

We succeeded in finding temporary posts for these well-behaved children. After the children were taken care of, the mother obtained support and housing from the Refugee Office so that the conditions of her life were once again on a straight path. The mother paid us a brief visit and explained radiantly and full of gratitude, that she had, in the meantime, together with her daughter, who now had a good job nearby, put together a cosy domesticity. The mother is, in the meantime, contented with the fact that she has brought up her son well, but hopes that she will later live together with both of her children.[22]

The Roman Catholic Church also provided food for refugees, through its various parishes in Osnabrück.[23]

While charities played some role in helping the refugees, the local state took the lead in the attempt to integrate them into Osnabrück society, assisting them in their search for shelter, food, and jobs. Their first and most pressing need consisted of securing accommodation, which they generally achieved with the help of the refugee office. The refugees initially had three housing solutions open to them as they moved into urban areas with acute shortages consequent upon allied bombing. These consisted of living in camps, setting themselves up in a shed, or sharing the homes of natives.

Camps, which characterised the Nazi years, also became a feature of the German landscape during the late 1940s as local authorities tried to find quick fixes to the problem of housing thousands of newcomers. Some of these camps lasted into the 1950s. Often, particulary in the short term, they simply consisted of places previously used by the Nazis.[24] One of the first places which housed refugees in Osnabrück, from the autumn of 1945 until February 1946, consisted of the isolation unit of the city hospital.[25] A woman who arrived from Pomerania remembered her first few days in a camp in Osnabrück, which had formerly housed foreign workers:

We did not have a bed although we had bed linen. They had to give us covers so that we could cover ourselves up. We thought we could wash ourselves, but we could not yet. Nobody could with cold water: look it was March, and it was cold, and we were supposed to wash ourselves with cold water. We washed our hands and then we crawled up. And the next morning came and nobody wanted to get up.[26]

The Osnabrück refugee office established some long term camps. One of the most important of these lay near to the railway station in the suburb of Lüstringen while Fernblick was located next to a synonymous coffee house. Others lay in the immediate hinterland of Osnabrück.[27] A report from 14 May 1947 gives some information about Lüstringen. Situated on the site of a paper factory, which still operated, it began housing refugees from November 1945. The camp utilised a total of 1,525 square metres on two floors. 'The roof is a wooden roof and finds itself in a bad situation. The roof is rotten and leaking in many places, so that water falls into the top floor during rainy weather'.[28] Fernblick seems to have come into existence on 15 April 1949. By July of that year it housed 190 people. An article in the *Neues Tageblatt* described life here in fairly positive terms. It portrayed the 'barracks' as 'painfully clean and tidy'. The refugees described the food as 'sufficient and nice tasting'. They paid DM1.10 per day for accommodation, although most of them did not have jobs. As a result they had much leisure time, which meant, for instance, that they had painted the dining room with pictures of their homeland. However, as many as six couples sometimes lived in the same room, meaning that relationships suffered.[29] By October 1949 the number of people in Fernblick had increased to 210, although others had moved on to similar, but roomier, accommodation in Schinkel. Those who remained continued to live in small spaces, sharing large rooms with complete strangers, which often led to conflict.[30] An investigation by the regional refugee care worker looked into conditions in the camp in November 1949, following complaints about it by inmates.

> On 18/11/49 I visited the Fernblick camp... The camp is occupied by 98 tenants made up of 227 persons, including 41 single people...6 families with 28 people have recently been accommodated in their own homes. 4 further families with 17 people are likewise moving into self standing homes in the next few days. There will then remain 182 people in the genuine transit camp. From the 98 tenants 30 are employed.

The rest lived off various types of welfare. The rooms of 50 square metres divided into four and housed a total of twelve people.[31]

Refugees who did not live in camps often found themselves in other forms of temporary accommodation, as illustrated in an article in the *Neues Tageblatt* of 30 September 1948 which carried the title of 'The Hut Man' and described the conditions in which such an individual had to reside, including 'finger thin' walls, doors which did not close and coal and potatoes stored in the living room.

Other refugees found themselves billeted in the homes of natives. Renate Schlosser remembered one particular family, who moved into a five bedroom home of 220 square metres, 'with father, mother and grandmother'. Her father built one 'apartment by joining together two rooms'.[32] Anneliese Diehl claimed that a mother with her grown up daughter lived with her and her parents at the end of the war. 'And then we had a couple from Silesia, who also fled.' They left when Mrs Diehl's sister arrived from East Prussia with her family.[33]

Table 6.3 provides a statistical snapshot of the reality of refugee housing in Osnabrück in March 1947 indicating that, at this stage, some of the newcomers did not have even the most basic necessities of life including heating, beds, and, in two cases, toilets. A couple of individual experiences help to illustrate the difficulties which existed. First, the case of Paul Teichert, who wrote to Bishop Berning in July 1949. He had arrived in the Fernblick camp the previous month from Uelzen. He had lived in camps with his wife and three children, between the ages of 7 and 11, since 1945 and complained about the lack of space available to himself and his family. The priest of St Josephs took up his case, pointing to the problems of children living in close proximity with adults.[34] Meanwhile, the refugee office investigated the case of Walter Bösel:

Bösel lives with his wife in a ground floor flat with three rooms in Veilchenstrasse, namely:

Kitchen,	about 5 square meters		
Salon,	" 10	"	"
Closet,	" 8	"	"
	" 23	"	"

All the rooms have very thin walls, the kitchen and the closet top hung windows that open out on the roof. Only the room has a proper window. With regard to furniture and equipment the house owner has made available to the couple a cupboard, a bedstead with a mattress, a chest of drawers, a table in the salon, two chairs, an oven, a kitchen table, two kitchen chairs, a bucket and a saucepan.

Rent totalled DM30 per month, together with DM1.50 for electricity in the summer and DM3 in the winter for a single lamp with a 25 watt bulb.[35]

As many refugees eventually reached Osnabrück with virtually no possessions, other than the clothing they wore on their backs, the refugee office had to provide them with the absolute basics of life before they could think of moving towards the more complex task of finding employment. With the help of local firms, the refugee office came up with clothing of all sorts for men (particularly released soldiers who had nothing but their uniforms) women and children. In addition, the refugee office also made efforts to provide newcomers with furniture and cooking utensils.[36] In August 1946 the military authorities launched a campaign involving local charities for the purpose of distributing clothing to refugees.[37] This had limited success. The section on refugees from the monthly medical report of March 1947 recording the experiences of 2,173 persons, pointed out that 648 people did not have shoes, while 740 did even not possess underwear.[38]

Along with housing, the most difficult problem facing refugees and the office which cared for them, consisted of the search for employment, although in many cases the newcomers found jobs fairly quickly.[39] Together with Hildesheim, Osnabrück had the lowest refugee unemployment rate in Lower Saxony,[40] reflecting the picture for the town's population as a whole. Refugees in Osnabrück actually had a diverse employment experience, which makes generalizations difficult. One of the groups which suffered most, in terms of the loss of status, consisted of professionals. The *Neues*

Tageblatt carried one story under the headline of 'Professor Hawks Shaving Cream'. The same article also carried details of a chief laboratory technician with four children, expelled from Prague, who had served a period as a prisoner of war and who could not secure a job in any of the hospitals in Osnabrück.[41] On the other hand, significant numbers of refugees opened up their own businesses by the end of the 1940s. A total of 44 such enterprises already existed in Osnabrück by October 1946.[42] In 1949 a total of 44 refugee enterprises had established themselves in the textile industry, particularly as merchants. By this time the overall number of refugee businesses had reached 210, of which 138 had previously existed.[43]

Table 6.3: Housing Conditions of 2,173 Osnabrück Refugees
(1,053 households) in March 1947

1. Type of Housing	a) Self-standing	2,138
	b) Mass Quarters	35
2. Heating	a) With	1,642
	b) Without	87
3. Sleeping Arrangements	a) With beds	1,642
	b) Without beds	531
4. Cooking Arrangements	a) Independent	512
	b) Communal	472
	c) No possibility	69
5. Water	a) In own rooms	986
	b) Communal	53
	c) Special arrangements	14
6. Toilet	a) Own	15
	b) Communal	1,036
	c) Without	2

Source: NSO   Rep-430-303-19/56-101,   Monatsbericht   des
Gesundheitsamtes, Osnabrück Stadt, March 1947.

The health of refugees suffered as a consequence of the deprivations which they experienced.[44] A report by the chief medical officer from 1 February 1947 pointed out that, in comparison with natives, they had a worse nutritional situation, experienced a significantly higher infection and death rate from tuberculosis, and suffered more from lice and scabies.[45] Statistics from the *Heil- und Pflegeanstalt* in Osnabrück in 1945-6 reveal that a high percentage of women admitted suffering from mental illness consisted of refugees, peaking at 66.7 per cent in June 1946. Between May 1945 and December 1946 this hospital admitted 100 refugee women and 135 natives with such ailments, meaning that the former were vastly over-represented considering refugees made up less than nine per cent of Osnabrück's population.[46] These statistics point to the trauma which the experience of flight and loss had caused.

Apart from assisting with the search for employment and the provision of housing and clothing, the local state also made efforts to help refugees develop a social life. In June 1949 the Osnabrück *Regierungsbezirk* spent DM1,200 on activities for refugees.[47] In April 1949 the Minister for Refugee Affairs in Lower Saxony suggested that camps should have libraries, which would help to relieve the boredom of those stuck in them.[48] By 1949 the city theatre also put on special performances for refugees, with free and discounted tickets paid by the Minister for Refugee Affairs in Lower Saxony.[49]

By 1949 refugees, with the assistance of the local state, had made some progress on the path towards integrating themselves in Osnabrück society and economy. Most had found employment, even if, in some cases, they had suffered a significant loss of social status, and most had homes. While the refugees may have had more difficulties than natives in getting on their feet, because they had no familiarity with their surroundings, they had developed lives which resembled normality by the end of 1949.

Refugee 'Ethnicity'?

As the majority of refugees had faced a forced expulsion they could not automatically erase the memories of home, particularly in a situation which disorientated them in unfamiliar surroundings in difficult economic circumstances. While they were not foreigners, they behaved as if they were in some of their actions, because of a sense of alienation. Furthermore, some of them experienced discrimination because of their origins. Once they began to cope with the problems of everyday life and started to reflect on their situation, they developed a sense of injustice at the forcible expulsion from their homes.

This combination of disorientation, discrimination and perceived victimization led refugees on both a local and national scale to establish organizations. These aimed at memorialising their areas of origin and also had the futile desire of reclaiming them. These bodies partly represented a manifestation of pride in the difference of eastern Germans from natives even though the newcomers did not all come from the same places. Klaus J. Bade has regarded the refugees from the East as one of the many streams of migrants that have moved towards core Germany during the nineteenth and twentieth centuries.[50] Indeed, one of his edited books, carrying the title of 'Strangers in the Land', focuses upon Germans who moved from the East throughout the post-War period.[51] Similarly, Lutz Hoffmann pointed out that West Germany had obtained one third of its population through immigration in 1989, made up of both foreign and German streams.[52]

Some Germans from the east perceived themselves as foreign partly as a reaction against prejudice from natives who wanted to protect the meagre resources they had saved through bombing and invasion. Government authorities did everything possible to ease the path of refugees into native society. As we have seen, the local state in Osnabrück put much effort into this process. The national authorities mirrored this work. In 1947 the Office for Expellee Issues came into existence in Frankfurt, which, two years later, moved to Bonn as the Federal Ministry for Expellees, Refugees and War Victims. In 1948 the newcomers received a Bill of Rights. Most importantly, the Federal Constitution of 1949 recognized them as full citizens.[53] It proves very difficult to find any examples of official hostility towards Germans from the east in the immediate post-War period, contrasting with the experience of other minorities in post-War Germany, particularly foreign workers, who did not receive this type of pampering.[54] There consequently existed few reasons for alienation from the new rump German state.

Does the same apply to the populations of German towns, who had suffered loss of property and family and now had to share their limited resources with complete strangers who had even less than they did? A more complex picture emerges which involves both negative and positive reactions, as a series of contradictory sources in Osnabrück illustrate. Police reports from the immediate post-War years carry little on the connections between natives and refugees. An exception is the following negative comment from September 1946:

> The relationship of the refugees to the native population is very bad. The native population views the refugees with mistrust as they want to keep the most essential necessities of life. These necessities are not there though. The native population sticks to the old traditions and is completely opposed to anything new. The refugees can't understand these completely ingrained prejudices and label the natives as hard-

hearted, whereas the natives, on the other hand, view the refugees as a horde.[55]

Interviews carried out for the project on refugees in Osnabrück led by Klaus Bade confirm that refugees faced hostility. A woman from Silesia, born in 1931, believed that she was a second-class citizen.

Although one was always conscious of oneself, refugee was a bitter word at the beginning…In school the children and so on suffered because of that, refugee, that was a bad word, that was used very often at first. Also they, if I can still remember, the boys in the school, they dealt with them as second-class citizens. I did not have personal experiences, because I didn't go to school here but I know that when my brother came home they often howled at him. 'They beat me up today', 'You dopey refugee', 'You rucksack German'.

Other refugees recorded similar memories.[56]

In the context of racism in twentieth century Germany such experiences would not even register on point one of a Richter scale of hostility. Just as much evidence exists to suggest that refugees received a warm welcome from Osnabrückers. The press, central in the spread of twentieth century racism, welcomed the refugees. A typical headline is the following, which reported a speech given by the Minister for Refugees in Lower Saxony delivered in Osnabrück: 'The Fate of the Refugees is the Fate of Each of Us.'[57] Natives interviewed for this project revealed little lingering hostility, although we would hardly expect them to admit to this. Anneliese Diehl, referring to the refugee family which lived in her house, claimed that: 'We lived wonderfully together. A home with a corridor, three rooms facing the street, one in the middle and three rooms facing the garden'.[58] Cilly Stein, on the other hand, asserted that 'They were not very welcome here, the refugees. And we had to share the little we had with them. They were viewed in a distorted way at first'.[59] Two interviewees remembered the dialects and accents of the refugees. Referring to the family which she knew, Renate Schlosser stated: 'The boy spoke in such a funny way' suggesting some sort of hostility, but she then went on to say, 'He was a very intelligent boy'.[60] Herman Thiem remembered that refugees came to buy pots and pans from his father's hardware store, asking for Polish items, which they did not stock, in Silesian German, which he found difficult to understand. However, Thiem revealed no overt animosity.[61]

The refugees therefore experienced little hostility in any true sense of the word.[62] Perhaps they were the 'victims' of German regionalism. They felt different enough to band together, motivated by the feeling that they had lost everything (which the German authorities recognized), their alienation from their new and unfamiliar surroundings, their linguistic and other 'cultural' differences from natives and their desire to see and reclaim their homes despite the finality of Potsdam, the treaty under which the Allies accepted the expulsion of Germans from eastern Europe in the summer of 1945.[63] The refugees therefore created a quasi-ethnicity by establishing their own organizations. On a national scale, especially during the course of the 1950s, all manner of groups evolved. Some represented the specific areas from where refugees originated, while others brought them all together.[64]

Reflecting the national picture, the exiles in Osnabrück did not begin to organize themselves properly until 1948. Due to the relatively small numbers of refugees in the town, the bodies which came into existence aimed at bringing individuals from a wide range of geographic origins together. A meeting involving 89 people occurred in the *Grüner Jäger* pub on 7 June to establish the first grouping in the form of the *Gemeinschaft der Ostvertriebenen* (GDO). It developed connections with a larger national body established in 1949 in the form of the *Zentralverband der Vertriebenen Deutschen* (Central Organization of Expelled Germans). The first public meeting of this organization took place in the *Blumenhalle* on the first Sunday of August 1948. One of the speakers declared that the group had two major tasks: 'The greatest aim for the future is the winning back of the homeland, the second aim is the fight for human rights, housing, work and reparations'.[65]

The largest event organised by the GDO during the late 1940s occurred on Sunday 31 July 1949, involving over 10,000 people from throughout the *Regierungsbezirk*. It lasted for the whole day and involved both Roman Catholic and Evangelical services, collective meals in restaurants in the centre of Osnabrück, a procession through the town, meetings of *Landmannschaften* (which united people from specific parts of Eastern Europe), speeches to the whole gathering in front of the Cathedral, and songs about the lost homeland. The gathering, in view of its size, received much coverage in local newspapers, which carried articles describing the events which took place during the course of the day. 'The meeting was opened with a service'.

> Love of the homeland and collective need united more than 10,000 expellees from the east at a large rally in Osnabrück. From near and distant surroundings countless expellees had already joined together in the cathedral during the morning.

There then followed a procession through the streets of Osnabrück after lunch, in which wagons with symbols referring back to areas in the 'homeland', such as East Prussia or Danzig, proceeded. People reassembled again upon the Domhof.

The meeting was started with a recollection of the many who had lost their lives as a result of the gruesome expulsion from the homeland. *Minister Rat* Goebel, from Lippstadt, declared that this meeting was more than a protest, it was a recognition of the homeland, of Germany and of a free Christian Europe. He demanded the same right of self-government for the east German provinces that west German regions had, the end of administration through foreign peoples and the return of the people who had their homes there.

The meeting closed with '15,000 larynxes' united in the song 'I would like to return home again'.[66] By the time this meeting had taken place the GDO claimed that it had 35,000 members.[67] It organized other events during the remainder of the year.[68]

The proceedings of 31 July 1949 reflect the reality of refugee life in Osnabrück during the late 1940s. They point to the extent to which integration had already occurred, as the proceedings took place with the full blessing of the Roman Catholic Church.[69] The rhetoric pointed to their centrality in remembrance of the War. They represented the German victims in memorialization of the conflict. The official level of their acceptance indicates the way in which all manner of organizations made great efforts to assist in their integration.

This support could not, of course, cover up the loss which refugees had experienced. The organizations which came into existence, as well as the central government departments established to assist them, served two tasks. On the one hand they attempted to integrate them into their new surroundings. On the other, they did this by keeping alive the memory of their homelands in the East, which they could not easily forget. The refugees eased the pain of their loss by coming together with people of similar experiences.

Only with the passage of time could they put the tragedy which they had experienced to the back of their minds, as they became increasingly integrated into west German society, helped by the economic miracle which began to improve everyone's life. Increasingly, they came to accept that the desire to return home became more and more of a dream as a result of the Cold War freeze and the West German government acceptance of Potsdam. The refugee organizations reached their zenith during the course of the 1950s, but subsequently declined in importance due to a combination of increasing integration and consequent forgetting.[70]

PART III

ETHNIC MINORITIES

THE PERSECUTION AND ELIMINATION OF THE JEWS

Introduction

The experience of the Jews in Osnabrück, as well as in the rest of Germany, during the Nazi years meant a bleak realization of the realities of racial policy. It resulted in the implementation of measures which even the most pessimistic of Jews could not have believed possible in the years before 1933. The rise to power of an overt antisemite became a possibility from the end of the nineteenth century. As the effects of the late Weimar economic crisis increasingly made themselves felt, this started to look more and more like reality. Some Jews had already decided to emigrate even before 1933, while others would risk staying on longer. Those who did so quickly realized that the worst of all possible nightmares would materialize.

Three phrases sum up the experiences of German Jewry in the years between 1933 and 1945. In chronological order Jews faced loss of civil rights, expulsion and extermination.[1] From a community remaining, in some ways, distinct from mainstream German society because of its ethnic and economic differences, precisely the reasons why the Nazis and their antisemitic predecessors had singled out the group, Jews virtually disappeared from German towns by the early stages of World War Two as a result of emigration, deportation and murder. Our concern lies with the realities of the deprivation of civil rights, deportation and extermination for both German Jews and gentiles.

This chapter fits into an enormous historiographical tradition, which has encompassed virtually all aspects of the life of German Jewry in the years 1933-45. On the one hand we have studies examining the national picture.[2] On the other, virtually every Jewish community of any size has had its history written in the period 1933-45, usually by a local enthusiast or enthusiasts, who have often produced empirical studies of the highest quality, although on other occasions outsiders, including Americans, have written such works.[3] From our own perspective, Marion Kaplan has produced a major study which looks at the everyday life of Jews in Nazi Germany based upon a wide range of primary and secondary sources.[4]

The Jews of Osnabrück have received considerable attention from local historians, which eases the reconstruction of their lives in the years 1929-

49. The survival of official documentation also facilitates this process. Similarly, the history of Osnabrück Jewry in the Nazi period remains fresh in the minds of people who lived in the town at the time. The people interviewed for this project nearly all had some memory of the local Jews, usually revealing abhorrence at their treatment.

The earliest significant work consists of a brief narrative covering the whole history of the local community commemorating the reopening of the Synagogue in 1969.[5] There then followed another brief, unpublished, account by K. Brenner, held in the local archive, covering the whole history of the community.[6] The first significant and detailed book, by Karl Kühling, which moves from the medieval period to 'The Great Death', appeared in 1983, a standard political and social history of the type produced by this writer.[7] The year 1988 saw the appearance of the volume focusing on the Nazi period by Junk and Sellmeyer. This will remain the standard work on the subject and represents an excellent local study of a German Jewish community under the Nazis because of the meticulous detail and thorough research involved. In an appendix, the authors provided details of the fate of every Jew living in the town at the start of the Nazi period. The volume reappeared in 1989 and 2000.[8] Perhaps because of the rigour of this volume, relatively little has appeared on Osnabrück Jewry since 1988, with the exception of an article jointly authored by Martina Sellmeyer (now Krause) and Michael Gander.[9] Osnabrück's most significant Jewish son, and one of the major artists of the Holocaust, Felix Nussbaum, has also had a large book published about him.[10]

The availability of both published and unpublished material on Osnabrück Jewry allows us to reconstruct its history from the 1920s until the 1940s. While the original Jewish community virtually disappeared by the end of the War, a rebirth in Osnabrück occurred almost immediately, as a result of the return of a small number of survivors and the presence of some Polish and Yugoslav Jews imported as foreign workers and prisoners of war respectively between 1939 and 1945. We can contextualize the history of Osnabrück Jewry in the years 1929-49 against the national background.

Osnabrück Jewry before 1929

The history of Osnabrück Jewry until the end of the Weimar Republic reflects that of German Jews elsewhere. This involved medieval settlement, persecution and expulsion, resettlement at some time in the early modern or modern period, and emancipation and movement into the local business elites during the nineteenth century.[11] During the first three decades of the twentieth century, German Jewry reached its zenith. While antisemitism remained a potent force, both before and during the Weimar Republic, people of Jewish faith or origins had become central in the economic, cultural and political establishment of the Weimar Republic. Although the economic crisis affected them, they remained a section of the population over represented in the higher echelons of German society and overwhelmingly concentrated in urban areas, particularly the big cities. Their middle class status also meant that they had an older age structure than the rest of the population.[12]

Osnabrück Jewry in the early part of the twentieth century reflects the national picture. One of the main differences consists of the small size of the local population, although, as 1,600 synagogue communities existed in the country as a whole, living outside the bigger populations of Berlin, Frankfurt, Breslau and Munich also represented normality for Jews in the three decades before the Nazis came to power.[13] The size of Osnabrück Jewry would determine some aspects of its development, although the general picture after 1933 remained similar to that in other parts of Germany.

Following the national pattern, Osnabrück Jewry witnessed an increase in numbers during the first three decades of the twentieth century from 397 in 1900 to 435 in 1933, although its proportion of the population of the town fell from 0.9 to 0.45.[14] While the size of the local community differs in scale and proportion of population from the larger ones,[15] it mirrors the national pattern. The declining proportion would reflect the middle class status of the local Jews, meaning lower birth rates, exogamy, and, after 1925, migration to other locations.

The occupational patterns of Osnabrück Jewry reflect the national picture, with an overwhelmingly middle class community, which had moved into commercial occupations during the emancipation era. Two lists of members of the Jewish community in the NSO[16] suggest that the Jewish community involved themselves almost entirely in middle class occupations by the 1920s. Osnabrück Jewry found itself highly concentrated in the commercial sector, with the largest occupational group consisting broadly of businessmen. Unlike other locations in Germany, Jews made relatively limited inroads into the professions, with few doctors or lawyers.[17] The presence of just one person involved in the arts points to the status of Osnabrück as a cultural backwater compared with some of the other major cities where Jews had a profound impact.[18] The information available also concentrates on male occupations. The list of Jewish parishioners for 1927 also lists women and children. The overwhelming majority of women simply attract the description of 'wife'. The two exceptions consist of a managing clerk, Johanna Blumenfeld, of Markt 18, and a doctor, Sophie Prag, of Wesereschstraße 22.

As local antisemites would emphasise, Osnabrück Jewry played a large role in local retailing, particularly the ownership of department stores, concentrated in Grosse Straße, the main shopping street in the town. In 1927, at the age of 23, the artist Felix Nussbaum still lived with his father, the businessman Philip Nussbaum, in the family villa in Schlossstraße. Philip ran an ironware business with his cousin Simon Coessels. The success of the concern allowed Philip to build the residence in Schlossstraße in 1922.[19]

The files listing the occupations of Osnabrück Jews also give information on their residential patterns, pointing to a concentration in the city centre and reflecting the national pattern with at least two thirds of German Jewry 'living in sophisticated, upper-middle class districts' of cities.[20] In the case of Osnabrück the main area of residence lay around the palace, as the list of synagogue members from 1927 indicates. Johanisstraße represented a particularly popular street. Jews remained largely absent from the working class areas of Sutthausen or Schinkel.[21]

The list of synagogue members from 1927 also provides information on the family structure of Osnabrück Jewry. In all 165 units existed, many of them with several children, although, at the same time, the information also suggests the presence of numerous households with just one person, often a widow. The local community had a typically bourgeois family structure. Of the 84 family units, making up half of the total, the most common consist of either one or two children, far outnumbering those with three or more offspring. At the end of the Weimar Republic German and Osnabrück Jewry therefore consisted of a mature middle class community, distinct in terms of its occupational structure, its residence patterns and its family structure.

In addition, the existence of distinct ethnic organizations, partly developed as a reaction against antisemitism and partly evolving for religious reasons, also helped to distinguish Jews from their German neighbours. While the Jewish community of Osnabrück may have divided into Orthodox, Reform and Conservative, its size prevented the evolution of separate services. Individual families chose the extent to which they practiced and adhered to their religion and its rituals, including attendance at services. The synagogue school played an important role in the maintenance of Jewish identification. The local community had evolved all manner of secular organizations, partly as a reaction against antisemitism. The fact that the Osnabrücker Tennis Association did not allow Jews as members led to the establishment of a Jewish Tennis Association. Similarly, the expulsion of Jewish members from the Osnabrück Sports Association in 1924 led to the foundation of Jewish Sports Association. However, we would be wrong to view Jewish society as completely distinct from the rest of the population. Jews played a major role in the Osnabrück economy, while some members of the minority joined the numerous *Vereine* in the town and had predominantly gentile friends.[22]

In fact, acculturation, assimilation and conversion played a major role in Jewish life from the emancipation period until the Third Reich, when Nazi racial policy ostracized Jews by creating a racial rather than a purely religious community. The above narrative has essentially focused upon the religious community which still recognized itself as such when the NSDAP seized power. But Jews also interacted positively with their Christian neighbours. Taking the example of Breslau, which had a much larger Jewish population than Osnabrück, Till van Rahden examined the relationship of its members with Protestants and Roman Catholics in the period 1860-1925. Although he admitted that antisemitism existed, he also demonstrated how the predominantly middle class grouping interacted with Christians by joining the same societies, developing friendships and, most significantly, intermarrying. He has spoken of a. situational ethnicity, which involved individuals holding multiple identities.[23] During the Weimar Republic between a tenth and a quarter of Jewish marriages involved a Christian partner, while the figure for Düsseldorf varied from 18 to 37 per cent,[24] again illustrating how well integrated Jews had become in German society by the 1920s. Between 1875 and 1932 a total of 53,000 mixed marriages occurred in Germany, while the Nazi census of 1939 listed 56,327 'fully Jewish' married couples and 20,454 mixed ones.[25]

Antisemitism During the Weimar Republic

Despite the level of acculturation, assimilation and multiculturalism which may have existed in Germany before 1933 'antisemitism was endemic to Weimar Germany'[26] and its manifestations countless, most potently in the form of violence,[27] although many Jews accepted it as part of their everyday life during this period.[28] In Osnabrück, the small size of the Jewish minority meant that it could offer less resistance than the more substantial communities in the larger cities. It appears that both the synagogue and the cemetery faced desecration in 1927.[29] Just before Christmas 1928 the NSDAP launched a campaign against Jewish shops, which involved the distribution of leaflets, one of which declared: 'Whoever gives his money to Jews, strikes himself with his own fists'. The leaflet asked: 'In fifty years time will the productive German live in backhouses and cellars?' Other leaflets called for a demonstration against department stores.[30]

In the last years of the Weimar Republic Jews still had power to defend themselves, which the Third Reich would take away. Following a pattern established at the end of the nineteenth century by the *Centralverein Deutscher Staatsbürger Jüdischen Glaubens*, an Osnabrück businessman, Ischel Schleimer took legal action against Otto Marxer and his publisher, Wilhelm Hildebrandt, for libelling him and other Jewish businessmen. He won the case resulting in a fine of RM220 for Marxer and RM20 for Hildebrandt.[31]

Although the Nazis continued their antisemitic activity between 1929 and 1933, the *Stadtwächter* became equally responsible for the spread of hatred of the Osnabrück Jews. Antisemitism represented a core theme in the propaganda of the group. It did not develop the racial sophistication of the Nazis, although similar ideas certainly surfaced, but focused, instead, upon the issues which concerned the local lower middle classes such as the financial power of the Jews, which would have played a large role in the spread of popular hostility towards this minority in the town. The front page of the *Stadtwächter* of 9 June 1929 declared: 'Germany in the Paws of International Capital'. A few weeks later the newspaper published an article which linked Jews with venereal disease amongst Germans.[32] Even more startling, pointing to the direction which the *Stadtwächter* would take, a text box appeared on 25 August, reading: 'Warning! Every Christian who takes even a penny to a Jew is a traitor to his religion and his people. He strengthens the power of the brutal Jewish slave holder.' In December 1929 the *Stadtwächter*, imitating the NSDAP campaign of the previous year declared: 'It is a true Christian duty to buy the symbols of love and the celebration of Christ's birth from Christians.'[33] In electioneering during the summer of 1930 the newspaper turned to another classic antisemitic stereotype, linking Jews with left wing politics and the SPD. An article on 'Jews in German Politics', spoke of their influence from Karl Marx to Walther Rathenau,[34] while another wrote of 'Social Democracy, the Guards of Jewish Capital'.[35] More menacingly, a piece entitled: 'The Jewish Question and its Solution' declared: 'the Jewish question violently demands a solution'.[36]

Such writing would have made Jews more conspicuous to those who had not thought about the position of this minority within the town. While documentary evidence does not survive to allow us to break down the readership of the *Stadtwächter*, we can assume that it was, to some extent, preaching to the converted, i.e. small shopkeepers, who felt threatened by the presence of Jewish department stores, a constituency to which the Nazis appealed.

The Elimination of the Jews

The antisemitism of the final years of the Weimar Republic prepared the way for the more dramatic actions of the Nazis. Germans elected a regime which turned the clock back. Initially, it simply went back to the middle of the eighteenth century, the period before emancipation but with the *Kristallnacht* pogrom of 1938, Germany had returned to medieval barbarity.

Once the War broke out, the Nazis moved forward to methods of murder unseen in European history as their march into Poland and the Soviet Union resulted in the introduction of factory killing. As Nazi racial policy would make clear, and as propaganda had indicated, the progress which Jews had made over the previous two centuries had become irrelevant. Although the NSDAP may have recognized that Jewish difference lay in religion, the basis of persecution lay in the racialization of this minority which drew upon the antisemitic ideas which had circulated since the end of the nineteenth century.[37] The evolution of legislation made sure that the Jews became a racial group. Under such circumstances the interaction between Jews and Gentiles which had characterized Weimar society, despite the rising Nazi party, became difficult.

The NSDAP acted against the Jews immediately after seizing power, using both legislation and force, a combination which directed all aspects of Nazi policy until the outbreak of the War.[38] Violence intensified throughout the country in the first few months of 1933,[39] although it does not seem to have surfaced in Osnabrück. However, the town, like the rest of the country, participated in Boycott Day on 1 April, called against Jewish businesses on 28 March, with the aim of forcing out Jews for the benefit of their rivals. Previous publicity, particularly in newspapers and posters outside Jewish shops, had alerted local residents in settlements throughout Germany, of the action before 1 April.[40]

The Osnabrück press reported the events. On 31 March we learn:

> The protest movement against Jewish businesses, lawyers and doctors began yesterday afternoon in Osnabrück, as in many other cities. At 4 pm SA people went to the businesses in question and erected display boards outside the entrances. At the same time a large gang marched through the streets with placards encouraging a boycott.[41]

On the day itself:

> At 10 o'clock there appeared SA people in uniform outside the shops in question carrying placards in their hands and placing them outside the shop windows advising about the character of the boycott and its necessity as a defence against the Jewish-Marxist foreign propaganda. In total 42 businesses in the town were affected by these measures. At the same time various persons who, despite the boycott, made purchases in the shops, had their pictures taken. In the morning the pictures taken on Friday were already being displayed in Kolkmeyer in Georgstrasse...

During the course of the morning a number of Jewish businessmen, doctors and lawyers were taken into protective custody and handed over to the political police.[42]

But those arrested soon regained their liberty as the Nazi regime did not use concentration camps for any length of time at this stage. Although some Germans displayed indignation at these actions,[43] the activities of 1 April did 'legitimise anti-Jewish measures in the economic field'. [44]

The street actions went together with legislation against the Jewish communities. The most significant measure at this stage consisted of the Law for the Restoration of the Professional Civil Service, which dismissed non-Aryans, overwhelmingly Jews, from government, including academic, employment.[45] This had a limited impact on Osnabrück Jewry because, as we have seen, the overwhelming majority of the local community worked as self employed businessmen. Perhaps the most important of the 400 measures introduced against the Jews were the Nuremberg Laws, which forbade Germans from marrying or having sexual relations with Jews, Romanies or black people and restricted citizenship to those with 'German blood'.[46] Those people who had mixed German and Jewish ancestry could claim citizenship depending on their level of Germanness.[47] The Nuremberg laws did more than any other legislation during the Third Reich to confirm the racialization of German society.

Between 1933 and 1938 Jews in most towns in the Reich lived a life which involved a level of stability despite a deterioration in their economic position and their constant victimization through propaganda, which could result in outbreaks of violence against them.[48] *Der Stürmer*, available in every town and village, made the status of the minority clear. Similarly, the entire population would have received reports of speeches by Hitler attacking Jews through the well developed newsreel and radio broadcasts.[49] Furthermore, numerous books appeared on them.[50]

Local antisemitic initiatives also emphasised the pariah status of the Jews, particularly through the publication of newspaper articles and the holding of rallies. While articles on the Jews did not appear on a regular basis in the Osnabrück press before November 1938, a daily trawl through the newspapers reveals some pieces attacking the Jews. Antisemitism also worked retrospectively, as revealed in an article in the *Osnabrücker Tageblatt* from 23 July 1936 linking an outbreak of theft in the town in 1769 with the arrival of 'Begging Jews'. Two years later, on 17 July 1938, the *Neue Volksblätter* published a piece from the *Völkische Beobachter* of the previous day, claiming to have discovered a paper revealing a Jewish plan to take over Germany and published with the front page headline of: 'A Document of Jewish Hatred'.

Antisemitic meetings must have terrified the local Jewish community. 'A Mass Rally on the Jewish Question' attracting 'between twenty-five and thirty thousand comrades' took place on 20 August 1935.[51] The main speakers at the meeting, Münzer and Kolkmeyer, concentrated upon the international and national power of the Jews, but also singled out local Jewish residents for attention.[52] Peter Longerich has described the events of 1935 as the 'second antisemtic wave', after the first when the Nazis seized power, representing the prelude to the Nuremberg Laws, passed in September, while the third phase lasted from the end of 1937 until the outbreak of the War, culminating in the pogrom of 1938.[53]

The economic existence of Jews changed fundamentally as a result of violence and measures passed in the first years of the Nazi regime. Former doctors and lawyers found that they could only make a living by turning to the pre-emancipation occupation of itinerant peddling. Others found themselves in poverty and consequently had to live off welfare benefits from the American Joint Distribution Committee and *Jüdische Winterhilfe* (Jewish Winter Help).[54] In Osnabrück those Jews who decided to stay made a living. Dr Fritz Lowenstein, for instance, continued to work as a medical practitioner until 1936, while Dr Ernst Jacobson still carried on as a lawyer until he committed suicide in October 1938 following the introduction of the ban on Jewish attorneys.[55] Despite pressure to persuade Germans to stop purchasing at Jewish establishments and attempts to pass all businesses into Aryan hands, many of the larger Jewish shops in Osnabrück survived until November 1938 but with a reduced turnover.[56] A police report covering August 1935 mentioned an organised boycott. 'People who set foot in Jewish shops were photographed. The pictures were displayed in public. Placards were placed outside Jewish businesses with inscriptions such as: "Jewish Shop! Whoever buys from here is a traitor to the people and will be publicly denounced"'. As the same report states, such actions had consequences:

In the first place the boycott has had an impact on the clothing shop Alsberg and Co. We are dealing with a concern which employs 151 people – including eight non-Aryans. The business has today witnessed a fall of 70 per cent in its daily takings and even more compared with the period before the boycott. The owner has already informed the *Regierungspräsident* in Osnabrück that he cannot carry on running the business under these circumstances.[57]

In September 1935 we learn that:

The propaganda for the purpose of defence against the Jews reported in the previous month has to a certain extent not failed in its aim. It is to be observed that the majority of the population are avoiding Jewish shops. Several Jewish business owners have consequently been struggling with business difficulties and some of them intend to sell their businesses.[58]

While the Nazi measures had a significant impact upon the economic activities of German Jews even before *Kristallnacht*, religious and social life continued to proceed almost as normal. Attendance at services rose amongst some individuals and communities who turned to God as the way to salvation. Meanwhile, theatre, music, art, film and sport continued, especially in larger Jewish centres with well developed cultural activities.[59] The Jewish organizations established before 1933, including the *Central Verein*, continued to exist and still displayed some defiance.[60]

Osnabrück police reports also reveal Jewish social and religious activity, most of which involved the Synagogue. On 1 October 1934 the Osnabrück branch of the Cultural League of German Jews held a meeting attended by 75 people and addressed by Dr Singer from Berlin on *Judas Macabaeus* with the help of a gramophone and a piano.[61] In January 1935 we learn of meetings held by the National League of Jewish Frontline Soldiers together with another organized by a Zionist group. The speaker at the latter, Dr Hans Capell from Düsseldorf, suggested emigration to Palestine as the only future for European Jews in view of the strength of antisemitism on the continent. Meanwhile, 'A Jewish religious teacher has established a history circle in Osnabrück, which meets on a weekly basis. Furthermore, the Cultural League of German Jews organized a chamber music evening'.[62]

The activities pursued by the Osnabrück Jews in 1934 and 1935 point to continuities with the late Weimar period. Yet the Zionist meeting suggests one possible means of salvation. Osnabrück Jews, like their counterparts throughout Germany, also reacted in other ways to the crisis facing them. Suicide became one way out. Although higher amongst Jews than Gentiles even before the Nazi era, it 'took on the character of a mass phenomenon' after 1933.[63] An inquiry into 230 suicides in Osnabrück between 1932 and 1942 revealed that three Jews had taken their lives, making up 1.2 per cent of such deaths when they counted under 0.5 per cent of the population.[64]

Osnabrück Jews challenged Nazi legislation, particularly those who had Aryan ancestors, as revealed in several case files in the city archive. The muddled nature of Nazi policy towards '*Mischlinge*' encouraged such challenges, which occurred at all levels and through all possible means, including the use of the courts. Success would allow 'half-Jews' not only to escape from Nazi racial legislation but also, in consequence, to survive persecution.[65] However, the challenges sometimes failed. For instance, the Osnabrücker Moritz Vogel failed to have his adopted son Günther, born illegitimately to a Jewish mother in 1920, freed from the clauses of the Nuremberg Laws, meaning that Günther could not carry out labour service or progress to University. The decision by the Ministry of the Interior was made after a medical examination and a reconstruction of the family tree of Günther. The doctor who carried out the medical examination commented:

> Because of the good physical and personal disposition I have no hesitation in recommending the request to enter into labour service. I would also like to recommend the request to study at a German University. On the other hand I have hesitations about the request for later entry into the civil service. In any case from my own personal point of view despite the positive characteristics of Günther Vogel I am not sympathetic to the idea that German girls and boys may in future be taught by a half Jew.[66]

Some Jews simply ignored Nazi legislation, or actually stood up to the regime, which would result in a prison sentence. For instance, 'On 23/7/35 a Jewess was arrested and taken into custody for seven days for disturbing the peace. She insulted the SA in the foulest way.'[67] Two years later Siegmund Storch received a prison sentence of 1 year and five months for having sexual relationships with 2 women.[68]

Table 7.1: Decline of the Size of Osnabrück Jewry.

Date	Number of Synagogue Members
1 January 1933	457
22 November 1934	403
1 October 1936	198
15 November 1937	186
26 October 1938	182
17 May 1939	119
15 February 1941	69

Source: Peter Junk and Martina Sellmeyer, *Stationen auf dem Weg nach Auschwitz: Entrechtung, Vertreibung, Vernichtung: Juden in Osnabrück* 3rd edition (Osnabrück, 2000), p. 73.

Many Jews decided to emigrate,[69] a path which many from the Osnabrück community followed, largely due to its small size, which meant that it could not rely on safety in numbers. Movement from the town did not simply take place abroad, but to other German cities with more significant Jewish populations. Osnabrück Jewry therefore shrunk dramatically by the time of *Kristallnacht*, in contrast to the larger communities, which survived. The percentage decline in Munich, for instance, was less than thirty per cent during the whole period.[70] About 150,000 of the 520,000 Jews living in Germany in 1933 had left the country by the start of 1938.[71] Peaks of emigration occurred at times of greatest fear for the Jewish community such as the spring of 1933 and the immediate aftermath of the passage of the Nuremberg Laws.[72]

Surviving *Gestapo* index cards allow the reconstruction of the decline of Osnabrück Jewry before 1938, as well as a tabulation of the destinations of individuals.[73] The most striking fact about emigration is that most of it occurred between November 1934 and October 1936. This period witnessed the antisemitic campaign of the summer of 1935 and the passage of the Nuremberg Laws in November of that year, both of which clearly had an impact. From their detailed researches on individual Jewish residents of Osnabrück, Junk and Sellmeyer have divided the fate of Jews according to their different geographical destinations as indicated in Table 7.2, which confirms the picture in Table 7.1 of most Jews escaping from Osnabrück but not necessarily, in the longer run, surviving the Nazis if they moved to other German towns or to Holland.

An examination of a few individuals will bring to life the emigration statistics. The Katzmann family of Möserstrasse 43 fell apart as a result of emigration. The parents Hermann and Paula still lived in Osnabrück at the start of the War. The first son, Siegfried, born in 1912, moved to Münster on 19 June 1933 and then further on to Basel on 10 June 1936. Their daughter Emmi, born in 1913, eventually migrated to Palestine in March 1938, where she probably joined her younger siblings Frietel and Liesel, who had already moved there. Hete-Margret, born in 1919, went to Wartebach in 1936 and then on to Cologne.[74] The Oppenheimer family also experienced a similar fate. The widow Emma moved to Cloppenburg in April 1935. She followed her eldest daughter who initially went to Berlin in 1933 and then to Cloppenburg where she got married in April 1934. Ingeborg Oppenheimer moved to Ludwigshaven in 1933, then returned to Osnabrück after a stay of six months, before migrating to Bremen in May 1935. Siegfried Oppenheimer eventually moved to South Africa, while W. Oppenheimer went to Hengelo on 10 September 1935.[75]

Table 7.2: The Fate of Osnabrück Jewry

Remained in Osnabrück	**106**
Number who died in the town	27
Number who committed suicide	2
Number murdered in Buchenwald in 1938	1
Number deported to Poland in 1938 and murdered there	4
Deported	66
Victims of euthanasia	1
Survived in Osnabrück	5
Migrated to other towns	**189**
Number who died there	5
Number who emigrated	82
Number deported	38
Fate unknown	64
Emigrated to Holland	**83**
Number who died in Holland	5
Number who committed suicide	1
Number who emigrated further	20
Number deported	40
Number who survived	11
Fate unknown	6
Emigrated to France	**4**
Number who emigrated further	3
Emigrated to Spain	**3**
Number who emigrated further	3
Emigrated to Shanghai	**3**
Number who emigrated further	3
Emigrated to Palestine	**44**
Emigrated to the USA	**43**
Emigrated to South America	**17**
Emigrated to Austria	**3**
Emigrated to Sweden	**4**
Emigrated to Denmark	**1**
Emigrated to Italy	**5**
Emigrated to England	**19**

Source: Peter Junk and Martina Sellmeyer, *Stationen auf dem Weg nach Auschwitz: Entrechtung, Vertreibung, Vernichtung: Juden in Osnabrück* 3rd edition (Osnabrück, 2000), pp. 72-3.

Those Jews remaining in Osnabrück in November 1938 would experience the full rage of Nazism. After the passage of the Nuremberg Laws in November 1935 Nazi antisemitism had reached something of a lull in the following two years, partly due to the desire not to alienate international opinion during the 1936 Berlin Olympics. However, by the end of 1937 and, more especially, the start of 1938, this had changed, partly because, despite the official antisemitism and the violence which had taken place, 'Jews in Germany at the end of 1937 were still relatively well off in economic terms'.[76] Although the 50,000 Jewish businesses which existed in Germany at the start of 1933 had declined to 9,000 by July 1938, this was too many for the Nazi leadership.[77]

The invasion of Austria and the subsequent *Anschluss* gave a boost to antisemitism in 1938. It had allowed antisemitism there, historically as strong as in Germany, to bring forth resentments which had boiled for decades, to overflowing, resulting in public humiliation of the most exalted Jews, as well as widespread violence and property damage.[78] These events gave momentum to antisemitic policy, as further measures followed during the summer and autumn, making it increasingly difficult for Jews to continue their businesses, banning them from practising as doctors and lawyers, forcing them to take the name Israel for males and Sara for females, and making it compulsory for them to have their passports stamped with a 'J'.[79]

On 7 November Herschel Grynzpan, a Polish Jew, murdered Ernst vom Rath, an official at the German Embassy in Paris. The Nazi press publicised this event and the party hierarchy communicated with local SA branches suggesting that they attack Jewish property.[80] This led to a nationwide explosion of antisemitic violence on the night of 9-10 November, which resulted in the destruction of 7,500 shops and more than 250 synagogues, as well as 236 deaths, affecting Jewish communities throughout the country.[81]

A series of sources allow us to reconstruct the lead up and aftermath of *Kristallnacht* in Osnabrück. Just before the murder of Ernst vom Rath the local newspapers had carried stories about Jews. For instance, on 5 November the *Neue Volksblätter* reported 'Thousands of Jews Expelled Over the Border. Energetic Measures of the Slovakian Government – Boycott Movement By the Population'. On 11 November its main front page headline declared: 'Saturday Funeral Service for Ernst vom Rath'. Meanwhile, the *Osnabrücker Tageblatt* had as its front page headline on 8 November: 'Cowardly Jewish Murder Attempt. Attack in the German Embassy in Paris – German Embassy Secretary Severely Injured by Two Shots'.

As to the actual damage caused to Jewish property, the two newspapers carried short stories. The *Neue Volksblätter*, under the headline of 'Thus Answer The People. Justified Revolt in Osnabrück', ran an article, which began: 'The sad news from Paris that a young life full of hope had fallen victim to a cowardly treacherous Jewish murder led to justified and remarkable rage even in Osnabrück.' It then described the damage caused by rioters:

> The inside of the Synagogue was destroyed and burnt out. The spontaneous Jew hating demonstration then turned against the last Jewish businesses and wholesale firms in Osnabrück. The shop windows were smashed and the goods put in safe keeping. In the earliest hours of the morning the justifiably enraged comrades gathered before the Jewish businesses in order to see how the goods were taken to safety on lorries.[82]

The report of the violence in the *Osnabrücker Tageblatt* provided less rhetoric and more information on the damage caused by the rioters.

> The spontaneous anti-Jewish actions were initiated shortly after midnight with the 'smoking out' of the synagogue in Rolandstrasse. A part of the interior decorations and the pews were burnt. The Star of David was taken away from the dome. Enormous placards indicating the status of the Jews as the enemy of the world were placed before the synagogue. The demonstration then turned against the still existing Jewish businesses, whose windows were destroyed: shop and shop window display contents remained undisturbed, however. The furious crowd also turned its attention against the homes of individual Jews. The Jews still resident here were taken from their homes during the course of the night and placed into protective custody; without causing them any injury; women and children were obviously left in their homes.[83]

The events of the night of 9-10 November represented the high point of pre-War antisemitism. They combined with official measures to speed up persecution and eradication of Jews from the German economy. The newspaper campaign which had begun in early November continued throughout the month. The *Neue Volksblätter* carried stories about the decision to eliminate Jews from German economic life,[84] as well as another one about the sentencing of Hermann Behr to five years in prison for having a sexual relationship with a German woman.[85] The *Osnabrücker Tageblatt* printed stories about international opinion and the Jews.[86]

As many as 30,000 German Jews faced arrest after the pogrom. They found themselves taken to the camps in Dachau, Buchenwald and Sachsenhausen. Although the surviving internees were released by the spring of 1939, up to 2,500 may have died within them due to a typhus epidemic and mistreatment by guards.[87] Those who faced arrest included the Osnabrücker Sigfried Heimbach, who was actually in Münster at the time. His daughter, Irmgard, recalled: 'The *Gestapo* knocked on our door and wanted to know where my father is. My mother had to give the address. He was put in jail in a really small prison in a village. We travelled there and could take him food every day.'[88]

The other major consequence of *Kristallnacht* consisted of the decision to eliminate Jews from German economic life. On 12 November Goebbels compelled Jews to sell all their enterprises and valuables. On the same day Göring ordered that all Jewish business activity should cease from 1 January.[89] A list from 1 November indicates the existence of 13 surviving Jewish commercial establishments in Osnabrück but a report from 23 December indicates that virtually none of these functioned by then.[90] A communication of 9 March 1939 indicates that: 'The warehouse of the firm Samson David has been sold for RM77,000. Of this sum the retail trade organization must pay RM27,000 and the firm Nobbe RM50,000. RM67,000 of the entire price has been payed up to now.'[91] By the outbreak of War the local state, following the national pattern, had 'aryanized' virtually all business activity in Osnabrück.[92] On 2 March even the land upon which the synagogue stood faced auction.[93] An examination of the businesses in Grosse Strasse indicates some of the changes which took place in ownership during the Nazi years. Most notably, one of the largest department stores in the town, at numbers 27-9, had changed from Alsberg and Co. to Lengermann and Trieschmann.[94]

After November 1938 Jews also faced expulsion from schools and from the general welfare system and could not enter some public spaces. Furthermore they could no longer drive or use university libraries and faced segregation.[95] A dramatic increase therefore occurred in the level of Jewish emigration. Despite obstacles put up by the Nazis and the reluctance of other states to accept Jews, about 115,000 left in the final ten months of peace.[96] As Table 7.1 indicates, 63 people fled from Osnabrück in the six months after *Kristallnacht*, leaving a community of just 119 by May 1939.

The outbreak of War meant a further deterioration in the position of those Jews remaining in German towns. In Osnabrück the local newspapers continued to peddle antisemitic propaganda against the background of the decision making process which would result in the deportation of German Jewry to death and labour camps in eastern Europe. The propaganda peaked in August and September 1941 centring around an exhibition and mass meeting on the theme of 'The Enemy of the World'.[97] Some normality continued in the everyday life of Jews, although this remained confined within the boundaries set by the Nazis. Irmgard Ohl still attended school in Münster until 1941, while her father, who had previously worked as a railway employee, found himself employed in a factory and then stone breaking. As a result of the implementation of a curfew for Jews, 'One had to be at home by 8, by 7 in the winter.'[98]

The deportation of Osnabrück Jewry occurred in several stages, the main one on 13 December 1941. Irmgard Ohl and her parents received a letter about a month beforehand informing them that they would face transportation to Riga and that they could take 50 kilos of luggage with them:

> We were picked up by the *Gestapo* a few days beforehand and taken to the elementary school in Pottgraben. The children were told that they had a few days off school because the heating was busted. Straw was spread out in the gym. We spent the night there. The next day we had to get on the train.

She eventually reached Riga three days later without her luggage and worked in various camps during the War. When asked how the *Gestapo* explained the events in Osnabrück, she replied: 'To labour service. But how, what for and where to didn't really exist.'[99] The Osnabrück *Kriegs-Chronik* described the deportation of 13 December in matter of fact terms:

> In the whole of the Reich people have set about to expel the Jews, if they still remain, beyond German borders and to send them to the eastern zones. Osnabrück also got rid of its Jews today. At 9.30 today the transport started moving out of the station with Riga as its destination. Only those who were over sixty years old, or who were married to an Aryan person as well as those who were sick were allowed to remain.[100]

A total of 34 Osnabrück Jews left on this day, joined by others from locations throughout the *Regierungsbezirk*, so that 205 people boarded the train.[101] On 31 July 1942 another transport took 28 Osnabrück Jews to Theresienstadt.[102] Of those people deported during the War, 35 had died in the Baltic states and 27 in Theresienstadt, while 5 had returned from Riga, together with 4 from Auschwitz and Theresienstadt.[103] The Nazis also intensified their efforts against '*Mischlinge*' after the outbreak of War which meant the arrest of people with mixed ethnic origins and the loss of employment for others.[104] The Osnabrück `half-Jew', Paul Wiesenthal, lost his position as a teacher and found himself forced to work in armaments production with the Teutonwerk.[105]

Osnabrück Jewry therefore virtually disappeared by 1945, following the pattern throughout Germany. At the close of 1944 just 14,574 full Jews lived within the German borders of 1937.[106] At the end of the War the number of Jews in Germany actually began to increase. Releases from concentration camps meant that about 50,000 lived within the territories of pre-War borders, although this had fallen to just 30,000 within a few weeks because of high death rates.[107] By 1947 the number of Jews in Germany had actually grown to about 200,000, originating mostly from Poland, which experienced serious antisemitic pogroms. The Jews in Germany at the end of the War, particularly those who had spent time in concentration camps, were barely alive because of the physical and psychological trauma from which they had emerged.[108]

Although just a handful of Jews survived in Osnabrück, their numbers increased in the early post-War years. By February 1946 a total of 64 lived in the city, consisting of 31 with German nationality and 33 foreigners.[109] The second figure receives partial explanation from the presence of Jewish prisoners of war amongst Yugoslavs held in a camp in the suburb of Eversburg during the conflict.[110] Those with German nationality included Irmgard Ohl who returned to Osnabrück with her mother in July 1945 and would subsequently marry a Christian.[111] On 19 August the opening ceremony of the synagogue took place in Rolandstrasse, which then held weekly services.[112]

The history of Osnabrück Jewry from the end of the Weimar Republic until the late 1940s therefore resembles Jewish communities throughout Germany, particularly smaller ones. To use the phrases of Junk and Sellmeyer, they lost their civil rights and then faced expulsion and extermination. Nevertheless, these phrases do not account for every Osnabrück Jew, as some survived through emigration. Unlike other locations, Jewry did not vanish forever from the town as a result of the actions of the Nazis but survived, albeit much smaller in size, to continue after the War.

Individual Action and the Persecution and Elimination of Osnabrück Jewry

Osnabrück Jewry did not disappear simply because of the passage of legislation but also as a result of the actions of ardent bureaucrats and Nazis. Documentation from two trials which took place after the War allows a reconstruction of the burning of the synagogue in 1938 and the deportations to eastern Europe. The evidence available would point to the efficiency of the bureaucratic machine, and particularly the individuals who controlled it, as central for the elimination of Osnabrück Jewry.

The trial of those involved in the burning of the synagogue occurred in December 1949 and included most of the leading figures in the Nazi hierarchy in Osnabrück, identified at the scene of the action by witnesses. The most surprising decision reached by the court concerned *Kreisleiter* Münzer, whom the jury accepted did not play a role in the burning and may not even have had knowledge of the event. The main culprit consisted of Erwin Kolkmeyer, who, however, received a prison sentence of just ten months because much of the evidence against him was rejected. Seven other men faced sentences of ten months or less for participating in the *Kristallnacht* disturbances and their aftermath.[113]

Between 1965 and 1967 in the aftermath of the Frankfurt Auschwitz Trial[114] an investigation took place into those responsible for the deportation of Osnabrück Jews, in connection with the trial of Anton Weiß-Bollandt, head of the local *Gestapo* between 1940 and 1942. The enquiry placed the blame on the shoulders of *Gestapo* employees, who seem to have totalled no more than 47, covering the entire *Regierungsbezirk* during the period 1938-45 and confirming the small numbers of people actually needed for the enforcement of racial policy as revealed by Gellately in his study of Düsseldorf.[115] To Gellately this indicated the compliance of the local population in racial policy. The investigation into Osnabrück provided more information on the fate of the Jews, as well as the mechanics of deportation and its precise dates, than it did on the work of local officials. Nevertheless, it concluded that 9 individuals had direct responsibility for the transportations. The two responsible for Jewish matters had died by then. As to the others, the investigation declared that they could not have had full knowledge of the fact that the deportees would die when they reached their final destination. Section 2 of the Osnabrück *Gestapo*, responsible for the 'Control of Political Opponents' had organized the deportations. The investigation interviewed twenty *Gestapo* employees, together with 14 of their victims. As in the case of all such trials of former Nazis, most of those questioned did not admit to having knowledge of the ethnic cleansing of the local Jewish population, and none of them accepted responsibility.[116] Fritz Kicker, a criminal secretary and an SS leader, admitted to knowing about the deportation which took place to Riga in December 1941, but claimed that the *Gestapo* office had never discussed this action. He also stated that he did not know about the ultimate fate of those making the journey.[117]

The death of the two *Gestapo* employees directly responsible for Jewish matters allowed their *Gestapo* colleagues to blame them. But the final report of the investigation connected with the trial of Weiß-Bollandt concluded that, while *Gestapo* employees knew of the deportations to eastern Europe, they did not necessarily know the fate of the Jews once they arrived at their destination. The report listed sixteen people who had knowledge of the transportation including Weiß-Bollandt, and the leader of the section 2 of the Gestapo, Heinrich Landwehr. While the process of eliminating Osnabrück Jewry may have followed the national pattern, these individuals had clearly overseen the implementation of Nazi antisemitic policy.

The Death of Inter-Ethnic Relations:
Attitudes Towards Jews After 1933

According to Raul Hilberg, 'In the course of the onslaught on European Jewry, some people in the non-Jewish population helped their Jewish neighbours, many more did or obtained something at the expense of the Jews, and countless others watched what had come to pass'.[118] Other scholars who have focused more directly upon Germany have recognized different levels of compliance and varying reactions at different stages of the antisemitic campaign and ethnic cleansing within Germany.[119] As the case of Osnabrück has revealed, the local population played a role in the campaigns which took place, either by not buying at Jewish shops or by attending some of the local rallies. If 25,000 people really did turn up at the meeting held in August 1935, this would have meant a high level of local participation even if they came from throughout the *Regierungsbezirk*. Others clearly benefited from the sale of Jewish businesses. On the other hand, some individuals ignored the wishes of the Nazis and continued to purchase at Jewish shops as long as they survived.

The researches of Kershaw, Bankier and Gellately suggest limited resistance to Nazi antisemitic policies.[120] Bankier, who points out that it 'was much easier to conform than to swim against the stream' also states that, although 'in general the public recognized the necessity of some solution to the Jewish problem, large sectors found the form of persecution abhorrent.'[121] Thus, for instance, after *Kristallnacht*: 'All sections of the population reacted with deep shock', confirmed by Kershaw in his study of Bavaria.[122] Nevertheless, this negative reaction did not go as far as to manifest itself in public hostility towards the regime, especially after the Germans had seen what the NSDAP could do with its enemies. When moving on to the War, Bankier claims that the majority of Germans were openly hostile to Jews and that they knew of the deportations, especially in small communities where 'people do not just vanish unnoticed'.[123] Kershaw concludes that most Germans did not care about the fate of the Jews in the War, although they probably knew about what happened to them.[124] Gellately, who also devotes much attention to informers, concludes that knowledge of what was happening 'got through in bits and pieces'.[125]

How does the population of Osnabrück fit into these patterns? The lack of archival material of the type used by Kershaw and Gellately, makes our task difficult. Few police reports survive after 1936, as in the case of Bavaria, while we do not have the extant *Gestapo* files from Düsseldorf and Würzburg used by Gellately. However, cards kept by the local *Gestapo* do survive. A sample of 80 revealed two individuals dealt with by the secret police for matters relating to the persecution of the Jews. For instance, during the peak of antisemitism in the summer of 1935, Pastor Johannes Bornschein, held a sermon in which he declared: 'The Jews, yes we can relate to them as we wish. The Jews are the chosen people of the Lord'. Bornschein does not seem to have paid any penalty for this.[126] On the other hand Paul Gerhardus was 'warned in the severest of terms' in March 1939 for describing the 'action against the Jews' as 'vulgar'.[127] Informers must have reported on both of these individuals.

Interviews represent another way of gauging reaction to antisemitic policies. These present problems, above all the time lag. More importantly, the sample proves problematic. Jew haters would not wish to speak about their views in the Federal Republic, which has made antisemitism illegal. In addition, all of those interviewed were either adolescents or children for much of the regime, so we cannot really expect them to have carried out heroic acts. As 'bystanders', their views do confirm the ideas of Bankier, Kershaw and Gellately. Most were disgusted by *Kristallnacht*, although some stared at the synagogue. As a mostly middle class sample, many had Jewish friends or acquaintances, and knew of their persecution and often their fate. Some of them carried out small acts of resistance.

The interviewees either brought up the subject of the Jews themselves or were directly asked about them. The most vivid memories concern *Kristallnacht*, which remained fixed for several people, most notably Maria Grün, born in 1922:

We found out about it at very close quarters because we lived in Arndtstraße. There was a crossroads, Rolandstraße, in which a very big synagogue stood...My mother woke us in the night and said children come now the synagogue is burning. It was an unbelievable atmosphere...In front of the synagogue sat the synagogue director and all who belonged to it in one corner and we all knew that they were to be taken away, we all knew it more or less. It was terrible.[128]

The younger Karl Mosse, born in 1930, remembered making his way to school the morning after *Kristallnacht*.

One morning – I still really remember very exactly – we were going through the shopping streets of Osnabrück to school, my friend and I, and we saw how the Jewish businessmen were destroyed and plundered...

We were terrified and did not know what had happened but there were people who whispered and explained what they had experienced. We also heard that and we also then soon learnt that the synagogue had been set alight. That did not lie on our way to school but on the way back we passed by because we wanted to know what had happened and it was really terrible.[129]

Günther Adam, meanwhile, claimed that he had been at the synagogue the night it burnt down and remembers a man from the SA or SS climbing on to the roof and throwing down the star of David.[130]

All interviewees knew of the persecution of the Jews and were aware of their disappearance or their emigration, especially if they had connections with them. Werner Funk, for instance, recalled the fate of several personal and family Jewish friends.[131] Similarly Heinrich and Elisabeth Wand spoke of Jews whom they knew simply not being there anymore.[132]

Hilde Scholl, born in 1920, went out of her way to avoid conforming to Nazi racial policies on a couple of occasions:

My mother and I were travelling with the tram and on one seat sat a Jew. One could tell. And in front of me stood such an SA man, so clothed in brown and the woman said to him: 'Sit yourself down on this empty seat'. He said to her: 'You can't expect me to sit next to a Jew!' And what did I do there? I sat down there. Because I felt sorry for the Jew. That really didn't have anything to do with politics. It only made me sorry because he said that.

She also recalled:

Once my friend and I wanted to buy a swimming costume. That was that, that one shouldn't buy from Jews. And in the window of the shop that is now Lengermann, lay a swimming costume that she wanted. I then said to her: 'Then let's just go in. Then you can buy it.' The big shop was empty. Nobody was inside. Then a salesman came and said to us, although we knew, that we should not buy from him. 'Yes', said my friend, 'we have also already heard that, but I want to have the swimming costume'.[133]

These were fairly petty childish acts, which made little difference to Nazi policy, but suggest the extent of inter-ethnic relations in a state which forbade them.

Conclusion

The history of Osnabrück Jewry reflects the development of communities in urban locations throughout Germany between the 1920s and the 1940s, particularly smaller settlements. The example of Osnabrück allows us to trace the rise of antisemitism, the emigration movement, the deportations and the situation immediately after the end of the War.

Osnabrück Jewry in this period remained isolated during the years under consideration. While some of the middle class interviewees had Jewish friends, the majority of the population had little contact with this minority other than when they used their shops, a pattern reflected in the country as a whole. Local newspaper and police reports suggest that much of the population harboured antisemitic grudges, indicated by the campaign which reached its peak in the summer of 1935. Similarly, while some individuals continued to buy from Jewish shops, many did not.

When it comes to actual participation in antisemitic acts only a small percentage of people involved themselves in Jew baiting or violence in 1933 or 1938. All of the evidence from *Kristallnacht* points to the fact that a small number of local Nazis carried out the destruction. As Kershaw and Bankier make clear, most of the population found such acts intolerable, even though they may have sympathised with milder forms of antisemitism.

It also seems obvious that the population of Osnabrück knew what was happening. Certainly before 1939 when the propaganda meant that people could not get away from the fact that the new regime hated the Jews. Similarly, responses to interview questions also make it clear that local residents had a fairly good idea that Jews were disappearing even though they may not have known what happened to them. However, inter-ethnic relations had virtually ceased after 1933, certainly in contrast to the Weimar Republic, when intermarriage had been normal.

Osnabrück may differ from some of the larger Jewish communities in the country because the small numbers meant that people had more desire to get out, even if this just meant moving to a larger Jewish community somewhere else in the country. Nevertheless, the Jews here did not completely disappear. A few survived at the end of the War, partly helped by the presence of Yugoslav officers. Consequently, a small community developed after 1945, based on the one which existed before 1933.

8

THE CONTINUITY OF ANTI-ROMANY DISCRIMINATION

Historical and Historiographical Background

The mass of research by local historians which has focused upon both ethnic majorities and minorities in Osnabrück during the Nazi period has ignored the Romanies. This does not reflect the situation on the national level because, although this minority may not have received the same amount of attention as its Jewish contemporaries, scholars have increasingly looked at it. Interestingly, many of the studies published about the Romanies have not simply concentrated upon the Nazi years, but have contextualized the genocidal events of the War within the history of persecution both before and after the Third Reich, bringing out the continuities. Local studies have also begun to appear, although these tend to concentrate simply upon the Nazi period.

Any discussion of the Romanies in Germany before, during and after the Nazis has to recognize that, in contrast to Jews, they did not have an ambivalent relationship with German society. We could not say that a dichotomy existed between integration and rising hostility towards them. The nineteenth century did not witness the emancipation of the Romanies, who remained outsiders. Part of the reason for this lay in their social status, which meant that they did not impact upon the higher echelons of German society in the same way as Jews did. When contact took place between the ethnic majority and Romanies, it usually did so either because of itinerant trading or because of arrest and persecution by the police.[1]

All of the scholars who have worked upon the German Romanies have recognized the continuation in their position, especially those who have taken a longer term perspective. But even those who have 'just' written on the Nazi period recognize the importance of the historical background for the evolution of NSDAP policy towards this group. Unlike the persecution of the Jews, which needed a series of legal measures to expel them from the mainstream, Romanies already lived a marginal existence, as modernization had largely passed them by. The first major academic study to focus just upon the Nazi persecution of Romanies appeared in 1964, written by Hans-Joachim Döring.[2] In 1972 there followed a volume written by two English scholars, Donald Kenrick and Grattan Puxon.[3] Ulrich König also focused upon the Third Reich in his 1989 book.[4] More recently, two books have appeared on the subject, one in German and one in English. The former, by Michael Zimmermann, a monumental work, will probably remain the standard volume on the subject for some time to come.[5] These national studies are unusual in their focus upon the Nazi period because most volumes on the Gypsies contextualize their persecution within the history of the German nation state.[6] The leading authority on the continuity of persecution of this group consists of Joachim S. Hohmann, who has produced numerous volumes on this ethnic minority in Germany.[7] Hohmann represents just one example of the many scholars taking the long-term approach. This assertion applies to both general histories of the Romanies,[8] as well as books which focus upon specific aspects of their development.[9] Scholars working in the English language have equally taken this approach. In addition to Kenrick and Puxon these have included Ian Hancock, David M. Crowe, Susan Tebbutt and Gilad Margalit.[10]

This long term perspective points to an acceptance amongst scholars working on German Romanies that the crimes of the Nazis simply represent the pinnacle of persecution. This position not only accepts that hostility existed before the Third Reich, but that it has also remained into the post-War period. Indeed, as Kirsten Martin-Heuß pointed out, some of the same researchers who carried out work on Romanies under the Nazis continued to do so after 1945.[11] Margalit's recent pioneering study has outlined in detail the difficulty which Gypsies have had in persuading the German authorities about the persecution which they suffered during the War, particularly compared with the Jews.[12]

The local studies of Sinti and Roma in Germany have not usually taken such a long-term perspective. Several have appeared on the consequences of the Third Reich for the local Romanies, but not to the extent to which they have done for the Jews. Good examples exist on Frankfurt, Munich and Düsseldorf.[13] The explanation for this fact may simply lie in the absence of material for any period outside the Third Reich. In addition, it would also point to the lack of interest in the Romanies compared with the Jews and probably also indicates the continuing hostility towards Sinti and Roma at the local level. Furthermore, as one of the least literate groups in German society, they are unlikely to write their own history, in contrast to the Jews, one of the most educated.

We therefore come to the history of the Osnabrück Romanies. No single reason exists for the lack of attention which local historians have devoted to them. Certainly, the points made in the previous paragraph may apply. The most important explanation may simply lie in the small numbers of people concerned, although this seems an inadequate justification in view of the fact that only 435 Jews lived in the town when the Nazis came to power. It proves difficult to find the exact number of Romanies resident in Osnabrück, but, as the documents below make clear, they appear to have totalled around fifty in the early stages of the War. This, however, has not prevented the city administration from erecting the plaque in the town square which commemorates those deported to Auschwitz. The lack of attention devoted to the Gypsies may be connected with the more general attitudes which exist towards them, although whether this extends to academics remains difficult to prove. The most convincing explanation may simply consist of a lack of evidence, although we would need to link this with the smaller numbers and, just as importantly, the relative social position of the Romanies when compared with the Jews, as the latter represented the richest ethnic group in the town, which meant that their disappearance made more of an impact than that of the Sinti and Roma, the poorest. In the time spent researching on Osnabrück, little information materialized on the Romanies other than the few specific, but extremely revealing, official documents directly relating to them, discussed below.

Local newspapers, tightly controlled under the Nazis, paid little attention to the Romanies between 1929 and 1949. Of the people interviewed only Gerhard Strauß, born in 1936, claimed that he could remember, what he described as, burning Gypsy wagons following an allied bombing raid in 1942, but had no recollection of the people who owned them. Like the rest of the interviewees, he had no other memories of this group.[14]

Not even the local *Gestapo* cared much about the Gypsies, as the published reports edited by Steinwascher indicate. The main concerns of the security police essentially consisted of public order, sedition and reactions to Nazi policies. Only one reference to Romanies seems to exist, concerned with security issues, although the extract below indicates that the local *Gestapo* regarded them as a longstanding problem:

The Gypsy plague remains a recurring complaint of the police authorities. It is nothing short of astonishing, how the Gypsies have managed to succeed in the Third Reich. The rural population is regularly cheated by the swindling of the Gypsies. In addition, there exists in the same region the problem that the Gypsies may develop connections with prisoners and concentration camp inmates and help them to escape. The possibility of espionage in the Krupps rifle range in Meppen also cannot be ignored. I have therefore for the time being put through an order to the local authorities which are adjacent to shooting galleries or camps forbidding the passage of Gypsies and travelling foreigners. Apart from that I will make extensive use of the forthcoming police information week in March to instruct the population on the way of behaving towards Gypsies. Even if the living space of Gypsies can be limited in this way, the Gypsy mischief must be treated at the Reich level in order to bring an end to it.[15]

The historical context illustrates the reality of life for Romanies in the modern German nation state, involving exclusion and persecution. Sinti and Roma first reached German soil at the start of the fifteenth century. Despite the level of hostility which they have experienced throughout their presence in German lands, their numbers have always remained small. At the end of the nineteenth century about 2,000 lived in the country, a figure which had increased to 14,000 by 1926 and 30,000 by the outbreak of the War after the incorporation of Austria and the Sudetenland into the Nazi Empire.[16]

Under the *Kaiserreich*, the issue of the 'Gypsy plague' received attention in *Reichstag* debates, as well as in the discussions of local assemblies.[17] The Bavarian police displayed particular hostility towards the Romanies.[18] Legislation under the *Kaiserreich* required Sinti and Roma to have a trading licence, while another act separated Romany children from their parents if they did not attend school. Such measures had the traditional underlying anti-Romany aim of forcing the group to become sedentary.[19]

The attitude towards and, consequently, the position of Romanies did not change under the more liberal Weimar Republic. At the end of the First World War the opponents of this minority claimed that its members had done well out of the conflict as a result of currency and horse dealing. More generally, stereotypes circulated about Romanies as aimless wanderers who were dirty and lazy and made their living from begging, stealing and prostitution.[20] In 1926 the Bavarian Law for the Combatting of Gypsies, Travellers and the Workshy focused particularly on movement and the education of children.[21] Meanwhile, in 1927 the Prussian interior ministry decided to fingerprint all itinerant persons living within its borders. Two years later the police centre for the control of Gypsies set up in Munich under the *Kaiserreich* began operating upon a national level.[22] Despite the implementation of such measures no documents seem to exist in local, regional or national archives on the Romany population of Osnabrück before 1933, although we must assume that they fell victim to similar official persecution.

Early Nazi Measures

The legitimisation of persecution as a result of the racialization of the state formed the background to the implementation of new measures. Although Hitler said little about the Gypsies in *Mein Kampf*, they represented a racial enemy and, after 1933, the Nazis devoted much 'scientific' attention towards them. Nazi ideology regarded Romanies, like Jews, as a sexual threat, whose blood would corrupt that of Germans, although much of the hostility towards the Romanies lay in the historical suspicion of them as an asocial unassimilated group, which pursued an itinerant life style different from the sedentary population. A 1937 publication, written by an employee of the Racial Political Office of the NSDAP, Dr Otto Finger, which appeared in a series of books edited by the Institute for Inheritance and Race in Gießen, examined the lifestyles and make up of two Gypsy 'clans', detailing all the members of the two groups, which Finger claimed totalled several hundred people. Finger displayed concern about both the activities of the people he studied and their origins.[23] In fact, much of the new research of the Third Reich focused specifically upon the racial make up and antecedents of the Romanies, partly in an attempt to explain their 'asocial' behaviour. Several academics made their careers in this expanding field, most notably Robert Ritter, who, in 1936, established a Racial Hygiene and Population Biology Research Unit within the Ministry of Health in Berlin, which subsequently transferred to the Central Police Headquarters. Although Ritter became the most prominent Romany researcher in the Third Reich, several other scholars who held Chairs at German universities jumped on the bandwagon, including scientists, anthropologists and sociologists. Much dispute developed over the purity of the Romanies as a racial grouping. Consequently, many academics carried out physical measurements of Gypsies. In 1939-40, for instance, Karl Morawek worked on a research project in Austria which involved measuring the colour of 113 Romanies for the purpose of determining their racial characteristics. The work of these 'scientists' provided the 'evidence' for Nazi anti-Romany policy. During the War Ritter worked as an adviser deciding whether individuals constituted Romanies and whether they should face deportation to Auschwitz.[24]

Sterilization represented a pre-War method of dealing with the Romanies. In fact, about 2 per cent of those between the ages 14 and 50 may have undergone this operation under the Law for the Prevention of Hereditary Diseased Offspring passed in 1933, which aimed at all ethnic groups. This new form of ethnically based persecution went together with older, more traditional varieties of hostility towards the Romanies, which prevented movement and also meant inacarceration.[25] In September 1933 the SA and the SS arrested a small number of Romanies for begging and placed them in the concentration camps at Buchenwald, Dachau and Sachsenhausen.[26] The first years of Nazi rule also meant the extension of the 1926 Bavarian Law to cover the whole country, although several other regions introduced additional measures.[27]

Persecution of the Romanies increased from 1936. In that year, in the lead up to Olympic games, the police escorted all Berlin Romanies with their caravans and horses to a camp established in the suburb of Marzahn, where they would remain to carry out forced labour.[28] Another camp for Romanies also came into existence in Frankfurt in 1936 which was tightly controlled by the local police and whose inhabitants became subject to examination by a Frankfurt biological research institute.[29]

By the outbreak of the War the Nazis had prepared the way for the deportations and murders which would take place during the conflict. The year 1938 meant an intensification of persecution for Romanies as well as Jews. The Imperial Police Office in Berlin took over the task of dealing with the former on a nationwide basis.[30] In both 1938 and 1939 the number of Romanies in concentration camps, especially Buchenwald, Dachau and Sachsenhausen, increased.[31]

Nevertheless, a degree of normality remained so that 200 Romanies still lived in Munich at the outbreak of War, either in houses or caravans,[32] despite the history of Bavaria as the centre of Gypsy persecution in Germany. Missionary work also continued, certainly in the early years of the Nazi regime.[33] Similarly, the traditional Romany occupation of peddling survived until at least the late 1930s.[34] But Romanies lived in constant fear.[35]

How did the measures introduced by the Nazis manifest themselves in Osnabrück? The local sterilization files, which I consulted did not suggest that any of the victims consisted of Romanies, either from the names or from the information about the victims contained in the individual paperwork.[36] Most of the relevant files which survive from the pre-War Nazi years consist of police documentation and concern themselves particularly with the movement and activities of Romanies and other itinerants in the town and its surrounding areas. One file, covering the years 1933-41, gives details of people arrested for begging, although it does not seem clear if these consist of Romanies or not. A letter from the local police authorities to the *Regierungspräsident*, dated 10 October 1933, states that:

> ...a total of 58 persons have been brought to the attention of the police and passed on to the district court. Members of the SA, the SS and the *Stahlhelm* were brought in to fight the problem of begging in the second half of September...As a result of the measures introduced begging in the area covered by the city has declined very considerably.
>
> Begging, which until now took place under cover of musical events on public streets, paths and public spaces is scarcely to be seen any more.

In December the province of Hanover required all itinerants to have a registration book (*Wanderbuch*) in their possession. During 1935 and 1936 the Osnabrück police congratulated themselves on the success of the measures which they had taken against begging so that in 1937 only 12 people had faced arrest for this offence.[37]

At least one newspaper article appeared expressing hostility towards Romanies in the middle of the 1930s. Written by Ludwig Hoffmeyer, it points to the ingrained nature of anti-gypsy prejudice. Clearly influenced by the events occurring at the time, it carried the title of 'The Gypsy Plague 200 Years Ago'. Written in academic prose, rather than Nazi racial language, the piece provided details of Romanies in the Osnabrück region who had faced persecution during the eighteenth century. The article viewed the group as criminals who needed control.[38]

The Deportation of the Osnabrück Romanies

Measures introduced during the course of the 1930s meant the Romanies found themselves persecuted, stigmatised and marginalized in a more pronounced way than they had under previous systems of government. The War meant an intensification of all of the developments which the Nazis had begun before 1939 so that the racial state reached perfection during the War years, as revealed in the most startling documents on the Romanies in Osnabrück from our period.

Just after the outbreak of war a decree prevented Romanies from travelling within German territory and plans emerged to deport them to Poland, a process which began in April and May 1940 with the rounding up of Romanies in western Germany. As German troops marched into the Soviet Union at the end of 1941 the *Einsatzgruppen* began murdering Sinti and Roma there. By this time Romanies also faced deportation to concentration and forced labour camps established in eastern Europe, although most of those in Germany remained to face continually deteriorating conditions. The Nazis decided upon the 'final solution' to the Gypsy question in December 1942, which involved deportation to camps throughout Europe, including Auschwitz BIIe, which accounted for the death of 20,078 Sinti and Roma.[39]

Following the decision of December 1942, the major deportation of Romanies occurred in March of the following year resulting in the transportation of 22,600 people or 90 per cent of the German Romany population by the end of that month. German towns and smaller settlements therefore witnessed the eradication of this group from their midst. In Frankfurt, for instance, the action took place in the early morning of 9 March, resulting in the deportation of 99 people from a local camp and private houses to Auschwitz.[40]

Documentation in the NSO reveals that the major deportation of the Romanies from Osnabrück occurred on 1 March 1943.[41] The first paper gives a list of the 54 Sinti and Roma deported and comes with a covering note from the *Gestapo* in nearby Münster to the *Regierungspräsident* in Osnabrück, dated 24 May.

<u>List</u>

of gypsy persons deported to the concentration camp in Auschwitz on 1/3/1943.

<u>Osnabrück</u>
Weiß, Karl, 17.6.85, Blankenberg
 --, Berthold, 11.12.12 Wesel
 --, Elisabeth, 26.5.25 Osnabrück
 --, Bernhard, 26.7.30 Billstedt
 --, Karl Joseph, 29.12.26 Wissenbach
Lutz, Hulda, 24.8.1919 Riestedt
Weiß, Jakob, 20.6.08 Dortmund
 --, Johann, 3.1.07 Bernie
Schmidt, Anna, 7.3.06 Neudorf
 --, Berthold, 29.10.1935 Hamm
 --, Karl Heinz, 29.10.1935 Hamm
 --, Violetto, 21.2.1942 Osnabrück
Dusbaba, August, 13.7.1909, Breukeln
 --, born Weiß, Anna, 2.6.1910 Elberfeld
 --, Elisabeth, 26.2.1932 Osnabrück
 --, Ludwig, 26.7.1936 Osnabrück
 --, Karl, 24.5.1938 Osnabrück
 --, Anita, 29.6.1942 Osnabrück
 --, August, 15.5.1941 Osnabrück
Schmidt, Maria, 18.3.1902 Neuenkirchen
 --, Franziska, 25.9.1917 Ellingen
 --, Alma, 1.4.1919 Esens
 --, Josef, 16.8.1929 Hochstede
 --, Klara, 14.4.1931 Marx
 --, Adolf, 14.5.1933 Syke
 --, Lilly, 1.5.1936 Bosel
 --, Christa, 23.12.42 Osnabrück
 --, Maritta, 16.10.1939 Osnabrück
 --, Clemens, 1.9.1941 Osnabrück
Winter, Heinrich, 13.1.1891 Hermannsburg

--, Karoline, 12.10.1911 Karlstedt
--, Sybille, 13.6.1913 Aschendorf
--, Oskar, 30.5.1921 Stettin
--, Helmut, 5.6.1926 Lübben
--, Otto, 19.12.1939 Osterholz-Scharmbeck
--, Margott, 8.9.1941 Barssel
--, Oswald, 26.9.1918 Osnabrück
Schmidt, Marie-Lina, 1.1.1910 Hartum
--, Ramona, 14.7.1939 Osnabrück
--, Werner, 17.2.1942 Osnabrück
Strauß, Heinrich, 14.9.1896 Thieme
--, born Schmidt, Sibilla, 26.10.1896 Wulkau
--, Anna, 21.6.1920 Lengerich
--, Walter, 8.11.1925 Osnabrück
--, Hildegard, 23.5.1934 Osnabrück
--, Margot, 28.6.1939 Osnabrück
Imker, Robert, 19.9.1883 Wachtendonk
--, born Hoffman, Anna, 17.4.1884 Wangen
--, Alois, 16.12.1927 Bersenbruck
--, Willem, 24.12.1906 Kathelyne
--, born Christ, Maria, 20.12.1907 Braunschweig
--, Gertrud, 24.3.1932 Osnabrück
--, Adelheid, 10.7.1938   "
--, Kostantin, 17.4.1942   "

The above document clearly provides much detail on the 54 Romanies deported to Auschwitz in March 1943 in terms of their ages, places of birth and relationships to each other. The same file from which it originates also contains an equally chilling six page document, which gives details of the property of the deported Gypsies. It begins as follows:

List

Of the property left behind by Gyspy persons who were assigned to the concentration camp in Auschwitz (in Upper Silesia) as a result of the order of RFSSuChdDtPol from 16/12/42

     1. <u>West,[42] Karl, recently resident at Sandstrasse 31</u>
         1. Estate (five bedroom family house)
            Kamp 48, rateable value   =   6800,oo RM
            (Debt: Mortgage from the Stadtsparkasse
            Osnabrück of over 1000 RM to finance

the payment of the rental tax).

2. Estate (three bedroom family house)
   Sandstrasse 31, rateable value = 3030,oo RM
   (Debt: Mortgage from the Stadtsparkasse
   Osnabrück of over 700RM to finance the
   payment of rental tax, and a 3000RM loan
   of the wife Bernhardine West, born
   Stahlschmidt (daughter in law of Karl West),
   resident in Spindelstraße 34

3. Bed and body linen, some of which
   is new or hardly used = 200,oo RM

4. Bed and body linen, used = 20,oo RM

5. A room fitting, buffet, sofa, 1 large table,
   2 small tables, 1 chair and 1 armchair = 160,oo RM

6. 1 food cupboard = 40,oo RM

7. Porcelain and nick-nacks = 70,oo RM

8. 1 oven (originating from Jewish property) = 10,oo RM

9. 1 oven = 15,oo RM

10. 1 clock (regulator) = 25,oo RM

11. 1 case with haberdashery = 50,oo RM

12. 1 chest of clothes draws = 50,oo RM

13. 3 dresses and 2 coats = 70,oo RM

14. 2 bedsteads with mattresses = 80,oo RM

15. 1 guitar = 20,oo RM

16. 1 radio (Lumophon) with loudspeaker for
    the annual market stall = 1000,oo RM

17. 1 bicycle = 10,oo RM

18. 3 lamps = 25,oo RM

19. 2 sets of suiting material
    (Manchester) @ 4 and 6 m = 45,oo RM

20. 1 set of kitchen furnishings
    (cupboard, table, 3 chairs) = 80,oo RM

21. 1 oven = 10,oo RM

22. 1 gas cooker = 5,oo RM

23. 1 electric iron = 8,oo RM

24. 1 washing trunk = 10,oo RM

25. 1 washing basket = 3,oo RM

26. 3 clay pots = 5,oo RM

27. 10 glasses of preserves = 10,oo RM

28. Kitchen porcelain and housekeeping
    materials = 30,oo RM

= 11881,oo RM

The document continues in the same detail about the possessions (or lack of them) of West's wife and children. It asserts, in all cases, 'Property left behind was not established'. There then follow a further four and a half pages, listing the belongings of the other Romany families resident in Osnabrück. None of them have quite the same number of possessions as the West family. The value of the property of the others totalled 249, 140, 150, 82, 16, 47, 32, 135, 197, 308, 45 and 97 *Reichsmarks*, therefore fitting into the typical picture of the poor economic status of most Romany families in twentieth century Europe.[43]

The file from which the above two lists originate, also contains one other interesting, if very brief, document in the form of a letter from the criminal police headquarters in Hanover to the *Regierungspräsident* in Osnabrück. In chilling, matter of fact, bureaucratic language, this runs as follows:

> The deportation of Gypsy persons as a result of the decree of the RHSA of 19/1/43 is complete. 54 persons from the region, that is the city of Osnabrück, have been assigned to the concentration camp in Auschwitz. There were no complications in the implementation of the action.[44]

Having examined the extant official material on the deportation of the Romanies in some detail, we need to pause and analyse it. We can clearly extract some information on the nature of the Romany community in Osnabrück in the first half of the twentieth century. To begin with, the total of 54 persons points to its small size, which fits in with the national picture. In addition, the property of all but one of the families deported reveals a poor ethnic minority. The information on birthplaces also points to the fact that while most of the Romanies resident in Osnabrück were born in the vicinity of the town, indicating that the community did not wander far, a few originated some distance from the region, suggesting otherwise. But these remain small in number, the most striking including Oskar Winter born in Stettin in Prussia.

A statistical breakdown of the ages of the Osnabrück Romanies deported to Auschwitz also makes chilling reading, because of the youth of this group, fitting in with the fertility of the Sinti and Roma throughout Europe during the twentieth century.[45] The 54 people moved to the death camp consisted of a handful of families. Half of them were 18 or under and, as the birth dates reveal, also included babies and toddlers. The Dusbaba family consisted of the parents August and Anna, and five children. The oldest, Elisabeth, was born in 1932, and was therefore just 11 on being deported to Auschwitz, while August and Anita were only 1 and 2 years old respectively.

Nevertheless, the police officers Julius and Wittern, who compiled the details of the estates of the all of the families recorded the fact that none of the Dusbaba children had any property, and also did the same for all of the other children sent to their deaths. The desire of these Nazi officials to fulfil their bureaucratic tasks represents the other major observation we can make about these documents. Those producing these papers seem oblivious to and unconcerned about the fact that they are facilitating the deaths of children. These are simply matter of fact everyday affairs in the documentation. They reflect the countless similar papers from the Nazi period sending people to their deaths, which exist in regional and national archives throughout Europe. In this sense the documentation on the deportation of the Osnabrück Romanies perfectly illustrates the issues about the centrality of bureaucracy, modernity and German efficiency in the implementation of the Holocaust illustrated by a stream of writers including Hannah Arendt, Zygmunt Bauman, Jonathan Steinberg and Omar Bartov.[46] The dehumanisation of individuals on paper meant that the bureaucrats responsible for the planning and implementation of Nazi racial goals could sleep well in their beds, as they had no human contact with the individuals whom they sent to their deaths. These documents perfectly illustrate the 'banality of evil', as well as a complete lack of inter-ethnic relations between Romanies and ethnic minorities.

A Survivor's 'Revenge'

Like the vast majority of the Romany population of pre-War Germany, those deported from Osnabrück to Auschwitz died. A few survived to return home including the members of one family from Munich, which, however lost its mother.[47] One Romany also returned to Osnabrück to exact an interesting 'revenge' on the wife of a *Gestapo* officer, in a fully documented legal case in a file in the NSO. Two sides exist to this story, resolved in court. According to Anna Braun,[48] the following happened in her house in Kornstraße 40:

> At midday on 20 June 1945 an unknown man appeared in my house and demanded pieces of clothing from me. He said that he had come out of a concentration camp and had the right to completely plunder my house. As I had to take the behaviour of the person seriously on the assumption that he would carry out his threats, I gave him 2 good suits, 1 shirt and 1 hat belonging to my husband.

However, the other side of the story, recorded on 27 June 1945, was somewhat different and also provides brief insights into the wartime and immediate post-War experiences of one Osnabrück Romany.

> The allegation about my behaviour in the house of Mrs Braun is correct.
>
> In February of 1943 I was taken to the concentration camp. My release from the camp at Belsen occurred in the middle of April this year as the English military occupied the area. I did not take any clothing with me during my absence from Osnabrück. With regard to my clothing I find myself in a desperate situation at the moment. It was known to me that a Mrs Braun, whose husband was employed by the *Gestapo*, lived at Kornstraße 40.

He then went to the house on 20 June: 'I introduced myself with the remark that I had come from the annihilation camp at Auschwitz. At the same time I said that the husband had worked for the secret police'. West stated that he asked for some clothes belonging to Mrs Braun's husband, as detailed by Mrs Braun, but that he did not threaten her. He continued: 'We spoke about how life in the concentration camp went. I therefore mentioned that our children were thrown at the wall.' West said that he would be happy to give the clothing back.

A report from West's lawyer, Dr Winkler, dated 16 November 1945, reveals the experiences of one German Romany family during the Second World War:

> The whole of the West family were taken to the concentration camp as Gypsies. The wife of the accused was killed there. The accused also lost his twins there. These children were used in experiments in the camp. As he was transported from Auschwitz he made a request that his children should be given to him, as they had already lost their mother in the camp. This request was rejected. The accused never heard anything from his children again. As he has been informed from various sources, his children died in the crematorium. The father of West also lost his life in the concentration camp. West therefore lost his entire family.
>
> Twenty-seven members of the West family lost their lives, ten of them from his immediate family.

The case went to court on 31 March 1947, with the following verdict:

The accused is charged with having visited Mrs Braun in her house in Kornstraße 40 in Osnabrück on 21 [sic] June 1945 and to have threatened her to such an extent, by stating that he could throw her children against the wall where they would remain hanging, plunder her home and chase her out, that she gave him two suits, one shirt and a hat.

The facts are not, however, considered to have been established. The accused was certainly in the house of the witness Braun on the day mentioned, and allowed himself to be handed the items, but whether he received them through threats or by describing his concentration camp experiences could not be established. The witness Braun, the single adult eye witness deviating from her earlier statements – and her sworn statement before the requested judge – stated that the accused did not exactly behave cheekily. He told her that he would not deal with what happened to his relatives in the concentration camp, although he could do that. He could also have ransacked her house, but he would not do that. She then became scared because she was a woman alone in her house and because the Russians had plundered elsewhere. She gave him things because she sympathised with him. The suspicion certainly remains that the accused alluded to his experiences in the concentration camp with the purpose of making the witness pliable. Using the evidence available from today's statements from the single witness the court has not adduced from the evidence, that the accused had beyond doubt threatened her.

The court therefore decided to release the prisoner.

The above documentation from the West file[49] offers an excellent insight into Romany life in Germany during World War Two. It indicates that the vast majority of Osnabrück and German Romanies deported to Auschwitz died there. The file also gives evidence of the fact that twins faced experimentation before being killed. West may have wished to exact some kind of revenge on the people responsible for the death of his whole family or may simply, as the court decided, have wanted to tell the wife of a member of the *Gestapo*, about the realities of Romany life in a German death camp. The court did not reach a definite decision about the way he secured clothing. Even so, like freed concentration camp inmates immediately after liberation, West felt that he had the right to take his own form of 'revenge', in an act of 'natural justice'. Surely, he was entitled to two suits, a shirt and a hat from someone whom he believed had sent his family to their deaths in Auschwitz. West would understandably have rationalized his actions, in visiting Mrs Braun, in this way, whether or not he threatened her.

Post-War Persecution

The leniency of the court proves unusual in view of the continuity of both official and unofficial anti-Romany feeling in twentieth century Germany. Hostility towards Sinti and Roma remained at the end of the War even though only a few hundred members of this community had survived the death camps and continued to live in the Allied occupation zones in the 1940s. The city authorities in several locations, including Bremen and Cologne had, however, implemented measures to control movement and register Sinti and Roma.[50] Exclusion of the Romanies also continued in Osnabrück as revealed in another letter dated 28 May 1946 from the police commander in the Osnabrück *Regierungsbezirk* to the chief executives in the areas which made up the region, including the town of Osnabrück. The letter is entitled 'Gypsy Matters' and begins thus:

> For some time an increasing number of Gypsies and people who rove like Gypsies has been observed in the *Regierungsbezirk*. One part of the court cases begun in the region, particularly the recent horse thefts, can be attributed to this category of persons. All Gypsies and people who rove like Gypsies are to have their papers checked and their wagons searched for stolen goods by all members of the police.

The document continued with details about the procedures to be followed if members of the policing authorities came across particular types of Romanies. First, 'native Gypsies':

> Various papers such as identity cards, trading licences of every variety etc are to be immediately examined. They are to be confiscated and sent to the issuing offices and authorities if they have expired or the conditions imposed have not been adhered to by the owner. Furthermore, also to be established is whether the person with the documentation matches the one which is printed upon it.

The letter further stated that under a ministerial decree passed by the criminal police office in Hanover in 1938 all people without homes were to be arrested and taken to prison. The residents of caravans 'make themselves liable to arrest if they move from place to place for more than three days...Housing offices are requested to issue exemption certificates only in exceptional circumstances'. A section on native Romanies concluded: 'Arrested Gypsies in need of support etc are, if necessary, to be entrusted to the responsible welfare office. Correctional education is to be applied in the case of neglected gypsy children'. A section on 'foreign Gypsies' emphasised the need to keep them out of Germany, in language which could come from any period in German history between 1870 and 1950: 'These are to be prevented from crossing the imperial border with all permissible means. Foreign Gypsies are to be recognized as such when they cannot prove their German nationality beyond doubt'. Arrested foreign Romanies were to be 'deported in an easterly direction'. The document continued that all responsible authorities would work together to control the Gypsies. Any arrested people would have their details noted in view of the fact that the criminal police office of Hanover was preparing an index of this group.[51]

Conclusion

The documents quoted at length above reveal the experiences of Sinti and Roma in Osnabrück during the first half of the twentieth century and provide an insight into a series of aspects of Romany life. The centrality and continuity of exclusion and persecution represents the first reality. The documents confirm the marginal position of this group before 1950, while a comparison between the attitudes of the Nazi and post-War authorities demonstrates similarities in attitudes. The language used and the policies pursued in the documents quoted above from 1933 and 1946 essentially remain the same. We could interchange them. Arrest, prosecution and control of movement represented central experiences in the lives of Romanies before, during and after the Third Reich. The Nazis resorted to policies of deportation and murder as their 'final solution' to a 'problem' which had existed in Germany since the first Romanies had arrived on German soil at the start of the fifteenth century.[52] As revealed in the documents concerning the case of Johann West, this meant the complete annihilation of his family.

The documents quoted above also reveal the coldness of the German bureaucratic regime, its determination to control Romanies, both during and after the Third Reich, and its matter of fact reporting of the deportation of Romanies to a death camp in 1943. On the other side of the story, we see the realities of deportation for Johann West, an everyday victim of the Nazi bureaucratic machine.

In view of surviving information in the NSO it seems surprising that the Romanies have not previously attracted attention from historians. We may partly explain this from the location of the papers within the archive. The details of the deportations to Auschwitz lie within a file entitled 'Confiscation of the Property of Organizations Hostile to the State, 1933-1943', while the West file makes up one of a group of court cases. This particular one has the title of 'Trader Johann West in Osnabrück because of Armed Robbery, 1945-7'. The main problem consists of the fact that neither file contains the word 'Gypsy' in the title. At the same time, because of the personal nature of the information involved, the archive director needs to grant written permission for their use.

While historians do not appear to have made much use of the Romany files, the city authorities seem to have based their plaque in the town square on the list of those deported to Auschwitz in 1943, a pattern repeated elsewhere in Germany.[53] This indicates that the civic memory of the ethnic cleansing of Jews and Romanies remains central in the official memorialization of World War Two. However, this applies more to Jews in the popular memory as indicated by the publications of Kühling and Junk and Sellmeyer and the Nussbaum Museum. Works such as those by Wido Spratte issued by the leading Osnabrück publisher, Wenner, concern themselves with the experiences of the ethnic majority. The exclusion of Romanies from the popular memory may have much to do with their small numbers before 1945, which means that people could not remember them. On the other hand it may symbolize their continuing marginalization in German society. Inter-ethnic relations between Germans and Romanies have proved problematic throughout the twentieth century, no matter what the nature of the regime in power. Unlike Jews, Romanies have remained a more distant group, which has not moved into the higher echelons of German society, but has, instead, lived a marginalized existence. Contact with the majority society has occurred either as a result of peddling or the actions of officialdom.

9

FOREIGN WORKERS AND PRISONERS OF WAR

Historical and Historiographical Background

Following the principles of Hitler's racial ideology and satisfying the labour needs of the German war economy, foreign workers and prisoners of war replaced the deported and exterminated Jews and Romanies. During World War Two Germany reached an ethnic diversity which it had never experienced before in its history. The sheer volume of people involved meant that parts of the country which had few experiences with foreigners before 1939, including Osnabrück, now dealt with them on a daily basis.

German and American historians began to focus upon the issue of foreign workers under the Nazis from the 1960s. The pioneering studies included those by Eva Seeber, Edward L. Homze and Hans Pfahlmann,[1] although Ulrich Herbert has done more than anyone else to give this topic scholarly respectability,[2] followed, more recently, by Mark Spoerer.[3] Wolfgang Jacobmeyer, meanwhile, has produced a series of studies examining the reality of life for foreign labourers in Germany following the cessation of hostilities.[4] We now also have an important volume on migration under the Weimar Republic by Jochen Oltmer.[5] Major studies of labour importation in German history have contextualized the War period within the overall development of this policy from the *Kaiserreich* to the Federal Republic, bringing out continuities.[6]

The issue of foreign workers came to the forefront of the historical memory of Nazism at the turn of the twenty first century, connected with the attempt to gain compensation for those affected. After the German government agreed to payments in 2000,[7] all manner of organizations, including both major Churches, admitted to having employed foreign workers during the War,[8] illustrating their importance to the economy between 1939 and 1945.

Against this background the local impact of forced labourers and prisoners of war has received attention in the smallest of areas.[9] Osnabrück provides a good illustration of this process. As early as 1982 the *Antifaschistischer Arbeitskreis* published a pamphlet on the subject.[10] By the end of the 1990s, coinciding with the move for compensation of former Nazi labourers, they began to receive considerable attention. Volker Issmer published two books focusing on his Dutch compatriots who found themselves working for the Nazis in the town during the War, one of which dealt with the camp in Ohrbeck, just outside Osnabrück.[11] In addition Michael Gander and Ute Weinmann have travelled to Belorussia and the Ukraine to interview people who had formerly worked in the town.[12] Foreign workers and prisoners of war have also had an impact upon the civic memory of Osnabrück. The Ohrbeck camp has become a museum. Similarly, Germans who lived through the Nazi period have memories of foreigners during the War.

Germany imported labour from the end of the nineteenth century as the country began to industrialize. As Germans moved from the eastern agricultural to the western industrial areas, labour shortages ensued in the regions which lost population. Consequently, a system of labour importation evolved, particularly in the east, which involved the issue of short term contracts, often seasonal in the case of agriculture, to foreign workers, particularly those from eastern Europe. Between 1871 and 1919 millions of men and women made their way to Germany to work either in agriculture or industry. A 1907 census revealed a total of 882,515, including 212,326 Russians, 380,393 Austro-Hungarians and 129,556 Italians. These migrants endured the harshest of living and working conditions.

World War One cut off the supply of Russian labour, but the imperial authorities decided to keep the 300,000 'hostile aliens' living in the country employed in industry. By the end of the conflict the German War machine, in desperate need of labour, turned its attention to those areas which it had conquered. The 715,770 foreign workers employed in the country in 1918 included 178,911 Russians (mostly Poles) and 110,177 people from Holland and Belgium. Many of the latter had faced forced deportation, laying down the template for recruitment procedures in World War Two. Also anticipating developments which occurred after 1939, the imperial authorities exploited the 2.5 million prisoners of war which they had acquired, particularly Russians. Consequently, foreigners made an appearance throughout the country, living and working in difficult conditions.[13]

The economic problems of the Weimar Republic meant that foreigners largely disappeared from Germany because of unemployment, although some certainly lived in the country, especially in the east, peaking at 236,870 in 1928.[14] The campaign for full employment of the early Nazi years did not have any need for foreign workers. But as the armaments based economic recovery got into full swing, labour shortages began to appear, which necessitated the importation of foreigners. In 1938-9 the 435,903 present in the country made up 2.12 per cent of the German workforce, divided fairly equally between agriculture and industry, working long hours and originating in Poland, Italy, Yugoslavia, Bulgaria and Hungary.[15]

World War Two meant dramatic changes in the ethnic composition of the German workforce. The labour shortages caused by full military mobilization for the *Wehrmacht*, the needs of the German economy, together with the reluctance to increase the numbers of women in employment, created a huge demand for more supplies. The conquest of large sections of western and, more especially, eastern Europe opened up to the Nazis vast reserves of labour which they willingly exploited. The total numbers of prisoners of war and foreign workers used by the regime increased from 301,000 in 1939 to 7,126,000 in 1944, or from 0.8 to 19.9 per cent of all workers employed in Germany.[16] The 1944 total included 5,295,000 civilians and 1,831,000 prisoners of war. While those in the latter category consisted almost exclusively of men, the Nazis made much use of female foreign labourers. At the end of 1943 they employed 3,631,000 males and 1,714,000 females.[17]

Table 9.1: Major Nationalities of Civilians and Prisoners of War Employed by the Nazi War Economy, August 1944.

Nationality	Civilians	Prisoners of War	Total
Belgian	203,262	50,386	253,648
French	654,782	599,967	1,254,749
Italian	158,099	427,238	585,337
Soviet	2,126,753	631,559	2,758,312
Polish	1,659,764	28,316	1,688,080
Others	919,223	192,621	1,111,844
Total	5,721,883	1,930,087	7,651,970

Source: Ulrich Herbert, *A History of Foreign Labour in Germany, 1880-1980: Seasonal Workers/Forced Labourers/Guest Workers* (Ann Arbor, MI, 1990), p. 154.

As Table 9.1 indicates, those employed by the Nazis came from all over Europe and moved to Germany through a combination of force and, to a much smaller extent, willingness.[18] Even if people moved to Germany voluntarily from western European states, part of the reason for this lay in the economic consequences of the Nazi invasion for their country.[19] Those who arrived from eastern Europe, particularly Poland and the Soviet

Union, had made their way to Germany either as a result of transportation or conscription.[20]

Underlying the decision to employ foreign workers, particularly from eastern Europe, lay not simply economic needs and historical precedents, but also ideological motivations, as outlined in *Mein Kampf*. While Jews represented the antithesis of the Aryan, eastern Europeans had a role to play as labourers. As the Nazis moved eastwards in the quest for *Lebensraum*, they would come into contact with what they perceived as inferior people, to whom they would act as masters and whose labour power they would exploit.[21] The labour needs of the economy played a larger role than ideological ones because the Nazis used people from both eastern and western Europe, although, under regulations for control of the different nationalities the latter, in theory at least, received better treatment than the former.

While the growth in the number of foreign workers and prisoners of War after 1939 drastically changed the ethnic composition of Osnabrück, the town had experienced little contact with foreigners since the Napoleonic invasions, unlike regions such as East Prussia and the Ruhr. Only during World War One had Osnabrück witnessed the presence of some prisoners of war.[22] Little international migration took place in and out of Osnabrück during the inter-War years. In 1931, for instance, 254 people left the town, while 181 moved in, giving an overall loss of 73. In 1936, 213 people emigrated, while 306 entered Osnabrück, meaning a net gain of 107. The 692 foreigners living in Osnabrück in September 1930 therefore declined during the course of the 1930s.[23] Although limited information has survived about them, the local press devoted attention, on various occasions, to visits made by schoolchildren, as well as adults, particularly those from Italy, Holland and England, reported in a positive way, either because of their political or religious credentials.[24]

Unlike other towns in Germany, Osnabrück had therefore experienced little contact with foreigners before 1939. During the Weimar Republic much of the immigration which had taken place had done so towards the eastern agricultural provinces, continuing those patterns which had developed before World War One.[25] Osnabrück did not experience the migration of Poles towards the Ruhr which had occurred before the 1914 and which, in the Weimar Republic, totalled hundreds of thousands people, if we include those born in the area of Polish parents, now facing racist and assimilationist pressures, although before the Third Reich they developed a rich ethnicity.[26] Inter-ethnic relations certainly developed here, most notably through mixed marriages so that, by 1939, the percentage of Polish unions involving a Pole and a German in the Ruhr town of Bottrop had increased to 39.5 per cent.[27] Osnabrück therefore contrasts with some parts of Germany in the early years of Nazi rule. It experienced relatively little labour migration but welcomed parties of schoolchildren and other visitors.

Experiences in Osnabrück During Wartime

After the War broke out foreigners found themselves employed all over Germany, wherever the needs of the German economy dictated that they should work. In April 1941 the areas with the highest concentrations consisted of Lower Saxony and Pomerania, where foreign workers made up over 13 per cent of all employees.[28] Many of those working in industry and mining lived in the Ruhr. The 39,388 foreigners in Essen in December 1944 made up 10.5 per cent of the entire population of 375,179.[29] Elsewhere, 6,000 workers found themselves in Bremen at the end of the War, employed especially by six firms.[30]

At the outbreak of War Osnabrück contained a small number of foreigners, which only increased gradually. A report from 22 September 1939 gave a list of just 8 Polish speakers who lived in the town.[31] By April 1943 a publication entitled *Der Arbeitseinsatz in Niedersachsen*, stated that 83,908 people worked in Osnabrück (presumably the *Regierungsbezirk*), of whom 15.8 per cent (12,578) consisted of foreigners, while 7,199 were prisoners of war, made up of 4,967 French people, 1,504 Soviets, 461 Belgians, 244 Yugoslavs and just 19 Poles.[32] In November 1944 the *Gestapo* provided a list of sixteen factories, including the engineering firms of Klöckner and the OKD which employed 8,199 people, of whom 4,552 consisted of foreigners, giving a proportion of over half. Klöckner used 1,964 non-Germans, out of a total workforce of 2,283, making 86 per cent.[33] At the end of the War Karl Kühling estimated that 10,000 of the 50,000 people who still lived in Osnabrück consisted of foreigners and prisoners of war from Russia, Poland, Holland, Belgium, France, Italy, Yugoslavia and Czechoslovakia.[34]

However inaccurate, these figures point to the centrality of foreign workers in the economy of Osnabrück during the War. Without them, the streets would have remained clogged with air raid rubble and the armaments factories would have ground to a halt. The above figures point to the range of national origins of foreigners and prisoners of war, originating both in eastern Europe and closer to Osnabrück in France, Holland and Belgium. In 1943 the *Kriegs-Chronik* claimed that order in the camps housing foreigners was maintained through nineteen different languages including Turkish, Rumanian and 'Indian' and also claimed the presence of Bulgarians and Spaniards in the town.[35]

Foreigners in wartime Germany lived in all manner of accommodation, most typically in camps.[36] At the start of the War Poles in Osnabrück had a certain amount of liberty,[37] but as the conflict progressed accommodation increasingly came to consist of camps. An article in the *Neue Volksblätter* from 1 May 1943 claimed that 'over two dozen camps' existed in Osnabrück. In the same month the *Kriegs-Chronik* elaborated upon these bare facts. It claimed that these camps, often situated next to factories, held an average of 30-40 people, but, in some cases, up to 200. The account listed nineteen places of accommodation dotted throughout the town and its immediate hinterland. They included two schools in Schinkel. The largest camp lay in the north west of the town. 'Down Landwehrstraße, in fact on Westfalian land, there literally extends a camp city with streets and central squares. Here live Yugoslav officers, totalling about 1,500 to 2,000, including nine generals.' The account concluded that 'the situation of all these camps can be described as first class'.[38]

Table 9.2: Nationalities of Foreigners Held
in Camps in Osnabrück in July 1943.

Nationality	Total Number
Ukrainian	2,488
Dutch	1,082
French	659
Eastern Workers	648
Russians	565
Belgians	275
Germans	242
White Russians	190
'Children'	128
Italians	124
Poles	118
Others	30
Serbians	13
Lithuanians	5
Bulgarians	3
Estonians	3
Czechs	2
Croats	1
Tartars	1
Total	6,940

Source: NSO Rep-430-303-19/56-230, Liste der Ausländerlager im Stadtkreis Osnabrück, 31 July 1943

A list produced in July 1943, gave details of thirty camps with their addresses, the name of the establishment running them, the number of people held and their nationality. The DAF ran three of these, the railways controlled four, the city authorities another two, while Osnabrück firms held responsibility for the rest. In this month the total number of foreigners and prisoners of war living in camps within the city stood at 6,940. The largest camp run by the DAF, held 1,039 people, while the smallest one acted as a home to ten Russians. Although the larger places of internment tended to house a variety of groups, the smaller ones usually held either just one nationality or a small number. The most numerous group, Ukrainians, made up nearly 36 per cent of the total, while all Soviets counted over half of those in Osnabrück. Nevertheless, significant numbers of western Europeans also lived in the town, including 1,082 Dutch, 659 French and 275 Belgians.[39] Table 9.2 provides details of the camp inmates, constructed in an unscientific manner by the responsible Nazi official.

Ursula Fisser-Bömer's account of forced labour in Osnabrück claimed that at least fifty camps existed during the entire duration of the war, providing a list of 49. Most of these were attached to individual concerns, in terms of the work which inmates carried out, although they did not necessarily lie near them. She states that while most of the camps consisted of barracks built to a standard pattern, others existed in 'dance halls, schools, empty buildings and similar makeshift accommodation'.[40] Another account produced by the *Antifaschistischer Arbeitskreis* lists 100 camps which existed in the town and its immediate hinterland during the War, dividing them into various categories, including those run by firms, above all Klöckner, which controlled twelve camps of various types between 1939 and 1945. Similarly, the railways ran fourteen camps, while many smaller firms had their own individual locations where they kept foreigners, often a house.[41]

The consequences of bombing, which sometimes resulted in direct hits upon accommodation situated next to armaments factories, meant that the authorities constantly had to change the places where foreigners lived, often housing them on the outskirts of the town and marching them in to work.[42] The makeshift accommodation included St Gertrude's nunnery, which housed people employed by the OKD for most of the War.[43]

Those lucky enough to live in private homes included Antonina Moskalenko, who stayed with the Thiem family and initially helped in the running of their hardware store. She arrived at the end of 1941. Hermann Thiem, born in 1929, recalled:

> She stayed in Osnabrück until the autumn of 1945, but she could only remain as a housemaid with us until 1943. We had her for two years

here. She then had to work for the Osnabrücker Kupfer- und Drahtwerk...When she was free, she came to us, and said: 'Oh Mrs Thiem, I would like to help you a bit, can I come?' 'Yes, certainly'. And so she came every evening and helped us, because she did not want to stay in the barracks. And because we got on so well with her. At half past nine in the evening she had to go because she had to work in the factory the following morning.[44]

The experience of Antonina Moskalenko probably represented the best of all possible worlds for an eastern European in wartime Osnabrück. At the other end of the scale, foreigners and prisoners of war could find themselves in the 'Work Correction Centre' in Ohrbeck, just outside the town. As many as 200 such camps existed throughout the country, particularly concerned with foreign workers, although they also housed other groups perceived as undesirable by the Nazis.[45] Using the 4,000 cards kept by the Osnabrück *Gestapo* and now held in the NSO, Volker Issmer has painstakingly established that over 1,000 foreigners faced a spell of incarceration in the camp for various misdemeanours.[46] He paints a negative picture of conditions in Ohrbeck using a variety of sources.[47] While those held here mostly worked in the nearby settlement of Georgsmarienhütte, some laboured in Osnabrück, especially for the purpose of clearing up after air raids.[48] Similarly, prisoners of war, together with German internees from camps in the Emsland, found themselves working in Osnabrück during the latter stages of the War, which meant that they temporarily remained in all manner of accommodation including dance halls, schools and hospitals.[49]

One of the best accounts of prisoner of war life in Osnabrück comes from a letter written by Karl Reinert to the British military authorities in March 1946. Reinert had served as a sergeant guarding a camp set up for Russian prisoners of war working for Klöckner. His narrative covered a variety of themes. He claimed that the camp held 620 people, 380 of whom had specialist skills. Beginning with the health of the internees, he claimed that the doctor responsible for them passed sick people as healthy. The examples given by Reinert included that of one prisoner who lost his fingers. Reinert further claimed that the internees were always thirsty and that bad nourishment meant that they could not carry out the type of heavy work required of them. In July 1944, for instance, the 620 prisoners received no bread for two days.

Reinert also focused much attention upon the ways in which the SS maintained discipline within the camp,[50] a theme touched upon by another eyewitness, Heinrich Voßgröne, a bricklayer's apprentice in the suburb of Piesberg, where three camps existed at various stages. He claimed that those who had not fulfilled their daily work quota of stone breaking found themselves in a company of 100 men who faced punishment. 'They had to load seven wagons a day.' Voßgröne also claimed that members of this company, entirely Russian, run by the SS, were regularly shot and killed.[51] In view of the absence of other evidence for such practices, we might wish to question the accuracy of some of Voßgröne's testimony, without denying, by also using the account of Reinert and placing the experience of Osnabrück within previous research on the national scale, that Russian prisoners of war faced harsh and often brutal treatment.[52]

Perhaps the most reliable document of all for the experiences of foreigners in Osnabrück comes from a report written for the *Regierungspräsident* on 26 January 1945 about the Backhausschule camp, which had come into operation in November of 1944.

> The Backhausschule is occupied by 320 foreigners of various nationalities. The body responsible for the camp is the Berlin firm of Glatz.
>
> The rooms are completely dark.
>
> The gym is completely dark. In the middle an open fire is burning. Straw is lying around in heaps on the ground, with foreigners lying upon it.
>
> In several classrooms one finds a pile of straw on the ground. The foreign inmates are standing or lying about everywhere, although it is working time…
>
> The clothing of the inmates present is meagre, dirty and partly torn. They only own what they are wearing on their backs…
>
> From information from the camp commandant and the representative of the firm only 150-160 of the 320 inmates went to work today; 120 remained in the camp because they have no footwear (they have developed lumps on their feet). About forty have colds.

The report concluded, in damning language: 'The Backhausschule camp is dirty and disorderly, the care of the provision of clothing for the inmates is inadequate, the heating is insufficient, the inmates are covered in lice. Only about 50 per cent of them go to work.'[53]

Another reliable indicator of the harshness of the treatment received by foreigners may be death rates. For instance, between 17 October 1942 and 16 March 1943, 86 of them died.[54] Any talk of death rates amongst foreigners, however, would have to recognize that Allied bombs killed more of them than Nazi mistreatment, even though this has much to do with the Nazi racial policy of forbidding them from entering air raid shelters.

Volker Issmer's work on Ohrbeck has examined the lack of food provision and poor medical care.[55] Issmer focused upon his Dutch compatriots and carried out interviews to bring home his point.[56] While we should take Nazi newspaper reports with a pinch of salt, they suggest that some degree of normality existed in the lives of internees, especially Dutch ones. In most situations of wartime internment, prisoners of war usually have much time to themselves, which allows them to develop a social life. Some evidence exists in the *Neue Volksblätter* to suggest that this happened in Osnabrück. In September 1941, for instance, we learn that a musical evening took place in a Dutch camp. In the following month another newspaper report spoke of an officially approved parade through the streets of women in wooden shoes who worked at the same camp.[57]

Little evidence exists after the end of 1941 to suggest any level of 'normality' in camp life as foreigners lived in Osnabrück for the purpose of working. They tended to find employment in armaments factories or helped to clear up the debris after Allied bombing raids, although others worked for the local state in a wide variety of employment. An examination of some of the larger Osnabrück armament firms demonstrates the extent to which they had become dependant upon foreigners, as well as illustrating working conditions. First, the OKD, which used non-Germans from the early stages of the conflict.[58] By April 1944 it employed 3,600 people. The 308 white collar workers all consisted of Germans, while the 3,292 manual labourers counted a majority of Germans (2,183), together with 1,109 foreigners, made up of 326 'western' workers, including 29 women, 486 labourers from the east, of whom 296 consisted of women, and 297 prisoners of war. The industrial report which provided these figures gave no indication of any difference in working times or hours between Germans and foreigners as both laboured between eleven and twelve hours per day, with total break times of 1 hour.[59] In fact, those who worked more than 57 hours per week, in the case of women, or 60 hours, in the case of men, received extra rations of pulses, whether foreigners or natives, at the same rate, according to the management of the OKD.[60] In February 1945 the local industrial inspectorate authorized an increase in hours for both Germans and foreigners to 69 per week.[61] Foreigners working for Klöckner complained about the wages they received in June 1941, claiming that they had been promised about RM1 per hour, which meant that they worked 'very irregularly'.[62] In November 1944 the management of the firm obtained permission to increase working hours to 69, as well as the rations of employees, for both foreigners and prisoners of war.[63] By May 1944 Karmann employed 111 German white collar workers and 1,109 manual labourers, made up of 543 Germans, 33 male 'western' workers, 420 female 'eastern workers' and 58 French prisoners of war. In March 1944 the firm had obtained permission to employ the eastern European women at night.[64]

In October 1940 the Osnabrück local authority drew up conditions for the treatment of foreigners and prisoners of war. These included: working times which would not exceed that of other employees; a weekly break of at least 24 consecutive hours; and the same treatment as Germans in the case of accidents. An undated list of 66 foreigners employed by the city authorities, originating in Poland, France, Spain, Rumania, Holland, Belgium and Italy indicated that they worked in the waterworks, gasworks and trams, mostly in manual employment, although one Dutch woman, Sophie Baumann, worked as a tram conductress.[65]

Clearing up after air raids became increasingly common in 1944 and 1945 as foreigners and prisoners of war essentially became a surplus labour supply, which the local authorities could call upon at a moment's notice. Karl Mosse remembered that, following the massive air raids of 1944, 'large columns of prisoners of war or political prisoners or forced labourers were brought in to clear premises and to make the streets clear again'.[66] On 19 October 1944, 180 men found themselves involved in a variety of activities including clearing up and the distribution of food following a large attack on 12 October which resulted in 10,000 people losing their homes. Of this total, 150 consisted of foreigners from a camp for Klöckner employees.[67] In addition, the SS controlled special units which they used for repairing the damage caused by Allied bombers as well as involving them in other forms of basic manual labour. These people often came from camps outside Osnabrück including Neuengamme and Esterwegen.[68]

As the NSDAP had imported so many foreigners into the country, it recognized that, in order to maintain racial distinctions, it would have to introduce rules and regulations to keep them apart from Germans, as foreigners would often have to leave camps in the course of carrying out their work. Once in factories, they often worked close to Germans in confined spaces.[69] Both natives and foreigners could face punishment if they broke the regulations, which distinguished between eastern and western workers, as the former came lower down the Nazi racial hierarchy.

Several documents in the NSO indicate the types of regulations introduced and the distinctions between Germans and different types of foreign workers. In 1941 the senior police chief and SS leader in Düsseldorf sent out a circular distinguishing 'employees of German descent' from 'workers of foreign peoples'. Those in the first category included Dutch, Danish, Norwegians and Flemish people, while everyone else fell into the second group. Those of 'German descent' had rights similar to natives, but all would face incarceration in camps. The regulations forbade sexual relations between Germans and foreigners. They further mentioned the 'lack of willingness to work', 'behaviour hostile to the Reich' and 'search and arrest' of those who tried to escape or did not work.[70]

Table 9.3: Foreigners Killed in Osnabrück Air Raids.

Date of Air Raid	Number of Foreigners Killed (Percentage in Brackets)	Number of Germans Killed (Percentage in Brackets)	Total Killed
10 August 1942	17 (27.4)	45 (71.6)	62
6 November 1942	1 (33.3)	2 (66.6)	3
23 March 1944	9 (34.6)	17 (65.4)	26
7 May 1944	30 (23.8)	96 (76.2)	126
8 May 1944	0	34 (100)	34
13 May 1944	67 (28.0)	172 (72.0)	239
31 May 1944	11 (46.0)	13 (54.0)	54
13 September 1944	29 (25.6)	84 (74.4)	113
26 September 1944	15 (21.4)	55 (78.6)	70
12 October 1944	28 (73.7)	10 (26.3)	38
21 November 1944	3 (9.7)	28 (90.3)	31
6 December 1944	8 (20.5)	31 (79.5)	39
16 February 1945	15 (71.4)	6 (78.6)	21
9 March 1945	2 (100)	0	2
17 March 1945	10 (58.8)	7 (41.2)	17
23 March 1945	7 (26.9)	19 (73.1)	26
25 March 1945	10 (5.9)	160 (93.1)	170
Totals Killed (Percentage in Brackets)	262 (25.1)	779 (74.9)	1,041

Source: NSO Dep-3b-XIX-79, 85, 93, 99, 103, 105, 106, 107, 108, 110, 113, 119, 124, 126, 132, 147, 154, 155, 158, 159.

During 1940 the Lord Mayor of Osnabrück had circulated a list of regulations, issued on a national level on 8 March, to deal with the treatment of Poles.[71] The most important measures included the wearing of a 'P' symbol on clothing, the issuing of a pass in two languages and the guarding of Polish workers by the local police. Further controls, reflecting national developments, followed in March 1942 because the local authorities believed that contact still took place between Poles and Germans, especially in shops. These regulations controlled the times when Poles could leave camps. Furthermore, they could only use bicycles or public transport for the purpose of travelling to and from work. They could not change address without permission, attend social and cultural activities, use photographic equipment, eat in restaurants, purchase alcohol, smoke, or use German hairdressers and barbers.[72] Poles and other foreign workers, could, however, use public swimming baths, but not at the same time as Germans.[73] On 7 July 1943 a further measure distinguished Germans from eastern European workers as the latter had to wear a symbol of 3.7 cm in height, declaring 'Ost'.[74]

Foreigners had some working rights, at least in the early stages of the war, although these largely aimed at ensuring that they did not have better working conditions than Germans. Most notably, several decrees and ordinances ensured that prisoners of war could not earn more than natives. Regulations also existed guaranteeing living conditions. In January 1943 the Osnabrück city authorities issued instructions to employers to limit hours and ensure that foreigners had breaks from work and received sufficient rations.[75] Despite such apparently protective regulations, evidence in Osnabrück suggests that the town reflected the national pattern, whereby 'for most of the eastern workers and some of the western workers, life was one continual nightmare of hard work, insufficient food, inadequate quarters, personal discrimination, hardship and cruelty.'[76]

Perhaps the cruellest aspect of all consisted of their exclusion from public air raid shelters, which meant that a considerable percentage of those killed in Allied attacks upon Osnabrück consisted of foreigners. Gerhard Strauß, born in 1936, recalled his shock at the fact that they could not take shelter:

What I found terrible was that at the railway embankment there was a sort of street in a field to the left of which was a tunnel and to the right of which was a place with barbed wire, where the so-called foreign workers, the Russians, were, and they could not come into the bunker. However, it was an area which was heavily bombarded because the platforms had to be attacked. And I found that terrible. We could go into the shelter and they had to remain outside, behind the barbed wire. And as children we sometimes went there and put half a loaf of bread through the fence, and the Russians had toys ready for us...They gave us toys for the bread.[77]

Karl Reinert recalled what happened to foreign workers in the camp he guarded:

As there was no shelter available for prisoners of war or other workers at the works, I arranged the following with the understanding of colonel Behrends: in the event of the siren sounding all the prisoners of war should proceed to the camp. From there we marched together to the wood which lay about 5km away.[78]

Herbert has claimed that 'in Essen, 7.7 per cent of the German inhabitants were killed by bombs during the war, contrasted with 13.8 per cent of the foreign workers'.[79] Surviving evidence for Osnabrück does not allow such definite conclusions as not all air raid reports broke down deaths into Germans and foreigners. Table 9.3 summarises the available statistics. Given the fact that Kühling estimated that there were five times more Germans than foreigners in Osnabrück at the end of the War, foreigners clearly had a considerably higher death rate than Germans.

The death rates of foreign workers and prisoners of war raises the issue of the ethics of Allied bombing. Should we blame the Nazis for bringing foreign workers to Osnabrück and not providing suitable air raid shelters for them, or should we blame the equally callous disregard for life of British and US bombing tactics? A balanced answer would have to point the finger at both parties. If the Allies aimed at undermining morale, they certainly did so, although those who worked in Osnabrück and other German cities already had little self esteem, living hundreds or thousands of miles from their homes in difficult housing conditions working long hours. The bombing simply emphasized the wretchedness of their existence.

The Reaction of Foreigners to their New Surroundings

Many foreigners simply could not bear the conditions under which they lived and chose to escape. Others committed petty acts of criminality recorded in detail by *Gestapo* cards in Osnabrück, as well as in several court cases, whose proceedings survive in the NHH. Herbert has viewed such acts of criminality as resistance, together with: 'bartering and black marketeering'; 'loafing'; and absconding. In addition, he has also written about more political forms of opposition, including sabotage and networks planning uprisings.[80] No evidence exists about organized opposition in Osnabrück, but 'resistance' formed part of everyday life. Twentieth century prisoners of war have traditionally viewed escape attempts as an occupational duty and hazard.[81]

'Petty criminality' certainly took place in Osnabrück as it does in any system of government, and as it did in locations throughout Germany during the War. A total of 456 foreigners faced persecution in Oldenburg, for instance, most commonly (in 201 cases) for theft, and leaving work places without permission (102).[82] Alienation caused by inhumane treatment which could last for years in a country far away from home probably made such acts more likely. The Osnabrück criminal statistics for the second quarter of 1944 reveal the arrest of eight foreigners for theft, consisting of 1 Pole, 3 Dutch people, 1 French person and 3 eastern Europeans.[83] Two Dutchmen faced prosecution at the higher special court[84] in Celle for stealing from hundreds of packages while employed by the post office. The judge described them as 'people's vermin' and sentenced them both to death, although this later went down to ten years each. The verdict stated:

> From November 1942 the accused went to the post office at the railway station for the purpose of carrying out thefts from public transportation. They used every opportunity which presented itself to steal from packets, small parcels and letters. They mainly focused upon packages which they believed to contain tobacco and food. They carried out the thefts during the day as well as the night, in the parcel room, in the elevator and on the platforms and did not take into consideration whether the parcels were damaged or undamaged.[85]

Similar cases to this include those of a French and Belgian prisoner of war, who faced jail sentences of three years for stealing rabbits and chickens.[86] The four individuals involved in these two cases may have acted at least partly out of hunger, bearing in mind the inadequate rations which they received. But this explanation would not apply to a Polish worker who stole several valuable items from a house in which he worked, including two gold chains.[87]

Numerous people faced prosecution for disobeying the countless measures which the Nazis had introduced to control foreign workers. We should probably accept that the range of regulations which existed made criminality inevitable because of the impossibility of living within such constraints. Take the case of a Czech, who received a sentence of nine months imprisonment for listening to a station from his homeland.[88] Or the Belgian who 'was arrested on 13/5/44 because he did not carry out his work in an orderly manner and left his employment without reason'.[89]

Similarly, a Polish woman had committed a similar 'offence' on three occasions, eventually making her way to Cracow.[90] A Frenchman, meanwhile, endured ten days in prison for illegally sending letters to his wife in France.[91] The *Gestapo* dealt with one Russian prisoner on three occasions, the second time for not wearing his 'Ost' badge.[92]

Herbert estimates that '500,000 or more escapes per year' took place on a national level, while Andreas Heusler has pointed to the regularity of this form of resistance, especially, for western workers, in Munich from 1942.[93] Osnabrück contains numerous cases of such 'escapes', particularly from Dutchmen, in view of the proximity of their homeland, although other western Europeans, as well as *Ostarbeiter*, also fled. For instance, two French prisoners of war left a labour battalion on 24 August 1943. On the same day another French prisoner fled, although the two cases appear unconnected.[94] A Dutchman meanwhile, who worked for Klöckner, faced arrest on the Dutch border near Nordhorn, while trying to cross it.[95] Another *Gestapo* card gives the following details:

> K. left his place of work without authorization and tried, with the help of a forged passport, to travel to Holland. He was arrested and was handed over after authorization from the town attorney in Osnabrück. He was sentenced to six months in prison and had to pay the cost of the proceedings.[96]

Issmer has provided more details on escaping Dutchmen, whom he traced using the *Gestapo* cards in Osnabrück. Anton Knoop, for instance, simply did not return after being granted leave to Holland in 1943.[97] Meanwhile, Marc Edelstein and his brother tried to flee because of the consequences of Allied bombing and the treatment they received from Germans, eventually facing arrest near the Dutch border, meaning a return to Osnabrück.[98] One of the most persistent 'foreign criminals' in the town during the war, Josef Kaminski, faced prosecution in July 1942 on eight charges of theft, two cases of breaking and entering, one of escape from a work camp, one of fleeing from a prison and another of attempted escape from a different jail.[99]

Inter-Ethnic Relations in Wartime

In view of the numbers of measures trying to prevent contact between Germans and foreigners, the Nazi authorities came down particularly severely on anyone who transgressed. Both natives and foreign workers could find themselves facing serious penalties, particularly if any sort of relationship involving a German woman had occurred. Between 18 April 1941 and 7 January 1942 a total of 9 Polish males were hanged in Baden and Alsace simply because they were seen with German women, while the latter faced incarceration in a concentration camp after having their hair shaved in public.[100] But as large numbers of German males disappeared from the home front, 'male foreign workers became a focus of sexual interest for German women.'[101]

Relationships took place between foreigners and Germans in Osnabrück, although the *Gestapo* and courts did not impose sentences as harsh as those in Alsace and Baden. The *Gestapo* cards contain a few examples of 'sexual deviance'. For instance, a Polish prisoner of war was arrested and given 'special treatment' in May 1942 because he had sexual intercourse with a German.[102] In addition, two women faced prosecution at the higher special court in Celle for having relationships with foreigners. Erna Oldenburg who worked for the OKD was born in 1915 and had actually been sterilized in 1936. Her crime, for which she received a prison sentence of fifteen months, consisted of entering into a sexual relationship with a Belgian prisoner of war, whom she got to know at work.[103] Meanwhile, the court in Celle described the behaviour of Gertrud Bergmann as 'shameless and unworthy of a German woman'. Married with eight children, she had a sexual relationship with a French prisoner of war while her husband served in the *Wehrmacht*. Like Oldenburg, she faced a prison sentence of fifteen months.[104] Neither case file provides any indication of the fate of the prisoners of war involved.

Some Osnabrückers simply displayed empathy with the position of foreign workers in their midst, whose wretched position they could see for themselves. These positive feelings often resulted in simple acts of kindness, as the case of Gerhard Strauß indicated. Similarly, Josefa Herz, who worked in the Klöckner offices, recalled:

> In the production there were really a lot of Russian prisoners of war. Our office faced the street and the permanent road while other offices faced the yard. There was a very nice woman there, who I also knew, and I also saw it once. The Russian prisoners of war, they were starving, they could scarcely walk but they had to work. And this woman often left bread and butter lying on the windowsill in the morning.[105]

Similarly, Hilde Scholl claimed that she and some of her female relatives had given food to French prisoners of war and also made space for them in air raid shelters.[106]

Despite the measures introduced by the Nazis to prevent inter-ethnic relations during the War, it proved difficult to stop contact between Germans and foreigners both in Osnabrück and elsewhere in the country.

This is hardly surprising when we considered that mixed marriages between Germans and Poles had become normal before 1933. The lack of German males increased the possibility of relationships, no matter what the penalties. But then so did, more importantly perhaps, the fact that the two groups of workers laboured in close proximity in armaments factories experiencing the same fate of long hours as Allied bombs fell from the sky. Under such circumstances it was hardly surprising that Germans developed sympathy for their fellow workers. Inter-ethnic relations, manifesting themselves in a range of responses, whether love, sex or simply providing a piece of bread, continued under the most extreme conditions.

Freedom, Criminality and Revenge

At the conclusion of hostilities, however, thousands of foreign workers remained in Osnabrück, most of them desperate to return home, after taking out their vengeance on the German population. In 1945 15,000 foreigners from the entire *Regierungsbezirk* faced repatriation from a camp set up for this purpose.[107] At the end of April 1945, the month of the British invasion of Osnabrück, the *Stadt-Chronik* estimated that around 20,000 of these 'unloved guests' lived in the town.[108] The entire repatriation lasted into the late 1940s.

Many remained in camps changing, in the words of the main authority on the subject, 'from forced labourers to homeless foreigners', often with no desire to return to the Eastern Bloc where they would face charges of treachery. They chose, instead, to remain or move west.[109] In July 1947 two repatriation camps still existed in Osnabrück, housing about 2,700 people. In January 1949, 739 prisoners remained in the camp in Eversburg made up of: 505 Poles; 24 Estonians; 75 Latvians; 1 Turk; 3 Armenians; 3 stateless people; 11 Lithaunians; 51 Yugoslavs; 5 Hungarians; 57 Polish Ukrainians; 1 Russian; and 3 Czechs.[110]

In the latter stages of the war, as bombing reduced the urban landscape to rubble, criminality increasingly became a fact of everyday life, affecting both Germans and foreigners. Looting and thieving soared as the basics of everyday life became increasingly difficult to secure. In this situation, especially during the last few months of the war, gangs of criminals, consisting of Germans and foreigners, terrified middle class natives who tried to hold on to what they had.[111] At the same time, those foreigners who had survived the war years also had a desire for revenge similar to that which motivated the returning Romany Johann West in the summer of 1945. Middle class opinion may have exaggerated the scale of the problem, as official racism disappeared and more traditional forms of unofficial hostility towards foreigners became normal, but crime certainly did take place. In Württemberg, for instance, the US authorities arrested 31 people in the week between 22 and 29 July, while the Mayor of Aachen registered 124 instances of crimes involving foreign workers on 9 July.[112]

Osnabrück reveals a similar pattern. Looting, involving both Germans and foreigners, began as British troops approached from the west. On 5 April the *Stadt-Chronik* focused upon crimes carried out by 'an unchained gang of foreigners – Italians, Ukrainians Yugoslavians, and above all, however, Poles and Russians' who wondered through the streets 'and plundered businesses and warehouses'. They were 'absolutely starving and mostly badly clothed' and used the opportunity to 'satisfy their instincts'. On the following day the *Stadt-Chronik* reported that:

> Hordes of east European workers of both sexes are wandering through the streets in order to plunder businesses. A gang of about 100 people broke into the cellar of the Leffers warehouse in Johannisstraße, which is packed with textile goods. They are stealing to their heart's content...

The narrative asserted that the police remained powerless. All bicycles fell into the hands of east European workers, who simply stopped and took them from Germans. The *Stadt-Chronik* also mentioned house burglaries as well as assaults upon women at gunpoint. On 30 May, it spoke about 'The Plague of Foreigners', although by this time excesses seem to have declined as the British military authorities had taken control, eventually placing most foreigners in camps ready for repatriation. The British also ordered the city authorities to provide for them which the writer of the *Stadt-Chronik* resented. As late as 28 June Dr Glenewinkel wrote that 'many Russians' preferred to remain in Osnabrück and continue their 'free life of robbery' rather than return home. On 19 August he reported an attack on a house in the suburb of Dodesheide by a group of Italians and Yugoslavs who tied up the residents and took all of their possessions.[113]

While the compiler of the *Stadt-Chronik* revealed his racism in his narratives, other documents from the summer of 1945 support his reporting, often in more graphic detail. For instance, the Roman Catholic Church in the suburb of Haste became victim to several crimes carried out by Russians in June 1945, which included attacks on the vicar, the chaplain and 'several nuns', while 'religious events...could not take place because of the Russian plague'. Furthermore, 'The Russians gather together on various street corners in groups of 20 men and attack all churchgoers and remove all watches, jewellery and pieces of clothing which they carry on their bodies, so that the believers are too afraid to attend services and religious events'.[114]

Police reports from August 1945 provide even more disturbing information. One from the 16th provides the following details of events which occurred in the previous week:

1.Murder.
A German man was shot in Iburger Strasse after being ambushed by Poles.
2. Rape.
In the month of July 1945 a young woman was raped by a Serb.
3. Dangerous Attacks.
Ten Poles attempted to stop a motorcycle in Osnabrück-Haste. The driver drove further. The Poles shot him and hit the passenger on the motorbike. The person shot at died from his injuries.
4. Burglaries.
The number of robberies has increased. In two cases the perpetrators were reported. In three cases it was asserted that the robberies were carried out by Poles.
The following were stolen:
3 pigs, 2 geese, 10 chickens, 11 rabbits, machines, tools, clothing and groceries.
5. Robberies
Sixteen robberies of bicycles and five other robberies were carried out. These robberies were committed in:
9 cases by Poles
5 cases by Italians
4 cases by Russians
3 cases by foreigners of unknown nationalities
1 case by a German
2 cases by people in English uniforms.
The following cases committed were armed robberies:
In three cases Russians
In three cases Italians
In three cases Poles
In two cases people in English uniforms.[115]

The police report of the following week told a similar story.[116]

The crimes carried out by freed foreigners reached their height in the few months after liberation and then subsided as the British authorities gained control by interning those foreign workers and prisoners of war awaiting repatriation. In fact, after the summer of 1945 little criminality occurred involving foreigners, as confirmed by the interviewees for this project, few of whom had any personal memories of such crimes. The only two Osnabrückers who did consisted of Lora Kraft and Hermann Thiem. The former remembered the fear caused by the activities of 'the Russians' on the streets, which meant that she only went out with several of her friends but, nevertheless, still had her bicycle taken away.[117] More interesting is a story told by Hermann Thiem. Antonia Moskalenko returned to live with his family for six months after the end of the War, together with one of her friends. Thiem claimed that their presence in the house of his parents prevented an attack by Russians, who wanted to loot a bakery opposite their shop. 'Antonia opened the window and said something in Russian – what I don't know – in any case they went away.'[118]

Conclusion

After several years of confinement or forced labour, foreign workers had disappeared from Osnabrück by the 1950s. The multicultural town, at least in outward appearance, which had developed during the course of the War, again became overwhelmingly German. During their time in this provincial German outpost, foreigners and prisoners of war had endured difficult living conditions combined with long working hours and exposure to bombing. A combination of Nazi and Allied policy had made their lives a constant struggle for survival. One of their main forms of resistance, one of the few open to them, consisted of criminality, which encompassed all manner of activities in the tightly controlled state in which they found themselves. While much of this consisted of petty activities such as theft, others carried out the ultimate act of resistance in the form of escape. Once freed, and perhaps influenced by news about activities by the Russian army to the east, many foreigners decided to enact their own revenge for the treatment they had received from Germans.

Relationships with natives were not completely antagonistic as the recollections of Hermann Thiem indicate. Furthermore, we cannot establish how many foreigners participated in criminality. It became endemic amongst them both during and after the War, although we could make the same assertions about Germans.[119] In fact, similarities exist in the experiences of both Germans and foreigners, despite the racial hierarchy established by the Nazis. During the war both groups had to endure long working hours, poor nutrition and, at the end, bombing, although Germans had slightly more protection. Nevertheless, while *some* Germans *may* have received what they deserved, foreigners simply found themselves in a strange land in extreme circumstances, which largely explains the acts of criminality carried out both before and after 1945.

EPILOGUE

10

THE EMERGENCE FROM CRISIS

Anyone born in Germany between about 1860 and 1940 would have lived through dramatic changes, whatever their ethnicity. Individuals finding themselves within German borders during the second quarter of the twentieth century could not have escaped the upheavals which the country experienced, whether they consisted of the consequences of economic collapse, the effects of a revolutionary racist regime, the impact of one of the most brutal wars in European history, or the aftermath of this conflict. Every individual living on German soil during some or all of the period 1929-1949 would have experienced at least some of these events.[1]

The two central themes of this book have consisted of the impact of the dramatic developments of the years 1929-49 upon individuals from different ethnic backgrounds and, especially in Part III, the consequences of these changes for relationships between the different ethnic groups which lived in Osnabrück. With regard to both of these, it was virtually impossible for anybody not to have noticed the transformations which occurred around them. The economic, political and social changes profoundly impacted upon members of all ethnic groups living in the town, while the variations in racial policy had consequences for the way in which different ethnic groups related to each other.

From Pain to Prosperity – For Survivors

We can begin by looking at the impact of the economic, social and political transformations upon the different ethnic groups which lived within the town, using the four chronological periods which have taken the narrative forward: the end of the Weimar Republic, 1929-33; the peacetime Nazi years, 1933-9; the Second World War, 1939-45; and the post-War crisis, 1945-9. The first and last of these periods resulted in the most equal level of transformation between the population groupings.

The Wall Street Crash meant a collapse of businesses throughout the country, which affected members of the middle classes, whether they consisted of Jews or gentiles. Unemployment impacted upon different ethnic groupings and social classes in varying ways but blue collar workers bore the brunt of the crisis. Romanies, living on the edge of society, may have experienced the least direct consequences of the late Weimar crisis, but even here falling levels of disposable income amongst Jews and gentiles

would have affected their lives. Politically, this crisis had little impact upon
the Romanies, an ethnic group which has traditionally remained distant
from politics. On the other hand the rise of the Nazis completely
transformed political life for active ethnic groups and classes. Many
contemporary accounts have demonstrated the fear which the rise the
NSDAP inflicted upon Jews, whether or not they actually had personal
experiences of violence.[2] The growth of the Nazi party also transformed
the level of political activity, both in terms of the numbers of election
meetings which took place, as polls at all levels occurred, and because of
the increase in violence. Certainly, political life in Osnabrück, and in
Germany as a whole, intensified between 1929-33, compared with the mid-
Weimar years, 1924-9, but in the context of the political transformations
which occurred in twentieth century German history, we might view it as
one of many such intensifications, which has also involved revolution in
1918 and 1989 and foreign occupation after 1945.[3]

The peacetime Nazi years had dramatic consequences for all ethnic
groups and all of the individual sections who made up the ethnic majority.
Romanies again witnessed the least dramatic changes because the level of
persecution which they experienced during the period 1933-9 would not
have differed significantly from what they had lived through for centuries,
as a completely marginalized and persecuted group in German society.
Forced sterilization may have represented a new departure, as did the use of
concentration camps, but the new measures to control Romanies simply
continue policies from the establishment of the German nation state at the
end of the nineteenth century.

Jews, on the other hand, saw their lives destroyed and experienced the
most dramatic transformations of any ethnic group under peacetime
Nazism. Antisemitism had been a fact of life for Jews throughout the
history of modern Germany, including the Weimar Republic. But this had
not prevented them from making progress into the highest echelons of
German society, especially as a result of the emancipation process of the
nineteenth century. In the early years of their rule the Nazis aimed at
reversing this process, which they essentially did through the hundreds of
antisemitic measures which they introduced depriving Jews of their civil
rights. Even worse, members of this group would experience Nazi violence
for the first time. Many therefore chose to emigrate rather than wait for the
NSDAP to destroy their lives, meaning that those who chose to move, took
control of their own lives. Those who remained would experience the
nightmare of the War.

All members of the ethnic majority also witnessed dramatic
transformations during the early Nazi period, but not on the same scale as
Jews. Experiences varied according to any number of factors including

political orientation, gender, class and health. Economically, the years 1933-9 meant positive changes for most members of the ethnic majority population because of the elimination of unemployment, which, however, partly resulted from the introduction of work creation and forced labour schemes. The reduction in unemployment went together with an increase in working hours. As a result of public works and then rearmament, businesses also got back on their feet again, although large companies did better than smaller ones.

Politically, the peacetime Nazi years also resulted in dramatic transformations, especially during 1933 when the new regime killed the Weimar constitution, abolishing democracy and eliminating its opponents. Members of groupings other than the NSDAP therefore witnessed dramatic changes in their political lives which now consisted, for those who chose to continue the fight, of some form of, usually illegal, activity, particularly for members of the SPD and KPD. In small locations such as Osnarbück this became especially difficult because of the lack of any support mechanisms in such a locality compared with those which could survive in urban conurbations such as the Ruhr or Berlin.

Economic and social change in the years 1933-9 proved more dramatic for some sections of the majority ethnic grouping than others. Some women found themselves out of the labour market, especially those who had previously worked in the professions, although the overall fall in the number of women workers proved quite limited. Children found themselves drawn into the activities of the Hitler Youth, which, as we have seen from the experiences of the Osnabrück interviewees, could prove an exciting or repulsive experience, largely dependant upon the political and religious persuasion of parents.

But one of the most important determining factors for the fate of the ethnic majority population of Osnabrück between 1933 and 1939 consisted of the 'racial health' of individuals. Healthy mothers and families would find themselves receiving all types of welfare benefits, even though these often continued Weimar traditions and reflected policies in other European states. The new departure came for those regarded as racially unfit to reproduce, following the passage of the Law for the Prevention of Hereditary Diseased Offspring of 14 July 1933. Although sterilization had its origins in the *Kaiserreich* and the Weimar Republic, it now became official policy and affected 320,000 people, or 0.5 percent of the German population, by the outbreak of War, including hundreds of patients in Osnabrück, despite complaints from parents.

Although all of the four periods under consideration resulted in dramatic changes, it was the War during which the most extraordinary developments occurred. For ethnic minorities, these years meant changes of which they could not have conceived before the Nazis came to power. Even the perennially and blatantly persecuted Romanies could not have believed that they would have been systematically murdered. In some ways the impact of the War may have proved less dramatic for Jews, because of the rapidity with which their position had already deteriorated between 1933 and 1939.

While the Romanies and Jews found themselves transferred to concentration camps, in their place came foreign workers, entering German cities of which they had no knowledge. Finding themselves on German soil for the purpose of working in a situation in which Allied bombs threatened their lives, their experiences differed dramatically from those of their land of origin, even though they may have originated in the Stalinistic USSR to which many of them would return. Continuities with their former lives seemed to vanish in the alienating land in which they found themselves, although they would have developed friendships with those around them and, as we have seen from the case of Atonina Moskalenko, they sometimes received help and sympathy from Germans.

While natives certainly did endure dramatic changes before 1939, the War meant new experiences of a different magnitude. The central development for Germans who remained on the home front consisted of the Allied bombing. All those who lived through it have some memories of it, which is not surprising, in view of the fear it caused and the physical damage which resulted. Furthermore, the Air War, together with the consequences of mobilization, meant the basics of everyday life, such as shelter, a regular supply of food and a division between the spheres of work and non-work, disappeared for many by 1945. Those Germans whom the Nazis regarded as outside the national community, whether on political or health grounds, would face further persecution, especially, in the case of the former, after the failed assassination attempt on Hitler of 20 July 1944. At the same time, reflecting the attempted 'final solutions' to other 'racial problems', the Nazis instituted a euthanasia programme.

The years which followed the conflict represented an attempt to return to some sort of stability, to the extent that such a concept existed in view of the changes which had occurred since 1929, for both ethnic majorities and minorities. Part of this process consisted of an attempt to eradicate memories and legacies of the Nazi past, whether through prosecution of the perpetrators, as Donald Bloxham has shown[4] or though denazification led by the Allies. However, as Robert G. Moeller has demonstrated, the early post-War years, but more especially the 1950s, also saw the German memorialization of the victims of Allied invasion, victory and bombing.[5]

Despite this, ethnic minorities had the most dramatic life changes to face after 1945. In a town such as Osnabrück, with small non-German communities, returning Jews such as Irmgard Ohl or Romanies such as

Johannn West found nothing left of their previous lives because their families and communities had disappeared. For them the post-War experience almost did represent 'life after death',[6] but in both cases they did manage to get back on their feet again, as new communities of sorts developed. This proved easier for Jews than Romanies because of the sympathy which the former now experienced, despite the continued survival of antisemitism,[7] in contrast with the overt persecution experienced by the Romanies, which did not differ substantially from that which existed before 1933. For foreign workers the immediate post-War years represented a period in which they had the initial desire, in some cases, to take revenge on the Germans, but the ultimate one, in most cases, to return to their homelands, even though in the case of those from the Soviet Union, they faced allegations of collaboration with their captors.[8]

Refugees from eastern Europe, like returning Jews and Romanies, had to begin their lives from scratch. This was not so much because they had lost their families, although many did, or a lack of community, because migration patterns meant that refugees from the same area usually reached the same destination, but more because of the new surroundings in which they found themselves. They reached what seemed to them an alien land (even though their new neighbours consisted of people with the same nationality as themselves) an alienation intensified by the desolation of the surroundings which faced them, so that they too would have felt that they were experiencing 'life after death'. While we should not underestimate the difficulties which the refugees faced, the west German state, supported by the bulk of public opinion, did everything to assist their integration, contrasting with the attitude towards foreigners after 1945. Their early years in Osnabrück proved a disorientating period when they lacked the basics of life such as sufficient food and proper housing. But as Bade, Meier and Parisius have written: 'The integration of refugees and expellees in the town of Osnabrück was determined by the development of the labour market and therefore proceeded relatively quickly and silently.'[9]

While natives may have had the 'easiest' experiences after 1945, they too had to face dramatic changes before life resembled anything which we can describe as normality. Soldiers, like refugees, returned to an alienating and devastated landscape, although they usually found work quite quickly. Housing also improved as did the general economic condition of the town, which had recovered by the 1950s and subsequently experienced the 'German economic miracle'. Only the first couple of years after the end of the War represented a particularly painful period for Germans in economic terms. The introduction of the *Deutschmark* in 1948 virtually meant the elimination of poverty from Germany.

How have those who lived through the period 1929-49 viewed these years? In the project led by Lutz Niethammer on the Ruhr between 1930 and 1960, respondents focused upon a variety of issues depending upon their gender, geographical, social and political background.[10] I asked interviewees to give their impression of the period as a whole and also obtained a series of responses. Few saw themselves as victims although most recalled them as the worst years of their lives, without bitterness. Werner Funk stated: 'I would say, it was a time of need, disappointment, hope and catastrophe'.[11] Similarly, Hermann Thiem replied: 'they were bad times, they were lean times'.[12] Three interviewees with left wing backgrounds gave some of the most interesting and varied impressions of the years 1929-49. First, Inge Walter, born in 1925:

> Yes, how shall I put it. My childhood was very poor. My parents never had very much money...
> I do not remember my childhood fondly. We never had very much to eat...
> The war years were even worse for me because my mother died in 1940 when I was 15 years old.

Werner Lorenz, meanwhile, gave various answers, believing that the years 1929-49 were the most important in German and European history. Most pertinently of all, he stated: 'When you live through such times, you have to cope with them'. Lilo Meyer, born in 1926, viewed the period positively in contrast to her friend Inge Walter: `I find that I had such a nice childhood, because one lived in solidarity, not only in the family, but in the surroundings in which we lived, where people stood up for one another.'[13] Heinrich Wand, meanwhile, stated: 'Since 1949 we have had a golden era. It was a gruesome terrible time.'[14] The two sentences, juxtaposed, sum up the experience of most ethnic Germans born in the first half of the twentieth century. While Allied bombers killed 600,000 people,[15] the overwhelming majority survived to live through and enjoy the most prosperous period in German history.

For survivors, the post-war period, whether or not we include the years 1945-9, represents a move from 'pain' to 'prosperity' in the words of Paul Betts and Greg Eghigian, who have used these two words to describe twentieth century German history.[16] While the years before 1949 had been characterized by pain in Osnabrück, prosperity best describes the post-War history of the town. In this period Osnabrück has experienced a complete recovery. Rebuilding allowed the town to surpass it former glory. By the 1970s it had become the third largest settlement in Lower Saxony, with a sound industrial base, excellent communications and a thriving cultural life, reflecting the 'economic miracle' which had restored West Germany to its place as the leading power on the European continent. Setbacks have occurred as a result of the oil crisis of the middle of the 1970s and reunification in the 1990s, which has meant industrial decline and the arrival of endemic unemployment.[17] But the economic difficulties of recent decades remain minor compared with the crises which affected Osnabrück between the late 1920s and the late 1940s. Despite a rise in support for the extreme right during the 1990s, this in no way threatened democracy either in Osnabrück or Germany, as the country has emerged into a mature liberal democratic state, which has left the demons of its Nazi past behind.[18]

Inter-Ethnic Relations

Osnabrück therefore reflects other towns in the Federal Republic, which have become centres of urban political and economic stability, despite the relatively minor crises which have occurred, at least in the western half of Germany, since 1945. The second major theme of this volume consisted of the impact of Nazism upon inter-ethnic relations, which, clearly, in view of the consequences of the policies implemented, was dramatic, although we need to recognize that continuities exist in the marginaliztion of ethnic minorities, if not the methods in which this marginalization occurred.

Between 1929 and 1949 Osnabrück counted, at various times, six major population groupings along ethnic grounds consisting of: native Christian Germans; Jews, either born within the town or coming from further afield; Romanies; foreign workers; German refugees; and British invaders. Power relationships between the ethnic majority and the various 'minority' groups proceeded along two different paths. Native Germans represented the dominant group in terms of both numbers and hold over power vis a vis Jews, Romanies, refugees and, for most of the period under consideration, foreign workers. For a short spell at the end of the War, the last group appeared to have the upper hand against the German majority, although we should not let the Osnabrück *Stadt-Chronik* colour our perception too much because, while crime against Germans occurred, the interviewees for the project reveal that they had little personal experience of it. However, the relationship with the British invaders did remain significantly different from that with the other groups considered here because although they remained a numerical minority, they held power over the local population.

In the years leading up to the Nazi takeover of power, inter-ethnic relations between the majority and their neighbours did not present a uniform pattern. Although antisemitism in Osnabrück clearly existed, as revealed by the rise of the *Stadtwächter*, as well as instances of everyday prejudice towards Jews, this community had come a long way since its return to the town following an absence of almost four centuries between

1431 and 1800. In the hundred and thirty years between their readmission and the Nazi seizure of power, Jews had made inroads here, as elsewhere in the country, into the local social, economic, political and artistic establishment. Just as importantly, they had intermarried with Christians. This contrasts significantly with Romanies. No emancipation movement had liberated this uneducated group of economic, social and political outsiders who had little contact with the majority population. Before 1933 Osnabrückers had relatively little experience of foreigners, in contrast with the larger urban conurbations of the Ruhr, where assimilation continued apace.

The peacetime Nazi years completely changed relationships between the ethnic majority and Jews. Middle class gentiles had less and less to do with this group due to the introduction of antisemitic legislation and the fact that the community had shrunk to a fraction of its previous size by the outbreak of War. Only a few Osnabrückers actively participated in the violence against the local Jewish community which occurred on 1 April 1933 and 9-10 November 1938. Most remained passive, largely through fear of the consequences of standing up to the Nazis. Relationships with Romanies continued as they did before 1933, with few Osnabrückers having anything to do with them. The local police authorities continued implementing the type of exclusionary measures which had characterised their history in the town and in the province of Hanover for centuries.[19] We have little information on the relationship of Germans with foreigners in the town between 1933 and 1939, although we have seen that Osnabrückers welcomed those with the right ethnic credentials.

The disappearance of the Jewish and Romany population during the War meant that relations with these groups ceased. The documentation in the NSO reveals that a small number of local *Gestapo* officials, most of whom originated from outside the locality, actually carried out the task of deporting these two ethnic minorities to eastern Europe. The rest of the population remained oblivious to the fate of the Romanies, but, from the evidence provided by interviewees, clearly had knowledge of the consequences of antisemitism on both a local and national scale. Because of their sheer numbers, making up as much as twenty per cent of the population of Osnabrück at the start of 1945, foreign workers inevitably became the group with which Germans had most contact during the War, despite the measures brought in to prevent any sort of relations between the two populations. Evidence reveals that Osnabrückers went out of their way to help foreigners, while, here, as elsewhere, sexual relationships developed, with serious consequences for those caught.

At the end of the conflict relationships between Germans and ethnic minorities changed again. The early post-War period witnessed foreign workers taking out acts of revenge against the German majority which had suppressed them during the conflict, but, by the foundation of the Federal Republic, the overwhelming majority of this group had returned home. In their place came a variety of others. In the first place the Jewish community reconstituted itself in a supportive and remorseful atmosphere. Irmgard Ohl's marriage to a gentile continued pre-Nazi patterns. Meanwhile, the enduring persecution of the Romanies reflects the twentieth century relationship of this minority to ethnic Germans. New groups also arrived. Evidence in Osnabrück suggests that hostility existed between natives and refugees. But the efforts of the national and local refugee offices meant that they became integrated quicker than any newcomers in twentieth century Germany, even though they still had more difficult life experiences than natives in the decades to come.[20] The British were dissimilar to any of the ethnic outsiders in Osnabrück during the twentieth century because of their power relationships to the Germans. In the early post-War years things ran relatively smoothly for the invaders, despite their policy of denazification, although Osnabrück indicates that hostility did sometimes explode against them.

Since the 1950s relationships between Germans and outsiders have developed in a fairly smooth way, largely because individual groups have adhered to their majority or minority status. While genocidal policies disappeared from Germany with the elimination of the Nazis, *ethnic differentiation did not*. The real winners from the economic miracle have consisted of native ethnic Germans living in the western half of the country. Foreign migrants have remained a marginalized group with no political rights working in worse conditions, with a lower social and economic status than Germans. By 1991 the foreign percentage of the Osnabrück population had reached 8.5 per cent, with an unemployment rate over twice as high as Germans. Those employed in the town carried out manual work to a greater extent than Germans. Interestingly, in 1993 a total of 19.44 per cent of Karmann employees consisted of foreigners. Furthermore, only 4.64 per cent of foreigners in this firm had office jobs, compared with 24.22 per cent for Germans, displaying close similarities with the wartime situation.[21]

The two groups which became victims of genocide under the Nazis have had vastly different experiences since the end of World War Two. On the one hand, Jews have become a thriving, organized middle class minority, fed by immigration from further east, at least in the towns in which local communities have resurfaced, albeit on a smaller scale than previously.[22] These include Osnabrück, whose Jewish community reconstituted itself immediately after the end of the War and which opened an impressive new synagogue in 1969.[23] This contrasts dramatically with the situation of

Romanies. While they may no longer experience state violence, they remain the most marginalized group in German society facing a raft of measures aimed at controlling them, pointing to the clear continuities in their persecution, which the leading scholars working on them have stressed.[24]

At least, in the case of Osnabrück, the local state has remembered Jews and Romanies equally, by establishing plaques to members of both communities who perished at the hands of the Nazis. Similarly, the Ohrbeck camp has become a museum to commemorate foreigners who worked in the town during the War. In fact, Osnabrück represents a site of international importance for those interested in the memory of Nazism and the Holocaust because of the Nussbaum collection in the museum.[25]

Despite the setbacks which have occurred since the end of the War, those Osnabrückers who survived have emerged from the crisis to enjoy the full fruits of the German 'economic miracle'. In the early twenty first century the memory of the consequences of Nazism remains central in both the serious and popular history of the town, assuring that the Third Reich continues to cast its shadow over its development. But it was not simply the Nazis who influenced inter-ethnic relations in Germany or Osnabrück as a whole. While intermarriage may continue apace, so does some level of ethnic segregation, witnessed not simply by the continuing marginalization of Romanies and foreign workers, but also the lowly social position of a new group of Germans from eastern Europe who fled to the country following the end of the old order in eastern Europe.[26] Yet it is likely they will become increasingly integrated as ethnic Germans. Osnabrück in the early twenty first century has therefore fully recovered from the traumas of the second quarter of the twentieth, although the memories of these years survive clearly in the civic and historiographical memory of the town.

NOTES

Preface

1 See, for, instance: *Inside Nazi Germany: Conformity, Opposition and Racism in Everyday Life* (London, 1993); *Die KPD im Widerstand: Verfolgung und Untergrundarbeit am Rhein und Ruhr 1933 bis 1945* (Wuppertal, 1980); *Die Edelweißpiraten: Protestbewegung jugendlicher Arbeiter im dritten Reich* (Cologne, 1988).

2 Robert Gellately, *The Gestapo and German Society: Enforcing Racial Policy 1933-1945* (Oxford, 1990).

3 Ian Kershaw, *Popular Opinion and Political Dissent in the Third Reich: Bavaria 1933-1945* (Oxford, 1983).

4 William Sheridan Allen, *The Nazi Seizure of Power: The Experience of a Single German Town, 1922-1945* (London, 1966).

5 Walter Struve, *Aufstieg und Herrschaft des Nationalsozialismus in einer industriellen Kleinstadt: Osterode am Harz, 1918-1945* (Essen, 1992).

6 Michael Burleigh and Wolfgang Wippermann, *The Racial State: Germany 1933-1945* (Cambridge, 1991) cover the Nazi period.

Chapter 1

1 Michael Burleigh, *The Third Reich: A New History* (London, 2000), p. 21.

2 These changes are stressed by Hans-Ulrich Wehler, *Deutsche Gesellschaftsgeschichte*, Vol. 4, *Vom Beginn des Ersten Weltkrieges bis zur Gründung der beiden deutschen Staaten, 1914-1949* (Munich, 2003).

3 Eric Hobsbawm, *Age of Extremes: A Short History of the Twentieth Century* (London, 1994), pp. 6-7, taking a global approach, has described the 'decades from the outbreak of the First World War to the aftermath of the Second' as 'an Age of Catastrophe'.

4 Robert Gellately, *The Gestapo and German Society: Enforcing Racial Policy 1933-1945* (Oxford, 1990).

5 William Sheridan Allen, *The Nazi Seizure of Power: The Experience of a Single German Town, 1922-1945* (London, 1966).

6 Walter Struve, *Aufstieg und Herrschaft des Nationalsozialismus in einer industriellen Kleinstadt: Osterode am Harz, 1918-1945* (Essen, 1992).

7 As he pointed out in 'Das "Dritte Reich" aus der "Alltags"-Perspektive', *Archiv für Sozialgeschichte*, vol. 26 (1986), p. 534.

8 See: *Inside Nazi Germany: Conformity, Opposition and Racism in Everyday Life* (London, 1993); *Die KPD im Widerstand: Verfolgung und Untergrundarbeit am Rhein*

und Ruhr 1933 bis 1945 (Wuppertal, 1980); *Die Edelweißpiraten: Protestbewegung jugendlicher Arbeiter im dritten Reich* (Cologne, 1988).

9   See, for example: Wolfgang Schneider, ed., *Alltag unter Hitler* (March, 2000); Werner Mazur, *Das Dritte Reich: Alltag in Deutschland von 1933 bis 1945* (Munich, 1998); and Harald Focke and Uwe Reimer, *Alltag unterm Hakenkreuz: Wie die Nazis das Leben der Deutschen veränderten* (Hamburg, 1979).

10 Johannes Volker Wagner, *Hakenkreuz über Bochum: Machtergreifung und Nationalsozialistische Alltag in einer Revierstadt*, 3rd Edition (Bochum, 1993).

11 Annette Kuhn, ed., *Frauenleben im NS-Alltag* (Pfaffenweiler, 1994); Margarete Dörr, *Vertrieben, Ausgebombt auf Sich Gestellt: Frauen meistern Kriegs- und Nachkriegsgeschichte* (Frankfurt am Main, 1998).

12 Asmus Nitschke, *Die 'Erbpolizei' im Nationalsozialismus: Zur Alltagsgeschichte der Gesundheitsämter im Dritten Reich* (Opladen, 1999); Berhnard Richarz, *Heilen, Pflegen, Töten: Zur Alltagsgeschichte einer Heil- und Pflegeanstalt bis zum ende des Nationasozialismus* (Göttingen, 1987).

13 Tobias Engelsing, *'Wir Sind in Deutschland und nicht in Russland': Eine Alltagsgeschichte der Volksschule in den jahren 1933-1949 am Beispiel der Stadt Radolfzell am Bodensee* (Constance, 1987).

14 Geoff Eley, 'Foreword', in Alf Lüdtke, ed., *The History of Everyday Life: Reconstructing Historical Experiences and Ways of Life* (Princeton, New Jersey, 1995), p. vii; David F Crew, '*Alltagsgeschichte*: A New German Social History "from Below?"', *Central European History*, vol. 22 (1989), p. 395; Winfried Schulze, ed., 'Einleitung' in Winfried Schulze, ed., *Sozialgeschichte, Alltagsgeschichte, Mikro-Historie: Eine Diskussion* (Göttingen, 1994), p. 6.

15 Wolfgang Hardtwig, 'Alltagsgeschichte Heute: Eine kritische Bilanz', in Schulze, ibid., p. 21.

16 Hans Medick, '"Missionaries in the Rowboat"? Ethnological Ways of Knowing as a Challenge to Social History', in Lüdtke, *Everyday Life*, pp. 41-71.

17 Alf Lüdtke, 'What is the History of Everyday Life and Who are its Practitioners', in Lüdtke, *Everyday Life*, p. 3.

18 See Berliner Geschichtswerkstatt, ed., *Alltagsgeschichte, Subjektivität und Geschichte: Zur Theorie und Praxis von Alltagsgeschichte* (Münster, 1994), pp. 157-234.

19 Stefan Risenfellner, ed., *Arbeitswelt um 1900: Texte zur Alltagsgeschite von Max Winter* (Vienna, 1988).

20 Gerhard A. Ritter, *The New Social History in the Federal Republic of Germany* (London, 1991), p. 36.

21 See, for instance, Johannes Hesse, *Carolinger 1939 bis 1947: Erinnerungen eines ehemaligen Schülers* (Osnabrück, 1997) as well as those in NSO Slg-54.

22 Institut für Zeitgeschichte, *Alltagsgeschichte der NS-Zeit: Neue Perpspektive oder Trivialisierung?* (Munich, 1984).

23 Ibid, p. 17.

24 Ibid, pp. 29-32.

25 Peukert, *Inside Nazi Germany*, p. 22.

26 Schulze, *Sozialgeschichte*.

27 Brigitte Berlekamp and Werner Röhr, eds, *Terror, Herrschaft und Alltag: Probleme eine Sozialgeschichte des deutschen Faschismus* (Münster, 1995).

28 The major exception at a national level is Michael Burleigh and Wolfgang Wippermann, *The Racial State: Germany 1933-1945* (Cambridge 1991) but this simply covers the Nazi years.

29 See ibid. for an introduction to racial differences.

30 See Ruth Gay, *The Jews of Germany: A Historical Portrait* (London, 1992).

31 Joachim S. Hohmann, *Geschichte der Zigeunerverfolgung in Deutschland*, 2nd edn (Frankfurt, 1988).

32 See Martin Broszat, *Zweihundert Jahre deutsche Polenpolitik*, 2nd Edn (Frankfurt, 1972).

33 Klaus J. Bade, *Vom Auswanderungsland zum Einwanderungsland? Deutschland 1880-1980* (Berlin, 1983); Ulrich, Herbert, *A History of Foreign Labour in Germany, 1880-1980: Seasonal Workers/Forced Workers/Guest Workers* (Ann Arbor, MI, 1990); Lothar Elsner and Joachim Lehmann, *Ausländische Arbeiter unter dem deutschen Imperialismus, 1900 bis 1985* (Berlin, 1988).

34 But see: Peter Junk and Martina Sellmeyer, *Stationen auf dem Weg nach Auschwitz: Entrechtung, Vertreibung, Vernichtung: Juden in Osnabrück, 1900-1945* (Osnabrück, 1989); and Michael Gander, 'Beziehungen zwischen sowjetischen Zwangsarbeitern und deutscher Bevölkerung in Osnabrück', in Babette Quinkert, ed., *'Wir sind die Herren dieses Landes': Ursachen, Verlauf und Folgen des deutschen Überfalls auf die Sowjetunion* (Hamburg, 2002), pp. 154-65.

35 As an introduction see Thomas Nipperday, *Deutsche Geschichte 1866-1918*, 2 Volumes (Munich, 1990-2).

36 See contributions to Klaus Larres and Panikos Panayi, eds, *The Federal Republic of Germany Since 1949: Politics, Society and Economy Before and After Unification* (London, 1996)

37 See, for instance, Roger Chickering, *Imperial Germany and the Great War* (Cambridge, 1998).

38 Richard Bessel, *Germany After the First World War* (Oxford, 1993).

39 These crises are covered in chapters 2-9 below.

40 The project resulted in three volumes under the collective title of *Lebensgeschichte und Sozialkultur im Ruhrgebiet 1930 bis 1960*. The details of the inidividual volumes are: Lutz Niethammer, ed., *'Die Jahre weiß man nicht, wo man die heute hinsetzen soll': Faschismus Erfahrungen im Ruhrgebiet* (Bonn, 1983); Lutz Niethammer, ed., *'Hinterher merkt man, daß es richtig war, daß es schiefgegangen ist': Nachkriegserfahrungen im Ruhrgebiet* (Bonn, 1983); Lutz Niethammer and Alexander von Plato, eds, *'Wir Kriegen jetzt andere Zeiten': Auf der Suche nach der Erfahrungen der Volker in Nachfaschistischen Ländern* (Bonn, 1985).

41 This project also resulted in three volumes edited by Klaus-Michael Mallmann, Gerhard Paul and Hans-Walter Hermann under the collective title of *Widerstand und Verweigerung im Saarland, 1933-1945*, as follows, *Das zersplitterte Nein: Saarländer gegen Hitler* (Bonn, 1989); *Herrschaft und Alltag: Ein Industrierevier im Dritten Reich* (Bonn, 1991); *Milieus und Widerstand: Eine Verhaltensgeschichte der Gesellschaft im Nationalsozialismus* (Bonn, 1995).

42 Niethammer, *'Die Jahre weiß man nicht'*, p. 7.

43 Ibid.

44 Ulrich Herbert, 'Apartheid Nebenan: Erinnerungen an die Fremdarbeiter im Ruhrgebiet', in ibid., pp. 233-66.

45 NSO Rep 430-201.

46 NSO Rep 439-19; Gellately used case files from both towns in his *Gestapo and German Society*, while Peukert utilised the Düsseldorf files for several studies including *KPD im Widerstand* and *Edelweißpiraten*.

47 Gerd Steinwascher, ed., *Gestapo Osnabrück Meldet: Polizei und Regierungsberichte aus dem Regierungsbezirk Osnabrück aus den Jahren 1933 bis 1936* (Osnabrück, 1995).

48 NSO Rep 430-303.

49 NSO Rep 727.

50 NSO Dep 3b

51 NSO Dep 3b XIX.

52 These are mostly contained under the general references NSO Erw and NSO Slg.

53 See Raimond Reiter, '"Heimtücke" und "Volksschädlinge": Osnabrücker vor dem Sondergericht Hannover in der NS-Zeit', *Osnabrücker Mitteilungen*, vol. 103 (1998), pp. 267-76.

54 Werner Delblanco, et. al, eds, *Archivalische Quellen zur politischen Krisensituation während der Weimarer Zeit in den ehemaligen Territorien des Landes Niedersachsen*, 4 Vols (Göttingen 1984-97), Vol. 4, pt. 3 *Akten staatlicher und kommunaler Dienstellen sowie privater Herrkunft im Regierungsbezirk Osnabrück* (Göttingen, 1991), p. xvii; Stefan Matysiak, 'Die britischen Heeresgruppenzeitungen und die Wiedergeburt der niedersächsischen Lokalpresse 1945/6', *Osnabrücker Mitteilungen*, vol. 107 (2002), pp. 233-51.

55 Struve, *Aufstieg*, pp. 39-40, points out that Osterode *Kreis* had a population of 48,500 in 1933, while Allen, *Nazi Seizure of Power*, p. 12, states that Northeim contained 10,000 residents in 1930.

56 *Statistisches Jahrbuch deutscher Städte*, vol. 26 (Jena, 1931), pp. 11-12.

57 *Statistisches Jahrbuch deutscher Gemeinde*, vol. 35 (Jena, 1940), pp. 235-7.

58 *Statistisches Jahrbuch deutscher Gemeinde*, vol. 37 (Schwäbisch Gmünd, 1949), pp. 14-30.

59 *Osnabrücker Volkszeitung*, 30 November 1930.

60 Panikos Panayi, *Ethnic Minorities in Nineteenth and Twentieth Century Germany: Jews, Gypsies, Poles, Turks and Others* (London, 2000), pp. 133-4.

61 This was the number deported to Auschwitz, as indicated in NSO Rep 430-201-16B-65-39-Bd.1.

62 Hans Joachim Döring, *Die Zigeuner im nationalsozialistischen Staat* (Hamburg, 1964), p. 18.

63 Friedrich Lehmann, 'Siedlung und Wohnungsbau nach dem Kriege', in Lehmann, ed., *Osnabrück* (Berlin, 1928), pp. 35-42.

64 Ibid., pp. 15-21; Ludwig, Hoffmeyer, et. al., *Chronik der Stadt Osnabrück* 6th Edn (Osnabrück, 1995), pp. 422-46; Edgar Schröder, *Osnabrück: So Wie Es War*, 2nd Edn, Vol. 1 (Düsseldorf, 1982), p. 84; Günther Höfelmann, Wilhelm van Kampen and Alfred Lindner, 'Industrialisierung und Arbeiterbewegung in Osnabrück vor dem Ersten Weltkrieg', in Wilhelm van Kampen and Tilman Westphalen, eds, *100 Jahre SPD in Osnabrück, 1875-1975: Ausgewählte Kapitel zur Geschichte der Arbeiterbewegung in Osnabrück* (Osnabrück, 1975), p. 19.

65 This is described by Höfelmann, Kampen and Lindner, ibid., pp. 24-50.

66 Ibid., pp. 51-81; Edgar Schroeder, *Osnabrück im 19. Jahrhundert* (Düsseldorf, 1995), p. 82.

67 Hoffmeyer, *Chronik*, pp. 496-503.

68 Ibid., pp. 504-7; Wilhelm Van Kampen and Heiko Schulze, 'Kriegsende und November Revolution', in van Kampen and Westphalen, *100 Jahre SPD*, pp. 89-95.

69 Senator Schulte, 'Die Entwicklung der städtischen Finanzen seit der Stabilisierung der Währung', in Lehmann, *Osnabrück*, pp. 99-101.

70 Heinrich Brinkmann, 'Handwerk und Gewerbe in Osnabrück', in Lehmann, ibid., pp. 101-3; Herbert Budde, 'Die Stadt Osnabrück und der Ortsverein der SPD, 1924-1933', in van Kampen and Westphalen, *100 Jahre SPD*, p. 98.

71 Walter Kolkmeyer, *Die Wirtschaftliche Verflechtung der Stadt Osnabrück* (Hanover, 1931), pp. 26-32.

72 Senator Schulte, 'Die Wohlfahrtspflege der Stadt', *Osnabrücker Jahrbuch*, vol. 2 (1929), pp. 137-41.

73 Karl Kühling, *Osnabrück, 1925-1933* (Osnabrück, 1963), pp. 65-72.

74 Ibid., pp. 33-6.

75 Karl Kühling, *Theater in Osnabrück: Im Wandel der Jahrhunderte* (Osnabrück, 1959).

76 Hoffmeyer, *Chronik*, pp. 484-8.

77 Hoffmeyer, ibid., pp. 515-18; Kühling, *Osnabrück, 1925-1933*, pp. 14-15, 36-42.

78 Budde, 'Die Stadt Osnabrück und der Ortsverein der SPD', pp. 99, 101.

79 See Anja Carl, 'Der Landesverband Osnabrück der Deutschnationalen Volkspartei (DNVP) von 1918 bis zum Ende der Weimarer Republik: Geschichte, Organisation, Politik' (unpublished University of Osnabrück MA thesis, 1995).

80 M Dumkow and Frank Roland, 'Geschichte der KPD Ortsgruppe Osnabrück, 1919-1933', 2 volumes (unpublished manuscript, 1975), vol. 1, pp. 37-9.

81 Franz Gartmann and Wolfgang Reichel, 'Aufstieg und Machtübernahme der NSDAP in Osnabrück' (unpublished manuscript, Osnabrück, 1974), pp. 9-28; Hoffmeyer, *Chronik*, p. 530.

82 NSO Dep 3b XV, Parts 1-7, Kriegs-Chronik, September 1939 – April 1945.

83 NSO Dep 3b XV, parts 41-60, cover the period from the end of the War until 1962.

84 *Osnabrück 1925-1933*; *Osnabrück 1933-1945: Stadt im Dritten Reich* (Osnabrück, 1964)

85 The tiltes are: *Im Anflug auf Osnabrück: Die Bombenangriffe, 1940-1945* (Osnabrück, 1985); and *Zwischen Trümmern: Osnabrück in den Jahren 1945 bis 1948* (Osnabrück, 1990).

86 Klaus J. Bade, Hans-Bernd Meier and Bernhard Parisius, eds, *Zeitzeugen im Interview: Flüchtlinge und Vertriebene im Raum Osnabrück nach 1945* (Osnabrück, 1997).

87 Abeitsgruppe des Graf-Stauffenberg-Gymnasiums, Osnabrück, *Ein anderer Stadtführer: Verfolger und Verfolgte zur Zeit des Nationalsozialismus in Osnabrück*, 4th edition (Osnabrück, 2000); Arbeitsgemeinschaft der Ursulaschule, *Osnabrück 1933-1945* (Osnabrück, 1983); Pax Christi – Basisgruppe Osnabrück und dem Antifaschistischen Arbeitskreis Osnabrück, eds, *SpureNsuche: Osnabrück 1933-1945* (Osnabrück, 1995).

88 The titles include: Antifaschistischer Arbeitskreis Osnabrück, ed., *Osnabrücker Arbeiter im Widerstand* (Osnabrück, 1987); Ursula Fisser-Bömer, *Zwangsarbeit in Osnabrück* (Osnabrück, 1982); Emil Jagusch, *Leben Hinter Stacheldraht: Ein Osnabrücker überlebt der KZ Sachsenhausen* (Osnabrück, 1978); Ludwig Landwehr, *'interresant war's eigentlich immer!': Aus dem Lebenserringungen der Ludwig Landwehr* (Osnabrück, 1987).

89 Ulrich von Hehl, 'Bischof Berning und das Bistum Osnabrück im Dritten Reich', *Osnabrücker Mitteilungen*, vol. 86 (1986), pp. 83-104; Heinrike Uhrmacher, '"Resistenz" oder Akzeptanz? Die evangelische Kirche im Osnabrück während der Zeit des Nationalsozialismus', *Osnabrücker Mitteilungen*,vol. 100 (1995), pp. 229-50.

90 Klemens-August Recker, *'Wem wollt ihr Glauben?': Bischof Berning im Dritten Reich* (Paderborn, 1998).

91 Dirk Glufke, 'Richard Karwehls "Politisches Messiastum: Zur Auseinandersetzung zwischen Kirche und Nationalsozialismus"', *Jahrbuch der Gesellschaft für niedersächsische Kirchengeschichte*, vol. 90 (1992), pp. 201-17; Heidrun Becker, 'Der Osnabrücker Kreis 1931-1939', in Heinrich Grosse, Hans Otte and Joachim Perels, eds, *Bewahren oder Bekennen? Die hannoversche Landeskirche im Nationalsozialismus* (Hanover, 1996), pp. 43-104.

92 Steinwascher, *Gestapo Osnabrück Meldet.*

93 Eva Berger, *Wer bürgt für die Kosten? Zur Sozialgeschichte des Krankenhauses: 125 Jahre Stadt-Krankenhaus Osnabrück* (Bramsche, 1991); *Die Würde des Menschen ist unantastbar: Niedersächsisches Landeskrankenhaus Osnabrück: Eine Psychiatriegeschichte* (Bramsche, 1999). See also Raimond Reiter, 'Das Erbgensundheitsgericht Osnabrück und die Sterilisationsverfahren nach dem "Gestz zur Verhütung erbkranken Nachwuchses" vom 14. Juli 1933', *Osnabrücher Mitteilungen*, vol. 110 (2005), pp. 211-22.

94 Gartmann and Reichel, 'Aufstieg'.

95 Carl, 'Landersverband Osnabrück'.

96 Paul-Josef Heuer, 'Die "Stadtwächterbewegung" in Osnabrück von 1929 bis 1931' (Osnabrück, 1984).

97 Jeremy Noakes, *The Nazi Party in Lower Saxony, 1921-1933* (Oxford, 1971), pp. 136-8.

98 Van Kampen and Westphalen, *100 Jahre SPD.*

99 SPD Osnabrück, *1933-1983: Machtergreifung der Nationalsozialisten in Osnabrück* (Osnabrück, 1983).

100 Geschichtsgruppe Arbeit und Leben in Osnabrück, *Freiheit-Krise-Diktatur: Zur Verfolgung der Gewerkschaften in Osnabrück 1933* (Bramsche, 1983).

101 Dumkow and Roland, 'Geschichte der KPD Ortsgruppe Osnabrück'.

102 Karl Kühling, *Die Juden in Osnabrück* (Osnabrück, 1969).

103 Junk and Sellmeyer, *Stationen.*

104 See, for instance, Eva Berger, Inge Jaehner, Peter Junk, Karl Georg Kaster, Manfred Meinz and Wendelin Zimmer, *Felix Nussbaum: Art Defamed, Art in Exile, Art in Resistance* (Bramsche, 1995).

105 Fisser-Blömer, *Zwangsarbeit in Osnabrück.*

106 *Niederländer in Verdammten Land: Zeugnisse der Zwangsarbeit von Niederländern im Raum Osnabrück während des Zweiten Weltkrieges* (Osnabrück, 1998); and *Das*

Arbeitserziehungslager Ohrbeck bei Osnabrück: Eine Dokumentation (Osnabrück, 2000).

107 *Neue Osnabrücker Zeitung*, 10, 16 May 2000.

108 But see Panikos Panayi, 'The Persecution of German Romanies: The Case of Osnabrück, 1933-46', *Patterns of Prejudice*, vol. 37 (2003), pp. 377-99.

109 See Mary Fulbrook, *German National Identity After the Holocaust* (Cambridge, 1999).

110 The works of Edgar Schroeder include: *Osnabrück: So Wie Es War*, 3 Volumes (Düsseldorf, 1981-1987); and *Osnabrück im 19. Jahrhundert*.

111 See, for instance, Karl Ordelheide, *Am Ende War der Anfang: Osnabrück, 1945-1948* (Osnabrück, 1982), together with two essays by Ernst Helmut Segschneider, 'Osnabrück im "achten Kriegsjahr": Zwei Skizzen nach Zeitzeugenberichten', in Nils-Arvid Bringéus, ed., *Wandel der Volkskultur in Europa*, vol. 2 (Münster, 1988), pp. 855-65, and 'Not kennt kein Gebot: Formen der Nahrungsbeschaffung nach dem Zweiten Weltkrieg im Raum Osnabrück', *Rheinisch-Westfälische Zeitschrift für Volkskunde*, vols 34-5 (1989-90), pp. 205-38.

Chapter 2

1 Richard Bessel, *Political Violence and the Rise of Nazism: The Storm Troopers in Eastern Germany, 1925-1934* (London, 1984); Dirk Schumann, *Politische Gewalt in der Weimarer Republik, 1918-1933: Kampf um die Straße und Furcht vor dem Bürgerkrieg* (Essen, 2001); Sven Reichardt, *Faschistische Kampfbünde: Gewalt und Gemeinschaft im italienischen Squadrismus und in der deutschen SA* (Cologne, 2002); Eve Rosenhaft, *Beating the Fascists: The German Communists and Political Violence, 1929-1933* (Cambridge, 1983).

2 Erberhard Kolb, *The Weimar Republic* (London, 1988), pp. 96-126.

3 Niall Ferguson, 'The German Inter-War Economy: Political Choice Versus Economic Determinism', in Mary Fulbrook, ed., *German History Since 1800* (London, 1997), p. 262.

4 Dietmar Petzina, 'Was There a Crisis Before the Crisis? The State of the German Economy in the 1920s', in Jürgen Baron von Kruedener, ed., *Economic Crisis and Political Collapse: The Weimar Republic, 1924-1933* (Oxford, 1990), pp. 1-19.

5 Detlev J. K. Peukert, *The Weimar Republic: The Crisis of Classical Modernity* (Harmondsworth, 1993), p. 118.

6 Ibid., pp. 119-24.

7 See Ferguson, 'German Inter-War Economy', pp. 264-73.

8 Richard Overy, 'The German Economy, 1919-1945', in Panikos Panayi, ed., *Weimar and Nazi Germany: Continuities and Discontinuities* (London, 2001), p. 39.

9 Ibid., p. 41.

10 Theo Balderston, *The Origins and Course of the German Economic Crisis, 1923-1932* (Berlin, 1993), pp. 43-8.

11 Peukert, *Weimar Republic*, p. 252.

12 Ibid., pp. 253-4; Heinrich August Winkler, *Weimar, 1918-1933: Die Geschichte der Ersten Deutschen Demokratie* (Munich, 1998), pp. 481-3.

13 Ludwig Hoffmeyer, et. al., *Chronik der Stadt Osnabrück* 6th Edn (Osnabrück, 1995), p. 522.

14   Karl Kühling, *Osnabrück, 1925-1933* (Osnabrück, 1963), p. 130; *Osnabrücker Zeitung*, 24, 25 June 1930.

15   *Osnabrücker Zeitung*, 18 May 1930.

16   *Freie Presse*, 21 January 1931.

17   *Osnabrücker Tageblatt*, 27 January 1929.

18   R. Friess, *75 Jahre Osnabrücker Kupfer und Drahtwerk* (Melle, 1948), p. 17.

19   *Freie Presse*, 15 November 1932.

20   Susanne Meyer, 'Die Streikbewegung in der Osnabrücker Montan- und Metalindustrie, 1859-1933', in Dirk Thierbach and Thomas Blömer, eds, *Vom Deutschen Metallarbeiterverband zur Industriegewerkschaft Metall: Texte und Dokumente aus der Geschichte der Metallarbeiter in Osnabrück* (Bramsche, 1990), p. 77.

21   NSO Rep 430-101-7-43-331-Band 6, 'Politische Wochenberichte über die wirtschaftliche und politische Lage in der Stadt Osnabrück u.a. an die Polizeidirektion Bremen, 1929', 14 January 1929.

22   *Freie Presse*, 18 January 1930.

23   NSO Rep 430-303-19-56-222, Betreuung für Säuglinge und Kleinkinder, 1928-43.

24   NSO Rep 430-303-19-56-49, Bd 1, Jahresgesundheitsbericht, 1932, Bd. 1.

25   David F. Crew, *Germans on Welfare: From Weimar to Hitler* (Oxford, 1998), p. 25.

26   Ibid., p. 152, described the situation in Hamburg.

27   Young-Sun Hong, *Welfare, Modernity and the Weimar State, 1919-1933* (Princeton, NJ, 1998), pp. 207-9.

28   *Osnabrücker Zeitung*, 26 January 1930.

29   Ibid, 27 February 1930.

30   Ibid., 21 October 1930; *Freie Presse*, 20 October 1930; *Osnabrücker Tageblatt*, 21 October 1930.

31   *Freie Presse*, 14, 28 October 1931; *Osnabrücker Zeitung*, 14 October 1931.

32   *Osnabrücker Zeitung*, 25 December, 1931.

33   *Freie Presse*, 3 June 1932.

34   Richard J. Evans, 'Introduction: The Experience of Unemployment in the Weimar Republic', in Richard J. Evans and Dick Geary, eds, *The German Unemployed: Experiences and Consequences of Mass Unemployment from the Weimar Republic to the Third Reich* (London, 1978), pp. 7-8.

35   *Osnabrücker Tageblatt*, 12 May 1931; *Osnabrücker Zeitung*, 20 December 1930, 12 May 1931.

36   *Mitteilungen des Osnabrücker Vereins für Innere Mission im Regierungsbezirk Osnabrück und des Evangelischen Wohlfahrtdienstes der Stadt Osnabrück*, November 1931.

37   *Friedensbote: Gemeindeblatt für St. Katharinen II Osnabrück*, 1 November 1931.

38   Crew, *Germans on Welfare*, p. 191; Winkler, *Der Weg in die Katastrophe*, pp. 53-5; Heidrun Homburg, 'From Compulsory Unemployment Insurance to Compulsory Labour: The Transformation of the Benefit System in Germany', in Evans and Geary, *German Unemployed*, pp. 73-107; Michael Schneider, 'The Development of State Work-Creation Policy in Germany, 1930-1933', in Peter D. Stachura, ed., *Unemployment and the Great Depression in Weimar Germany* (London, 1986), pp. 163-86.

39 *Freie Presse*, 5 November 1929, 20 September 1930, 12 February 1932; *Osnabrücker Tageblatt*, 2 October, 24 November, 1932; *Osnabrücker Volkszeitung*, 12 February 1932.

40 *Osnabrücker Zeitung*, 21 February, 30 April, 3 November 1931; *Osnabrücker Tageblatt*, 30 April, 11 July 1931.

41 Jürgen W Falter, 'Unemployment and the Radicalization of the German Electorate, 1928-1933: An Aggregate Data Analysis with Special Emphasis on the Rise of National Socialism', in Stachura, *Unemployment*, pp. 187-208.

42 Jürgen W. Falter, *Hitlers Wähler* (Munich, 1991), pp. 290-300.

43 See contributions to: Ian Kershaw, ed., *Weimar: Why Did German Democracy Fail* (London, 1990); and von Kruedener, *Economic Crisis*.

44 As considered, by amongst others, Ian Kershaw, *The 'Hitler Myth': Image and Reality in the Third Reich* (Oxford, 1987), pp. 13-47.

45 As argued most recently by Michael Burleigh, *The Third Reich: A New History* (London, 2000).

46 Kühling, *Osnabrück, 1925-1933*, pp. 91-2; Paul-Josef Heuer, 'Die "Stadtwächterbewegung" in Osnabück von 1929 bis 1931' (unpublished manuscript, 1984), p. 43; Jeremy Noakes, *The Nazi Party in Lower Saxony, 1921-1933* (Oxford, 1971), p. 136.

47 Carsten Glüsenkamp, 'Die Gleichschaltung der Presse in Osnabrück, 1933-34' (unpublished MA thesis, University of Münster, 1992), pp. 16, 29.

48 Kühling, *Osnabrück, 1925-1933*, pp. 98-9; Noakes, *Nazi Party in Lower Saxony*, pp. 138-9.

49 *Stadtwächter*, 28 April 1929. The theatre crisis is discussed in Kühling, *Osnabrück, 1925-1933*, pp. 58-63.

50 The party's antisemitism is discussed in chapter 7 below.

51 The various legal cases can be traced in Kühling, *Osnabrück, 1925-1933*, pp. 102-12. They are also detailed in *Osnabrücker Tageblatt*, 21 25 February, 2, 4, 9, 22 April, 8, 15, 21 May, 22 August, 12 September, 4, 5 November 1930.

52 Noakes, *Nazi Party in Lower Saxony*, p. 137.

53 A *Stadwächter* existed in nearby Bielefeld, as mentioned in Kühling, *Osnabrück, 1925-1933*, p. 103.

54 *Osnabrücker Tageblatt*, 25 August 1930; *Stadtwächter*, 31 August 1930.

55 See, for instance, *Stadtwächter*, 14 September 1930. The relationship between the Stadtwächter and the Nazis is dealt with by Heuer, 'Stadtwächterbewegung', pp. 68-70.

56 Heuer, ibid., pp. 138-40.

57 *Reichswächter*, 25 September 1931.

58 *OD-AL*, 1 July, 13 November 1932; Heinrich Schierbaum, *Die "Weiße Wehr" und ihr Kampf ums Deutsche Reich und den 5. Weltwirtschaftsraum* (Osnabrück, 1933); Kühling, *Osnabrück, 1925-1933*, p. 111.

59 Falter, *Hitlers Wähler*, pp. 167-75.

60 Carl, 'Der Landesverband Osnabrück der Deutschnationalen Volkspartei', pp. VI-XXI.

61 Klaus-Michael Mallmann, *Kommunisten in der Weimarer Republik: Sozialgeschichte einer revolutionären Bewegung* (Darmstadt, 1996), pp. 84-164; Conan Fischer, *The*

German Communists and the Rise of Nazism (London, 1991); Ben Fowkes, *Communism in Germany under the Weimar Republic* (London, 1984).

62 M. Dumkow and Roland Funk, 'Geschichte der KPD Ortsgruppe Osnabrück, 1919-1933', Part II (unpublished manuscript, Osnabrück 1975), pp. 4-39.

63 Donna Harsch, *German Social Democracy and the Rise of Nazsim* (London, 1993), p. 28; Herbert Budde, 'Die Stadt Osnabrück und der Ortsverein der SPD, 1924-1933', in Wilhelm van Kampen and Tilman Westphalen, eds, *100 Jahre SPD in Osnabrück, 1875-1975: Ausgewählte Kapitel zur Geschichte der Arbeiterbewegung in Osnabrück* (Osnabrück, 1975), pp. 102-3.

64 See Noel D. Cary, *The Path to Christian Democracy: German Catholics and the Party System from Windhorst to Adenauer* (London, 1996), pp. 1-145.

65 Carl, 'Der Landesverband Osnabrück der Deutschnationalen Volkspartei', pp. 19, 28; Christian F. Trippe, *Konservative Verfassungspolitik, 1918-1923: Die DNVP als Opposition in Reich und Ländern* (Düsseldorf, 1995), pp. 28-32.

66 Ludwig Richter, *Die Deutsche Volkspartei, 1918-1933* (Düsseldorf, 2002), pp. 585-800.

67 Josef Engelman, 'Die Politik der DNVP im Landesverband Osnabrück, 1930-1933' (unpublished manuscript, Osnabrück, 1970), p. 21.

68 Falter, *Hitler's Wähler*, pp. 110-17.

69 Theodore Abel, *Why Hitler Came into Power* (Cambridge, MA, 1986 edition), p. 311. Membership statistics for Osnabrück have not survived.

70 Franz Gartmann and Wolfgang Reichel, 'Aufstieg und Machtübernahme der NSDAP in Osnabrück' (unpuplished manuscript, Osnabrück, 1975), pp. 31-2; Noakes, *Nazi Party in Lower Saxony*, p. 139; Martin Broszat, *The Hitler State: The Foundation and Development of the Internal Structure of the Third Reich* (Harlow, 1981), p. 29.

71 Studies of the support base for the Nazis up to the seizure of power include: Michael H. Kater, *The Nazi Party: A Social Profile of Members and Leaders, 1919-1945* (Oxford, 1983), pp. 19-71, 169-89; Detlef Mühlberger, *Hitler's Followers: Studies in the Sociology of the Nazi Movement* (London, 1991); Richard F. Hamilton, *Who Voted for Hitler?* (Princeton, 1982); Falter, *Hitlers Wähler*; and Abel, *Why Hitler Came into Power*. Most of these studies are locally based. Useful national statistics can be found in Jeremy Noakes and Geoffrey Pridham, eds, *Nazism, 1919-1945*, Vol. 1, *The Rise to Power, 1919-1934: A Documentary Reader* (Exeter, 1983), pp. 81-7.

72 Gartmann and Reichel, 'Aufstieg und Machtübernahme', pp. 31, 37, 53, 54.

73 NSO Rep 430-201-5-66-12, Bd. 1, Report from the Police Office in Osnabrück, 28 August 1929.

74 See Chapter 7 below.

75 The above political events from 1929 are reconstructed from NSO Rep 430-101-7-43-331-Band 6, 'Politische Wochenberichte über die wirtschaftliche und politische Lage in der Stadt Osnabrück u.a. an die Polizeidirektion Bremen, 1929'. For more detail on May Day see Konrad Nettelnsrot, 'Der 1. Mai in Osnabrück: Die "Arbeiter-Maifeier" als Kampf- und Festtag der Arbeiterbewegung', *Osnabrücker Mitteilungen*, vol. 93 (1988), pp. 151-78.

76 NSO Rep 430-101-7-43-331-Band 7, 'Politische Wochenberichte über die wirtschaftliche und politische Lage in der Stadt Osnabrück u.a. an die Polizeidirektion Bremen', 20 January 1930.

77 NSO Rep 430-101-7-43-331-Band 7, 'Politische Wochenberichte über die wirtschaftliche und politische Lage in der Stadt Osnabrück u.a. an die Polizeidirektion Bremen', 10 February 1930.

78 See, for instcance, NSO Rep 430-101-7-43-331-Band 7, 'Politische Wochenberichte über die wirtschaftliche und politische Lage in der Stadt Osnabrück u.a. an die Polizeidirektion Bremen', 7 April, 5 May, 7, 28 July 1930.

79 NSO Rep 430-101-7-43-331-Band 7, 'Politische Wochenberichte über die wirtschaftliche und politische Lage in der Stadt Osnabrück u.a. an die Polizeidirektion Bremen', 8 September 1930; *Osnabrücker Zeitung*, 5 September 1930.

80 See the reports for October, November and December in NSO Rep 430-101-7-43-331-Band 7, 'Politische Wochenberichte über die wirtschaftliche und politische Lage in der Stadt Osnabrück u.a. an die Polizeidirektion Bremen'.

81 *Osnabrücker Tageblatt*, 5, 25, 30 January 1931; NSO Rep 430-101-7-43-331-Band 8, 'Politische Wochenberichte über die wirtschaftliche und politische Lage in der Stadt Osnabrück u.a. an die Polizeidirektion Bremen', 12, 26 January 1931.

82 NSO Rep 430-101-7-43-331-Band 8, 'Politische Wochenberichte über die wirtschaftliche und politische Lage in der Stadt Osnabrück u.a. an die Polizeidirektion Bremen', 22 June 1931.

83 *Freie Presse*, 19 September 1931.

84 NSO Rep 430-201-5-66-12-Band 2, 'Polizei, Überwachung der NSDAP, 1930-32'.

85 NSO Rep 430-101-7-43-331-Band 9, 'Politische Wochenberichte über die wirtschaftliche und politische Lage in der Stadt Osnabrück u.a. an die Polizeidirektion Bremen', 8 January 1932.

86 NSO Rep 430-101-7-43-331-Band 9, 'Politische Wochenberichte über die wirtschaftliche und politische Lage in der Stadt Osnabrück u.a. an die Polizeidirektion Bremen', 7 and 14 March 1932.

87 *Freie Presse*, 23 July 1932. The Iron Front was established to counter the growing threat of the Nazis. See Harsch, *German Social Democracy*, pp. 169-73.

88 NSO Rep 430-101-7-43-331-Band 9, 'Politische Wochenberichte über die wirtschaftliche und politische Lage in der Stadt Osnabrück u.a. an die Polizeidirektion Bremen', 11 July 1932.

89 NSO Rep 430-101-7-43-331-Band 9, 'Politische Wochenberichte über die wirtschaftliche und politische Lage in der Stadt Osnabrück u.a. an die Polizeidirektion Bremen', 25 July 1932 gives the figure of 25,000 people.

90 *Osnabrücker Volkszeitung*, 25 July 1932.

91 NSO Rep 430-201-5-66-12-Band 2, Police Report of 21 October 1932; NSO Rep 430-101-7-43-331-Band 9, 'Politische Wochenberichte über die wirtschaftliche und politische Lage in der Stadt Osnabrück u.a. an die Polizeidirektion Bremen', 24 October, 7 November 1932.

92 William L. Patch, Jr, *Heinrich Brüning and the Dissolution of the Weimar Republic* (Cambridge, 1988); Richard J Evans, *The Coming of the Third Reich* (London, 2003), pp. 296-308; Winkler, *Weimar*, pp. 521-94; Rudolf Morsey, 'Die

Deutsche Zentrumspartei', in Erich Matthias and Rudolf Morsey, eds, *Das Ende der Parteien 1933: Darstellungen und Dokumente* (Düsseldorf, 1960), pp. 302-44.

93 See Dieter Ohr, *Nationalsozialistische Propaganda und Weimarer Wahlen: Empirische Analysen zur Wirkung von NSDAP Versammlungen* (Opladen, 1997), p. 233, who concluded that 'a strong positive connection' existed between the rise in Nazi support and the level of their political activity, particularly meetings.

94 Mallmann, *Kommunisten*, pp. 165-240.

95 Eve Rosenhaft, 'Links gleich Rechts? Militante Straßengewalt um 1930', in Thomas Lindenberger and Alf Lüdtke, eds, *Physische Gewalt: Studien zur Geschichte der Neuzeit* (Frankfurt, 1995), pp. 259-70; Anthony McElligot, *Contested City: Municipal Politics and the Rise of Nazism in Altona* (Ann Arbor, 1998).

96 Enso Traverso, *The Origins of Nazi Violence* (London, 2003).

97 Peter H Merkl, *Political Violence Under the Swastika: 581 Early Nazis* (London, 1975), pp. 142-53.

98 The legacy of violence after 1918 is critically examined by Richard Bessel, *Germany After the First World War* (Oxford, 1993), pp. 254-84.

99 Schumann, *Politische Gewalt*, p. 11.

100 Ibid., pp. 359-68.

101 Adolf Hitler, *Mein Kampf* (London, 1939 edition), pp. 334-78; Merkl, *Political Violence under the Swastika*, pp. 446-9; Bessel, *Political Violence*, pp. 75-82.

102 Reichardt, *Faschistische Kampfbünde*; Rosenhaft, *Beating the Fascists*, p. 3.

103 Harsch, *German Social Democracy*, pp. 20-1, 104-5; Rosenhaft, ibid., p. 4.

104 NSO Rep 430-201-5-66-22, Letter from Polizei-Direktion to Regierungspräsident, 29 August 1930.

105 The events of May 1931 can be traced in NSO Rep 430-201-10-43-20. See also the report of the trial following the events of 30 May in *Freie Presse*, 14 July 1931.

106 NSO Rep 430-201-5-66-13-Bd 1, Letter from Regierungspräsident to Polizeibehörden des Bezirks, 11 April 1931.

107 *Sonder-Ausgabe Amtsblatt der Preussischen Regierung in Osnabrück*, 9 July 1930.

108 Evans, *Coming of the Third Reich*, p. 274.

109 NSO Dep 3b-IV-671, Letter from Dr Filbry to Dr Gaertner, 26 September 1931.

110 NSO Rep 430-201-10-43-10, Letter from the Polizeidirektion to the Regierungspräsident, 26 August 1931.

111 *Osnabrücker Zeitung*, 12 November 1931; *Freie Presse*, 13 November, 1931.

112 Patch, *Heinrich Brüning*, pp. 247-56.

113 *Osnabrücker Zeitung*, 18 March 1932.

114 *Osnabrücker Tageblatt*, 22 June 1933; NSO Rep 430-201-5-66-26, Letter of Ortspolizeibehörde to Regierungspräsident, 22 June 1932.

115 *Osnabrücker Zeitung*, 24 June 1932.

116 *Freie Presse*, 5 July, 28 July, 28 September 1932.

117 Ibid., 2 September 1932.

118 See: Bessel, *Political Violence*, especially pp. 75-96; and Rosenhaft, *Beating the Fascists*.

119 Winkler, *Weimar*, pp. 489-90.

120 Rosenhaft, *Beating the Fascists*.

121 Ludwig Hoffmeyer, *Chronik der Stadt Osnabrück*, 6th edition (Osnabrück, 1995), pp. 504-15.

Chapter 3

1 David Schoenbaum, *Hitler's Social Revolution: Class and Status in Nazi Germany, 1933-39* (London, 1967), pp. 1-42, outlines the Nazi promises.

2 Gerd Steinwascher, ed., *Gestapo Osnabrück Meldet: Polizei und Regierungsberichte aus dem Regierungsbezirk Osnabrück aus den Jahren 1933 bis 1936* (Osnabrück, 1995), pp. 6-34; Peter Junk and Martina Sellmeyer, *Stationen auf dem Weg nach Auschwitz: Entrechtung, Vertreibung, Vernichtung: Juden in Osnabrück, 1900-1945* (Osnabrück, 1989), pp. 249-57; Ludwig, Hoffmeyer, et. al., *Chronik der Stadt Osnabrück* 6th Edn (Osnabrück, 1995), pp. 534-49; Karl Kühling, *Osnabrück 1933-1945: Stadt im Dritten Reich* (Osnabrück, 1964), pp. 42-61, 137-51; Rainer Hehemann, *Biographisches Handbuch zur Geschichte der Region Osnabrück* (Osnabrück, 1990).

3 Junk and Sellmeyer, *Stationen*, p. 257; Hehemann, ibid., p. 169.

4 Richard Overy, *War and Economy in the Third Reich* (Oxford, 1994), p. 169.

5 NSO Rep 430-101-7-43-331-Band 9, 'Politische Wochenberichte über die wirtschaftliche und politische Lage in der Stadt Osnabrück u.a. an die Polizeidirektion Bremen, 1929', 13 February 1933; *Osnabrücker Tageblatt*, 23 July 1933, 20 April 1934.

6 *Neue Volksblätter*, 19 December 1938.

7 For a variety of interpretations of the Nazi economy see: Overy, *War and Economy*, pp. 1-256; Schoenbaum, *Hitler's Social Revolution*, pp. 77-119; Rüdiger Hachtmann, *Industriearbeit im 'Dritten Reich': Untersuchungen zu den Lohn- und Arbeitsbedingungen in Deutschland* (Göttingen, 1989); Timothy W. Mason, *Social Policy in the Third Reich: The Working Classes and the 'National Community'* (Oxford, 1993); Hartmut Berghoff, 'Did Hitler Create a New Society? Continuity and Change in German Social History Before and After 1933', in Panikos Panayi, ed., *Weimar and Nazi Germany: Continuities and Discontinuities* (London, 2001), pp. 74-104; Dan P. Silverman, *Hitler's Economy: Nazi Work Creation Programmes, 1933-1936* (London, 1998); Anja Bagel-Bohlen, *Hitlers Industrielle Kreigsvorbereitungen, 1936-1939* (Coblenz, 1975); Fritz Blaich, *Wirtschaft und Rüstung im Dritten Reich* (Düsseldorf, 1987), pp. 15-32; Avraham Barkai, *Nazi Economics: Ideology, Theory and Policy* (Oxford, 1990); Arthur Schweitzer, *Big Business in the Third Reich* (Bloomington, IN, 1964); and Lothar Gall and Manfred Pohl, eds, *Unternehmen im Nationalsozialismus* (Munich, 1998).

8 NSO Dep-3b-IV-6518, Dr Kolkmeyer, 'Wirtschaftsänderungen in Osnabrück'.

9 Kühling, *Osnabrück 1933-1945*, p. 64.

10 *Osnabrücker Zeitung*, 22, 30 November 1933.

11 Ibid., 4, 6, 8, 20 March 1934.

12 Ibid., 20 May 1934.

13 *Osnabrücker Tageblatt*, 11 October 1934.

14 Ibid., 6 June 1935.

15 Kühling, *Osnabrück, 1933-1945*, pp. 61-75.

16 *Osnabrücker Tageblatt*, 11 October 1936.

17 Ibid., 12 May 1939.

18 Ibid.; *Neue Volksblätter*, 6 August 1938.

19 Karin Klaus Patel, *'Soldaten der Arbei': Arbeitsdienst in Deutschland und den USA* (Göttingen, 2002); Schoenbaum, *Hitler's Social Revolution*, pp. 96-7; *Osnabrücker Zeitung*, 19 April 1935.

20 Wolfgang Ayaß, *'Asoziale' im Nationalsozialismus* (Stuttgart, 1995), pp. 57-104.

21 See the correspondence in NSO Dep-3b-XXI-119.

22 NSO Dep-3b-XXI-131, Geheime Staatspolizei, Staatspolizeistelle Osnabrück, to Städt. Wohlfahrtsamt Osnabrück, 17 May 1938.

23 NSO Rep-610-Osn-33, Gewerbeaufsichtsamt Osnabrück, Jahresbericht, 1934.

24 For the national picture see Bagel-Bohlau, *Hitlers Industrielle Kriegsvorbereitung*, pp. 82-131.

25 NSO Rep-610-Osn-33, Gewerbeaufsichtsamt Osnabrück, Jahresbericht, 1934; NSO Rep-610-Osn-310, Erster Gewerberat to OKD, 28 December 1938; R.Friess, *75 Jahre Osnabrücker Kupfer und Drahtwerk* (Melle, 1948), pp. 17-19; *OKD Werkzeitung*, 22 March 1935.

26 See NSO Rep-610-Osn-277.

27 See the details in NSO Rep-610-Osn-248.

28 Dieter Kunst, *The Karmann Story: Germany's Coachbuilder to the World*, 2nd Edn (Osnabrück, 1996), pp. 46-52; NSO Rep-610-Osn-251.

29 Schweitzer, *Big Business*; Gall and Pohl, *Unternehmer*; Mason, *Social Policy*, pp. 128-50; Michael Schneider, *Unterm Hakenkreuz: Arbeiter und Arbeiterbewegung 1933 bis 1939* (Bonn, 1999), pp. 591-638.

30 See Berghoff, 'Did Hitler Create a New Society?', pp. 80-4; A. R. L. Gurland, Otto Kirchheimer and Franz Neumann, *The Fate of Small Businesses in the Third Reich* (New York, 1975); Schweitzer, ibid., pp. 156-96.

31 *Osnabrücker Zeitung*, 23 October 1933.

32 Institut für deutsche Wirtschaftspropaganda, *'Braune Messe Osnabrück': vom 2. bis 10. September 1933 der Reichsführung der NS `Hago'* (Osnabrück, 1933); *Osnabrücker Tageblatt*, 3 September 1933; *Osnabrücker Zeitung*, 3 September 1933.

33 Hartmut Fackler, 'Gleichgeschaltet: Der Handel im Dritten Reich', in Michael Haverkamp and Hans-Jürgen Teuteberg, eds, *Unterm Strich: Von der Winkelkrämerei zum E-Commerce: Eine Austellung des Museums Industriekultur im Rahm des 175. Bestehen der Sparkasse Osnab*rück (Bramsche, 2000), p. 248.

34 Heinz-Günther Borck, 'Chronik der Handwerkskammer Osnabrück, 1900-1975', in Handwerkskammer Osnabrück, ed., *Geschichte des Osnabrückder Handwerks* (Osnabrück, 1975), p. 438.

35 Schoenbaum, *Hitler's Social Revolution*, pp. 79-80; Alf Lüdtke, 'The "Honour of Labour": Industrial Workers and the Power of Symbols Under National Socialism', in David F. Crew, ed., *Nazism and German Society* (London, 1994), pp. 67-109.

36 *Osnabrücker Tageblatt*, 2 May 1933.

37 Ibid., 2 May 1937.

38 Shelley Baranowski, *Strength Through Joy: Consumerism and Mass Tourism in the Third Reich* (Cambridge, 2004); Schneider, *Unterm Hakenkreuz*, pp. 168-243; Ronald Smelser, *Robert Ley: Hitler's Labour Front Leader* (Oxford, 1988).

39 NSO Rep-725a-40, An die Wirtschaftsführer im Kreise Osnabrück, 1 June 1934.

40 Deutsche Arbeiter Front, *Arbeitsschule, Osnabrück 1936* (Osnabrück, 1936).

41 *Neue Volksblätter*, 5 May 1939.

42 *Osnabrücker Zeitung*, 22 July 1933.

43 NSO Rep-725a-40, Kraft Durch Freude to Betriebsführer des Kreises Osnabrück-Stadt, 8 December 1934; Baranowski, *Strength Through Joy*, pp. 118-98.

44 Deutsche Arbeitsfront, Kraft Durch Freude, Gau Weser-Ems, Sportamt Osnabrück, *Sportsprogramm*, April, Mai, Juni 1936.

45 *Osnabrücker Tageblatt*, 24 November 1935; *Neue Volksblätter*, 21 March 1937.

46 *Neue Volksblätter*, 21 April 1938; *Osnabrücker Tageblatt*, 2 September 1934, 21 September 1936.

47 Hartmut E. Lissina, *Nationale Sportsfeste in nationalsozialistischen Deutschcland* (Mannheim, 1997).

48 *Festschrift zur Fünfzigjahrfeier Zweigverein Osnabrück des Deutschen Alpenvereins, 1888-1938* (Osnabrück, 1938), pp. 14-15, 104.

49 Sportverein Eversburg, *75 Jahre, 1894-1969* (Osnabrück, 1969), p. 11.

50 Carl Diem, *Der deutsche Sport in der Zeit des Nationalsozialismus* (Cologne, 1980), pp. 9-10; Horst Ueberhorst, *Frisch, Frei, Stark und Treu: Die Arbeitersportbewegung in Deutschland, 1893-1933* (Düsseldorf, 1933), pp. 250-78.

51 *Festschrift Anlässlich des 100. jährigen bestehens des Osnabrücker Turnvereins ev* (Osnabrück, 1961), p. 37; Günter Wienhold, *150 Jahre Osnabrücker Sportclub* (Osnabrück, 1999), pp. 34-8; *Osnabrücker Tageblatt*, 27 September 1938.

52 Christoph Sachse and Florian Tennsedt, *Der Wohlfahrtstaat im Nationalsozialismus* (Stuttgart, 1992), especially pp. 11-13, 51-3.

53 Ibid., pp. 110-33; Michael Burleigh and Wolfgang Wippermann, *The Racial State in Germany, 1933-1945* (Cambridge, 1991), pp. 68-71.

54 *Osnabrücker Zeitung*, 15 July 1934; *Osnabrücker Tageblatt*, 1 September 1934.

55 *Osnabrücker Zeitung*, 10 May 1936.

56 NSO Dep-3b-XXI-74, Amt für Volkswohlfahrt Osnabrück to Städtische Wohlfahrtsamt, 14 January 1938.

57 NSO Dep-3b-XXI-74, Amt für Volkswohlfahrt Osnabrück to Bezirksfürssorgeverband, 29 May 1939.

58 NSO Dep-3b-XXI-737, Verzeichnis derjenigen Personen, die von der Stadt Osnabrück eine Siedlerbeihilfe erhalten haben (Siedlung Bremer Strasse der Niedersächsischen Heimstätte).

59 NSO Rep-430-303-19/56-19, Gesundheitsamt to Regierungspräsidenten, 24 October 1936.

60 *Osnabrücker Zeitung*, 1, 23 October 1933; *Neue Volksblätter*, 13 October 1937.

61 Robert Proctor, *The Nazi War on Cancer* (Princeton, 1999).

62 Margret Osege, 'Vergleichende Untersuchung über sozialhygienische Probleme in der Stadt Osnabrück vor und nach dem zweiten Weltkrieges' (unpublished University of Münster medical dissertation, 1949), pp. 9-10, 14, 16.

63 NSO Rep-430-303-19-56-53-Bd 1, Jahresgesundheitsbericht, Vol. 1, 1938.

64 Werner Pelster, 'Selbstmord im Stadt-u. Landkreis Osnabrück' (unpublished University of Münster medical dissertation, 1943), p. 10.

65 See the discussions in Richard Grunberger, *A Social History of the Third Reich* (London, 1991), pp. 155-68 and Michael Burleigh, *The Third Reich: A New History* (London, 2000), pp. 158-77, which mainly deal with 'political crime' and,

in Burleigh's words, 'The Demise of the Rule of Law'. Hans-Jürgen Eitner, *Hitlers Deutsche: Das Ende einer Tabus* (Gernsbach, 1991), pp. 176-87, considers both crime statistics and the issues tackled by Grunberger and Burleigh.

66 Burleigh, ibid., p. 166, points to the passage of the 1933 Law Against Dangerous Habitual Criminals and Measures for Their Detention and Improvement.

67 Claudia Koonz, *Mothers in the Fatherland: Women, the Family and Nazi Politics* (London, 1987), p. 25.

68 Ibid., pp. 19-49; Ute Frevert, *Women in German History: From Bourgeois Emancipation to Sexual Liberation* (Oxford, 1989), pp. 168-204.

69 Jill Stephenson, *The Nazi Organization of Women* (London, 1981).

70 Martin Klaus, *Mädchen im 3. Reich: Der Bund Deutcher Mädel* (Cologne, 1998), p. 82; Lisa Pine, 'Creating Conformity: The Training of Girls in the *Bund Deutscher Mädel*', *European History Quarterly*, vol. 33 (2003), pp. 367-85.

71 Dorothee Klinksiek, *Die Frau im NS-Staat* (Stuttgart, 1982), pp. 48-51, 122.

72 Interview with Agnes and Annie Adel, 5 July 2000.

73 Interview with Aneliese Diehl, 15 August 2001.

74 Interview with Maria Grün, 8 August 2000.

75 Interview with Werner Lorenz, Inge Walter and Lilo Meyer, 21 August 2000.

76 Koonz, *Mothers in the Fatherland*, p. 108.

77 *Neue Volksblätter*, 23 February, 17 May 1939.

78 See the list in NSO Rep-430-19/56-20, Oberburgermeister to Regierungspräsident, 27 June 1939.

79 Burleigh and Wippermann, *Racial State*, p. 250.

80 NSO Dep-3b-XXI-135, Bund der Kinderreichen to the Oberbürgermeister, 20 August 1935. It is not clear how many, if any, of these became operational in Osnabrück.

81 See NSO Dep-3b-XXI-138.

82 See the letter to the Städtische Wohlfahrtsamt of 21 July 1930 in NSO Dep-3b-XXI-135.

83 Rita Thalmann, *Frausein im Dritten Reich* (Munich, 1984), p. 124; Peter Marschalck, *Bevölkerungsgeschichte Deutschlands im 19. und 20. Jahrhundert* (Frankfurt, 1984), pp. 75-83.

84 Osege, 'Vergleichende Untersuchung', pp. 9-10. This source asserts that in 1938 the birth rate was 18 per thousand in Osnabrück, compared with 18.7 in the Reich.

85 Thalmann, *Frausein*, p. 124.

86 *Osnabrücker Tageblatt*, 7 October 1934.

87 NSO Rep-430-15-65-74, Städtisches Wohlfahrtsamt to Regierungspräsidenten, 1 April 1935.

88 *Neue Volksblätter*, 20 June 1937.

89 See Dörte Winkler, *Frauenarbeit im 'Dritten Reich'* (Hamburg, 1977), pp. 38-65.

90 Thalmann, *Frausein*, pp. 158-9.

91 *Osnabrücker Zeitung*, 9 November 1934; NSO Dep-3b-XXI-119, `Pflichtarbeit der Frauen', 18 December 1934.

92 NSO Rep-610-Osn-278-66.

93 NSO Rep-610-Osn-278-107.

94 As Ian Kershaw, *The Hitler Myth: Image and Reality in the Third Reich* (Oxford, 1987), argues.

95 David Welch, *The Third Reich: Politics and Propaganda* (London, 1993), pp. 23-49.

96 *Ein anderer Stadtführer: Verfolger und Verfolgte zur Zeit des Nationalsozialismus in Osnabrück*, 4th edn (Osnabrück, 2000), p. 3.

97 Kershaw, *Hitler Myth*, p. 60.

98 *Osnabrücker Tageblatt*, 31 January 1935.

99 *Neue Volksblätter*, 31 January, 1 February 1937.

100 Ibid., 31 January 1938.

101 Ibid., 6 November 1937; *Osnabrücker Tageblatt*, 8, 10 November 1934, 7, 10 November 1937; *Osnabrücker Zeitung*, 9 November 1934, 11 November 1935.

102 Kershaw, *Hitler Myth*, pp. 57-9.

103 *Osnabrücker Zeitung*, 11 November 1933.

104 See Welch, *Third Reich*, pp. 30-4.

105 See *Neue Volksblätter*, 19, 21 July 1938.

106 Interview with Werner Funk, 16 August 2000.

107 Kershaw, *Hitler Myth*, p. 57.

108 *Osnabrücker Tageblatt*, 21 April 1933.

109 See, for instance, ibid., 22 April 1934, 21 April 1936, 21, 22 April 1937; *Neue Volksblätter*, 20 April 1937.

110 See, for instance, *Osnabrücker Zeitung*, 27 August 1934; *Osnabrücker Tageblatt*, 20, 21 June 1937.

111 See, for instance: *Osnabrücker Tageblatt*, 24 June 1937; *Osnabrücker Zeitung*, 23 June 1933.

112 Heinz Lauber and Dirgit Rothstein, *Der 1. Mai unter dem Hakenkreuz: Hitlers 'Machtergreifung' in Arbeiterschaft und in Betrieben* (Gerlingen, 1983).

113 *Osnabrücker Tageblatt*, 2 and 3 May, 1938.

114 *Neue Volksblätter*, 2 May 1938.

115 *Osnabrücker Zeitung*, 29 April, 2 May 1934.

116 *Was Bietet Osnabrück*, vol. 2, part 9, May 1936; Konrad Nettelnsrot, 'Der 1. Mai in Osnabrück: Die "Arbeiter-Maifeier" als Kampf- und Festtag der Arbeiterbewegung', *Osnabrücker Mitteilungen*, vol. 93 (1988), pp. 165-9.

117 For details of Stew Sundays in Osnabrück see, for instance: *Neue Volksblätter*, 11 January, 15 March, 11 November 1937, 10 Janaury, 11 February, 10 October 1938, 12 December, 13 March 1939; *Osnabrücker Tageblatt*, 15 November 1937; *Osnabrücker Zeitung*, 1 October, 4 December 1933, 7 November 1935, 9 November 1936. See also Detlef J. K. Peukert, *Inside Nazi Germany: Conformity, Opposition and Racism in Everyday Life* (London, 1993), pp. 49, 60, 83.

118 *Osnabrücker Tageblatt*, 24 March 1936.

119 Ibid., 26 March 1938.

120 But this caused concern which played a role in the purge of the SA on 30 June 1934. For the SA after the seizure of power see Peter Longerich, *Die Braune Bataillone: Geschichte der SA* (Munich, 1989), pp. 165-238.

121 *Osnabrücker Zeitung*, 3 February 1933.

122 *Neue Volksblätter*, 25 February 1937, 25 February 1939.

123 See, for instance, ibid., 7, 11, 14 February 1937.

124 Ibid., 15 January 1937.

125 Ibid., 27 March 1935; *Osnabrücker Tageblatt*, 27 March 1935.

126 *Neue Volksblätter*, 24 March 1937.

127 See the excellent introduction to Inge Marßolek and Adelheid von Soldern, eds, *Zuhören und Gehörtwerden: Radio im Nationalsozialismus* (Tübingen, 1988).

128 *Osnabrücker Tageblatt*, 20 December 1937; *Neue Volksblätter*, 20 December 1937.

129 David Welch, *Propaganda and the German Cinema, 1933-1945*, 2nd edn (London, 2001); David Stewart Hull, *Film in the Third Reich: A Study of the German Cinema, 1933-1945* (Berkeley, 1969), pp. 10-125.

130 Anne Paech, *Kino zwischen Stadt und Land: Geschichte des Kinos in der Provinz Osnabrück* (Marburg, 1985), pp. 71-91.

131 *Neue Volksblätter*, 19, 21 August 1938.

132 *Was Bietet Osnabrück*, vol. 3, part 13 (July, 1937), p. 9.

133 Welch, *Propaganda*, p. 36; Sabine Hake, *Popular Cinema of the Third Reich* (Austin, TX, 2001).

134 As an introduction see Marc A. Weiner, *Richard Wagner and the Anti-Semitic Imagination* (London, 1995).

135 Edward Bahr, 'Nazi Cultural Politics: Intentionalism vs Functionalism', in Glenn R. Cuomo, ed., *National Socialist Cultural Policy* (New York, 1995), pp. 5-22.

136 See: Erik Levi, *Music in the Third Reich* (Basingstoke, 1994); Michael Meyer, *The Politics of Music in the Third Reich* (New York, 1991); Michael H. Kater, *The Twisted Muse: Musicians and their Music in the Third Reich* (Oxford, 1997).

137 *75 Jahre Symphonieorchester (1919-1994): Festschrift* (Bramsche, 1994), p. 12.

138 *Kulturveranstaltungen 1938/39* (Osnabrück, 1938), pp. 4-5.

139 Bogusław Drewniak, 'The Foundation of Theatre Policy', in Cuomo, *National Socialist Cultural Policy*, p. 75.

140 Carsten Steuwer, 'Das Deutsche Nationaltheater in Osnabrück: Die Integration des Osnabrücker Theaters in die Nationalsozialistische Propagandamaschine', *Osnabrücker Mitteilungen*, vol. 106 (2001), pp. 261-4; Karl Kühling, *Theater in Osnabrück: Im Wandel der Jahrhunderte* (Osnabrück, 1959), pp. 70-5.

141 NSO ERW-A100-91, *Die Schriften des Deutschen Nationaltheaters*, Vol. 14, 1938-9.

142 This is contained in NSO ERW-A100-91.

143 John London, ed., *Theatre Under the Nazis* (Manchester, 2000).

144 See Paul Weindling, *Health, Race and German Politics Between National Unification and Nazism, 1870-1945* (Cambridge, 1989), pp. 378-9, 414-16.

145 *Osnabrücker Zeitung*, 18 February 1935.

146 *Neue Volksblätter*, 11 February, 19 March 1939.

147 *Osnabrücker Tageblatt*, 4 April 1934.

148 Peter Junk, '"Dann gehöre ich auf die Seite der Gefangenen und Unterdrückten": Kunst und Künstler im Nationalsozialismus', in Wilfried Wolf, ed., *Die Gründerzeit Osnabrücker Kunst* (Bramsche, 1986), pp. 24-30.

149 Alan E. Steinweis, *Art, Ideology and Economics in Nazi Germany: The Reich Chambers of Music, Theatre and the Visual Arts* (London, 1993); Jonathan A. Petropoulos, *Art as Politics in the Third Reich* (London, 1996).

150 Harald Scholtz, *Erziehung und Unterricht unterm Hakenkreuz* (Göttingen, 1985), p. 58; Klaus Kümmel, 'Zur schulischen Berufserziehung im Nationalsozialismus: Gesetze und Erlasse', in Manfred Heinemann (ed.), *Erziehung und Schulung im*

Dritten Reich, Vol. 1, *Kindergarten, Schule, Jugend, Berufserziehung* (Stuttgart, 1980), pp. 275-88.

151 Elke Nyssen, *Schule im Nationalsozialismus* (Heidelberg, 1979), pp. 28-32; Michael Buddruss, *Totale Erziehung für den totalen Krieg: Hitlerjugend und nationalsozialistische Jugendpolitik*, Vol. 1 (Munich, 2003), pp. 60-80.

152 Johannes Erger, 'Lehrer und Nationalsozialismus: Von den traditionallen Lehrerverbänden zum Nationalsozialistischen Lehrerbund (NSLB)', in Heinemann, *Erziehung und Schulung im Dritten Reich*, Vol. 2, *Hochschule, Erwachsenbildung* (Stuttgart, 1980), pp. 206-31; Ottwiln Ottweiler, *Die Volksschule im Nationalsozialismus* (Weinheim, 1979), p. 27.

153 *Osnabrücker Tageblatt*, 6 December, 30 May 1936.

154 Ottweiler, *Die Volksschule*, p. 4.

155 For all of the major educational measures introduced under the Third Reich see: Rolf Eilers, *Die nationalsozialistische Schulpolitik: Eine Studie zur Funktion der Erziehung im totalitären Staat* (Cologne, 1963); and Renate Fricke-Finkelnberg, ed., *Nationalsozialismus und Schule: Amtliche Erlasse und Richtlinien, 1933-1945* (Opladen, 1989).

156 St Ursula Osnabrück, *Festschrift zum Hundertjähriges Schuljubiläum* (Osnabrück, 1965), pp. 15-16.

157 *Neue Volksblätter*, 13 April 1939; *Osnabrücker Tageblatt*, 13 April 1939.

158 See NSO Rep-726-9.

159 Hartmut Ranke and Walter Moess, 'Das Ratsgymnasium von 1918 bis 1945', in Uwe Schipper, ed., *400 Jahre Ratsgymnasium Osnabrück* (Bramsche, 1985), pp. 211-12.

160 Hans Dietmar Beer, et. al., 'Das Gymnasium Carolinium und das Dritte Reich: Unsere Schule in den Jahren 1933/34', in *Schola Carolinium*, no. 108 (October 1984), pp. 6-7.

161 Interview with Margret Friedrich, 29 June 2000.

162 Interview with Josefa Herz, 26 July 2000.

163 Lorenz Peiffer, *Turnunterricht im Dritten Reich: Erziehung für den Krieg* (Cologne, 1987); NSO Dep-58b-1, 'Strukturwandel in Aufgaben und Ausgaben 1932 bis jetzt', 1938; Fricke-Finkelnburg, *Nationalsozialismus und Schule*, pp. 105-22.

164 NSO Dep-57b-87.

165 Presumably the *Ratsgymnasium*.

166 Lorenz Peiffer, 'Das Amt "K" und seine nachgeordneten regionalen Dienstellen: Kreissportlehrer im Regierungsbezirk Osnabrück: Ein Beitrag zur Alltagsgeschichte des Schulturnens im Nationalsozialismus', in Wolfgang Buss and Arnd Krüger, eds, *Sportgeschichte: Traditionspflege und Wertewandel* (Duderstadt, 1984), pp. 197-211; NSO Dep-57b-57.

167 NSO Dep-3b-IV-3306, Oberburgermeister to Regierungspräsident, 10 February 1939; *Osnabrücker Tageblatt*, 4 March 1935; *Neue Volksblätter*, 30 March 1938.

168 NSO Dep-3b-IV-2539, Oberstudiendirektor des Ratgymnasiums to the Oberpräsident, Abteilung für hoheres Schulwesen in Hannover, 14 April 1936; Gilmer W. Blackburn, *Education in the Third Reich: Race and History in Nazi Textbooks* (Albany, NY, 1985).

169 NSO Rep-726-1-91-81, `Staatlicher Reformsgymnasium in Osnabrück, Bericht über des Schuljahres 1933/4'.
170 Klemens-August Recker, '...meinen volke und meinen Herrgott dienen...': Das Gymnasium Carolinum zwischen partieller Kontinuität und Resistenz in der NS-Zeit (Osnabrück, 1989), pp. 193-4.
171 NSO Dep-3c-826, 'Lehrplan für Erdkunde', June 1936.
172 The above is based upon: Karl Heinz Jahnke and Michael Buddrus, eds, Deutsche Jugend, 1933-1945 (Hamburg, 1989); Arno Klönne, Jugend im Dritten Reich: Die Hitlerjugend und ihre Gegner (Cologne, 1999); Peter D. Stachura, The German Youth Movement, 1900-1945 (London, 1981); Hans-Christian Brandenberg, Die Geschichte der HJ: Weg und Irrwege einer Generation (Cologne, 1968); Fricke-Finkelnburg, Nationalsozialismus und Schule, pp. 237-56; Nyssen, Schule im Nationalsozialismus, pp. 33-82; Buddrus, Totale Erziehung; Michael H. Kater, Hitler Youth (London, 2004), pp. 13-69.
173 NSO Dep-3b-XV-12; Neue Volksblätter, 4 November 1937, 28 January, 5 March, 13 June 1938, 28 March 1939.
174 Osnabrücker Tageblatt, 2, 6 June 1933; Neue Volksblätter, 8 July 1938.
175 Neue Volksblätter, 27 March 1938.
176 Osnabrücker Tageblatt, 8 June 1937.
177 Ibid, 20 April 1936, 20 April 1937.
178 Neue Volksblätter, 18 February 1937.
179 Interview with Hugo Weiss, 19 June 2000.
180 Interview with Günther Adam, 2 August 2001.
181 Volker Issmer, 'Hitlerjungen – Flakhelfer – Edelweißpiraten: Jugendliche zwischen Anpassung und Widerstand, verdeutlicht an Beispielen aus der Region Osnabrück-Emsland', Osnabrücker Mitteilungen, vol. 107 (2002), pp. 207-32.
182 As an introduction to this issue see, Patrick von zur Mühlen, 'Exile and Resistance', in Wolfgang Benz and Walter H. Pehle, eds, Encyclopedia of German Resistance to the Nazi Movement (New York, 1997), pp. 91-100.
183 Detlev J. K. Peukert, Die KPD im Widerstand: Verfolgung und Untergrundarbeit an Rhein und Ruhr 1933 bis 1945 (Wuppertal, 1980).
184 Karl Dietrich Bracher, Wolfgang Sauer and Gerhard Schulz, Nationalsozialistische Machtergreifung: Studien zur Errichtung der totalitären Herrschaftsystem in Deustchland, 1933/4 (Cologne, 1960).
185 For the role of the SA in the Nazi seizure of power see: Longerich, Die Braune Battaillone, pp. 165-79; and Richard Bessel, Political Violence and the Rise of Nazism (London, 1984), pp. 97-118. Kristallnacht is dealt with in Chapter 7 below.
186 See contributions to Gerhard Paul and Klaus-Michael Mallmann, eds, Die Gestapo: Mythos und Realität (Darmstadt, 1996).
187 Wolfgang Sofsky, The Order of Terror: The Concentration Camp (Princeton, NJ, 1997); Nikolaus Wachsmann, Hitler's Prisons: Legal Terror in Nazi Germany (London, 2004); Harold Marcuse, Legacies of Dachau: The Uses and Abuses of a Concentration Camp, 1933-2001 (Cambridge, 2001), pp. 21-49.
188 The standard works on justice and the courts in the Third Reich include: Ralph Angermund, Deutsche Richterschaft, 1919-1945: Krisenerfahrung, Illusion, politische

Rechtsprechung (Frankfurt, 1990); and Lothar Gruchmann, *Justiz im Dritten Reich, 1930-1940* (Munich, 1990).

189 See, for instance, Peter Weidisch, *Die Machtergreifung in Würzburg, 1933* (Würzburg, 1990); Friedrich Keinemann, *Sieben Entscheidende Jahre: Hamm, 1928-1935* (Bochum, 1991); and Herbert Schwarzwälder, *Die Machtergreifung der NSDAP in Bremen, 1933* (Bremen, 1966).

190 See Table 2.2.

191 NSO Rep 430-101-7-43-331-Band 9, 'Politische Wochenberichte über die wirtschaftliche und politische Lage in der Stadt Osnabrück u.a. an die Polizeidirektion Bremen, 1932-3', 13, 20 February 1933; NSO Rep-430-201-5-66-2-Band 1; *Osnabrücker Zeitung*, 2 February, 2 March 1933; Rüdiger Griepenberg, '1933-1945: Illegalität und Verfolgung', in Wilhelm van Kampen and Tilman Westphalen, eds, *100 Jahre SPD in Osnabrück, 1875-1975: Ausgewählte Kapitel zur Geschichte der Arbeiterbewegung in Onsnabrück* (Osnabrück, 1975), pp. 107-11; Ludwig Hoffmeyer, et. al., *Chronik der Stadt Osnabrück* 6th Edn (Osnabrück, 1995), pp. 536-42; Dirk Thierbach, 'Der Deutsche Metallarbeiterverband in Osnabrück', in Thierbach and Thomas Blömer, eds, *Vom Deutschen Metallarbeiterverband zur Industriegewerkschaft Metall: Texte und Dokumente aus der Geschichte der Metallarbeiter in Osnabrück* (Bramsche, 1990), p. 64; Kühling, *Osnabrück, 1933-1945*, pp. 32-42; Geschichtsgruppe Arbeit und Leben in Osnabrück, *Freiheit-Krise-Diktatur: Zur Zerschlagung der Gewerkschaften in Osnabrück* (Bramsche, 1983); Ian Kershaw, *Hitler, 1889-1936: Hubris* (London, 1998), pp. 431-68; Schneider, *Unterm Hakenkreuz*, pp. 39-120; Dirk Erbe, ed., *Gleichgeschaltet: Der Nazi Terror gegen Gewerkschaaften und Berufsverbände, 1930 bis 1933* (Göttingen, 2001).

192 Keinemann, *Sieben entscheidende Jahre*, pp. 201-20, 281-303; Weidisch, *Die Machtergreifung in Würzburg*, pp. 98-156, 177-9; Hoffmeyer, *Chronik der Stadt Osnabrück*, pp. 539, 542; Thomas Grove, 'Die Entfernung des Osnabrücker Reichstagsabgeordneten Dr Johannes Drees aus seinem Amt 1933: Gleichschaltungsmaßnahme und politische Verfolgung', *Osnabrücker Mitteilungen*, vol. 103 (1998), pp. 259-66.

193 *Osnabrüker Tageblatt*, 29 March 1933; Antifaschistischer Arbeitskreis Osnabrück, ed., *Osnabrücker Arbeiter in Widerstand* (Osnabrück, 1987); Ludwig Landwehr, '*interresant war's eigentlich immer!': Aus dem Lebenserringungen der Ludwig Landwehr* (Osnabrück, 1987), p. 30; NSO Rep-430-201-5-66-3.

194 Günther Heuzeroth and Johannes Petrich, eds, *Unter der Gewaltherrschaft des Nationalsozialismus, 1933-1945, Vorgestellt an den Ereignissen in Weser-Ems*, Vol. 1, *Verfolgte aus politischen Grunden* (Osnabrück, 1989), pp. 1002-3; Landwehr, ibid.; Emil Jagusch, *Leben Hinter Stacheldraht: Ein Osnabrücker überlebt der KZ Sachsenhausen* (Osnabrück, 1978).

195 See Peukert, *Die KPD im Widerstand*.

196 *Osnabrücker Zeitung*, 1 August 1933.

197 NWSM Gen-STA-Hamm-Erstinstanz 11950, Vorbereitung zum Hochverrat: Besitzung kommunistische Druckschriften, Waffenbesitz zu kommunistische Zwecke in Bückeberg und Osnabrück.

198 NWSM Gen-STA-Hamm-Erstinstanz 1116, Vorbereitung zum Hochverrat: Verwohung kommunistischer Druckschriften in Osnabrück, 1933.

199 NWSM Gen-STA-Hamm-Erstinstanz 11278, Vorbereitung zum Hochverrat: Teilnahme an einer Strassenversamlung in Altenbögge, Transporte von Flugschriften in Osnabrück, 1933.

200 NWSM Gen-STA-Hamm-Erstinstanz 2882, Vorbereitung zum Hochverrat: Mitgliederschaft in der Roten SA in Osnabrück. Name has been changed.

201 NWSM Gen-STA-Hamm-Erstinstanz 2942, Vorbereitung zum Hochverrat: Illegaler Drusckscriften in Osnabrück.

202 'Lagebericht des Regierungspräsidenten von Osnabrück an den Reichsminister des Innern für den Monat Juli 1934 vom 10. September 1934', in Steinwascher, *Gestapo Osnabrück Meldet*, p. 72.

203 'Auszug aus dem Lagebericht der Staatspolizeistelle Osnabrück an das Geheime Staatspolizeiamt für den Monat Dezember 1934', in ibid., p. 126.

204 'Auszug aus dem Lagebericht der Staatspolizeistelle Osnabrück an das Geheime Staatspolizeiamt für den Monat Januar 1935 vom 4. Februar 1935', in ibid., pp. 134-5.

205 See the relevant reports in ibid.

206 NSO Rep-439-16, SS-Obersturmbahnführer to Zentralbüro der politischen Polizeikommandeurs, 4 October 1934.

207 NSO Rep-439-16, Gestapo Osnabrück to Gestapo Headquarters, 4 December 1934.

208 NWSM Gen-STA-Hamm-Erstinstanz 3436, Vorbereitung zum Hochverrat: Herstellung und Verbreitung kommunistischer Druckschriften in Osnabrück, 1934. Name has been changed.

209 General accounts of the churches under the Third Reich include: J. S. Conway, *The Nazi Persecution of the Churches, 1933-45* (London, 1968); Ernst Christian Helmreich, *The German Churches Under Hitler: Background, Struggle and Epilogue* (Detroit, 1979); Kurt Meier, *Kreuz und Hakenkreuz: Die evangelische Kirche im Dritten Reich* (Munich, 1992); Günther von Norden, 'Christen im Widerstand', in Löwenthal and von zur Mühlen, *Widerstand und Verweigerung*, pp. 111-28; Guenter Lewy, *The Catholic Church Under the Nazis* (London, 1964); Gerhard Besier, *Die Kirchen und das Dritte Reich: Spaltungen und Abwehrkämpfe, 1934-1937* (Munich, 2001); Manfred Galius, *Protestantismus und Nationalsozialismus: Studien zur nationalsozialistischen Durchdringung des protestantischen Sozialmilieus in Berlin* (Cologne, 2001).

210 Doris L. Bergen, *The German Christian Movement in the Third Reich* (London, 1996).

211 Conway, *Nazi Persecution of the Churches*, pp. 45-201; Helmreich, *German Churches*, pp. 133-235; Gunter van Norden, 'Widerstand im deutschen Protestantismus', in Klaus-Jürgen, Müller, ed., *Der Deutche Widerstand, 1933-1945*, 2nd edn (Paderborn, 1986), pp. 108-34.

212 Henrike Uhrmacher, '"Resistenz oder Akzeptanz? Die evangelische Kirche in Osnabrück während der Zeit des Nationalsozialismus', *Osnabrücker Mitteilungen*, vol. 100 (1995), pp. 232-6.

213 'Bericht der Staatspolizeistelle Osnabrück an das Geheime Staatspolizeiamt über Entstehung, Entwicklung und Lage des evangelischen Kirchenstreites im Regierungsbezirk Osnabrück vom 20. September 1934', in Steinwascher, *Gestapo Osnabrück Meldet*, p. 92; Kühling, *Osnabrück, 1933-1845*, pp. 75-88.

214 Dirk Glufke, 'Richard Karwehls "Politisches Messiastum": Zur Auseinandersetzung zwischen Kirche und Nationalsozialismus', *Jahrbuch der Gesellschaft für niedersächsische Kirchengeschichte*, vol. 90 (1992), pp. 201-6.

215 Richard Karwehl, 'Politisches Messiastum: Zur Auseinandersetzung zwischen Kirche und Nationalsozialismus', *Zwischen den Zeiten*, vol. 9 (1931), pp. 519-43. See other views put forward by Karwehl in LAH N86/4, Nachlaß Richard Karwehl, 'Kirchenkampf'.

216 Conway, *Nazi Persecution of the Churches*, pp. 83-5.

217 Heidrun Becker, 'Der Osnabrücker Kreis 1931-1939', in Heinrich Grosse, Hans Otte and Joachim Perels, eds, *Bewahren oder Bekennen? Die hannoverische Landeskirche im Nationalsozialismus* (Hanover, 1967), pp.43-104; Jutta Greiwe, 'Die evangelische Kirche in Osnabrück 1933-1939' (unpublished University of Osnabrück MA dissertation, 1992).

218 Conway, *Nazi Persecution of the Churches*, pp. 270-1.

219 LAH 51/916.

220 Ewald Hein-Janke, 'Die Gestapo und die Osnabrücker Kirchengemeinden 1934/5', *Junge Kirche*, vol. 39 (1978), pp. 287-90.

221 John Cornwell, *Hitler's Pope: The Secret History of Pius XII* (London, 1999).

222 Most notably in Lewy, *Catholic Church*.

223 Most recently Beth A. Griech-Polelle, *Bishop von Galen: German Catholicism and National Socialism* (London, 2002).

224 Conway, *Nazi Persecution of the Churches*; Ian Kershaw, *Popular Opinion and Political Dissent in the Third Reich: Bavaria, 1933-1945* (Oxford, 1983), pp. 205-23.

225 Heinz Hürten, 'Selbstbehauptung und Widerstand der katholischen Kirche', in Müller, *Der deutsche Widerstand*, pp. 135-56.

226 Klaus-Michael Mallmann and Gerhard Paul, *Milieus und Widerstand: Eine Verhaltensgeschichte der Gesellschaft im Nationalsozialismus* (Bonn, 1995), pp. 60-144.

227 Ulrich von Hehl, et. al., *Priester Unter Hitler's Terror*, 2 Volumes (Paderborn, 1996).

228 Wolfgang Seegrün, 'Bischof Berning von Osnabrück und die katholischen Lainverbände in den Verhandlungen um Artikel 31 des Reichskonkordates 1933-1936', *Osnabrücker Mitteilungen*, vol. 80 (1973), pp. 151-82; Ulrich von Hehl, 'Bischof Berning und das Bistum Osnabrück im Dritten Reich', *Osnabrücker Mitteilungen*, vol. 86 (1986), pp. 83-104.

229 Klemens-August Recker, *'Wem wollt ihr Glauben?' Bischof Berning im Dritten Reich* (Paderborn, 1998).

230 Kershaw, *Popular Opinion*, pp. 185-223; Lewy, *Catholic Church*, pp. 25-175; Helmreich, *German Churches*, pp. 237-73.

231 BAOS 03-17-72-32, Wilhelm Berning, Silvesterprädigten, 1933, 1937.

232 Recker, *'Wem wollt ihr Glauben?'*, pp. 124-267.

233 See above p. 64.

234 Heinz-Albert Raem, *Katholischer Gesellenverein und deutsche Kolpingfamilie in der Ära des Nationalsozialismus* (Mainz, 1982).

235 Willy Brinkwerth, 'Aus der Geschichte der Kolpingfamilie Osnabrück-Zentral', in Kolpingfamilie Osnabrück-Zentral, ed., *Festschrift zur Hundertjahrfeier der Kolpingfamilie Osnabrück-Zentral* (Osnabrück, 1959), pp. 10-14; *Neue Volksblätter*,

23 October 1937; NSO Rep-430-201-16B-65-160-Bd. 1, Gestapo letter dated 26 April 1939; BAOS 06-36-63-02.

236 The text is contained in BAOS 07-14-90.

237 Kühling, *Osnabrück, 1933-1945*, p. 100.

238 BAOS 04-61-00-5, Ferdinand Esser to Bishop Berning, 17 August 1932.

239 BAOS 04-63-00, Letter of Bishop Berning, 9 September 1933.

240 Hehl, *Priester*, pp. 1118, 1121, 1124.

241 See Paul and Mallmann, *Milieus*, pp. 60-144.

242 'Lagebericht der Staatspolizeistelle Osnabrück an das Geheime Staatspolizeiamt für den Monat Februar 1935 vom 7. März 1935', in Steinwascher, *Gestapo Osnabrück Meldet*, p. 139.

243 One of the longest reports on the Roman Catholic Church is 'Lagebericht der Staatspolizeistelle Osnabrück an das Geheime Staatspolizeiamt für den Monat Juni 1935 vom 4. Juli 1935', in ibid., pp. 191-7, which covers all of the above issues.

244 Erich Schmidt-Volkmar, *Der Kulturkampf in Deutschland, 1871-1890* (Berlin, 1962); Griech-Polelle, *Bishop von Galen*, pp. 23-41.

245 The Gestapo reports in Steinwascher, *Gestapo Osnabrück Meldet* make no mention of them.

246 Walter Struve, *Aufstieg und Herrschaft des Nationalsozialismus in einer industriellen Kleinstadt: Osterode am Harz, 1918-1945* (Essen, 1992), pp. 242-64.

247 See SPD Osnabrück, *1933-1983: Machtergreifung der Nationalsozialisten in Osnabrück* (Osnabrück, 1983), p. 7.

248 Detlef Garbe, *Zwischen Widerstand und Martyrium: Die Zeugen Jehovas im 'Dritten Reich'* (Munich, 1993); Gerhard Besier and Clemens Vollnhalls, eds, *Repression und Selbstbehauptung: Die Zeugen Jehovas unter der NS und der SED Diktatur* (Berlin, 2003).

249 Burleigh and Wippermann, *Racial State*, p. 253.

250 Gisela Bock, *Zwangssterilization im Nationalsozialismus: Studien zur Rassenpolitik und Frauenpolitik* (Opladen, 1986), pp. 28-41.

251 Hans-Walther Schmuhl, *Rassenhygiene, Nationalsozialismus, Euthanasie*, 2nd edn (Göttingen, 1987), pp. 23-125.

252 Weindling, *Health*, p. 424.

253 Burleigh and Wippermann, *Racial State*, pp. 33-4.

254 For which, see, for instance, Weindling, *Health*.

255 Adolf Hitler, *Mein Kampf* (London, 1939 edition), pp. 351-2.

256 Bock, *Zwangssterilization*, pp. 24-7.

257 Ibid., p. 183.

258 Christian Gansmüller, *Die Erbgesundheitspolitik des Dritten Reiches* (Cologne, 1987), pp. 57-9.

259 NSO Rep-430-19-56-241, Kreisarzt to Regierungpräsident, 2 June 1934.

260 Michael H. Kater, *Doctors Under Hitler* (London, 1989), p. 74.

261 Burleigh and Wippermann, *Racial State*, pp. 136-41; Robert Proctor, *Racial Hygiene: Medicine Under the Nazis* (London, 1988), pp. 95-112.

262 NSO Rep-727-62-83-2, Report on the Heil- und Pflegeanstalt, Osnabrück, 4 December 1933; NSO Rep-430-303-19-56-247, Oberlandesgerichtspräsident to Landesgerichtspräsident, 13 December 1938; NSO Rep-430-303-19-56-245,

Oberburgermeister to Regierungspräsident, 19 March 1939; Eva Berger, *Die Würde des Menschen ist unantastbar: 200 Jahre Psychiatriegeschichte im ehemaligen Königreich Hannover am Beispiel des Niedersächsischen Landeskrankenhaus Osnabrück* (Bramsche, 1999), pp. 183, 241; Hans Kremer, 'Erbhygienische Untersuchungen an Osnabrücker Hilfsschulen' (unpublished manuscript, Osnabrück, 1936); Raimond Reiter, 'Das Erbgensundheitsgericht Osnabrück und die Sterilisationsverfahren nach dem "Gestz zur Verhütung erbkranken Nachwuchses" vom 14. Juli 1933', *Osnabrücher Mitteilungen*, vol. 110 (2005), pp. 211-22..

263 This is one of the central arguments of Bock, *Zwangssterilisation*.

264 The figures are drawn together from NSO Rep-727-62-83-15.

265 NSO Rep 430-303-19-56-249-Band 4, contains annual reports relating to the Law for the Prevention of Hereditary Diseased Offspring.

266 Only first names are used in this section because of the sensitive nature of the material.

267 NSO Rep-727-13-85-M-1938-98.

268 See, for instance, NSO Rep-430-303-19-56-242.

269 The first names have been altered.

270 NSO Rep-430-303-35-71-2, Oberbürgermeiester der Stadt Osnabrück (Gesundheitsamt) to Regierungspräsident, 17 July 1936.

271 NSO Rep-430-303-35-71-2, Der Reichs- und Preußische Minister des Innern to Regierungspräsident Osnabrück, 12 November 1936.

272 Ayaß, '*Asoziale*'; Robert Gellately and Nathan Stolzfus, eds, *Social Outsiders in Nazi Germany* (Oxford, 2001). See above p. 57 for the workshy and below Chapter 8 for Romanies.

273 See, for instance: Richard Plant, *The Pink Triangle: The Nazi War Against Homosexuals* (Edinburgh, 1987); Till Bastian, *Homosexuelle im Dritten Reich: Geschichte einer Verfolgung* (Munich, 2000); Burkhard Jellonek, *Homosexuellen unter dem Hakenkreuz: Die Verfolgung Homosexuellen im Dritten Reich* (Paderborn, 1990). I found no material on homosexuals in Osnabrück.

274 Benz and Pehle, *Encyclopedia of German Resistance*.

Chapter 4

1   Hans-Ulrich Wehler, *Deutsche Gesellschaftsgeschichte*, Vol. 4, *Vom Beginn des Ersten Weltkrieges bis zur Gründung der beiden deutschen Staaten, 1914-1949* (Munich, 2003), p. 842.

2   Hans Mommsen, 'Kriegserfahrungen', in Ulrich Borsdorf and Mathilde Jamin, *Überleben im Krieg: Kriegserfahrungen in einer Industrieregion, 1939-1945* (Hamburg, 1989), pp. 7-14.

3   Wido Spratte, *Im Anflug auf Osnabrück: Die Bombenangriffe, 1940-1945* (Osnabrück, 1985); Ludwig Hoffmeyer, et. al., *Chronik der Stadt Osnabrück* 6th Edn (Osnabrück, 1995), pp. 589-603; Karl Kühling, *Osnabrück 1933-1945: Stadt im Dritten Reich* (Osnabrück, 1964), pp. 162-222.

4   Matthias Rickling, *Der Tag, an dem Osnabrück Unterging: 13. September 1944* (Gudensberg-Gleichen, 2004).

5   *Osnabrücker Tageblatt*, 25 March 1955.

6   See Table 4.2.

7   Spratte, *Im Anflug auf Osnabrück*, p. 155.

8   See Chapter 9 below.

9   Spratte bases his statistics on those provided by the air raid police immediately after the end of the War and contained in NSO Dep-3b-XIX-173. A memorial edition of the *Osnabrücker Tageblatt*, 25 March 1955, published on the tenth anniversary of the final and greatest attack on Osnabrück, gives slightly lower figures.

10 Interview with Hugo Weiss, 19 June 2000.

11 Neil Gregor, 'A *Schicksalgemeinschaft*? Allied Bombing, Civilian Morale, and Social Dissolution in Nuremberg, 1942-1945', *Historical Journal*, vol. 43 (2000), pp. 1051-1070.

12 This is touched on by ibid., p. 1052.

13 *United States Strategic Bombing Survey: Overall Report, European War* (Washington, DC, 1945); Denis Richards and Hilary St George Saunders, *Royal Air Force, 1939/1945*, 3 Vols (London, 1953); Sir Charles Webster and Noble Frankland, *The Strategic Air Offensive Against Germany, 1939-1945*, 4 Vols (London, HMSO, 1961).

14 Norman Macmillan, *The Royal Air Force in the World War*, 4 Vols (London, 1942-50); Sir Arthur Harris, *Bomber Offensive* (London, 1947).

15 Examples of this genre include: Max Hastings, *Bomber Command* (London, 1979); Robin Neillands, *The Bomber War: Arthur Harris and the Allied Bomber Offensive, 1939-1945* (London, 2001).

16 Mark Connelly, *Reaching for the Stars: A New History of Bomber Command in World War II* (London, 2001), pp. 1, 2.

17 The most important works include: Richard Overy, *The Air War, 1939-1945* (London, 1980); and Ronald Schaffer, *American Bombing in World War II* (Oxford, 1985). Both of these works deal with the Air War generally and not simply with events above Germany.

18 See, for example, Franz Kurowski, *Der Luftkrieg über Deutschland* (Düsseldorf, 1977).

19 Stephen A. Garrett, *Ethics and Airpower in World War II: The British Bombing of German Cities* (New York, 1993); A. C. Grayling, *Among the Dead Cities: Was the Allied Bombing of Civilians in WWII a Necessity or a Crime* (London, 2006).

20 The major exception is Earl R. Beck, *Under the Bombs: The German Home Front, 1942-1945* (Lexington, 1986).

21 Hans Rumpf, *Das War der Bombenkrieg: Deutsche Städte im Feuersturm* (Oldenburg, 1961); Erich Hampe, *Der Zivile Luftschutz im Zweiten Weltkrieg: Dokumentation und Erfahrungsberichte über Aufbau und Einsatz* (Frankfurt am Main, 1963); Michael Krause, *Flucht vor dem Bombenkrieg: Umquartierung im Zweiten Weltkrieg und die Wiedereingliederung der Evakuierten in Deutschland* (Düsseldorf, 1997).

22 Jörg Friedrich, *Der Brand: Deutschland in Bombenkrieg, 1940-1945* (Munich, 2002); Stephan Burgdorff and Christian Hobbe, eds, *Als Feuer vom Himmel Field: Der Bombenkrieg in Deutschland* (Munich, 2003); Lothar Kettenacker, ed., *Ein Volk von Opfern? Die Neue Debatte um den Bombenkrieg, 1940-45* (Berlin, 2003); Olaf Groehler, *Bombenkrieg gegen Deutschland* (Berlin, 1990).

23 See, for instance, Spratte, *Im Anflug auf Osnabrück*; Rolf Uphoff, *Als der Tag zur Nacht wurde - und der Nacht zum Tage: Wilhelmshaven im Bombenkrieg* (Oldenburg,

1992); Ralf Blank, 'Die Stadt Dortmund im Bombenkrieg', in Gerhard E. Sollbach, ed., *Dortmund – Bombenkrieg und Nachkriegszeit, 1939-1948* (Hagen, 1986).

24 Garrett, *Ethics and Airpower.*

25 *The Strategic Air Offensive Against Germany, 1939-1945: Report of the British Bombing Survey Unit* (London, 1998 reprint), pp. 70-1.

26 Ibid., p. 77.

27 Beck, *Under the Bombs*, p. 180.

28 *Strategic Air Offensive*, pp. 1-13.

29 Connelly, *Reaching for the Stars*, pp. 62-120.

30 *Strategic Air Offensive*, pp. 33-49.

31 Connelly, *Reaching for the Stars*, p. 13.

32 Garrett, *Ethics and Airpower*, pp. 19-20.

33 *Strategic Air Offensive*, p. 41.

34 Rumpf, *Das War der Bombenkrieg*, p. 191; Kurowkski, *Luftkrieg*, pp. 355-6.

35 Spratte, *Im Anflug auf Osnabrück*, pp. 156-7.

36 Rumpf, *Das War der Bombenkrieg*, pp. 195-200.

37 Garrett, *Ethics and Airpower*, pp. 17, 20.

38 Discussed in Chapter 3 above.

39 Hampe, *Der Zivile Luftschutz*, pp. 11-12, 16-49; Horst Adalbert-Koch, *Flak: Die Geschichte der deutschen Flakartillerie und der Einsatz der Luftwaffenhelfer*, 2nd Edition (Bad Nauheim, 1965), pp. 31-73.

40 NSO Dep-3b-XIX-3, Einsatz= und Verpflegungsstärken des Kommandos der Schutzpolizei Osnabrück.

41 NSO Dep-3b-XIX-168.

42 NSO Dep-3b-XIX-168, Bericht über den Stand der LS-Baumassnahmen, 1 January 1942, 1 July 1944.

43 Spratte, *Im Anflug auf Osnabrück*, p. 16.

44 NSO Dep-3b-XIX-168, Fliegeralarme für den Monat August 1944.

45 *Neue Volksblätter*, 11 July, 8 August 1943; NSO Dep-3b-IV-6492, Oberbürgermeister an alle Betriebe mit mehr als 50 Gefolgschaftsmitgliedern, 2 March 1943.

46 NSO Dep-3b-XIX-14, Stradtschulrat to Oberburgermeister, 29 February 1942.

47 Details exist in: NSO Dep-58b-157; NSO Dep-58b-158; NSO-Rep-726-32.

48 NSO SLG-54-5, 'Volk ans Gewehr: Eine Jugend im "Totalen Krieg", betr. Luftwaffenhelfer in Osnabrück'. For similar experiences elsewhere in Germany see: Ludger Tewes, *Jugend im Krieg: Von Luftwaffenhelfern und Soldaten, 1939-1945* (Essen, 1989); Kurt Abels, *Ein Held War Ich Nicht: Als Kind und Jugendlicher in Hitlers Krieg* (Cologne, 1998); and Koch, *Flak*, pp. 309-21.

49 Spratte, *Im Anflug auf Osnabrück*, p. 18.

50 Martin Middlebrook and Chris Everitt, *The Bomber Command War Diaries: An Operational Reference Book, 1939-1945* (London, 1985), p. 54.

51 NSO Dep-3b-XIX-53.

52 NSO Dep-3b-XV-1, Kriegs-Chronik, Band I, Sept. 1939 – Juni 1940, p. 340.

53 NSO Dep-3b-XIX-54; NSO Dep-3b-XIX-55; Middlebrook and Everitt, *Bomber Command War Diaries*, p. 61; NSO Rep-430-201-14-47-2, Report of 12 July 1940.

54 NSO Dep-3b-XIX-61; *Neue Volksblätter*, 20 September 1940.

55 Detailed in: NSO Dep-3b-XIX-67; NSO Dep-3b-XIX-70; NSO Dep-3b-XIX-72.

56 NSO Dep-3b-XIX-72.

57 NSO Rep 430-201-14-47-2, Police Report of 14 August 1942.

58 NSO Dep-3b-XIX-79; NSO Dep-3b-XIX-80.

59 NSO Rep 430-201-14-47-2, Police Report of 20 August 1942; NSO Dep-3b-XIX-81.

60 Middlebrook and Everitt, *Bomber Command War Diaries*, p. 314.

61 Spratte, *Im Anflug auf Osnabrück*, p. 156.

62 NSO Rep 430-201-14-47-2, Police Report of 20 August 1942.

63 See the list of attacks in NSO Dep-XIX-173.

64 NSO Dep-3b-XIX-103; NSO Dep-3b-XIX-105.

65 NSO Dep-3b-XIX-106; NSO Dep-3b-XIX-107.

66 NA AIR40/627.

67 NSO Dep-3b-XIX-108.

68 NSO Dep-3b-XIX-109.

69 NSO Dep-3b-XIX-113.

70 NSO Dep-3b-XIX-114, Oberbürgermeister to Ernährungsamt B, 17 September 1944.

71 NSO Dep-3b-XV-6, Kriegs-Chronik, Band VI, Juli 1944 - Okt. 1944, pp. 1854-5. For more detail see Rickling, *Der Tag*, pp. 26-41.

72 Interview with Agnes and Annie Adel, 5 July 2000.

73 Krause, *Flucht vor dem Bombenkrieg*, pp. 13-184; Kerstin Siebenborn-Ramm, *Die 'Butenhamborger': Kriegsbedingte Migration und Ihre Folgen im und nach dem Zweiten Weltkrieg* (Hamburg, 1996), pp. 1-221; Katja Klee, *'Im Luftschutzkeller des Reiches': Evakuierte in Bayern, 1939-1953: Politik, soziale Lage, Erfahrungen* (Munich, 1999), pp. 9-206.

74 NSO Dep-3b-XIX-116; NSO Dep-3b-XIX-118.

75 NSO Dep-3b-XIX-121; NSO Dep-3b-XIX-122; NSO Dep-3b-XIX-124.

76 NSO Rep 430-201-14-47-2, Police Report of 24 November 1944; NSO Dep-3b-XIX-128.

77 Spratte, *Im Anflug auf Osnabrück*, p. 157.

78 NSO Dep-3b-XIX-135; NSO Dep-3b-XIX-138; NSO Dep-3b-XIX-141.

79 NSO Dep-3b-XIX-147; NSO Dep-3b-XIX-149; NA AIR40/805; NA AIR40/807; NA AIR40/829, Interpretation Report No. K4142, 12 May 1945.

80 These figures come from NSO Dep-3b-XIX-159.

81 NSO Dep-3b-XV-7, Kriegs-Chronik, Band VII, Nov. 1944 – April 1945, pp. 2220-2221.

82 Details exist in NSO Dep-3b-IV-6495.

83 See Roswitha Poppe, 'Denkmalspflege in Osnabrücker Raum während und nach dem Kriege', *Mitteilungen des Vereins für Geschichte und Landkunde von Osnabrück*, vol. 62 (1947), pp. 221-32.

84 B. Robben, *Die Herz-Jesu-Kirche in Osnabrück: Enstehung, Zerstörung, Wiederaufbau* (Osnabrück, 1955), pp. 23-32; BAOS 04-79-10-04; BAOS 04-79-10-05.

85 Details can be found in LAH 51.

86 NSO Dep-3b-XXI-80, Städt. Wohlfahrtsamt to Oberbürgermeister, 2 October 1942.

87 Krause, *Flucht vor dem Bombenkrieg*.

88 See the correspondence in NSO Rep-430-108-11-67-II-114 and the relevant articles in *Osnabrücker Tageblatt*, 25 July 1942 and *Neue Volkslblätter*, 25 July, 1 August 1942.

89 NSO Rep-430-303-19-56-136, 'Auffangstellen für Obdachlose in den an das Stadtgebiet angrenzenden Landkreisen', 21 August 1943.

90 See NSO Dep-3b-IV-6401.

91 See *Neue Volkslblätter*, 10 September 1942, 15 October, 18 November 1944.

92 *Neue Volkslblätter*, 19 May 1944.

93 Ibid., 25 June 1942.

94 Ibid., 15 August 1942.

95 Ibid., 12, 19 May 1944; *Osnabrücker Tageblatt*, 12 May 1944.

96 Christoph Kleßmann, ed., *Nicht nur Hitlers Krieg: Der Zweite Weltkrieg in Deutschland* (Düsseldorf, 1989); Marlis G. Steinert, *Hitler's War and the Germans: Public Mood and Attitude during the Second World War* (Athens, OH, 1977); Martin Kitchen, *Nazi Germany at War* (London, 1995).

97 See Alan S. Milward, *The German Economy at War* (London, 1965); Dietrich Eichholtz, ed., *Krieg und Wirtschaft: Studien zur deutschen Wirtschaftsgeschichte, 1939-1945* (Berlin, 1999); Dietrich Eicholtz, *Geschichte der deutschen Kriegswirtschaft*, 3 Volumes (Berlin, 1971-96); Gregor Jannsen, *Das Ministerium Speer: Deutschlands Rüstung im Krieg* (Berlin, 1968).

98 Hoffmeyer, *Chronik der Stadt Osnabrück*, p. 576.

99 Interview with Werner Funk, 16 August 2000.

100 Interview with Agnes and Annie Adel, 5 July 2000.

101 Richard Overy, *War and Economy in the Third Reich* (Oxford, 1994), pp. 291-303, 343-75.

102 NSO Dep-3b-XV-18, Arbeitsamt Osnabrück to Verkehrs- and Presseamt, 23 July 1942.

103 R. Friess, *75 Jahre Osnabrücker Kupfer und Drahtwerk* (Melle, 1948), p. 19; NSO Rep-610-Osn-614, Report of inspection of OKD dated 14 April 1944.

104 See the 1944 correspondence in NSO Rep-610-Osn-283.

105 BA MA/RW/20-6-17, Lageberichte der Rüstungsinspektion VI, Heft I, 21.9.1939-21.2.1940, p. 209.

106 See, for instance, Neil Gregor, *Daimler Benz in the Third Reich* (London, 1998), pp. 109-32.

107 Dieter Kunst, *The Karmann Story: Germany's Coachbuilder to the World*, 2nd Edn (Osnabrück, 1996), pp. 53-7.

108 See correspondence in NSO Rep-610-Osn-251.

109 NSO Rep-610-Osn-252, Report of inspection of Karmann dated 8 May 1944.

110 BA MA/RW/21/51/5, Kriegstagebuch der Rüstungskommandos Osnabrück Bd. V, 1.3-51.5 1941, p. 21.

111 Deutsches Berufserziehungswerk, Gau Weser-Ems, Osnabrück, *Jeder macht mit – in den fördernden Lehrgemeinschaften für Berufstätige* (Osnabrück, 1941); Deutsches Berufserziehungswerk, *Übungsstätten für Berufstätige* (Osnabrück, 1942).

112 Daniel Wildmann, *Begehrte Körper: Konstruktion und Inszenierung des 'arischen' Männerkörpers im 'Dritten Reich'* (Zurich, 1998).

113 *Osnabrücker Tageblatt*, 16 October 1941.

114 NSO Dep-3b-IV-6493, DAF, Kraft Durch Freude an alle Betriebsführer, 8 May 1940.

115 *OKD Werkzeitung*, September/October 1940, October/November 1942.

116 Hartmut Fackler, 'Gleichgeschaltet: Der Handel im Dritten Reich', in Michael Haverkamp and Hans-Jürgen Teuteberg, eds, *Unterm Strich: Von der Winkelkrämerei zum E-Commerce: Eine Austellung des Museums Industriekultur im Rahm des 175. Bestehen der Sparkasse Osnabrück* (Bramsche, 2000), pp. 252-3; Heinz-Günther Borck, 'Chronik der Handwerkskammer Osnabrück, 1900-1975', in Handwerkskammer Osnabrück, ed., *Geschichte des Osnabrückder Handwerks* (Osnabrück, 1975), pp. 440-4.

117 NSO Dep-3b-XXI-165, Der Reichsstatthalter in Oldenburg und Bremen, Landwirtschaftsamt Weser-Ems, Bremen, to Betriebsführer der Firma Friedrich Zinn, Osnabrück, 24 February 1943.

118 NSO Dep-3b-XV-18, 'Bericht über die wirtschaftliche Lage des Handwerks im Regierungsbezirk Osnabrück während des vierten Kalendervierteljahres 1943'; *Osnabrücker Tageblatt*, 30 November 1943.

119 Avner Offer, *The First World War: An Agrarian Interpretation* (Oxford, 1989); Dietmar Petzina, 'Soziale Lage der deutschen Arbeiter und Probleme des Arbeitseinsatzes während des Zweiten Weltkrieges', in Waclaw Długoborski, ed., *Zweiter Weltkrieg und sozialer Wandel* (Göttingen, 1981), pp. 65-86; Rolf Dieter Müller, 'Die Konsequenzen der "Volksgemeinschaft": Ernährung, Anbeutung und Vernichtung', and Marie Luise Recker, 'Zwischen soziale Befriedung und industrielle Ausbeutung: Lohn- und Arbeitsbedingungen im Zweiten Weltkrieg', both in Wolfgang Michalka, ed., *Der Zweite Weltkrieg: Analysen, Grundzüge, Forschungsbilanz* (Munich, 1989), pp. 240-8, 430-4; Robert Kalt, *Rationierung der Nahrungsmittel und Schwarzer Markt in der Kriegswirtschaft* (Fribourg, 1951), pp. 9-87; Overy, *War and Economy*, pp. 281-5; Kitchen, *Nazi Germany at War*, pp. 79-84.

120 NSO Dep-3b-XV-1, Kriegs-Chronik, Band I, Sept. 1939 – Juni 1940, p. 2.

121 NSO Rep 430-201-14-47-2, Police Report of 11 December 1940.

122 NSO Dep-3b-XV-6, Kriegs-Chronik, Band VI, Juli 1944 – Okt. 1944, p. 1743.

123 NSO Rep 430-201-14-47-2, Lagebericht, 11 July 1944.

124 NSO Dep-3b-XV-7, Kriegs-Chronik, Band VII, Nov. 1944 – April 1945, p. 2101.

125 *Osnabrücker Tageblatt*, 3 March 1942.

126 *Neue Volksblätter*, 2 June 1940.

127 See Marie-Luise Recker, *Nationalsozialistische Sozialpolitik im Zweiten Weltkrieg* (Munich, 1985).

128 NSO Dep-3b-XXI-95, 'Vorlage wegen Erhöhung unserer Unterstützung für allgemeine Fürsorge'.

129 See NSO Dep-3b-XXI-96.

130 NSO Rep-726-27, WHW to Oberschule für Jungen, 4 March 1942.

131 BAOS 04-63-04, 'Bericht über die Seelsorgsstunden für die Kinder der Grundschule im Kriegswinter 1944/5'

132 Peter Marschalck, *Bevölkerungsgeschichte Deutschlands im 19. und 20. Jahrhundert* (Frankfurt, 1984), p. 84; Günter Steinberg, *Die Bevölkerungsentwicklung Deutschlands im Zweiten Weltkrieg* (Bonn, 1991).

133 Margret Osege, 'Vergleichende Untersuchung über sozialhygienische Probleme in der Stadt Osnabrück vor und nach dem zweiten Weltkrieges' (unpublished University of Münster medical dissertation, 1949), p. 14; G. Weinand, 'Die Tuberkulose vor, während und nach dem Kriege (1936-1946) im Stadt- und Landkreis Osnabrück' (unpublished manuscript, 1948); Werner Pelster, 'Selbstmord in Stadt-u. Landkreis Osnabrück' (unpublished University of Münster medical dissertation, 1943), p. 10.

134 Dörte Winkler, *Frauenarbeit im 'Dritten Reich'* (Hamburg, 1977), pp. 82-92, 102-10, 122-75; Ute Frevert, 'Frauen an der "Heimatfront", in Kleßmann, *Nicht nur Hitlers Krieg*, pp. 51-69; Elizabeth D. Heinemann, *What Difference Does a Husband Make? Women and Marital Status in Nazi and Postwar Germany* (London, 1999), pp. 44-74.

135 Irmgard Weyrather, *Muttertag und Mutterkreuz: Der Kult um die 'deutsche Mutter' im Nationalsozialismus* (Frankfurt, 1993).

136 *Osnabrücker Tageblatt*, 2 October 1939; *Neue Volksblätter*, 20 May 1940; NSO Rep 430-303-19-56-20, Oberburgermeister to Regierungs Präsident, 13 March 1940.

137 *Neue Volksblätter*, 4 March 1941.

138 Ibid., 23 September 1944.

139 Ibid., 16, 19 December 1939.

140 Ibid., 27 February 1943.

141 Overy, *War and Economy*, pp. 303-5.

142 Michael Burleigh and Wolfgang Wippermann, *The Racial State in Germany, 1933-1945* (Cambridge, 1991), p. 260.

143 Tim Mason, 'Women in Germany, 1925-1940: Family, Welfare and Work', in Jane Caplan, ed., *Nazism, Fascism and the Working Classes: Essays by Tim Mason* (Cambridge, 1995), p. 201.

144 Ibid., pp. 201-2; Richard Grunberger, *A Social History of the Third Reich* (London, 1991), pp. 326-7; Rita Thalmann, *Frausein im Dritten Reich* (Munich, 1984), pp. 179-80.

145 *Neue Volksblätter*, 28 May 1940.

146 NSO Rep-610-Osn-614, Report of inspection of OKD dated 14 April 1944.

147 Interview with Anneliese and Hate Berger, 12 July 2000.

148 Interview with Anneliese Diehl, 15 August 2001.

149 Interview with Lora Kraft, 20 August 2001.

150 Arbeitsgemeinschaft Sozialdemokratischer Frauen, Unterbezirk Osnabrück Stadt, *Vor 50 Jahren: Wie Frauen das Kriegsende erlebten* (Osnabrück, 1996), p. 13.

151 Interview with Agnes and Anni Adel, 5 July 2000.

152 Interview with Werner Lorenz, Inge Walter and Lilo Meyer, 21 August 2000.

153 Aristotle A. Kallis, *Nazi Propaganda and the Second World War* (Basingstoke, 2005).

154 See chapters 6-8 of Ian Kershaw, *The Hitler Myth: Image and Reality in the Third Reich* (Oxford, 1987).

155 David Welch, *The Third Reich: Politics and Propaganda* (London, 1993), pp. 90-124.

156 *Neue Volksblätter*, 31 January 1945.

157 Ibid., 14 November 1944.
158 Ibid., 21 April 1941, 21 April 1943, 22 April 1944.
159 Ibid., 6 November 1940.
160 *Osnabrücker Tageblatt*, 18 March 1941.
161 *Neue Volksblätter*, 28 January 1945.
162 Ibid., 23 April 1940, 30 June 1941.
163 *Osnabrücker Tageblatt*, 12 March 1941.
164 Ibid., 15 April 1942; *Neue Volksblätter*, 15 April 1942.
165 *Neue Volksblätter*, 8 September 1943.
166 David Welch, *Propaganda and the German Cinema, 1933-1945*, 2nd edn (London, 2001), pp. 159-203; Daniel Stuart Hall, *Film in the Third Reich: A Study of the German Cinema, 1933-1945* (Berkerley and Los Angeles, 1969), pp. 157-266.
167 Jürgen Diehl, 'Unterhaltung und Propaganda: Osnabrücker Filmtheater im Zweiten Weltkrieg', *Osnabrücker Mitteilungen*, vol. 105 (2000), pp. 155-99. *Ich Klage an* is discussed by Burleigh and Wippermann, *Racial State*, pp. 156-61, who state that 18 million people watched it, with mixed reactions. See also Udo Benzenhöfer and Wolfgang E. Eckert, eds, *Medizin im Spielfilm des Nationalsozialismus* (Tecklenburg, 1990).
168 Anne Paech, *Kino zwischen Stadt und Land: Geschichte des Kinos in der Provinz Osnabrück* (Marburg, 1985), p. 82.
169 Alan E. Steinweis, *Art, Ideology, and Economics in Nazi Germany: The Reich Chambers of Music, Theatre and the Visual Arts* (London, 1993); Jonathan A. Petropoulos, *Art as Politics in the Third Reich* (London, 1996).
170 *Neue Volksblätter*, 5 October 1940.
171 Carsten Steuwer, 'Das deutsche Nationaltheater Osnabrück: Die Integration des Osnabrücker Theaters in die Nationalsozialistische Kultur und Propagandamaschine', *Osnabrücker Mitteilungen*, vol. 106 (2001), p. 272.
172 NSO ERW A100 91, Deutsches Nationaltheater, Werbeheft, 1940-1.
173 NSO ERW A100 91, Die Schriften des Deutschen Nationaltheaters, Heft 1, 1940-1.
174 Deutsches Nationaltheater Osnabrück, *Rückblick auf der Spielzeit 1941-42* (Osnabrück, 1942).
175 Karl Kühling, *Theater in Osnabrück: Im Wandel der Jahrhunderte* (Osnabrück, 1959), p. 87; Klaus Kieser, *Das Gärtnerplatz-theater in München, 1932-1944: Zur Operette im Nationalsozialismus* (Frankfurt, 1991), p. 111.
176 *Kulturveranstaltungen 1940-1* (Osnabrück, 1940).
177 NSO ERW A100 91, Deutsches Nationaltheater, Werbeheft, 1940-1.
178 Boguslaw Drewniak, *Das Theater im NS-Staat: Szenarium deutscher Zeitgeschichte, 1933-1945* (Darmstadt, 1983), pp. 344-54.
179 *Neue Volksblätter*, 8 September 1943.
180 NSO Dep-3b-XV-20, `Gau Kulturtage Weser-Ems 1943'.
181 *Neue Volksblätter*, 23 May 1944.
182 Ibid., 3, 6 October 1940, 19 January, 30 March 1942.
183 Ibid., 5 December 1943.
184 Ibid., 5 October 1941; *Ausstellung im Schloss zu Osnabrück, Niederländische Kunst der Gegenwart, 5-26 Oktober 1941* (Osnabrück, 1941).

185 Hans Josef Horchem, *Kinder im Krieg: Kindheit und Jugend im Dritten Reich* (Hamburg, 2000); Karl Heinz Jahnke, *Hitlers letztes Angebot: Deutsche Jugend im sechsten Kriegsjahr, 1944/45* (Essen, 1993); Michael Buddruss, *Totale Erziehung für den totalen Krieg: Hitlerjugend und nationalsozialistische Jugendpolitik*, vol. 2 (Munich, 2003), pp. 651-741; Nicholas Stargardt, *Witnesses of War: Children's Lives Under the Nazis* (London, 2005).

186 NSO Dep-3b-XV-19, Verzeichnis der zum Heeresdienst einberufenen Volks-u. Mittelschullehrkräfte.

187 *Mitteilungsblatt der Staatlichen Oberschule für Jungen*, No. 4, January 1940, p. 3; Hartmut Ranke and Walter Moess, `Das Ratsgymnasium von 1918 bis 1945', in Uwe Schipper, ed., *400 Jahre Ratsgymnasium Osnabrück* (Bramsche, 1985), p. 223.

188 Guido Knopp, *Hitler's Children* (Stroud, 2000), pp. 173-284.

189 *Schola Carolina*, No. 35, May 1944.

190 *Mitteilungsblatt der Staatlichen Oberschule für Jungen*, No. 4, January 1940, p. 3

191 Ranke and Moess, 'Ratsgymnasium', pp. 223-4.

192 See NSO Dep-58b-114.

193 Interview with Karl Mosse, 10 August 2001; Johannes Hesse, *Carolinger 1939 bis 1947: Erinnerungen eines ehemaligen Schülers* (Osnabrück, 1997), pp. 99-109.

194 There is a large literature on evacuation, some of it local and some of it popular. A cross section includes: Martha Schlegel, *Von der Nordseeküste in die Kinderlandverschickung, 1940-1945* (Oldenburg, 1996); Martin Rüther, *`Zu Hause könnten sie es nicht schöner haben': Kinderlandverschickung aus Köln und Umgebung, 1941-1945* (Cologne, 2000); Thomas Gießmann and Rudolf Marciniak, *`Fast sämtliche Kinder sind jetzt Weg': Quellen und Zeitzeugenberichte zur Kinderlandverschickung aus Rheine, 1941-1945* (Münster, 2001); Gerhard Dabel, *KLV: Die erweiterte Kinder-Land-Verschickung: KLV-Lage, 1940-1945* (Freiburg, 1981); Claus Larass, *Der Zug der Kinder: Die Evakuierung 5 Millionen deutscher Kinder im 2. Weltkrieg* (Frankfurt, 1992); Gerhard Kock, *`Der Führer sorgt für unsere Kinder': Die Kinderlandverschickung im Zweiten Weltkrieg* (Paderborn, 1997); Jorst Hermand, *Als Pimpf in Polen: Erweiterte Kinderlandverschickung, 1940-1945* (Frankfurt, 1993).

195 *Neue Volksblätter*, 30 October 1941.

196 NSO Rep-726-26, 'Stand der Kinderlandverschickung' 15 August 1944; Klemens-August Recker, *`...meinen volke und meinen Herrgott dienen...': Das Gymnasium Carolinum zwischen partieller Kontinuität und Resistenz in der NS-Zeit* (Osnabrück, 1989), pp. 220-36.

197 NSO SLG-54-2, Dirk Siegel, 'Tagebuchnotizen über das letzte Schuljahr am Ratsgymnasium in Osnabrück, 1940/1'.

198 Interview with Karl Mosse, 10 August 2001.

199 St Ursula Osnabrück, *Festschrift zum Hundertjähriges Schuljubiläum* (Osnabrück, 1965), p. 16.

200 Renate Fricke-Finkelnberg, ed., *Nationalsozialismus und Schule: Amtliche Erlasse und Richtlinien, 1933-1945* (Opladen, 1989), pp. 72-85, 123-132; Karl Heinz Jahnke and Michael Buddrus, eds, *Deutsche Jugend, 1933-1945* (Hamburg, 1989), pp. 28-39.

201 NSO Dep-3b-IV-3306, 'Dienstbesprechung der Sacharbeiter für Leibeserziehung und Leiter der Hochschulinstitute für Leibesübungen an der Führerschule Neustrelitz vom 10. – 13. Oktober 1944'.

202 Ranke and Moess, 'Ratsgymnasium', pp. 227-33.
203 NSO Dep-58b-147, 'Zusammenstellung der von den Schulen gesammelten Altmaterialen im Jahre 1941'.
204 Matthias von Hellfeld and Arno Klönne, eds, *Die betragene Generation: Jugend im Faschismus* (Cologne, 1985), pp. 189-248; Hans-Christian Brandenburg, *Die Geschichte der HJ: Wege und Irwege einer Generation* (Cologne, 1968), pp. 227-33; Christoph Schubert-Weller, *Hitler-Jugend: Von 'Jungsturm Adolf Hitler' zur Staatsjugend des Dritten Reiches* (Weinheim, 1993), pp. 198-211; H. W. Koch, *The Hitler Youth: Origins and Development* (London, 1975), pp. 228-52; Michael H. Kater, *Hitler Youth* (London, 2004), pp. 167-246.
205 *Neue Volksblätter*, 23 October 1939, 29 September 1942, 16 April 1944.
206 Ibid., 26 June 1941, 2 June 1943; *Osnabrücker Tageblatt*, 28 May 1942.
207 NSO Rep-430-201-16B-65-12.
208 See three works by Peukert: *Inside Nazi Germany: Conformity, Opposition and Racism in Everyday Life* (London, 1993); *Die Edelweißpiraten: Potestbewegung jugendlicher Arbeiter im dritten Reich* (Cologne, 1988); 'Protest und Widerstand von Jugendlichen im Dritten Reich', in Richard Löwenthal and Patrick von zur Mühlen, eds, *Widerstand und Verweigerung im Dritten Reich, 1933-1945* (Berlin, 1982), pp. 177-201.
209 Volker Issmer, 'Hitler-Jungen – Flakhelfer – Edelweißpiraten: Jugendliche zwischen Anpassung und Widerstand, verdeutlicht an Beispielen aus der Region Osnabrück-Emsland', *Osnabrücker Mitteilungen*, vol. 107 (2002), pp. 207-32.
210 Raimond Reiter, '"Heimtücke" und "Volksschädlinge": Osnabrücker vor dem Sondergericht Hannover in der NS-Zeit', *Osnabrücker Mitteilungen*, vol. 103 (1998), pp. 267-76.
211 Ralph Angermund, '"Recht ist, was dem Volke nutzt": Zum Niedergang von Recht und Juztiz im Dritten Reich', in Karl Dietrich Bracher, Manfred Funke and Hans-Adolf Jacobsen, eds, *Deutschland, 1933-1945: Neue Studien zur nationalsozialistischen Herrschaft* (Düsseldorf, 1993), pp. 68-70; Nikolaus Wachsmann, *Hitler's Prisons: Legal Terror in Nazi Germany* (London, 2004), pp. 191-226.
212 Ralph Angermund, *Deutsche Richterschaft, 1919-1945: Krisenerfahrung, Illusion, politische Rechtsprechung* (Frankfurt, 1990), pp. 179-200.
213 Eric Johnson, *The Nazi Terror: Gestapo, Jews and Ordinary Germans* (London, 1999), p. 554, note 8.
214 Interview with Agnes and Annie Adel, 5 July 2000.
215 Interview with Elizabeth and Heinrich Wand, 16 August 2001.
216 Interview with Werner Lorenz, Inge Walter and Lilo Meyer, 21 August 2000.
217 Robert Gellately, *The Gestapo and German Society: Enforcing Racial Policy 1933-1945* (Oxford, 1990).
218 NHH Hann-171a-Hann-107-83-135. Names have been changed in this and subsequent files in this section.
219 NHH Hann-171a-Hann-107-83-162.
220 NHH Hann-171a-Hann-107-83-305.
221 NHH Hann-171a-Hann-107-83-729.
222 NSO Rep-430-201-16B-65-58.

223 *Neue Volksblätter*, 10 July 1942.

224 Ibid., 23 October 1942.

225 NHH Hann-171a-Hann-28-66-352. Name has been changed.

226 See, for instance, Roger Manwell and Heinrich Frankel, *The July Plot: The Attempt in 1944 on Hitler's Life and the Men Behind It* (London, 1964); Kurt Finker, *Der 20. Juli 1944: Militärpolitik oder Revolution* (Berlin, 1994); Joachim C. Fest, *Staatsreich: Der Lange Weg zur 20. Juli* (Berlin, 1994).

227 Rüdiger Griepenberg, '1933-1945: Illegalität und Verfolgung', in Wilhelm van Kampen and Tilman Westphalen, eds, *100 Jahre SPD in Osnabrück, 1875-1975: Ausgewählte Kapitel zur Geschichte der Arbeiterbewegung in Osnabrück* (Osnabrück, 1975), p. 114.

228 Interview with Werner Lorenz, Inge Walter and Lilo Meyer, 21 August 2000. For more on Neuengamme see Frank Bührmann-Peters, 'Dort Haben wir an und für sich gar nicht gemerkt, daß wir Gefangene waren: Der Arbeitzansatz von Strafgefangenen aus den Emlandslagern im Raum Osnabrück', *Osnabrücker Mitteilungen*, vol. 103 (1998), pp. 218-36; Fritz Bringmann, *Neuengamme: Berichte, Errinerungen, Dokumente* (Hamburg, 1993), pp. 38-50; Volker Issmer, 'Zum Bombenräumen nach Osnabrück: KZ-Häftlinge aus dem Lengerichen Tunnel in unserer Stadt', *Osnabrücker Mitteilungen*, vol. 108 (2003), pp. 179-88; and NSO Dep-3b-XIX-167.

229 See: J. S. Conway, *The Nazi Persecution of the Churches, 1933-45* (London, 1968), pp. 232-9, 254-90; Ernst Christian Helmreich, *The German Churches Under Hitler: Background, Struggle and Epilogue* (Detroit, 1979), pp. 303-46; Günther von Norden, 'Christen im Widerstand', in Richard Löwenthal and Patrick von zur Mühlen, eds, *Widerstand und Verweigerung im Dritten Reich, 1933-1945* (Berlin, 1982), pp. 124-7; Gunther van Norden, 'Widerstand im deutschen Protestantismus', in Klaus-Jürgen Müller, ed., *Der Deutche Widerstand, 1933-1945*, 2nd edn (Paderborn, 1986), pp. 123-7; Günther van Norden and Volkmar Wittmütz, eds, *Evangelische Kirche im Zweiten Weltkrieg* (Cologne, 1991).

230 *Kirchenbote der evangelisch-lutherischen Gemeinden Osnabrück*, May 1940.

231 The information in the above paragraph is gleaned from LAH 51/916.

232 Conway, *Nazi Persecution of the Churches*, pp. 254-90; Helmreich, *German Churches*, pp. 347-67; Guenter Lewy, *The Catholic Church Under the Nazis* (London, 1964), pp. 263-308.

233 Ian Kershaw, *Popular Opinion and Political Dissent in the Third Reich: Bavaria, 1933-1945* (Oxford, 1983), pp. 331-2; Beth A. Griech-Polelle, *Bishop von Galen: German Catholicism and National Socialism* (London, 2002), pp. 59-135.

234 BAOS 03-17-72-25, Bischöfliches Generalvikariat an allen hochwürdigen Herren Priester der Diözese Osnabrück, 22 September 1939.

235 Ulrich von Hehl, 'Bischof Berning und das Bistum Osnabrück im Dritten Reich', *Osnabrücker Mitteilungen*, vol. 86 (1986), p. 97.

236 Ulrich von Hehl, et. al., *Priester Unter Hitler's Terror*, Vol. 2 (Paderborn, 1996), pp. 1128, 1130, 1132.

237 BAOS 04-63-01, Beschlagnahmen, Enteinungen.

238 BAOS 08-52-22-13, Beschlagnahme der Klöster St. Angela in Osnabrück-Haste und St. Ursula in Osnabrück; NSO Rep-430-201-77-87-30.

239 NSO Rep 430-303-19-56-249-Band 4.

240 NSO Rep-727-62-83, Regierungspräsident an den Herrn Oberpräsident Hannover, 18 February 1941.

241 Kurt Nowak, *Euthanasie und Sterilization im 'Dritten Reich': Die Konfrontation der evangelischen und katholischen Kirchen mit dem Gesetz zur Verhutung Erbkranken Nachwuchses und der "Euthanasie"-Aktion* (Göttingen, 1984).

242 Hans-Walther Schmuhl, *Rassenhygiene, Nationalsozialismus, Euthanasie*, 2nd edn (Göttingen, 1987), p. 185.

243 Ibid., pp. 106-25.

244 Studies of the euthanasia programme include: ibid; Alice Platen-Hallermund, *Die Tötung Geistkranker in Deutschland* (Bonn, 1993 reprint); Ernst Klee, *'Euthanasie' im NS-Staat: Die 'Vernichtung lebensunwerten Lebens'* (Frankfurt, 1985); Michael Burleigh, *Ethics and Extermination: Reflections on Nazi Genocide* (Cambridge, 1997), pp. 113-29; Burleigh and Wippermann, *Racial State*, pp. 142-67.

245 Eva Berger, *Die Würde des Menschen ist unantastbar: 200 Jahre Psychiatriegeschichte im ehemaligen Königreich Hannover am Beispiel des Niedersächsischen Landeskrankenhaus Osnabrück* (Bramsche, 1999), pp. 252-4.

246 Raimond Reiter, *Psychiatrie im Dritten Reich in Niedersachsen* (Hanover, 1997), pp. 204-5; NHH Nds-721-Hannover-61-81-28-VI; NHH Nds-721-Hannover-61-81-28-VIII.

247 The list is contained in NHH Nds-721-Hannover-61-81-28-VIII. See also the details of Osnabrück patients who died in: NHH Nds-721-Hannover-61-81-28-II; and NHH Nds-721-Hannover-61-81-28-III.

248 See NHH Nds-721-Hannover-61-81-28-IV. Names have been changed.

249 Extensive details of the trial and the investigation which surrounded it exist in NHH Nds-721-Hannover-61-81-28-VI. Names have been changed.

250 NHH Nds-721-Hannover-61-81-28-VIII.

Chapter 5

1 See Osmar White, *Conqueror's Road: An Eyewitness Report of Germany, 1945* (Cambridge, 2003), pp. 31-52. Further good introductory sources on the end of the War in Germany are: Reimer Hansen, *Das Ende des Dritten Reiches: Die Deutsche Kapitulation, 1945* (Stuttgart, 1966); Jörg Hillmann and John Zimmermann, eds., *Kriegsende in Deutschland* (Munich, 2002); and Sabine Heise and Gerburg Harenbrock, eds, *Geschichte und Gespräch: Kriegsende 1945 und Nachkriegszeit in Münster* (Münster, 1997).

2 Sir Bernard Law Montgomery, *Normandy to the Baltic* (London, 1947), p. 212. See also: NSO Dep-3b-XV-41, Chronik von Dr Hans Glenewinkel, 5. April – 31. Dezember 1945, p. 1; and Günter Wegmann, *Das Kriegsende zwischen Ems und Weser* (Osnabrück, 1983).

3 Karl Ordelheide, *Am Ende war Anfang: Osnabrück, 1945-1948* (Osnabrück, 1982), p. 34; Gerd Steinwascher, 'Dr Johannes Petermann – Burgermeister und Regierungspräsident von Osnabrück', *Osnabrücker Mitteilungen*, vol. 106 (2001), pp. 247-59; Ludwig Hoffmeyer, et. al., *Chronik der Stadt Osnabrück*, 6th Edn (Osnabrück, 1995), pp. 616-17; Wido Spratte, *Zwischen Trümmern: Osnabrück in den Jahren 1945 bis 1948* (Osnabrück, 1990), pp. 14-21; Rudolf Schachtebek and

Wendelin Zimmer, *'die uns kein Teufel rauben kann': Vier Jahrzehnte Demokratie in Osnabrück seit 1945* (Bramsche, 1991), pp. 9-14.

4 As an introduction to this topic see: Ulrike Jordan, ed., *Conditions of Surrender: Britons and Germans Witness the End of the War* (London, 1997); and Patricia Meehan, *A Strange Enemy People: Germans under the British* (London, 2001).

5 Interview with Maria and Hans Grün, 8 August 2000. The lack of fear of western invaders, even amongst Nazi sympathisers, is revealed in Lutz Niethammer, 'Privat-Wirtschaft: Errinerungsfragmente einer anderen Umerziehung', in Lutz Niethammer, ed., *'Hinterher merkt man, daß es richtig war, daß es schiefgagenen ist': Nachkriegserfahrungen im Ruhrgebiet* (Bonn, 1983), pp. 17-34.

6 Interview with Heinrich and Elizabeth Wand, 16 August 2001.

7 Interview with Lora Kraft, 20 August 2001.

8 Meehan, *Strange Enemy People*, p. 15.

9 But see: White, *Conqueror's Road*, pp. 96-8, 128-34; and Atina Grossmann, 'A Question of Silence: The Rape of German Women by Occupation Soldiers', in Robert G. Moeller, ed., *West Germany Under Reconstruction: Politics, Society and Culture in the Adenauer Era* (Ann Arbor, 1997), pp. 33-52.

10 Ute Frevert, *Women in German History: From Bourgeois Emancipation to Sexual Liberation* (Oxford, 1989), p. 258.

11 NSO Dep-3b-XV-41, Chronik von Dr Hans Glenewinkel, 5. April – 31. Dezember 1945, p. 20.

12 Interview with Dick Roberts, 30 August 2001.

13 Interview with Lora Kraft, 20 August 2001.

14 Interview with Josefa Herz, 26 July 2000.

15 NA FO/1005/1683, Military Government, Regierungsbezirk Osnabrück, Monthly Report, 1 July to 31 July 1946, No. 15.

16 Details of these events exist in NSO Rep-430-201-16B-65-76.

17 Richard Overy, *Interrogations: The Nazi Elite in Allied hands, 1945* (London, 2001).

18 Donald Bloxham, *Genocide on Trial: War Crimes and the Formation of Holocaust History and Memory* (Oxford, 2001).

19 A. J. Nicholls, *The Bonn Republic: West German Democracy, 1945-1990* (Harlow, 1997), p. 16.

20 *Neues Tageblatt*, 1 June 1948. See also Chapter 7 below for Kolkmeyer's trial in December 1949.

21 Ibid., 31 August 1948.

22 Meehan, *Strange Enemy People*, pp. 67-87; Dennis L. Bark and David R. Gress, *A History of West Germany: From Shadow to Substance, 1945-1963*, Vol. 1, 2nd edn (Oxford, 1993), pp. 74-89; Alfred Grosse, *Geschichte Deutschlands seit 1945: Eine Bilanz* (Munich, 1974), pp. 61-77; Nicholls, *Bonn Republic*, pp. 15-19; Ian D. Turner, 'Denazification in the British Zone', in Turner, ed. *Reconstruction in Post-War Germany: British Occupation Policy and the Western Zones, 1945-1955* (Oxford, 1989), pp. 239-67; Constantine Fitzgibbon, *Denazification* (London, 1969); Justus Fürstenau, *Entnazifizierung: Ein Kapital deutscher Nachkriegspolitik* (Berlin, 1969); Irmgard Lange, *Entnazifizierung in Nordrhein-Westfalen: Richtlinien, Anweisungen, Organization* (Siegburg, 1976); Lutz Niethammer, *Entnazifizierung in Bayern: Säuberung und Rehabilitierung unter Amerikanisher Besatzung* (Frankfurt, 1972).

23   According to Hoffmeyer, *Chronik*, p. 628. The total must include the entire *Regierungsbezirk*.

24   Ibid.

25   NSO Rep 430-201-16B-65-165 Bd. 1, Der Polizei-Amtsleiter im Polizeibezirk Osnabrück to Militär-Regierung Det 604, 20 December 1947.

26   He participated in a meeting which took place on 4 March 1947, for instance.

27   *Osnabrücker Rundschau*, 26 March 1946.

28   This sample is taken from NSO Rep-980-169-4, Registrabuch der Polizeibeamtes Osnabrück für die in Kategorie III eingestuften Personen betr. Stadt Osnabrück, pp. 3-4, 6-8, 11-12, 17, 19, 22, 29, 31, 51, 55.

29   See examples in NSO Rep-980-120.

30   This is one example from NSO Rep-980-152, which contains forms filled in by teachers.

31   This is from another box concerned with education, NSO Rep-980-149.

32   NSO Rep-980-106.

33   This case is from NSO Rep-980-17. Unfortunately, we have no detailed information about the *Blockleiter* system in Osnabrück.

34   This is one of many category three cases contained in NSO Rep-980-169-4, which is a police registration book for such people.

35   NSO Rep-945-98.

36   For the national picture see: Theodor Eschenberg, J*ahre der Besatzung, 1945-1949* (Wiesbaden, 1989), pp. 171-209; and Wolfgang Benz, *Von der Besatzungsherrschaft zur Bundesrepublik: Stationen einer Staatsgrundung, 1946-1949* (Frankfurt, 1984).

37   Hoffmeyer, *Chronik*, p. 631.

38   NSO Rep-430-201-16B-65-78, Bd. 1, Chef der Polizei, Osnabrück Stadt, an den Herrn Kommandeur der Polizei im Reg. Bez., 26 September 1946.

39   'Protokol der Gründungsversammlung des Freien Deutschen Gewerkschaftsbundes', 13 August 1945, document in possession of Werner Lenz.

40   *Osnabrücker Rundschau*, 15 March 1946.

41   Ulrich Breuker, 'Wideraufbau und Politik der Osnabrücker SPD in den Nachkriegsjahren', in Wilhelm van Kampen and Tilman Westphalen, eds, *100 Jahre SPD in Osnabrück, 1875-1975: Ausgewählte Kapitel zur Geschichte der Arbeiterbewegung in Osnabrück* (Osnabrück, 1975), pp. 118-20.

42   Hoffmeyer, *Chronik*, p. 653; *Osnabrücker Rundschau*, 30 July 1946.

43   The democratic structures in Osnabrück are explained in J. F. Schneyder, *Wiedergeburt der Demokratie* (Osnabrück, 1946).

44   Hoffmeyer, *Chronik*, pp. 653-7; *Neues Tageblatt*, 15 October 1946, 22 April 1947, 16 August 1949; *Niederdeutscher Kurier*, 16 August 1949; Schachtebek and Zimmer, *'die uns kein Teufel rauben kann'*, pp. 9-73.

45   The above account is based upon: Peter Marschalck, *Bevölkerungsgeschichte Deutschlands im 19. und 20. Jahrhundert* (Frankfurt, 1984), pp. 83-93; Richard Overy, 'The Economy of the Federal Republic since 1949', in Klaus Larres and Panikos Panayi, eds., *The Federal Republic of Germany Since 1949: Politics, Society and Economy Before and After Unification* (London, 1996), pp. 3-9; A. J. Nicholls, *Freedom with Responsibility: The Social Market Economy in Germany, 1918-1963* (Oxford, 1994), pp. 122-36; Harald Winkel, *Die Wirtschaft im geteilten Deutschland,*

1945-1970 (Wiesbaden, 1974), pp. 1-65; Bark and Gress, *History of West Germany*, pp. 128-35; Werner Abelshauser, *Wirtschaft in Westdeutschland, 1945-1948: Rekonstruktion und Wirtschaftsbedingungen in der amerikanischen und britischen Zonen* (Stuttgart, 1975); Alan Kramer, *The West German Economy, 1945-1955* (Oxford, 1991), pp. 91-130; Heise and Harnebrock, *Geschichte in Gespräch*; Eschenberg, *Jahre der Besatzung*, pp. 265-9, 515-38; Günter Steinberg, *Die Bevölkekrungsentwicklung Deutschlands im Zweiten Weltkrieg* (Bonn, 1991), pp. 161-6; Benz, *Von der Besatzungsherrschaft*; Adelheid zu Castell, 'Die demographischen Konsequenzen des Ersten und Zweiten Weltkrieges für das Deutsche Reich, die Deutsche Demokratische Republik und die Bundesrepublik Deutschland', in Waclaw Długoborski, ed., *Zweiter Weltkrieg und sozialer Wandel* (Göttingen, 1981), pp. 117-47.

46   Helmut Segschneider, 'Osnabrück im "achten Kriegsjahr": zwei Skizzen nach Zeitzeugenberichten', in Nils-Arvid Bringéus, et. al., eds, *Wandel der Volkskultur in Europa: Festschrift für Günter Wiegelmann zum 60. Geburtstag*, Vol. 2 (Münster, 1988), p. 855.

47   Kerstin Siebenborn-Ramm, *Die 'Butenhamborger': Kriegsbedingte Migration und Ihre Folgen im und nach dem Zweiten Weltkrieg* (Hamburg, 1996), pp. 222-43.

48   NSO Dep-3b-XV-41, Chronik von Dr Hans Glenewinkel, 5. April – 31. Dezember 1945, pp. 23, 128

49   *Osnabrücker Rundschau*, 9 July 1946.

50   Ordelheide, *Am Ende war Anfang*, p. 167

51   *Statistisches Jahrbuch deutscher Gemeinden* (Schwäbisch Gmünd, 1949), p. 16.

52   For the national picture see Panikos Panayi, *Ethnic Minorities in Nineteenth and Twentieth Century Germany: Jews, Gypsies, Poles, Turks and Others* (London, 2000), pp. 200-12.

53   Albrecht Lehmann, *Gefangenschaft und Heimkehr: Deutsche Kriegsgefangene in der Sowjetunion* (Munich, 1986); Annette Kaminsky, ed., *Heimkehr, 1948* (Munich, 1998).

54   Interview with Heinz Frank, 13 August 2001.

55   Andrea Hilger, *Deutsche Kriegsgefangene in der Sowjetunion, 1941-1956: Kriegsgefangenenpolitik, Lageralltag und Errinerung* (Essen, 2000), pp. 353-64.

56   *Neues Tageblatt*, 16 November 1949.

57   *Niedersächsischer Kurier*, 20 April, 8 December 1948.

58   Spratte, *Zwischen Trümmern*, p. 72.

59   Sybille Meyer and Eva Schulze, eds, *Wie Wir das alles geschafft haben: Alleinstehende Frauen berichten über ihr Leben nach 1945* (Munich, 1988); Annette Kühn, ed., *Frauen in der Deutschen Nachkriegszeit*, 2 Volumes (Düsseldorf, 1984-6); Elizabeth D. Heinemann, *What Difference Does a Husband Make? Women and Marital Status in Nazi and Postwar Germany* (London, 1999), pp. 75-136.

60   *Niedersächsischer Kurier*, 21 July 1947.

61   *Neues Tageblatt*, 29 August 1947.

62   Ibid., 5 March 1949.

63   Robert G. Moeller, 'Reconstructing the Family in Reconstruction Germany: Women and Social Policy in the Federal Republic, 1949-1955', in Moeller, *West Germany Under Reconstruction*, pp. 109-33; Barbara Willenbacher, 'Zerrütttung und Bewährung der Nachkriegs-Familie', in Martin Broszat, Klaus Dietmar

Henke and Hans Woller, eds, *Von Stalingrad zur Währungsreform: Zur Sozialgeschichte des Umbruchs in Deutschland* (Munich, 1988), pp. 595-618.

64 NSO Typescript, Fol. 2184, 'Verwaltungsbericht der Stadt Osnabrück, 1945-6'; NSO Dep-3b-XV-45a, 'Eheschliesungen, Geburten und Sterbefälle in der Stadt Osnabrück'.

65 Heinemann, *What Difference?*, pp. 108-36.

66 Kramer, *West German Economy*, pp. 134-40; Hoffmeyer, *Chronik*, p. 668; *Neues Tageblatt*, 19 June 1948, 18 June 1949; *Niedersächsischer Kurier*, 23 June 1948.

67 Günther Schulz, *Wideraufbau in Deutschland: Die Wohnungspolitik in den Westzonen und der Bundesrepublik von 1945 bis 1957* (Düsseldorf, 1994), pp. 31-45, 134-74; Werner Durth, 'Vom Überleben: Zwischen Totalem Krieg und Währungsreform', in Ingeborg Flagge, ed., *Geschichte des Wohnens*, Vol. 5, *1945 bis Heute: Aufbau, Neubau, Umbau* (Stuttgart, 1999), pp. 17-79.

68 Interview with Dick Roberts, 30 Augusts 2001.

69 NA FO/1010/112, Monthly Report on Employment and Labour Supply, September and December 1945.

70 Hoffmeyer, *Chronik*, pp. 659-60; Spratte, *Zwischen Trümmern*, pp. 126-30; *Neues Tageblatt*, 6 May, 12 August 1947; NA FO1005/1721, Report No. 11, 26 June 1947.

71 NSO Dep-3c-650, Stadt Osnabrück to Walter Spitzbarth; NSO Dep-3c-655, Oberstadtdirektor to Franz Sommer, 27 July 1948.

72 Interview with Agnes and Annie Adel, 5 July 2000.

73 *Neues Tageblatt*, 7 April 1949.

74 Hoffmeyer, *Chronik*, pp. 677-82, 700-4.

75 NSO Typscript Z917/74, 'Jahresbericht der Stadtwerke Osnabrück, 1946', pp. 2, 39-40, 51-3.

76 *Neues Tageblatt*, 25 April 1947.

77 Ibid., 17 December 1946.

78 Hoffmeyer, *Chronik*, p. 626; Spratte, *Zwischen Trümmern*, pp. 133-7; *Osnabrücker Rundschau*, 6 August 1946; *Neues Tageblatt*, 6 May 1947, 14 October 1947, 12 May, 28 September 1949.

79 *Neues Tageblatt*, 11 July 1947, 10 February 1948; *Niedersächsischer Kurier*, 10 February 1948; Hoffmeyer, *Chronik*, p. 626; NSO Typscript Z917/74, 'Jahresbericht der Stadtwerke Osnabrück, 1946', p. 63.

80 NA FO1010/124, Appendix K(e) to Report No.2 made by Mil. Gov. Det. on Stadtkreis Osnabrück on 26 April 1945.

81 NSO Rep-640-Osn-14, Die Erwerbspersonen in September 1945 in Osnabrück.

82 *Nordwest-Nachtrichten*, 31 August 1945.

83 NA WO171/8021, Appx 'J' to 604 L/R Mil Gov Det Monthly Report No. 6, 1-31 October 1945, Confidential Light Industries.

84 NA WO171/8021, Weekly Report on OKD, 26 August 1945.

85 NSO Rep-640-Osn-12, Verzeichnis der Betriebe mit 50 und mehr Beschäftigten, Stand September 1945.

86 NSO Rep-430-108-26-73-447, 'Industrie, Handel und Gewerbe im Kreise: Osnabrück Stadt über 5 Beschäftige 1946'.

87 Heinz-Günther Borck, 'Chronik der Handwerkskammer Osnabrück, 1900-1975', in Handwerkskammer Osnabrück, ed., *Geschichte des Osnabrücker Handwerks* (Osnabrück, 1975), p. 458.

88 *Osnabrücker Rundschau*, 16 August 1946; R. Friess, *75 Jahre Osnabrücker Kupfer und Drahtwerk* (Melle, 1948), p. 19.

89 Dieter Kunst, *The Karmann Story: Germany's Coachbuilder to the World*, 2nd Edn (Osnabrück, 1996), pp. 58-82.

90 *Niedersächsischer Kurier*, 21 July 1948.

91 NSO Dep-3b-XXI-80, Betr. einmalige Beihilfe aus Fonds für Frau Krey, Stahlwerksweg 20, 17 April 1946.

92 BAOS 10/02/35, Frau Kifler to Bishop Berning, 3 December 1945.

93 Gabriele Stüber, *Der Kampf gegen den Hunger, 1945-1950: Die Ernährungslage in der Britischen Zone Deutschlands, insbesondere in Schleswig-Holstein und Hamburg* (Neumünster, 1984); Günter J. Trittel, *Hunger und Politik: Die Ernährungskrise in der Bizone (1945-1949)* (Frankfurt, 1990); Paul Ecker, *Ernährungskrise und Nachkriegsgesellschaft: Bauern und Arbeiterschaft in Bayern,1943-1953* (Stuttgart, 1990); Rainer Gries, *Die Rationen-Gesellschaft: Versorgungskampf und Vergleichsmentalität* (Munich, 1991); Karl-Heinz Rothenberger, *Die Hungerjahre nach dem Zweiten Weltkrieg: Ernährungs- und Landwirtschaft in Rheinland-Pfalz, 1945-1950* (Boppard, 1980); Winkel, *Die Wirtschaft im geteilten Deutschland*, pp. 29-36; Bark and Gress, *History of West Germany*, pp. 130-2.

94 NSO Dep-3b-XV-41, Chronik von Dr Hans Glenewinkel, 5. April – 31. Dezember 1945, pp. 23, 36.

95 NSO Dep-3c-380, Ernährungsamt Abt. A to Oberbergurmeister, 2 August 1945.

96 NSO Dep-3b-XV-41, Chronik von Dr Hans Glenewinkel, 5. April – 31. Dezember 1945, p. 130.

97 NSO Dep-3b-XV-42, Stadtchronik, Januar bis Dezember 1946, pp. 135, 154, 190.

98 Quoted in Spratte, *Zwischen Trümmern*, p. 32.

99 NSO Dep-3c-545, Beschluß-Niederschrift aus der Sitzung des Rates der Stadt Osnabrück am 6. August 1946.

100 Segschneider, 'Osnabrück im "achten Kriegsjahr"', p. 860; *Neues Tageblatt*, 4 March, 3 October 1947; NSO Dep-3b-XV-43 Stadtchronik, 1947, p. 270.

101 Spratte, *Zwischen Trümmern*, p. 33; NSO Rep-430-201-16B-65-165-Bd. 1, Monatsbericht über Moral und öffentliche Meinung, 20 December 1947.

102 NSO Rep-430-201-16B-65-165-Bd. 1, Monatsbericht über Moral und öffentliche Meinung, 17 May 1948.

103 NSO Rep-430-201-16B-65-78-Bd. 1, Monatsbericht über Moral und öffentliche Meinung, 21 July 1948.

104 Helmut Segschneider, 'Not kennt kein Gebot: Formen der Nahrungsbeschaffung nach dem Zweiten Weltkrieg im Raum Osnabrück', *Rheinisch-westfälische Zeitschrift für Volkskunde*, vol. 34-5 (1989-90), pp. 205-38; Spratte, *Zwischen Trümmern*, pp. 33-4.

105 See, for instance, Gries, *Die Rationen-Gesellschaft*.

106 Michael Wildt, *Der Traum vom Sattwerden: Hunger und Protest, Schwarzmarkt und Selbsthilfe* (Hamburg, 1986), pp. 76-123.

107 *Niedersächsischer Kurier*, 11 May 1948; *Neues Tageblatt*, 13 May 1948.

108 NSO Dep-3c-382; *Osnabrücker Rundschau*, 3 May 1946.

109 Interview with Werner Funk, 16 August 2000.

110 *Niedersächsischer Kurier*, 2 April 1948.

111 Interview with Renate Schlosser, 8 August 2000.

112 NSO Dep-3c-379, Bereitstellung von Kleingartenland, 13 April 1946.

113 NSO Dep-3c-379, Kreisgärtnerschaft (23) Osnabrück to Oberstadtsdirektor, Dr Vollbrecht, 26 March 1946.

114 NSO Rep-430-201-16B-65-165-Bd. 1, Monatsbericht über Moral und öffentliche Meinung, 20 December 1947.

115 Spratte, *Zwischen Trümmern*, pp. 54-61; NSO Rep-430-201-16B-65-78-Bd. 1, Volksunruhen-Bericht für den Monat Dezember 1946; *Osnabrücker Rundschau*, 19 March 1946.

116 NA FO1005/1683, Military Government, *Regierungsbezirk* Osnabrück, Monthly Report, 1 July 1946 – 31 July 1946, No. 15.

117 NSO Rep-430-201-16B-65-78-Bd. 1, Monatsbericht über Moral und öffentliche Ordnung, 17 January 1948.

118 Durth, 'Vom Überleben'; Heise and Harenbrock, *Geschichte im Gespräch*, pp. 74-91.

119 Segschneider, 'Osnabrück im "achten Kriegsjahr"', pp. 857-60.

120 Interview with Gerhard Strauss, 22 August 2001.

121 NSO Rep-430-201-16B-65-78 Bd. 1, Stimmung der örtlichen Bevölkerung, 26 September 1946.

122 Hans-Ulrich Sons, *Gesundheitspolitik während der Besatzungszeit: Das öffentliche Gesundheitswesen in Nordrhein-Westfalen, 1945-1949* (Wuppertal, 1983), pp. 75-159; Bark and Greiss, *History of West Germany*, p. 131; Victor Gollancz, *In Darkest Germany* (London, 1947), pp. 23-52.

123 NSO Rep-430-303-19-56-138-Bd 1, Letter from Gesundheitsamt, 17 July 1945; NSO Rep-430-303-19-56-10, Report of June 1946.

124 Interview with Cilly Stein, 28 June 2000.

125 'Bericht über die Tätigkeit der inneren Abteilung im Jahre 1946', in 'Verwaltungsberichte der Stadt Osnabrück, 1945-6'.

126 'Verwaltungsbericht des Gesundheitsamtes für die Jahre 1945/46/47' in 'Verwaltungsberichte der Stadt Osnabrück, 1945-7.'

127 NSO Rep-430-303-19-56-138-Bd. 3, Bericht über das gesundheitswesen vom 1. 15. 1. 1946; NSO Rep-430-303-14-61-1, Jahresgesundheitsbericht, Allgemeine gesundheitliche Verhältnisse für Osnabrück Stadt, 1947.

128 NA FO1050/694, Brief Notes on Niedersächsisches Landes Heil und Pflegeanstalt, Osnabrück, 5 May 1949.

129 *Osnabrücker Rundschau*, 2 August 1946.

130 NSO Rep-430-303-15/65-81, Chefarzt der Med. Klinik der Städt. Krankenanstalten Osnabrück to Regierungs Präsident, 24 September 1947.

131 NSO Rep-430-303-15-65-22-Bd.2, Jahresgesundheitsberichte, 1948, Teil A, Osnabrück Stadt, Abschnitt II, Allgemeine gesundheitliche Verhältnisse.

132 NSO Rep 430-303-15-65-22-Bd.4, Jahresgesundheitsberichte 1949, Teil A.

133 Willi A. Boelcke, *Der Schwarzmarkt, 1945-1948: Vom Überleben nach dem Kriege* (Braunschweig, 1986); Wildt, *Der Traum*, pp. 101-23.

134 NSO Rep-430-201-16B-65-76, Kommando der Schutzpolizei, Tätigkeitsbericht und Erläuterungen zum wöchentlichen Kriminalbericht vom 16.8.1945.

135 NSO Dep-3b-XIX-1-97-12, Tätigkeitsbuch 1. Polizei Revier, 25/2/45 – 11/1/46.

136 *Neues Tageblatt*, 24 January, 20 May 1947.

137 Ibid., 22 April 1947.

138 *Niedersächsischer Kurier*, 25 March 1948.

139 NSO Rep-430-201-16B-65-81, Chef der Polizei, Osnabrück Stadt, Schwarzhandel und Schwarzschlachtungen, 20 December 1945.

140 NSO Rep-430-201-16B-65-81, Chef der Polizei, Osnabrück Stadt, Bericht über den Schwarzhandel im Monat Mai 1947.

141 NSO Rep-430-201-16B-65-81, Chef der Polizei, Osnabrück Stadt, Bericht über Schwarzhandel für den Monat Juni 1946.

142 NSO Rep-430-201-16B-65-82, Razzia auf dem Augustenburgerplatz am 6.4.48; *Neues Tageblatt*, 8 April 1948.

143 See the relevant reports in NSO Rep-430-201-16B-65-81.

144 See the reports for Osnabrück in: NSO Rep-430-201-16B-65-81; and NSO Rep 430-201-16B-65-83.

145 See the case of four people who came from the Ruhr in NSO Rep-430-201-16B-65-81, Polizei Abschnitt C, Stadtpolizei Osnabrück, Bericht über den Schwarzhandel im Monat Dezember 1947.

146 *Neues Tageblatt*, 18 March 1948.

147 NSO Rep-430-201-16B-65-83, Polizeiabschnitt C, Überwachung des schwarzen Marktes, 30 October 1948.

148 Karl Heinz Füssl, *Die Umerziehung der Deutschen: Jugend und Schule unter dem Siegermächten des Zweiten Weltkrieges* (Paderborn, 1994); Rolf Lutzerbäck, *Die Bildungspolitik der Britischen Militärregierung im Spannungsfeld zwischen 'Education' und 'Re-Education' in ihrer Bezatzungszone, insbesondere in Schleswig-Holstein und Hamburg in den Jahren 1945-7*, 2 Volumes (Frankfurt, 1991).

149 Spratte, *Zwischen Trümmern*, p. 82.

150 BAOS 04-79-21, Registriert Osnabrück, den 30. Juni 1945.

151 Spratte, *Zwischen Trümmern*, p. 82; Hans Hinrichs, 'Das Ratsgymnasium seit dem Ende des Zweiten Weltkrieges', in Uwe Schipper, ed., *400 Jahre Ratsgymnasium Osnabrück* (Bramsche, 1985), p. 237.

152 Johannes Hesse, *Carolinger 1938 bis 1947: Erinnerungen eines Ehemaligen Schülers* (Osnabrück, 1997), p. 132.

153 'Verwaltungsberichte der Stadt Osnabrück, 1945-7'; 'Verwaltungsbericht der Stadt Osnabrück 1949'.

154 'Verwaltungsberichte der Stadt Osnabrück, 1945-7'.

155 NSO SLG-54-1, Alexander Dicke, 'Mir "Vorwärts, vorwärts…" war es nicht getan: Errinerungen von 1931 bis 1955', p. 157.

156 St Ursula Osnabrück, *Festschrift zum Hundertjähriges Schuljubiläum, 1865-1965* (Osnabrück, 1965), pp. 21-2.

157 *Schola Carolina*, December 1946, p. 1.

158 *Neues Tageblatt*, 18 January 1949; *Niedersächsischer Kurier*, 25 March 1949.

159 Bark and Greiss, *History of West Germany*, p. 168; 'Verwaltungsberichte der Stadt Osnabrück', 1945-7; NSO Dep-58b-40-89-440, Bericht über des Ratsgymnasiums zu Osnabrück von 1945 bis 31. 3. 1948.

160 Kathleen Southwell Davis, 'The Problem of Textbooks', in Arthur Hearnden, ed., *The British in Germany: Educational Reconstruction after 1945* (London, 1978), pp. 108-30; Hinrichs, 'Das Ratsgymnasium', p. 241.

161 *Neues Tageblatt*, 25 October 1946.

162 BAOS-05-55-61.

163 NSO Dep-58b-40-89-427.

164 *Nidersächsischer Kurier*, 4 August 1948.

165 NSO Rep-430-303-19-56-146, Städt. Gesundheitsamt, Schularzt to Regierungs Präsident, 16 February 1948.

166 Jutta Held, *Kunst und Kunstpolitik in Deutschland, 1945-49: Kulturaufbau in Deutschland nach dem 2. Weltkrieg* (Berlin, 1981); Hans Habe, *Im Jahre Null: Ein Beitrag zur Geschichte der deutschen Presse* (Munich, 1966); Stefan Matysiak, 'Die Britischen Heeresgruppenzeitungen und die Wiedergeburt der Niedersächsischen Lokalpresse, 1945/46', *Osnabrücker Mitteilungen*, vol. 107 (2002), pp. 233-51.

167 Jörg Echternkamp, 'Von Opfern, Heldern und Verbrechern: Anmerkungen zur Bedeutung des Zweiten Weltkrieges in den Errinerungskulturen der Deutschen, 1945-1955', in Hillmann and Zimmermann, *Kriegsende, 1945*, pp. 301-6.

168 *Niedersächsicher Kurier*, 20 September 1949.

169 Ibid., 22, 25 October, 1948; BAOS 03-17-72-11, 'Friedensgedächtniswoche der Stadt Osnabrück vom 16. bis 24. Oktober 1948'; NSO Rep-430-16B-65-72, Friedensgedächtniswoche.

170 Gabriele Clemens, *Britische Kulturpolitik in Deutschland, 1945-1949* (Stuttgart, 1997).

171 Spratte, *Zwischen Trümmern*, pp. 103-7; Matysiak, 'Die Britischen Heeresgruppenzeitungen'.

172 Spratte, *Zwischen Trümmern*, pp. 111-13; *Statistisches Jahrbuch Deutscher Gemeinde*, Vol. 37 (Schwäbisch Gmünd, 1949), pp. 198, 200; NSO Dep-3b-XV-43, Stadt-Chronik, 1947, pp. 289-90; Ordelheide, *Am Ende war Anfang*, p. 96; Karl Kühling, *Theater in Osnabrück: Im Wandel der Jahrhunderte* (Osnabrück, 1959), pp. 87-101.

173 NSO Dep-3b-XV-43, Stadtchronik, 1947, pp. 290-1; *50 Jahre Osnabrücker Symphonie Orchester* (Osnabrück, 1969); *50 Jahre Musikverein, 30 Jahre Städtischer Orchester Osnabrück* (Osnabrück, 1949), p. 5, 10-11; *Statistisches Jahrbuch Deutscher Gemeinde*, pp. 196-200.

174 NSO ERW-E4-1-89-7, Neue Liedertafel Osnabrück, Jahresberichte, 1943-7.

175 *30 Jahre Männergesangverein Osnabrücker Kupfer und Drahtwerk, 1922-1952* (Osnabrück, 1952).

176 Roger Smither, *'Welt im Film*: Anglo-American Newsreel Policy', in Nicholas Pronay and Keith Wilson, eds, *The Political Re-Education of Germany and Her Allies After World War II* (Beckenham, 1985), p. 151; Heide Fehrenbach, 'Cinema in Democratizing Germany: The Reconstruction of Mass Culture and National identity in the West, 1945-1960' (New Brunswick, Rugers Ph.D thesis, 1990), pp. 1-88.

177 Ordelheide, *Am Ende war Anfang*, p. 96; Spratte, *Zwischen Trümmern*, pp. 114-116; Sabine Hake, *Popular Cinema of the Third Reich* (Austin, TX, 2001), pp. 210-30.

178 Ilsetraut Lindemann, 'Künstlerisches Schaffen im Schatten einer zerstörten Stadt, 1945-1949', in Wilfried Wolf, ed., *Die Gründerzeit Osnabrücker Kunst* (Bramsche, 1986), pp. 36-57; 'Verwaltungsbericht der Stadt Osnabrück, 1948'.

179 Horst Höweler and Horst Hartelt, *100 Jahre Sport in Osnabrück: Die Erste reich illustrierte Osnabrücker Sportchronik* (Osnabrück, 1948), p. 138; Sportsverein Eversburg, *75 Jahre 1894-1969* (Osnabrück, 1969), p. 11; Günter Wienhold, *150 Jahre Osnabrücker Sportclub* (Osnabrück, 1999), pp. 40-1; Spratte, *Zwischen Trümmern*, pp. 120-2.

180 See above pp. 128-9.

181 Spratte, *Zwischen Trümmern*, pp. 90-4. For the national picture see, for instance, Karl Herbert, *Kirche zwischen Aufbruch und Tradition: Entscheidungsjahre nach 1945* (Stuttgart, 1989); Anton Rauscher, *Kirche und Katholismus, 1945-1949* (Munich, 1977); Armin Boyens, et. al., *Kirchen in der Nachkriegszeit: Vier Zeitgeschichtliche Beiträge* (Göttingen, 1979).

Chapter 6

1 A good narrative introduction to the expulsion of Germans from eastern Europe is Günter Böddeker, *Die Flüchtlinge: Die Vertreibung der Deutschen im Osten* (Berlin, 1997).

2 Siegfried Bethlehem, *Heimatvertreibung, DDR-Flucht, Gastarbeiterwanderung: Wanderungsströme und Wanderungspolitik in der Bundesrepublik Deutschland* (Stuttgart, 1982), p. 22.

3 Alexander von Plato and Wolfgang Meinecke, *Alte Heimat – Neue Zeit: Flüchtlinge, Umgesiedelte, Vertriebene in der sowjetischen Besatzungszone und in der DDR* (Berlin, 1991), pp. 25-6.

4 Robert G. Moeller, *War Stories: The Search for a Usable Past in the Federal Republic of Germany* (London, 2001), pp. 51-87; Theodor Schieder, *Dokumentation der Vertreibung der Deutschen aus Ost-Mitteleuropa*, 4 Volumes (Bonn, 1954-1961).

5 Paul Lüttinger and Rita Rossmann, *Integration der Vertriebenen: Eine Empirische Analyse* (Frankfurt, 1989); Paul Erker, *Vom Heimatvertriebenen zum Neubürger, 1945-1955* (Wiesbaden, 1988); David Rock and Stefan Wolff, eds, *Going Home to Germany? The Integration of Ethnic Germans from Central and Eastern Europe in the Federal Republic* (Oxford, 2002).

6 Alfred de Zayas, *Anmerkungen zur Vertreibung der Deutschen aus dem Osten* , 2nd Edn (Stuttgart, 1987), pp. 60-173; Rudolf Mühlfenzl, ed., *Geflohen und Vertrieben: Augenzeugen Berichten* (Königstein im Taunus, 1981); Frank Grube and Gerhard Richter, ed., *Flucht und Vertreibung: Deutschland zwischen 1944 and 1947* (Hamburg, 1980); Stefan Aust and Stefan Burgdorff, eds, *Die Flucht: Über die Vertreibung der Deutschen aus dem Osten* (Stuttgart, 2002).

7 Klaus J. Bade, Hans-Bernd Meier and Bernhard Parisius, eds, *Zeitzeugen im Interview: Flüchtlinge und Vertriebene im Raum Osnabrück* (Osnabrück, 1997), p. 13.

8 NSO Dep-3c-983, Monatlicher Nachweis der Bevölkerungsvorgänge, Osnabrück Stadt, 1 Juni 1949.

9 NSO Dep-3c-972, Städtisches Wohlfahrtsamt, Flüchtlingsstelle to Städt. Vekehrsamt, 23 November 1945.

10   Bade, Meier and Parisius, *Zeitzeugen*, p. 13.

11   Moeller, *War Stories*, pp. 51-87.

12   IMIS Expellee Interview No. 2, with Liselotte Burchardt, 26 January 1945.

13   See the relevant correspondence in NSO Dep-3c-962.

14   NSO Dep-3c-386, Prüfungsbericht über das Kriegsgefangenen-Entlassungslager Osnabrück, Hauswörmannsweg, 25 November 1946; *Neues Tageblatt*, 18 October 1946.

15   BAOS 06-08-00, Oberbürgermeister to Caritasverband, 19 October 1945.

16   *Nordwest-Nachrichten*, 30 October 1945.

17   Bade, Meier and Parisius, *Zeitzeugen*, p. 29.

18   Ibid., p. 33; 'Verwaltungsberichte der Stadt Osnabrück 1945-6'; NSO Dep-3c-972, Städtisches Wohlfahrtsamt – Flüchtlingstelle – to Städtisches Verkehrsamt, 23 November 1945.

19   These do not seem to have survived in the NSO.

20   'Verwaltungsberichte der Stadt Osnabrück 1945-6'; Regierung Osnabrück, *Die Aufgaben des Ortsflüchtlingsbetreuers* (Osnabrück, 1950).

21   *100 Jahre Rotes Kreuz in Osnabrück, 1870-1970* (Osnabrück, 1970), p. 40.

22   Caritasverband für die Diözese Osnabrück e.v., *Festschrift zum 50 jährigen Bestehen des Diözesan-Caritasverbandes Osnabrück 1916-1966: Berichte vom Dienst der Kirche an den Menschen* (Osnabrück, 1966), p. 86.

23   BAOS 10-02-51, Caritasverband to Bishop Berning, 16 October 1948.

24   Georg Müller and Heinz Simon, 'Aufnahme und Unterbringung', in Eugen Lemberg and Friedrich Edding, eds, *Die Vertriebenen in Westdeutschland: Ihre Eingliederung und ihr Einfluss auf Gesellschaft, Wirtschaft, Politik und Geistleben*, Vol. 1 (Kiel, 1959), pp. 300-446; Friedrich Käss, 'Die Arbeits- und Wohnraumbeschaffung', in Hans Joachim von Merkatz, ed., *Aus Trümmern wurden Fundamente: Vertriebene, Flüchtlinge, Aussiedler* (Düsseldorf, 1979), pp. 69-82; Hiddo M Jolles, *Zur Soziologie der Heimatvertriebenen und Flüchtlinge* (Cologne, 1965), pp. 131-41.

25   'Verwaltungsberichte der Stadt Osnabrück 1945-6'.

26   Interview with Frau Al. quoted in Bade, Meier and Parisius, *Zeitzeugen*, p. 134.

27   Wido Spratte, *Zwischen Trümmern: Osnabrück in den Jahren 1945 bis 1948* (Osnabrück, 1990), p. 75; 'Verwaltungsberichte der Stadt Osnabrück 1945-6'.

28   NSO Rep-304-15-65-28, Bericht über die am 13.5.47 im Flüchtlingsdurchgangslager Lüstringen ausgeführte Prüfung.

29   *Neues Tageblatt*, 16 July 1949.

30   Ibid., 14 October 1949.

31   NSO Rep-430-304-15-65-26, Bericht über die überprüfung des Lagerausschusses des Flüchtlinglagers Fernblick Osnabrück, 21 November 1949.

32   Interview with Renate Schlosser, 8 August 2000.

33   Interview with Anneliese Diehl, 15 August 2001.

34   BAOS 06-08-22-10.

35   NSO Rep-430-304-19-56-228.

36   'Verwaltungsberichte der Stadt Osnabrück 1945-6'; NSO Rep-430-304-15-65-75; NSO Rep-430-304-15-65-38, Regierungs Präsident to Flüchtlingsamt, Osnabrück Stadt, 2 September 1949.

37 NS0 Dep-3c-964, Bekleidungsaktion für Flüchtlinge, 20 August 1946.

38 NSO Rep-430-303-19-56-101, Monatsbericht des Gesundheitsamtes, Osnabrück Stadt, March 1947.

39 For the national picture see: Erker, *Vom Heimatvertriebenen*, pp. 67-86; Lüttinger, *Integration*, pp. 83-6; Eugen Lemberg and Freidrich Edding, eds, *Die Vertriebenen in Westdeutschland: Ihre Eingliederung und ihr Einfluss auf Gesellschaft, Wirtschaft, Politik und Geistleben*, Vol. 2 (Kiel, 1959).

40 Bade, Meier and Parisius, *Zeitzeugen*, p. 55.

41 *Neues Tageblatt*, 29 June, 28 October 1949.

42 NSO Dep-3c-982, Monatsbericht über Flüchtlinggeschäftsleute und Gewerbetriebende, 11.1.46.

43 See the relevant documentation on Osnabrück in NSO Rep-430-304-15-65-44.

44 Eugen Lemberg, 'Völkerpsychologie und Weltgeschichtliche Aspekte', in Eugen Lemberg and Friedrich Edding, eds, *Die Vertriebenen in Westdeutschland: Ihre Eingliederung und ihr Einfluss auf Gesellschaft, Wirtschaft, Politik und Geistleben*, Vol. 3 (Kiel, 1959), pp. 578-95; Albrecht Lehmann, *Im Fremden ungewollt zuhaus: Flüchtlinge und Vertriebene in Westdeutschland* (Munich, 1990).

45 NSO Rep-430-303-19/56-101, Der Rat der Stadt Osnabrück, Städt. Gesundheitsamt to Regierungspräsident, 1 February 1947.

46 Andrea Riecken, '"Der Kranke Flüchtling": Die gesundheitliche Behandlung von Flüchtlingen und Vertriebenen in Niedersachsen', in Klaus J. Bade and Jochen Oltmer, eds, *Zuwanderung und Integration in Niedersachsen seit dem Zweiten Weltkrieg* (Osnabrück, 2002), pp. 120-3.

47 NSO Rep-430-304-15-65-5, Niedersächsicher Minister für Flüchtlingsangelegenheiten to Regierungs Präsident, Osnabrück, 29 June 1949.

48 NSO Rep-430-304-15-65-5, Niedersächsicher Minister für Flüchtlingsangelegenheiten to Regierungs Präsident, Osnabrück, 6 April 1949.

49 See the relevant correspondence in NSO Rep-430-304-15-65-80.

50 See, for instance, Klaus J. Bade, ed., *Deutsche im Ausland - Fremde in Deutschland: Migration in Geschichte und Gegenwart* (Munich, 1992).

51 Klaus J. Bade, ed., *Fremde in Land: Zuwanderung und Eingliederung im Raum Niedersachsen seit dem Zweiten Weltkrieg* (Osnabrück, 1997).

52 Lutz Hoffmann, *Die Unvollendete Republik: Zwischen Einwanderungsland und Deutschem Nationalstaat*, 2nd edn (Cologne, 1992), pp. 28-9.

53 Hans W. Schoenberg, *Germans from the East: A Study of their Migration, Resettlement and Subsequent Group History* (The Hague, 1970), p. 37; Betty Barton, *The Problem of 12 Million German Refugees in Today's Germany* (Philadelphia, 1949), pp. 30-4; Marion Frantzioch, *Die Vertriebenen: Hemmnisse und Wege ihrer Integration* (Berlin, 1987), pp. 199, 201.

54 As an introduction see Ulrich Herbert, *A History of Foreign Labour in Germany, 1880-1980: Seasonal Workers/Forced Laborers/Guest Workers* (Ann Arbor, MI, 1990), pp. 193-254.

55 NSO Rep-430-201-16b-65-78 Bd. 1, Chef der Polizei, Osnabrück Stadt, an den Herrn Kommandeur der Polizei im Reg. Bez., 26 September 1946.

56 Bade, Meier and Parisius, *Zeitzeugen*, pp. 159-68.

57 *Niedersächsischer Kurier*, 17 December 1948.

58 Interview with Anneliese Diehl, 15 August 2001.

59 Interview with Cilly Stein, 28 June 2000.

60 Interview with Renate Schlosser, 8 August 2000.

61 Interview with Hermann Thiem, 10 June 2001.

62 But see: Rainer Schulze, 'Growing Discontent: Relations between Native and Refugee Populations in a Rural District in Western Germany after the Second World War', in Robert G. Moeller, ed., *West Germany Under Reconstruction: Politics, Society and Culture in the Adenauer Era* (Ann Arbor, 1997), pp. 53-72; and Lehmann, *In Fremden*.

63 For Potsdam see, Alfred Maurice de Zayas, *The German Expellees: Victims in War and Peace* (London, 1993).

64 Hermann Weiß, 'Die Organisation der Vertriebenen und ihre Presse', in Wolfgang Benz, ed., *Die Vertreibung der Deutschen aus dem Osten: Ursachen, Ereignisse, Folgen* (Frankfurt, 1995), pp. 244-64.

65 Bade, Meier and Parisius, *Zeitzeugen*, p. 79; *Niedersächsischer Kurier*, 4 August 1948.

66 BAOS 06-08-00, 'Großkundgebung der Ostvertriebenen in Osnabrück am Sonntag, dem 31. Juli 1949'; *Niederdeutscher Kurier*, 1 August 1949; *Neues Tageblatt*, 2 August 1949.

67 NSO Rep-430-304-56-87-61, Gemeinschaft der Ostvertrieben im Lande Niedersachsen, Interessengemeinschaft Stadt und Landkreis Osnabrück to Regierungs Präsident, 22 April 1949.

68 *Niederdeutscher Kurier*, 11 October 1949.

69 Both the Evangelical and Roman Catholic Churches played a central role in integration throughout the country. See the contributions by Walter Menges, Friedrich Spiegel-Schmidt and Adolf Kindermann in Lemberg and Edding, *Die Vertriebenen*, vol. 3.

70 Weiß, 'Die Organisation der Vertriebenen'; Max Hildebert Boehm, 'Gruppenbildung und Organisationswesen', in Lemberg and Edding', *Vetriebene*, vol. 1, pp. 524-7.

Chapter 7

1 From Peter Junk and Martina Sellmeyer, *Stationen auf dem Weg nach Auschwitz: Entrechtung, Vertreibung, Vernichtung: Juden in Osnabrück*, 3rd edition (Osnabrück, 2000).

2 Excellent examples include: Wolfgang Benz (ed.), *Die Juden in Deutschland: Leben unter nationalsozialistischer Herrschaft* (Munich, 1993); and Saul Friedlander, *Nazi Germany and the Jews: The Years of Persecution, 1933-39* (London, 1997).

3 Good local studies include: Dieter Goetz, *Juden in Oldenburg, 1933-1938* (Oldenburg, 1988); Henry Huttenbach, *The Destruction of the Jewish Community of Worms, 1933-1945: A Study of the Holocaust Experience in Germany* (New York, 1981); Regina Bruss, *Die Bremer Juden unter Nationalsozialismus* (Bremen, 1983); Frank Bajohr, *'Aryanization' in Hamburg: The Economic Exclusion of Jews and the Confiscation of their Property in Nazi Germany* (Oxford, 2002).

4 Marion A. Kaplan, *Between Dignity and Despair: Jewish Life in Nazi Germany* (Oxford, 1998).

5 Z. Asaria, *Zur Geschichte der Juden in Osnabrück und Umgebung: Zur Weihe der Synagoge in Osnabrück* (Osnabrück, 1969).

6   K. Brenner, 'Dokumentation über die Juden in Osnabrück' (unpublished manuscript, 1978).

7   Karl Kühling, *Die Juden in Osnabrück* (Osnabrück, 1983).

8   Junk and Sellmeyer, *Stationen*.

9   Martina Krause and Michael Gander, '"Ariesierung" des jüdischen Handels und Handel mit jüdischem Besitz im Regierungsbezirk Osnabrück', in Michael Haverkamp and Hans-Jürgen Teuteberg (eds), *Unterm Strich: Von der Winkelkrämerei zum E-Commerce: Eine Austellung des Museums Industriekultur im Rahm des 175. Bestehen der Sparkasse Osnab*rück (Bramsche, 2000), pp. 227-43. See also Panikos Panayi, 'Victims, Perpetrators and Bystanders in a German Town: The Jews of Osnabrück Before, During and After the Third Reich', *European History Quarterly*, vol. 33 (2003), pp. 451-92.

10   Eva Berger, Inge Jaehner, Peter Junk, Karl Georg Kaster, Manfred Meinz and Wendelin Zimmer, *Felix Nussbaum: Art Defamed, Art in Exile, Art in Resistance* (Bramsche, 1997).

11   Kühling, *Juden*, pp. 14-76; Junk and Sellmeyer, *Stationen*, pp. 10-11.

12   Panikos Panayi, *Ethnic Minorities in Nineteenth and Twentieth Century Germany: Jews, Gypsies, Poles, Turks and Others* (London, 2000), pp. 133-7; Donald Niewyk, *The Jews in Weimar Germany* (Baton Rouge, LO, 1980); Walter Grab and Julius H. Schoeps (eds), *Juden in der Weimarer Republik* (Stuttgart, 1986).

13   Avraham Barkai, 'Die Juden als sozio-ökonomische Minderheitsgruppe in der Weimarer Republik', in Grab and Schoeps, ibid., p. 331.

14   Junk and Sellmeyer, *Stationen*, p. 11.

15   In 1933 Frankfurt Jewry totalled 26,158, making up 4.7 per cent of the city's population, while the figures for Breslau stood at 20,202 and 3.2 per cent. No other community made up more than 2 per cent of the total population of any city. See the table in Goetz, *Juden in Oldenburg*, p. 24.

16   The reference numbers are NSO Dep-3b-IV-2169 and NSO Dep-3b-IV-2170. While they have no date, Junk and Sellmeyer, *Stationen*, p. 330, place them at 1927 and 1923 respectively.

17   Niewyk, *Jews in Weimar*, p. 15, points out that Jews made up 11 per cent of German doctors and 16 per cent of lawyers.

18   Jost Hermannd, 'Juden in der Kultur der Weimarer Republik', in Grab and Schoeps, *Juden in der Weimarer Republik*, pp. 9-37.

19   NSO Dep-3b-IV-2169; Berger, et. al., *Felix Nussbaum*, p. 29.

20   Niewyk, *Jews in Weimar*, p. 85.

21   NSO Dep-3b-IV-2169.

22   This paragraph is based on Junk and Sellmeyer, *Stationen*, pp. 24-30.

23   Till van Rahden, *Juden und andere Breslauer: Die Beziehungen zwischen Juden, Protestanten und Katholiken in einer deutschen Großstadt von 1860-1925* (Göttingen, 2000).

24   Anthony Kauders, *German Politics and the Jews: Düsseldorf and Nuremberg, 1910-1933* (Oxford, 1996), pp. 15, 26.

25   Beate Meyer, *'Jüdische Mischlinge': Rassenpolitik und Verfolgungserfahrung* (Hamburg, 1999), p. 25.

26   Daniel John Goldhagen, *Hitler's Willing Executioners: Ordinary Germans and the Holocaust* (London, 1996), p. 83.

27 Central-Verein Deutscher Staatsbürger Jüdischen Glaubens, *Friedhofsschändungen in Deutschland, 1923-32: Dokumente der politischen und kulturellen Verwilderung unserer Zeit*, 5th edn (Berlin, 1932).

28 Werner Bergmann and Juliane Wetsel, '"Der Miterlebende weiß nichts": Alltagsantisemitismus als zeitgenössiche Erfahrung und spätere Errinerung (1919-1933)', in Wolfgang Benz, Arnold Paucker and Peter Pulzer, eds, *Jüdisches Leben in der Weimarer Republik* (Tübingen, 1998), p. 176.

29 According to Junk and Sellmeyer, *Stationen*, p. 31 but not Central-Verein Deutscher Staatsbürger Jüdischen Glaubens, *Friedhofsschändungen*, pp. 8-10.

30 Junk and Sellmeyer, ibid, p. 35; NSO Erw-C3-26, Flugblatt der NSDAP, 1928.

31 *Osnabrücker Tageblatt*, 19 October 1929; NSO Rep 430-101-7-43-331-Band 6, 'Politische Wochenberichte über die wirtschaftliche und politische Lage in der Stadt Osnabrück u.a. an die Polizeidirektion Bremen, 1929', 21 October 1929. The two accounts give different facts and figures.

32 *Stadtwächter*, 30 June 1929.

33 Ibid., 8 December 1929.

34 Ibid., 27 April 1930.

35 Ibid., 3 August 1930.

36 Ibid., 7 July 1929.

37 Michael Burleigh and Wolfgang Wippermann, *The Racial State: Germany 1933-1945* (Cambridge 1991), pp. 23-73.

38 Peter Longerich, *Politik der Vernichtung: Eine Gesamtdarstellung der nationalsozialistischen Judenverfolgung* (Munich, 1998), pp. 23-226.

39 Huttenbach, *Destruction*, p. 14; Richard Bessel, *Political Violence and the Rise of the Nazis: The Storm Troopers in East Germany* (London, 1984), p. 105; Bajohr, '*Aryanization*', pp. 16-20.

40 Avraham Barkai, *From Boycott to Annihilation: The Economic Struggle of the German Jews, 1933-1945* (Hanover, NH, 1989), pp. 17-18.

41 *Osnabrücker Tageblatt*, 1 April 1933.

42 *Osnabrücker Zeitung*, 2 April 1933.

43 Kaplan, *Between Dignity and Despair*, p. 23.

44 Barkai, *Boycott to Annihilation*, p. 23.

45 Friedlander, *Nazi Germany and the Jews*, pp. 27-8; Longerich, *Politik der Vernichtung*, pp. 41-3.

46 Burleigh and Wippermann, *Racial State*, pp. 49-50; Longerich, ibid., pp. 102-11.

47 Jeremy Noakes, 'The Development of Nazi Policy Towards the German-Jewish "Mischlinge", 1933-1945', *Leo Baeck Institute Year Book*, vol. 34 (1989), pp. 306-15.

48 Micahel Wildt, 'Violence Against the Jews in Germany, 1933-39', in David Bankier, ed., *Probing the Depths of German Antisemitism: German Society and the Persecution of the Jews, 1933-1941* (Oxford, 2000), pp. 181-209.

49 Burleigh and Wippermann, *Racial State*, pp. 77-86.

50 See, for instance, Institut zum Studium der Judenfrage, *Die Juden in Deutschland* (Munich, 1937).

51 *Osnabrücker Zeitung*, 22 August 1935. We need to question the number of spectators.

52 *Osnabrücker Tageblatt*, 21 August 1935.

53 Longerich, *Politik der Vernichtung*, pp. 70-111, 153-226.

54 Barkai, *Boycott to Annihilation*, p. 77; Günther Plum, 'Wirtschaft und Erwebsleben', in Benz, *Die Juden*, pp. 292-313.

55 Junk and Sellmeyer, *Stationen*, pp. 60-1.

56 Krause and Gander, 'Ariesierung', p. 231.

57 'Lagebericht der Staatspolizeistelle Osnabrück an das geheime Staatspolizeiamt für den Monat August 1935 vom 4. September 1935', in Gerd Steinwascher, ed., *Gestapo Osnabrück Meldet: Polizei und Regierungsberichte aus dem Regierungsbezirk Osnabrück aus den Jahren 1933 bis 1936* (Osnabrück, 1995), p. 250.

58 'Lagebericht der Staatspolizeistelle Osnabrück an das Geheime Staatspolizeiamt für den Monat September 1935 vom 10. Oktober 1935', in ibid, p. 266.

59 Volker Dahm, 'Kulturelles und geistiges Leben', in Benz, *Die Juden*, pp. 125-222.

60 Alfred Hirschberg, 'Der Zentralverein deutscher Staatsürger jüdischen Glaubens', in *Wille und Weg des deutschen Judentums* (Berlin, 1935), pp. 12-29.

61 'Lagebericht der Staatspolizeistelle Osnabrück an das Geheime Staatspolizeiamt für den Monat Oktober 1934 vom 3. November 1934', in Steinwascher, *Gestapo Osnabrück Meldet*, p. 116.

62 'Auszug aus dem Lagebericht der Staatspolizeistelle Osnabrück an das Geheime Staatspolizeiamt für die Monate Dezember 1934 und Januar 1935 vom 4. Februar 1935', in ibid., p. 133.

63 Konrad Kwiet, 'The Ultimate Refuge: Suicide in the Jewish Community under the Nazis', *Leo Baeck Institute Year Book*, vol. 29 (1984), pp. 135-48.

64 Werner Pelster, 'Selbstmord in Stadt-u. Landkreis Osnabrück' (unpublished University of Münster medical dissertation, 1934), p. 34.

65 Noakes, 'Development of Nazi Policy'; Meyer, *'Jüdische Mischlinge'*.

66 NSO Rep 430-303-19-56-233.

67 'Lagebericht der Staatspolizeistelle Osnabrück an das Geheime Staatspolizeiamt für den Monat Juli 1935 vom 4. August 1935', in Steinwascher, *Gestapo Osnabrück Meldet*, p. 228.

68 *Neue Volksblätter*, 12 March 1937. Storch was a foreign Jew with the real name of Schlamon.

69 Juliane Wetzel, 'Auswanderung aus Deutschland', in Benz, *Die Juden*, pp. 413-98.

70 Werner Jacob Cahman, *German Jewry: Its History and Sociology* (Brunswick, NJ, 1984), p. 83.

71 Michael Marrus, *The Unwanted: European Refugees in the Twentieth Century* (New York, 1985), pp. 129-30.

72 Wetzel, 'Auswanderung', pp. 417-18.

73 Tables 7.1 and 7.2 refer to part of the reality, i.e. synagogue members, rather than those who had intermarried, about whom we cannot come to such definite conclusions.

74 NSO Dep-3b-IV-2167, Cards 216-216f.

75 NSO Dep-3b-IV-2167, Cards 341-341d.

76 Avraham Barkai, 'The Fateful Year 1938: The Continuation and Acceleration of Plunder', in Walter H. Pehle, ed., *November 1938: From 'Reichskristallnacht' to Genocide* (Oxford, 1991), p. 95.

77　Ian Kershaw, *Hitler, 1936-1945: Hubris* (London, 2001), p. 131.

78　Friedländer, *Nazi Germany and the Jews*, pp. 241-2; Longerich, *Politik der Vernichtung*, pp. 162-5.

79　Kershaw, *Hitler*, p. 131; Bruss, *Die Bremer Juden*, pp. 84-94.

80　Uwe Dietrich Adam, 'How Spontaneous was the Pogrom', in Pehle, *November 1938*, pp. 73-94.

81　Anthony Read and David Fisher, *Kristallnact: Unleashing the Holocaust* (London, 1991), pp. 73-4.

82　*Neue Volksblätter*, 11 November 1938.

83　*Osnabrucker Tageblatt*, 11 November 1938.

84　*Neue Volksblätter*, 13, 14 November 1938.

85　Ibid., 16 November 1938.

86　*Osnabrücker Tageblatt*, 15, 18, 20 November.

87　Read and Fisher, *Kristallnacht*, pp. 73, 134-5; Erika Weinzierl, 'Schuld durch Gleichgültigkeit? Zur Geschichte der Novemberpogrome 1938', in Günther Gorschenk and Stephen Reimers, eds, *Offene Wunden – Brennende Fragen: Juden in Detschland von 1938 bis Heute* (Frankfurt, 1989), p. 20.

88　Interview with Irmgard Ohl, 28 July 2000.

89　Friedländer, *Nazi Germany and the Jews*, pp. 281, 284.

90　NSO Rep-430-904-15-65-2, Letter from the Oberburgermeister to Regierungspräsident, 23 December 1938.

91　NSO Rep-430-904-15-65-2, Letter from the Oberburgermeister to Regierungspräsident of 9 March 1939.

92　Krause and Gander, 'Ariesierung', pp, 233-6; NSO Rep-430-904-15-65-9; NSO Rep-430-904-15-65-12.

93　*Neue Volksblätter*, 10 February 1939.

94　*Addressbuch der Stadt und Landkreis Osnabrück 1934-1935* (Osnabrück,1934); *Addressbuch der Stadt und Landkreis Osnabrück 1938-1939* (Osnabrück, 1938).

95　Friedländer, *Nazi Germany and the Jews*, pp. 284-5.

96　Konrad Kwiet, 'To Leave or not to Leave: The German Jews at the Crossroads', in Pehle, *November 1938*, p. 146.

97　*Neue Volksblätter*, 29, 31 August, 6 September 1941.

98　Interview with Irmgard Ohl, 28 July 2000.

99　Ibid.

100　NSO Dep-3b-XV-3, Kriegs-Chronik, Band III, Sept. 1941 – Okt. 1942, p. 779.

101　NSO Rep-439-21.

102　Junk and Sellmeyer, *Stationen*, p. 208.

103　Asaria, *Zur Geschichte der Juden in Osnabrück*, p. 32.

104　Meyer, *'Judische Mischlinge'*, pp. 52-62.

105　NSO Rep-726-16.

106　Benz, *Die Juden*, p. 733.

107　Wolfgang Jacobmeyer, 'Jüdische Überlebende als "Displaced Persons": Untersuchungen zur Besatzungspolitik in den deutschen Westzonen und zur Zuwanderung osteuropäischer Juden 1945-1947', *Geschichte und Gesellschaft*, vol. 9 (1983), p. 421.

108 Koppel S. Pinson, 'Jewish Life in Liberated Germany', *Jewish Social Studies*, vol. 9 (1947), pp. 103, 110; Ruth Gay, *Safe Among the Germans: Liberated Jews After World War II* (London, 2002).

109 NSO Rep-430-201-16B-65-27-1, Letter from Regierungspräsident of 8 February 1946.

110 The camp is discussed by: Junk and Sellmeyer, *Stationen*, pp. 212-16; and Asaria, *Zur Geschichte der Juden in Osnabrück*, pp. 33-9.

111 Interview with Irmgard Ohl, 28 July 2000.

112 BAOS 04-88-1; Asaria, *Zur Geschichte der Juden in Osnabrück*, p. 43.

113 The trial can be traced through the *Niederdeutscher Kurier*, 3, 7, 14, 15, 17 December 1949.

114 Rebecca Wittmann, *Beyond Justice: The Auschwitz Trial* (Cambridge, MA, 2005); Devin O. Pendas, *The Frankfurt Auschwitz Trial, 1963-1965: Genocide, History and the Limits of the Law* (Cambridge, 2006).

115 In March 1945 the Düsseldorf Gestapo employed 291 persons, 242 of then bureaucrats, to control a population approximately 500,000. Robert Gellately, *The Gestapo and German Society: Enforcing Racial Policy, 1933-1945* (Oxford, 1990), p. 45.

116 Wittmann, *Beyond Justice*.

117 Details of the investigation are contained in two files: NSO Rep-945-42; and NSO Rep-945-44.

118 Raul Hilberg, *Perpetrators, Victims, Bystanders: The Jewish Catastrophe, 1933-1945* (London, 1993), p. 212.

119 See, for instance: Ian Kershaw, *Popular Opinion and Political Dissent in the Third Reich: Bavaria 1933-1945* (Oxford, 1983), pp. 224-77, 358-72; David Bankier, *The Germans and the Final Solution: Public Opinion Under Nazism* (Oxford, 1992), pp. 67-88, 116-38; and Robert Gellately, *Backing Hitler: Consent and Coercion in Nazi Germany* (Oxford 2001), pp. 121-50.

120 Although Kershaw, ibid., pp. 246-57, indicates that the Nazis made relatively little headway in rural Bavaria because of the influence of the Roman Catholic clergy.

121 Bankier, *Germans*, pp. 68, 69.

122 Ibid., p. 86; Kershaw, *Popular Opinion*, pp. 262-3.

123 Bankier, ibid, pp. 121, 131.

124 Kershaw, *Popular Opinion*, pp. 358-72.

125 Gellately, *Backing Hitler*, p. 149.

126 NSO Rep-439-19-116.

127 NSO Rep-439-19-334.

128 Interview with Maria and Hans Grün, 8 July 2000.

129 Interview with Karl Mosse, 10 August 2001.

130 Interview with Günther Adam, 2 August 2001.

131 Interview with Werner Funk, 16 August 2000.

132 Interview with Heinrich and Elizabeth Wand, 16 August 2001.

133 Interview with Hilde Schüll, 3 September 2001.

Chapter 8

1   Michael Zimmermann, *Rassenutopie und Genozid: Die nationalsozialistische 'Lösung der Zigeunerfrage'* (Hamburg,1996), pp. 73-4; Leo Lucassen, *Zigeuner: Die Geschichte eines polizeilichen Ordnungsbegriffes in Deutschland, 1700-1945* (Cologne, 1996).

2   Hans-Joachim Döring, *Die Zigeuner im Nationalsozialistischen Staat* (Hamburg, 1964).

3   Donald Kenrick and Grattan Puxon, *The Destiny of Europe's Gypsies* (London, 1972).

4   Ulrich König, *Sinti und Roma unter dem Nationalsozialismus: Verfolgung und Widerstand* (Bochum, 1989).

5   Zimmermann, *Rassenutopie*; Guenter Lewy, *The Nazi Persecution of the Gypsies* (Oxford, 2000).

6   Even Till Bastian, *Sinti und Roma im Dritten Reich: Geschichte einer Verfolgung* (Munich, 2001), a brief history of persecution under the Nazis, has a substantial introduction on the years before 1933 and an 'Afterword' entitled `And Today?'.

7   These include *Geschichte der Zigeunerverfolgung in Deutschland*, 2nd edn (Frankfurt, 1988).

8   See, for example: Georg von Soest, *Zigeuner zwischen Verfolgung und Integration: Geschichte, Lebensbedingungen und Eingliederungsversuche* (Weinheim, 1979); Michael Schenk, *Rassismus gegen Sinti und Roma: Zur Kontinuität der Zigeunerverfolgung innerhalb der deutschen Gesellschaft von der Weimarer Republik bis in die Gegenwart* (Frankfurt, 1994); Katrin Reemstma, *Sinti und Roma: Geschichte, Kultur, Gegenwart* (Munich, 1996); Wolfgang Wippermann, *Geschichte der Sinti und Roma in Deutschland: Darstellung und Dokumente* (Berlin, 1993).

9   See, for instance: Kirsten Martin-Heuß, *Zur Mythischen Figur der Zigenuer in der deutschen Zigeunerforschung* (Frankfurt, 1983); and Mareile Krause, *Verfolgung durch Erziehung: Eine Untersuchung über die Jahrhundertlange Kontinuität staatlicher Erziehungsmaßnahmen im Dienste der Vernichtung kultureller Identität von Roma und Sinti* (Hamburg, 1989); Lucassen, *Zigeuner*.

10 Kenrick and Puxon, *Destiny of Europe's Gypsies*; Ian Hancock, *The Pariah Syndrome: An Account of Gypsy Slavery and Persecution* (Anne Arbor, MI, 1987); David M. Crowe, *A History of the Gypsies in Eastern Europe and Russia* (London, 1995); Susan Tebbutt, ed., *Sinti and Roma: Gypsies in German-Speaking Society and Literature* (Oxford, 1998); Gilad Margalit, *Germany and Its Gypsies: A Post-Auschwitz Ordeal* (Madison, WI, 2002).

11 Martin-Heuß, *Zur mythischen Figur der Zigeuner*.

12 Margalit, *Germany and its Gypsies*.

13 Wolfgang Wippermann, *Das Leben in Frankfurt zur NS-Zeit*, Vol. 2, *Die nationalsozialistische Zigeunerverfolgung: Darstellung und didaktische Hinweise* (Frankfurt, 1986); Peter Sander, *Frankfurt. Auschwitz: Die nationalsozialistische Verfolgung der Sinti und Roma in Frankfurt am Main* (Frankfurt, 1998); Eva von Hase-Michalik, and Doris Kreuzkamp, *Du kriegst auch einen schönen Wohnwagen: Zwangslager für Sinti und Roma während des Nationalsozialismus in Frankfurt am Main* (Frankfurt am Main, 1990); Karola Fings and Frank Sparing, '*z. Zt. Zigeunerlager': Die Verfolgung der Düsseldorfer Sinti und Roma in Nationalsozialismus* (Cologne,

1992); Ludwig Eiber and Michail Krausnick, '*Ich wußte, es wird schlimm*': *Die Verfolgung der Sinti und Roma in München, 1933-1945* (Munich, 1993).

14 Interview with Gerhard Strauß, 22 August 2001.

15 'Lagebericht des Regierungspräsidenten von Osnabrück an den Reichsminister des Innern für die Monate Dezember 1935 und Januar 1936 vom 4. Februar 1936', in Gerd Steinwascher, ed., *Gestapo Osnabrück Meldet: Polizei und Regierungsberichte aus dem Regierungsbezirk Osnabrück aus den Jahren 1933 bis 1936* (Osnabrück, 1995), pp. 326-7.

16 Panikos Panayi, *Ethnic Minorities in Nineteenth and Twentieth Century Germany: Jews, Gypsies, Poles, Turks and Others* (London, 2000), pp. 15, 175.

17 Rainer Hehemann, *Die 'Bekämpfung des Zigeunerwesens' in Wilheminischen Deutschland und in der Weimarer Republik* (Frankfurt am Main, 1979), pp. 214-17.

18 Alfred Dillmann, *Zigeuner-Buch* (Munich, 1905).

19 Hohmann, *Geschichte der Zigeunerverfolgung*, p. 75; Soest, *Zigeuner zwischen Verfolgung und Integration*, p. 30; Krause, *Verfolgung durch Erziehung*, pp. 81-2; Hehemann, *Die 'Bekämpfung des Zigeunerwesens'* pp. 261-2.

20 Reemstma, *Sinti und Roma, p.* 97; Hohmann, ibid., pp. 73-7; Zimmermann, *Rassenutopie,* pp. 66-71.

21 Michael Burleigh and Wolfgang Wippermann, *The Racial State: Germany 1933-1945* (Cambridge, 1991) pp. 114-15; Lucassen, *Zigeuner*, pp. 192-8.

22 Hehemann, *Die 'Bekämpfung des Zigeunerwesens',* pp. 273-7; Wippermann, *Geschichte der Sinti und Roma,* p. 25.

23 Otto Finger, *Studien an zwei asozialen Zigeunermischlings-Sippen* (Gießen, 1937).

24 Zimmermann, *Rassenutopie,* pp. 129-55; Burleigh and Wippermann, *Racial State,* pp. 118, 120, 125; Hohmann, *Geschichte der Zigeunerverfolgung*, p. 109.

25 Zimmermann, ibid., pp. 81-155.

26 Schenck, *Rassismus*, p. 114.

27 Sybil Milton, 'Antechamber to Birkenau: The *Zigeunerlager* after 1933', in H. Gubitz, H. Bästlein and J. Tuckel, eds, *Die Normalität des Verbrechers: Bilanz und Perspektiven der Forschung zu den national sozialistischen Gewaltverbrechen* (Berlin, 1994), pp. 241-3.

28 Ibid., p. 245.

29 Hase-Malik and Kreuzkamp, *Du Kriegst auch einen schönen Wohnwagen*, pp. 40-1, 46.

30 Milton, 'Antechamber to Birkenau', p. 249.

31 Zimmermann, *Rassenutopie,* pp. 118-24.

32 Eiber, Strauß and Krausnick, '*Ich wußte, es wird schlimm'*, p. 30.

33 See Maria Michalsky-Knak, *Zigeuner: Und was wir mit ihnen in Berlin erlebten* (Berlin, 1935).

34 Hans Weltzel, 'The Gypsies of Central Germany', *Journal of the Gypsy Lore Society*, vol. 17 (1938), pp. 9-24, 20-8, 73-80, 104-90.

35 Alfred Lessing, *Mein Leben im Versteck: Wie ein deutscher Sinti den Holocaust überlebte* (Düsseldorf, 1930), p. 30.

36 The relevant archival references are: Rep 430-303 and Rep 727-15-84-1.

37 NSO Rep 430-201-16B-65-21.

38 *Osnabrücker Zeitung*, 12 April 1934.

39   König, *Sinti und Roma*, pp. 80-9; Burleigh and Wippermann, *Racial State*, pp. 120-7; Bernhard Steck, 'Die nationalsozialistische Methoden zur Lösung des Zigeunerproblems', *Tribüne*, vol. 20 (1981), pp. 53-78; Soest, *Zigeuner zwischen Verfolgung und Integration*, p. 41-6; Zimmermann, *Rassenutopie*, pp. 172-3.

40   Sander, *Frankfurt. Auschwitz*, pp. 249-51.

41   The Osnabrück Gypsies do not appear to have faced deportation in the round up which occurred of 930 members of this minority in north west Germany in April and May 1940. According to Zimmermann, *Rassenutopie.*, p. 173, these consisted of 550 people from Hamburg, 160 from Bremen and 'locations such as Winsen an der Aller, Bremervörde and Wesermünde' and 200 from Schleswig-Holstein.

42   In view of the personal details involved here the real names have been changed.

43   While this statement does not apply to the West family, this individual case does not change the overall social and economic position of the Romanies in either Osnabrück or Germany as a whole.

44   All of the above documents come from NSO Rep 430-201-16B-65-39-Bd.1.

45   Panikos Panayi, *Outsiders: A History of European Minorities* (London, 1999), pp. 45-9; Panikos Panayi, *An Ethnic History of Europe Since 1945: Nations, States and Minorities* (London, 2000) pp. 29-31.

46   Hannah Arendt, *Eichmann in Jerusalem: A Report on the Banality of Evil* (Harmondsworth, 1963); Zygmunt Bauman, *Modernity and the Holocaust* (Cambridge, 1989); Jonathan Steinberg, *All or Nothing: The Axis and the Holocaust, 1941-3* (London, 1990); Omar Bartov, *Murder in Our Midst: The Holocaust, Industrial Killing and Representation* (Oxford, 1996).

47   The fate of the family of Konrad H. is described by Eiber, Strauß and Krausnich, '*Ich wußte, es wird schlimm*', p. 103. Sander, *Frankfurt. Auschwitz*, p. 251, asserts that about 15 per cent of Romanies survived.

48   The names in this file have been changed.

49   NSO Rep-945-85.

50   Josef Bura, 'Die unbewältigte Gegenwart: "Zigeunerpolitik" und alltäglicher Rassismus in der Bundesrepublik', in Rudolf Bauer, Josef Bura and Klaus Lang, eds, *Sinti in der Bundesrepublik: Beiträge zur sozialen Lage einer verfolgten Minderheit*, (Bremen, 1984), pp. 14-15; Sybil Milton, 'Persecuting the Survivors: The Continuity of "Anti-Gypsyism" in Post-War Germany and Austria', in Tebbutt, *Sinti and Roma*, pp. 36-7.

51   Rep-430-201-16b-65-10, Vol. 3.

52   Rainer Hehemann, '"…jederzeit gottlose böse Leute" : Sinti und Roma Zwischen Duldung und Vernichtung', in Klaus J. Bade, ed., *Deutsche im Ausland, Fremde in Deutschland: Migration in Geschichte und Gegenwart* (Munich, 1992), pp. 271-7.

53   The city authorities in Marburg unveiled a plaque to the Romanies deported to Auschwitz on the fiftieth anniversary of the event on 23 March 1993, although it does not seem to list the names of those involved. See Udo Engbring-Romang, *Marburg. Auschwitz: Zur Verfolgung der Sinti in Marburg und Umgebung* (Frankfurt, 1998), p. 11.

Chapter 9

1 Eva Seeber, *Zwangsarbeiter in der faschistischen Kriegswirtschaft* (Berlin, 1964); Edward L. Homze, *Foreign Labour in Nazi Germany* (Princeton, NJ, 1967); Hans Pfahlmann, *Fremdarbeiter und Kriegsgefangene in der deutschen Kriegswirtschaft, 1939-1945* (Darmstadt, 1968).

2 His most important volume, a translation of the original German work is *Hitler's Foreign Workers: Enforced Labour in Germany under the Third Reich* (Cambridge, 1997).

3 Mark Spoerer, *Zwangsarbeit unter dem Hakenkreuz: Ausländische Zivilarbeiter, Kriegsgefangene und Häftlinge im Deutschen Reich und im besetzten Europa* (Stuttgart, 2000).

4 Most importantly, *Vom Zwangsarbeiter zum heimatlosen Ausländer* (Göttingen, 1985).

5 Jochen Oltmer, *Migration und Politik in der Weimar Republik* (Göttingen, 2005).

6 See, for instance: Klaus J. Bade, ed., *Auswanderer – Wanderarbeiter – Gastarbeiter: Bevölkerung, Arbeitsmarkt und Wanderung in Deutschland seit der Mitte des 19. Jahrhunderts*, 2 Volumes (Ostfildern, 1984); Ulrich Herbert, *A History of Foreign Labour in Germany, 1880-1980: Seasonal Workers/Forced Laborers/Guest Workers* (Ann Arbor, MI, 1990); Johann Woydt, *Ausländische Arbeitskräfte in Deutschland: Vom Kaiserreich zur Bundesrepublik* (Heilbronn, 1987); and Lothar Elsner and Joachim Lehmann, *Ausländische Arbeitskräfte in Deutschland: Vom Kaiserreich zur Bundesrepublik* (Heilbronn, 1987).

7 http://www.stiftung-evz.de

8 For an introduction to these issues see Spoerer, *Zwangsarbeit unter dem Hakenkreuz*, pp. 233-51.

9 See, for instance: Gabriele Freitag, *Zwangsarbeiter im Lipper Land: Der Einsatz von Arbeitskräften in der Landwirtschaft Lippes, 1939-1945* (Bochum, 1996); and Heinrich Burgdorf, et. al., eds, *Zwangsarbeiterinnen und Kriegsgefangene in Blomberg (1939-1945)* (Bielefeld, 1996).

10 Ursula Fisser-Blömer, *Zwangsarbeit in Osnabrück* (Osnabrück, 1982).

11 The titles of the two books are: *Niederländer in Verdammten Land: Zeugnisse der Zwangsarbeit von Niederländern im Raum Osnabrück während des Zweiten Weltkrieges* (Osnabrück, 1998); and *Das Arbeitserziehungslager Ohrbeck bei Osnabrück: Eine Dokumentation* (Osnabrück, 2000).

12 For details of the project see *Neue Osnabrücker Zeitung*, 10, 16 May 2000. See also Michael Gander, 'Beziehungen zwischen sowjetischen Zwangsarbeitern und deutscher Bevölkerung in Osnabrück', in Babette Quinkert, ed., *'Wir sind die Herren dieses Landes': Ursachen, Verlauf und Folgen des deutschen Überfalls auf die Sowjetunion* (Hamburg, 2002), pp. 154-65.

13 For an introduction to labour importation before 1918 see Herbert, *History of Foreign Labour*, pp. 9-119.

14 Jochen Oltmer, '"Schutz des nationalen Arbeitsmarkts: Transnationale Arbeitswanderungen und protektionistische Zuwanderungspolitik in der Weimarer Republik', in Jochen Oltmer, ed., *Migration Steuern und Verwalten: Deutschland vom späten 19. Jahrhundert bis zur Gegenwart* (Göttingen, 2003), pp. 85-122.

15   Panikos Panayi, *Ethnic Minorities in Nineteenth and Twentieth Century Germany: Jews, Gypsies, Poles, Turks and Others* (London, 2000), p. 182.

16   Herbert, *History of Foreign Labour*, pp. 154, 156.

17   Homze, *Foreign Labour*, p. 195.

18   Jochen August, 'Die Entwicklung des Arbeitsmarkts in Deutschland in den 30er Jahren und der Masseneinsatz ausländischer Arbeitskräfte während des Zweiten Weltkrieges', *Archiv für Sozialgeschichte*, vol. 24 (1984), p. 305.

19   See, for instance, Gerhard Hirschfeld, 'Der "freiwillige" Arbeitseinsatz niederländischer Fremdarbeiter des Zweiten Weltkrieges als nicht-nationalsozialistischen Verwaltung', in Hans Mommsen and Winfried Schulze, eds, *Vom Elend der Handarbeit: Probleme historischer Unterschichtenforschung* (Stuttgart, 1981), pp. 499-500.

20   Herbert, *Hitler's Foreign Workers*, pp. 61-9, 137-51.

21   Adolf Hitler, *Mein Kampf* (London, 1939), pp. 250-2, 546-65; Michael Burleigh, *Germany Turns Eastwards: A Study of Ostforschung in the Third Reich* (Cambridge, 1988).

22   Ludwig Hoffmeyer, et. al., *Chronik der Stadt Osnabrück* 6th Edn (Osnabrück 1995), p. 497. See also Stefan Schubert, *Sainsonarbeit am Kanal: Rekrutierung, Arbeists- und Lebensverhältnisse ausländischer Arbeitskräfte beim Bau des Mittelandkanals im Osnbrücker Land 1910-1916* (Frankfurt, 2005), which looks at the employment of foreign workers in the construction of one stretch of the Mittellandkanal north of Osnabrück.

23   See NSO Rep-430-201-16B-65-121.

24   See, for instance, *Osnabrücker Tageblatt*, 30 July, 2, 3, 4 August, 27 September 1936.

25   G. Gross, 'Ausländische Arbeiter in der deutschen Landwirtschaft und die Frage ihrer Ersetzbarkeit', *Landwirtschaftliche Jahrbücher*, vol. 59 (1924).

26   See, for instance: Christoph Kleßmann, *Polnische Bergarbeiter im Ruhrgebiet, 1870-1945* (Göttingen, 1978), pp. 150-80; and Ralf Karl Oenning, '*Du da mitti polnischen Farben...*' *Sozialisationserfahrungen von Polen im Ruhrgebiet 1919 bis 1939* (Münster, 1991).

27   Richard Charles Murphy, 'Polish In-Migration in Bottrop, 1891-1933: An Ethnic Minority in a German Industrial City' (University of Iowa Ph.D thesis, 1977), p. 182.

28   Pfahlmann, *Fremdarbeiter*, p. 128.

29   Herbert, *Hitler's Foreign Workers*, pp. 205-22.

30   H. Weisfeld, 'Zwangsarbeit in Bremen', in Diethelm Knauf and Helga Schröder, eds, *Fremde in Bremen: Auswanderer, Zuwanderer, Zwangsarbeiter* (Bremen, 1993), pp. 119-20.

31   NSO Rep-430-201-16b-65-30, list dated 22 September 1939.

32   *Der Arbeitseinsatz in Niedersachsen* is contained in NSO Rep-430-201-16B-65-54-Bd. 1.

33   The details are in NSO Rep 439-22.

34   Karl Kühling, *Osnabrück, 1933-1945: Stadt im Dritten Reich* (Osnabrück, 1980), p. 214.

35   NSO Dep-3b-XV-4-5, Kriegs-Chronik, Bänder IV-V, Nov. 1942 – Juni 1944, p. 129.

36 Jehuda L. Wallach, 'Probleme der Zwangsarbeit in der deutschen Kriegswirtschaft', *Jahrbuch des Instituts für deutsche Geschichte*, vol. 6 (1977), pp. 483-91.

37 See correspondence in NSO Rep-430-201-16B-65-114.

38 NSO Dep-3b-XV-4-5, Kriegs-Chronik, Band IV-V, Nov. 1942 – Juni 1944, pp. 129-30.

39 NSO Rep-430-303-19/56-230, Liste der Ausländerlager im Stadtkreis Osnabrück, 31 July 1943

40 Fisser-Bömer, *Zwangsarbeit in Osnabrück*, pp. 45-59.

41 Pax Christi – Basisgruppe Osnabrück und dem Antifascistischen Arbeitskreis Osnabrück, eds, *SpureNsuche: Osnabrück 1933-1945* (Osnabrück, 1995), pp. 67-74.

42 See NSO Rep 430-201-14-47-2, Police Report of 11 June 1944.

43 See the correspondence in NSO Rep-727-62-83-10.

44 Interview with Hermann Thiem, 10 January 2001.

45 Issmer, *Arbeitserziehungslager*, p. 33; Gabriele Lofti, *KZ der Gestapo: Arbeitserziehungslager im Dritten Reich* (Stuttgart, 2000).

46 Issmer, ibid., pp. 171-312.

47 Ibid., pp. 45-91.

48 Ibid., pp. 108-21, 385-92

49 Frank Bührmann-Peters, 'Dort Haben wir an und für sich gar nicht gemerkt, daß wir Gefangene waren: Der Arbeitzansatz von Strafgefangenen aus den Emlandslagern im Raum Osnabrück', *Osnabrücker Mitteilungen*, vol. 103 (1998), pp. 218-32; Volker Issmer, 'Zum Bombenräumen nach Osnabrück: KZ-Häftlinge aus dem Lengerischen Tunnel in unserer Stadt', *Osnabrücker Mitteilungen*, vol. 108 (2003), pp. 179-88.

50 NSO ERW-A100-103, Karl Reinert to the Militärregierung, 18 March 1946. Sickness and fatigue affected workers throughout Germany as illustrated by those who worked for the Adler concern in Frankfurt, which had an absentee rate of close to a third by the beginning of 1945, as demonstrated by Ernst Kaiser and Michael Knom, *'Wir Lebten und Schliefen zwischen den Toten': Rüstungsproduktion, Zwangsarbeit and Vernichtung in den Frankfurter Adlerwerken*, 3rd edn (Frankfurt, 1998), pp. 227-8.

51 Quoted in Pax Christi, *SpureNsuche*, pp. 60-3.

52 For the national picture see Gerhard Hirschfeld, ed., *The Policies of Genocide: Jews and Soviet Prisoners of War in Nazi Germany* (London, 1986).

53 NSO Rep 430-303-19-56-230, Dr Fischer to Regierungspräsident, 26 January 1945.

54 Pax Christi, *SpureNsuche*, p. 65.

55 Issmer, *Arbeitserziehungslager*, 59-78.

56 Especially in *Niederländer in Verdammten Land*.

57 *Neue Volksblätter*, 14 September, 24 October 1941.

58 BA MA RW/21/51/8, 'Kriegstagebuch des Rüstungskommandos Osnabrück', Bd. 8, 1.12.1941 – 28.2.1942, p. 6.

59 NSO Rep-610-Osn-614, Report of inspection of OKD dated 14 April 1944.

60 NSO Rep-610-Osn-614, OKD to Ernährungsamt, 1 January 1944.

61 NSO Rep-610-Osn-315.

62 BA MA RW/21/51/6, Rüstungskommando Osnabrück, Band 6, 1.6.-31.8.1941.

63 NSO Rep-610-Osn-283.

64 NSO Rep-610-Osn-252.

65 This information comes from NSO-Dep-3b-IV-6496.

66 Interview with Karl Mosse, 10 August 2001.

67 NSO Dep-3b-XIX-124.

68 Pax Christi, *SpurenSuche*, pp. 65-6; Issmer, 'Zum Bombenräumen'.

69 Andreas Heusler, *Ausländereinsatz: Zwangsarbeit für die Münchener Kriegswirtschaft, 1939-1945* (Munich, 1996), p. 358.

70 NSO Rep 430-201-16b-65-100, Abschrift, Der Höhere SS- und Polizeiführer, West, 8 August 1941.

71 Herbert, *Hitler's Foreign Workers*, pp. 71-9.

72 See documents in NSO Rep 430-201-16B-65-114.

73 See NSO Dep-3b-IV-6531.

74 NSO Rep-430-201-16b-65-10 Bd. 3, Polizeiordnung über die in Reg.- Bezirk Osnabrück eingesezten Ostarbeiter und Ostarbeiterinnen, 7 July 1943.

75 See documents in NSO Dep-3b-IV-6496.

76 Homze, *Foreign Labour*, p. 297.

77 Interview with Gerhard Strauß, 22 August 2001.

78 NSO ERW-A100-103, Karl Reinert to Militärregierung, 18 March 1946.

79 Herbert, *Hitler's Foreign Workers*, p. 317.

80 Ibid., pp. 326-58.

81 As an introduction see Bob Moore and Kent Fedorowich, eds, *Prisoners of War and Their Captors in World War II* (Oxford, 1996).

82 Katharina Hoffmann, *Zwangsarbeit und ihre gesellschaftliche Akzeptanz in Oldenburg, 1939-1945* (Oldenburg, 2001), p. 176.

83 NSO Rep-430-201-16B-65-58, Abschrift, Kriminalpolizeistelle Bremen, Außendienststelle Osnabrück, 1 July 1944.

84 Nazi justice in discussed in Chapter 3.

85 NHH Hann-171a-Hann-107-83-254.

86 NHH Hann-171a-Hann-107-83-916.

87 NHH Hann-171a-Hann-107-83-630.

88 NHH Hann-171a-Hann-107-83-266.

89 NSO Rep-439-19-283.

90 NSO Rep-439-19-535.

91 NSO Rep-439-19-1011.

92 NSO Rep-439-19-1061.

93 Herbert, *Hitler's Foreign Workers*, pp. 340-5; Heusler, *Ausländereinsatz*, pp. 269-76.

94 NSO Rep-430-201-16B-65-107, Kriminalkomissar to Regierungspräsident, 24 August 1943.

95 NSO Rep-439-19-86.

96 NSO Rep-439-19-633.

97 Issmer, *Niederländer*, p. 34.

98 Ibid., pp. 185-212.

99 NSO Rep-950-Osn-18-54-33. Name has been changed.

100 Seeber, *Zwangsarbeiter*, 165, 179.
101 Jill Stephenson, 'Triangle: Foreign Workers, German Civilians and the Nazi Regime: War and Society in Württemberg', *German Studies Review*, vol. 15 (1992), p. 344.
102 NSO Rep-439-19-320.
103 NHH Hann-171a-Hann-107-83-933. Name has been changed.
104 NHH Hann-171a-Hann-107-83-956. Name has been changed.
105 Interview with Josefa Herz, 26 July 2000.
106 Interview with Hilde Scholl, 3 September 2001.
107 Gander, 'Beziehungen', p. 158.
108 NSO Dep-3b-XV-41, Chronik von Dr Hans Glenewinkel, 5. April – 31. Dezember 1945, p. 21.
109 Jacobmeyer, *Zwangsarbeiter*.
110 These statistics come from NSO Rep-430-201-16B-65-70-Bd. 2.
111 For the national picture, with a particular focus upon the Ruhr, see Herbert, *Hitler's Foreign Workers*, pp. 359-81.
112 Jacobmeyer, *Zwangsarbeiter*, p. 48; Marc Engels, *Zwangsarbeit in der Stadt Aachen: Ausländereinsatz in einer westdeutschen Grenzstadt während des zweiten Weltkrieges* (Aachen, 2002), p. 151.
113 NSO Dep-3b-XV-41, Chronik von Dr Hans Glenewinkel, 5. April – 31. Dezember 1945, pp. 1-4, 21, 35, 59, 80
114 BAOS 04-79-71.
115 NSO Rep-430-201-16B-65-76, Kommando der Schutzpolizei to Pol. Offz. B/ Det. 902, 16 August 1945.
116 NSO Rep-430-201-16B/65-76, Police-Headquarters to Public Safety Officer of the English Military Government, 23 August 1945.
117 Interview with Lora Kraft, 20 August 2001.
118 Interview with Hermann Thiem, 10 January 2001.
119 See the comparison of post-War criminality amongst Germans and foreigners in Jacobmeyer, *Zwangsarbeiter*, pp. 48-50.

Chapter 10

1   Konrad H. Jarausch and Michael Geyer, *Shattered Past: Reconstructing German History* (Princeton, 2003), pp. 317-25.
2   See, for instance, Hannele Zürndorfer, *The Ninth of November* (London, 1983), p. 45.
3   See Panikos Panayi, 'Continuities and Discontinuities in German History, 1919-1945', in Panikos Panayi, ed., *Weimar and Nazi Germany: Continuities and Discontinuities* (London, 2001), pp. 3-29.
4   Donald Bloxham, *Genocide on Trial: War Crimes and the Formation of Holocaust History and Memory* (Oxford, 2001).
5   Robert G. Moeller, *War Stories: The Search for a Usable Past in the Federal Republic of Germany* (London, 2001).
6   Richard Bessel and Dirk Schumann, 'Introduction: Violence, Normality, and the Construction of Postwar Europe', in Richard Bessel and Dirk Schumann, eds, *Life After Death: Approaches to a Cultural and Social History of Europe During the 1940s and 1950s* (Cambridge, 2003), pp. 1-13.

7   Frank Stern, *The Whitewashing of the Yellow Badge: Antisemitism and Philosemitism in Postwar Germany* (Oxford, 1992).

8   Bernd Bonwetsch, 'Sowjetische Zwangsarbeiter vor und nach 1945: Ein doppelter Leidensweg', *Jahrbücher für Geschichte Osteuropas*, vol. 41 (1993), pp. 537-42; Pavel Markovič Poljan and Žanna Antonovna Zajončkovskaja, 'Ostarbeiter in Deutschland und Daheim: Ergebnisse einer Fragenbogenanalyse', *Jahrbücher für Geschichte Osteuropas*, vol. 41 (1993), pp. pp. 556-61.

9   Klaus J. Bade, Hans-Bernd Meier and Bernhard Parisius, eds, *Zeitzeugen im Interview: Flüchtlinge und Vertriebene im Raum Osnabrück* (Osnabrück, 1997), p. 86.

10 Lutz Niethammer, 'Privat-Wirtschaft: Errinerungsfragmente einer anderen Umerziehung', in Lutz Niethammer, ed., *'Hinterher merkt man, daß es richtig war, daß es schiefgagenen ist': Nachkriegserfahrungen im Ruhrgebiet* (Bonn, 1983), pp. 17-105.

11 Interview with Werner Funk, 16 August 2000.

12 Interview with Hermann Thiem, 10 January 2001.

13 Interview with Werner Lorenz, Inge Walter and Lilo Meyer, 21 August 2000.

14 Interview with Elizabeth and Heinrich Wand, 16 August 2001.

15 Hans-Ulrich Wehler, *Deutsche Gesellschaftsgeschichte*, Vol. 4, *Vom Beginn des Ersten Weltkrieges bis zur Gründung der beiden deutschen Staaten, 1914-1949* (Munich, 2003), p. 932.

16 Greg Eghigian and Paul Betts, 'Introduction: Pain and Prosperity in Twentieth Century Germany', in Paul Betts and Greg Eghigian, eds, *Pain and Prosperity: Reconsidering Twentieth Century German History* (Stanford, CA, 2003), pp. 1-15.

17 For the development of post-War Osnabrück see Ludwig Hoffmeyer, et. al., *Chronik der Stadt Osnabrück* 6th Edn (Osnabrück, 1995), pp. 674-810.

18 For democracy in post-War Osnabrück see Rudolf Schachtebeck and Wendolin Zimmer, *'die uns kein Teufel rauben kann': Vier Jahrzehnte Demokratie in Osnabrück seit 1945* (Bramsche, 1991).

19 Leo Lucassen, *Zigeuner: Die Geschichte eines polizeilichen Ordnungsbegriffes in Deutschland, 1700-1945* (Cologne, 1996), pp. 139-73.

20 See contributions to Klaus J. Bade, ed., *Fremde in Land: Zuwanderung und Eingliederung im Raum Niedersachsen seit dem Zweiten Weltkrieg* (Osnabrück, 1997).

21 Norbert Böker, *Sozialräumliche Segregationstendenzen ausländischen Bevölkerung in Osnabrück: Eine empirische Untersuchung zu Aspekten der sozialen und räumlichen Ungleichheit zwischen ausländischer und deutscher Bevölkerung* (Aachen, 1996).

22 See Michael Brenner, *After the Holocaust: Rebuilding Jewish Lives in Postwar Germany* (Princeton, NJ, 1997).

23 Z. Asaria, *Zur Geschichte der Juden in Osnabrück und Umgebung: Zur Weihe der Synagoge in Osnabrück* (Osnabrück, 1969); Peter Junk and Martina Sellmeyer, *Stationen auf dem Weg nach Auschwitz: Entrechtung, Vertreibung, Vernichtung: Juden in Osnabrück* 3rd edition (Osnabrück, 2000), pp. 240-7.

24 Especially Joachim S. Hohmann, *Geschichte der Zigeunerverfolgung in Deutschland*, 2nd edn (Frankfurt, 1988); Michael Schenk, *Rassismus gegen Sinti und Roma: Zur Kontinuität der Zigeunerverfolgung innerhalb der deutschen Gesellschaft von der Weimarer Republik bis in die Gegenwart* (Frankfurt, 1994); and Katrin Reemstma, *Sinti und Roma: Geschichte, Kultur, Gegenwart* (Munich, 1996).

25 Eva Berger, Inge Jaehner, Peter Junk, Karl Georg Kaster, Manfred Meinz and Wendelin Zimmer, *Felix Nussbaum: Art Defamed, Art in Exile, Art in Resistance* (Bramsche, 1995).
26 Manuela Westphal, 'Die fremden Deutschen: Einwanderung und eingliderung von Aussiedlern in Niedersachsen', in Bade, *Fremde im Land*, pp. 167-212.

BIBLIOGRAPHY

A. PRIMARY SOURCES

1. Archival Material

Bistumsarchiv Osnabrück
03-17-72-11, Allgemeiner Schriftswechsel Bischof Bernings
03-17-72-32, Silvesterpredigten Bischof Berning
04-61, Kirche und Parteien
04-63, Bistum Osnabrück im NS-Staat
04-79, Die Kirche in der Lage des 2. Weltkrieges
04-88-1, Juden
05-55-61, Kinderheim St. Anna-Stift, Osnabrück, 1945-48
06-36-63-02, Kolpinghaus Osnabrück
06-08, Vetriebenenseelsorge
07-14, Schul und Bildungswesen
10-02, Caritasverband

Bundesarchiv, Militärarchiv, Freiburg
RW-20-6, Kriegstagebücher der Rüstungsinspektion VI
RW-21-51, Rüstungskommando Osnabrück, Kriegstagebücher

National Archives, London
AIR40, Minstry of Air
FO1005, Foreign Office
FO1010, Foreign Office
FO1050, Foreign Office
WO171, War Office

Niedersächsisches Hauptstaatsarchiv, Hannover
Hann-171a-107-83, Staatsanwaltschaft Hannover

Nds-721-Hannover-61-81-28, Akten der Staatsanwaltschaft beim Landgericht Hannover

Niedersächsisches Staatsarchiv Osnabrück
Dep-3b-IV, Stadtsachen
Dep-3b-V, Polizei und Gildesachen
Dep-3b-XV, Kriegs-und Stadt-Chronik, 1939-62
Dep-3b-XIX, Ortspolizeibehörder – Kommand der Schutzpolizei, 1938-45
Dep-3b-XX, Wahlen, Statistikern, 1918-38
Dep-3b-XXI, Wohlfahrtsamt, 1844-1955
Dep-3c, Neues Archiv
Dep-57, Oberschule für Mädchen in Osnabrück
Dep-58b, Ratsgymnasium zu Osnabrück
Erw-C3, Politische Flügblätter und Maueranschläge
Erw-E4, Neue Liedertafel, 1835-1985
Erw-A18, Zeitungsausschnitsammlung Waltermann, 1903-70
Rep-430-108, Regierung Osnabrück, Raumordung, Landesplannung
Rep-430-201, Regierung Osnabrück, Polizeidezernante
Rep-430-303, Regierung Osnabrück, Gesundheitswesen
Rep-430-304, Regierung Osnabrück, Sozialwesen, Vertriebenen- und Flüchtlingsangelegenheiten
Rep-439, Geheime Staatspolzei – Staatspolizestelle Osnabrück, 1934-45
Rep-610-Osn, Gewerbeaufsichtsamt Osnabrück
Rep-640-Osn, Arbeitsamt Osnabrück
Rep-725a, Landes- Frauenklinik zu Osnabrück
Rep-726, Ernst-Moritz-Arndt-Gymnasium zu Osnabrück
Rep-727, Landeskrankenhaus Osnabrück
Rep-945, Staatsanwaltschaft Osnabrück
Rep-980, Entnazifizierungsausschüsse
Slg-54, Erlebnisberichte, Manuskripte und sonstige Materielle der NS Zeit

Nordrhein-westfälisches Staatsarchiv, Münster
Gen-Sta-Hamm-Ertinstanz, Generalstaatsanwaltschaft Hamm, Strafsachen, 1933-1945

2. Oral Sources

(a) Interviews carried out by Panikos Panayi
Adam, Günther, 2 August 2001*
Adel, Agnes and Annie, 5 July 2000*
Berger, Anneliese and, Hate, 12 July 2000*

Bräkling, Anneliese, 31 July 2000
Diehl, Anneliese, 15 August 2001*
Frank, Heinz, 13 August 2001*
Friedrich, Margret, 29 June 2000*
Funk, Werner, 16 August 2000*
Grün, Maria and Hans, 8 August 2000*
Heermann, Helmut, 26 June 2000
Herz, Josefa, 26 July 2000*
Kraft, Lora, 20 August 2001*
Krüger, Gertrud, 8 August 2001
Lorenz, Werner, Meyer, Lilo and Walter, Inge, 21 August 2000*
Mosse, Karl, 10 August 2001*
Ohl, Irmgard, 28 July 2000
Roberts, Dick, 30 August 2001*
Schloßer, Renate, 8 August 2000*
Scholl, Hilde, 3 September 2001*
Semnet, Marianne, 10 July 2000
Stein, Cilly, 28 June 2000*
Strauß, Gerhard, 22 August 2001*
Thiem, Hermann, 10 January 2001*
Wahlbrink, Josef, 9 August 2001*
Weiss, Hugo, 19 June 2000*
Wand, Elizabeth and Heinrich, 16 August 2001*

An asterisk indicates the use of a pseudonym.

(b) Institut Für Migrationsforschung und Interkulturelle Studien, Universität Osnabrück
Transcripts of interviews carried out with German refugees in Osnabrück

3. Printed Works

(a) *Official Publications*
Addressbuch der Stadt und Landkreis Osnabrück 1934/1935 (Osnabrück, 1934).
Addressbuch der Stadt und Landkreis Osnabrück 1938/1939 (Osnabrück, 1938).
Deutsche Arbeiter Front, *Arbeitsschule, Osnabrück 1936* (Osnabrück, 1936).
Deutsches Berufserziehungswerk, Gau Weser-Ems, Osnabrück, *Jeder macht mit – in den fördernden Lehrgemeinschaften für Berufstätige* (Osnabrück, 1941).
Deutsches Berufserziehungswerk, *Übungsstätten für Berufstätige* (Osnabrück, 1942).

Institut für deutsche Wirtschaftspropaganda, *'Braune Messe Osnabrück': vom 2. bis 10. September 1933 der Reichsführung der NS 'Hago'* (Osnabrück, 1933).

Statistische Jahresberichte der Stadt Osnabrück 1932 und 1933 (Osnabrück, 1934).

Statistisches Jahrbuch deutscher Gemeinde, 1934-41, 1949.

Statistisches Jahrbuch deutscher Städte, 1929-33.

Steinwascher, Gerd, ed., *Gestapo Osnabrück Meldet: Polizei und Regierungsberichte aus dem Regierungsbezirk Osnabrück aus den Jahren 1933 bis 1936* (Osnabrück, 1995).

The Strategic Air Offensive Against Germany, 1939-1945: Report of the British Bombing Survey Unit (London, 1998 reprint).

United States Strategic Bombing Survey: Overall Report, European War (Washington, DC, 1945).

'Verwaltungsberichte der Stadt Osnabrück', 1945-9.

Was Bietet Osnabrück, 1936-9.

(b) Newspapers and Periodicals
Daily Mail
Freie Presse
Friedensbote: Gemeindeblatt für St. Katharinen II Osnabrück
Kirchenbote der evangelisch-lutherischen Gemeinden Osnabrück
Kirchliches Amtsblatt für die Diöseze Osnabrück
Mitteilungen des Osnabrücker Vereins für Innere Mission im Regiereungsbezirk Osnabrück und des Evangelischen Wohlfahrtdienstes der Stadt Osnabrück
Mitteilungsblatt der Staatlichen Oberschule für Jungen
Neue Osnabrücker Zeitung
Neue Volksblätter
Neues Tageblatt
Niederdeutscher Kurier
Niedersächsischer Kurier
Nordwest-Nachrichten
OD-AL
OKD Werkzeitung
Osnabrücker Rundschau
Osnabrücker Tageblatt
Osnabrücker Volkszeitung
Osnabrücker Zeitung
Reichswächter
Schola Carolina
Stadtwächter

(c) Contemporary Books, Articles, Pamphlets and Memoirs on Osnabrück
50 Jahre Musikverein, 30 Jahre Städtischer Orchester Osnabrück (Osnabrück, 1949).

Deutsches Nationaltheater Osnabrück, *Rückblick auf der Spielzeit 1941-42* (Osnabrück, 1942).

Festschrift zur Fünfzigjahrfeier Zweigverein Osnabrück des Deutschen Alpenvereins, 1888-1938 (Osnabrück, 1938).

Friess, R., *75 Jahre Osnabrücker Kupfer und Drahtwerk* (Melle, 1948).

Hesse, Johannes, *Carolinger 1939 bis 1947: Erinnerungen eines ehemaligen Schülers* (Osnabrück, 1997).

Jagusch, Emil, *Leben Hinter Stacheldraht: Ein Osnabrücker überlebt der KZ Sachsenhausen* (Osnabrück, 1978).

Karwehl, Richard, 'Politisches Messiastum: Zur Auseinandersetzung zwischen Kirche und Nationalsozialismus', *Zwischen den Zeiten*, vol. 9 (1931), pp. 519-43.

Kremer, Hans, 'Erbhygienische Untersuchungen an Osnabrücker Hilfsschulen' (unpublished manuscript, Osnabrück, 1936).

Kolkmeyer, Walter, *Die Wirtschaftliche Verflechtung der Stadt Osnabrück* (Hanover, 1931).

Kulturveranstaltungen 1938/39 (Osnabrück, 1938).

Landwehr, Ludwig, *'interresant war's eigentlich immer!': Aus dem Lebenserringungen der Ludwig Landwehr* (Osnabrück, 1987).

Lehmann, Friedrich, ed., *Osnabrück* (Berlin, 1928).

Pelster, Werner, 'Selbstmord im Stadt-u. Landkreis Osnabrück' (unpublished University of Münster medical dissertation, 1943).

Schierbaum, Heinrich, *Die 'Weiße Wehr' und ihr Kampf ums Deutsche Reich und den 5. Weltwirtschaftsraum* (Osnabrück, 1933).

Schulte, Senator, 'Die Wohlfahrtspflege der Stadt', *Osnabrücker Jahrbuch*, vol. 2 (1929), pp. 137-41.

B. SECONDARY SOURCES

1. Books, Articles, Pamphlets, Manuscripts and Theses on Osnabrück

30 Jahre Männergesangverein Osnabrücker Kupfer und Drahtwerk, 1922-1952 (Osnabrück, 1952).

50 Jahre Musikverein, 30 Jahre Städtischer Orchester Osnabrück (Osnabrück, 1949).

50 Jahre Osnabrücker Symphonie Orchester (Osnabrück, 1969)

100 Jahre Rotes Kreuz in Osnabrück, 1870-1970 (Osnabrück, 1970).

Antifaschistischer Arbeitskreis Osnabrück, ed., *Osnabrücker Arbeiter im Widerstand* (Osnabrück, 1987).

Arbeitsgemeinschaft der Ursulaschule, *Osnabrück 1933-1945* (Osnabrück, 1983).

Arbeitsgemeinschaft Sozialdemokratischer Frauen, Unterbezirk Osnabrück Stadt, *Vor 50 Jahren: Wie Frauen das Kriegsende erlebten* (Osnabrück, 1996).

Arbeitsgruppe des Graf-Stauffenberg-Gymnasiums, Osnabrück, *Ein anderer Stadtführer: Verfolger und Verfolgte zur Zeit des Nationalsozialismus in Osnabrück*, 4th edition (Osnabrück, 2000).

Asaria, Z., *Zur Geschichte der Juden in Osnabrück und Umgebung: Zur Weihe der Synagoge in Osnabrück* (Osnabrück, 1969).

Bade, Klaus J., Meier, Hans-Bernd, and Parisius, Bernhard, eds, *Zeitzeugen im Interview: Flüchtlinge und Vertriebene im Raum Osnabrück nach 1945* (Osnabrück, 1997).

Becker, Heidrun, 'Der Osnabrücker Kreis 1931-1939', in Heinrich Grosse, Hans Otte and Joachim Perels, eds, *Bewahren oder Bekennen? Die hannoversche Landeskirche im Nationalsozialismus* (Hanover, 1996), pp. 43-104.

Berger, Eva, *Wer bürgt für die Kosten? Zur Sozialgeschichte des Krankenhauses: 125 Jahre Stadt-Krankenhaus Osnabrück* (Bramsche, 1991).

Berger, Eva, *Die Würde des Menschen ist unantastbar: Niedersächsisches Landeskrankenhaus Osnabrück: Eine Psychiatriegeschichte* (Bramsche, 1999).

Berger, Eva, Jaehner, Inge, Junk, Peter, Kaster, Karl Jeorg, Meinz, Manfred, and Zimmer, Wendelin, *Felix Nussbaum: Art Defamed, Art in Exile, Art in Resistance* (Bramsche, 1995).

Borck, Heinz-Günther, 'Chronik der Handwerkskammer Osnabrück, 1900-1975', in Handwerkskammer Osnabrück, ed., *Geschichte des Osnabrücker Handwerks* (Osnabrück, 1975), pp. 355-509.

Brenner, K., 'Dokumentation über die Juden in Osnabrück' (unpublished manuscript, 1978).

Brinkwerth, Willy, 'Aus der Geschichte der Kolpingfamilie Osnabrück-Zentral', in Kolpingfamilie Osnabrück-Zentral, ed., *Festschrift zur Hundertjahrfeier der Kolpingfamilie Osnabrück-Zentral* (Osnabrück, 1959), pp. 10-17.

Bührmann-Peters, Frank, 'Dort Haben wir an und für sich gar nicht gemerkt, daß wir Gefangene waren: Der Arbeitseinsatz von Strafgefangenen aus den Emlandslagern im Raum Osnabrück', *Osnabrücker Mitteilungen*, vol. 103 (1998), pp. 205-36.

Caritasverband für die Diözese Osnabrück e.v., *Festschrift zum 50 jährigen Bestehen des Diözesan-Caritasverbandes Osnabrück 1916-1966: Berichte vom Dienst der Kirche an den Menschen* (Osnabrück, 1966).

Carl, Anja, 'Der Landesverband Osnabrück der Deutschnationalen Volkspartei (DNVP) von 1918 bis zum Ende der Weimarer Republik: Geschichte, Organization, Politik' (unpublished University of Osnabrück MA thesis, 1995).

Diehl, Jürgen, 'Unterhaltung und Propaganda: Osnabrücker Filmtheater im Zweiten Weltkrieg', *Osnabrücker Mitteilungen*, vol. 105 (2000), pp. 155-99.

Dumkow, M., and Roland, Frank, 'Geschichte der KPD Ortsgruppe Osnabrück, 1919-1933' (unpublished 2 volume manuscript, Osnabrück, 1975).

Engelman, Josef, 'Die Politik der DNVP im Landesverband Osnabrück, 1930-1933' (unpublished manuscript, Osnabrück, 1970).

Festschrift Anlässlich des 100. jährigen bestehens des Osnabrücker Turnvereins ev (Osnabrück, 1961).

Fisser-Bömer, Ursula, *Zwangsarbeit in Osnabrück* (Osnabrück, 1982).

Gander, Michael, 'Beziehungen zwischen sowjetischen Zwangsarbeitern und deutscher Bevölkerung in Osnabrück', in Babette Quinkert, ed., *'Wir sind die Herren dieses Landes': Ursachen, Verlauf und Folgen des Deutschen Überfalls auf die Sowjetunion* (Hamburg, 2002), pp 154-65.

Gartmann, Franz, and Reichel, Wolfgang, 'Aufstieg und Machtübernahme der NSDAP in Osnabrück' (unpublished manuscript, Osnabrück, 1974).

Geschichtsgruppe Arbeit und Leben in Osnabrück, *Freiheit-Krise-Diktatur: Zur Verfolgung der Gewerkschaften in Osnabrück 1933* (Bramsche, 1983).

Glufke, Dirk, 'Richard Karwehls "Politisches Messiastum: Zur Auseinandersetzung zwischen Kirche und Nationalsozialismus"', *Jahrbuch der Gesellschaft für niedersächsische Kirchengeschichte*, vol. 90 (1992), pp. 201-17.

Glüsenkamp, Carsten, 'Die Gleichschaltung der Presse in Osnabrück, 1933-34' (unpublished MA thesis, University of Münster, 1992).

Greiwe, Jutta, 'Die evangelische Kirche in Osnabrück 1933-1939' (unpublished University of Osnabrück MA dissertation, 1992).

Grove, Thomas, 'Die Entfernung des Osnabrücker Reichstagsabgeordneten Dr Johannes Drees aus seinem Amt 1933: Gleichschaltungsmaßnahme und politische Verfolgung', *Osnabrücker Mitteilungen*, vol. 103 (1998), pp. 259-66.

Haverkamp, Michael, and Teuteberg, Hans-Jürgen, eds, *Unterm Strich: Von der Winkelkrämerei zum E-Commerce: Eine Austellung des Museums Industriekultur im Rahm des 175. Bestehen der Sparkasse Osnabrück* (Bramsche, 2000).

Heheman, Rainer, *Biographisches Handbuch zur Geschichte der Region Osnabrück* (Bramsche, 1990).

Hehl, Ulrich von, 'Bischof Berning und das Bistum Osnabrück im Dritten Reich', *Osnabrücker Mitteilungen*, vol. 86 (1986), pp. 83-104.

Hein-Janke, Ewald, 'Die Gestapo und die Osnabrücker Kirchengemeinden 1934/5', *Junge Kirche*, vol. 39 (1978), pp. 287-90.

Heuer, Paul-Josef, 'Die "Stadtwächterbewegung" in Osnabrück von 1929 bis 1931' (unpublished manuscript, Osnabrück, 1984).

Hoffmeyer, Ludwig, et. al., *Chronik der Stadt Osnabrück* 6th Edn (Osnabrück, 1995).

Höweler, Horst and Hartelt, Horst, *100 Jahre Sport in Osnabrück: Die Erste reich illustrierte Osnabrücker Sportchronik* (Osnabrück, 1948).

Issmer, Volker, *Das Arbeitserziehungslager Ohrbeck bei Osnabrück: Eine Dokumentation* (Osnabrück, 2000).

Issmer, Volker, 'Hitlerjungen – Flakhelfer – Edelweißpiraten: Jugendliche zwischen Anpassung und Widerstand, verdeutlicht an Beispielen aus der Region Osnabrück-Emsland', *Osnabrücker Mitteilungen*, vol. 107 (2002), pp. 207-32.

Issmer, Volker, *Niederländer im Verdammten Land: Zeugnisse der Zwangsarbiet von Niederlanden im Raum Osnabrück während des Zweiten Weltkrieges* (Osnabrück, 1998).

Issmer, Volker, "'…Wegen Arbeitsbummlei für die Dauer von 8 Wochen in den AZL.-Ahaus/Westf. Eingewiesen": Frauen aus Osanbrück im Arbeitserziehungslager Ahaus', *Osnabrücker Mitteilungen*, vol. 106 (2001), pp. 303-11.

Issmer, Volker, 'Zum Bombenräumen nach Osnabrück: KZ-Häftlinge aus dem Lengerichen Tunnel in unserer Stadt', *Osnabrücker Mitteilungen*, vol. 108 (2003), pp. 179-88.

Junk, Peter, and Sellmeyer, Martina, *Stationen auf dem Weg nach Auschwitz: Entrechtung, Vertreibung, Vernichtung: Juden in Osnabrück, 1900-1945*, 3rd Edn, (Osnabrück, 1989).

Kühling, Karl, *Die Juden in Osnabrück* (Osnabrück, 1969).

Kühling, Karl, *Osnabrück, 1925-1933* (Osnabrück, 1963).

Kühling, Karl, *Osnabrück 1933-1945: Stadt im Dritten Reich* (Osnabrück, 1964).

Kühling, Karl, *Theater in Osnabrück: Im Wandel der Jahrhunderte* (Osnabrück, 1959).

Kunst, Dieter, *The Karmann Story: Germany's Coachbuilder to the World*, 2nd Edn (Osnabrück, 1996).

Matysiak, Stefan, 'Die britischen Heeresgruppenzeitungen und die Wiedergeburt der niedersächsischen Lokalpresse 1945/6', *Osnabrücker Mitteilungen*, vol. 107 (2002), pp. 233-51.

Nettelnsrot, Konrad, 'Der 1. Mai in Osnabrück: Die "Arbeiter-Maifeier" als Kampf- und Festtag der Arbeiterbewegung', *Osnabrücker Mitteilungen*, vol. 93 (1988), pp. 151-78.

Ordelheide, Karl, *Am Ende War der Anfang: Osnabrück, 1945-1948* (Osnabrück, 1982).

Osege, Margret, 'Vergleichende Untersuchung über sozialhygienische Probleme in der Stadt Osnabrück vor und nach dem zweiten Weltkrieges' (unpublished University of Münster medical dissertation, 1949).

Paech, Anne, *Kino zwischen Stadt und Land: Geschichte des Kinos in der Provinz Osnabrück* (Marburg, 1985).

Panayi, Panikos, 'Exploitation, Criminality, Resistance: The Everyday Life of Foreign Workers and Prisoners of War in the German Town of Osnabrück, 1939-49', *Journal of Contemporary History*, vol. 40 (2005), pp. 483-502.

Panayi, Panikos, 'The Persecution of German Romanies: The Case of Osnabrück, 1933-46', *Patterns of Prejudice*, vol. 37 (2003), pp. 377-99.

Panayi, Panikos, 'Victims, Perpetrators and Bystanders in a German Town: The Jews of Osnabrück Before, During and After the Third Reich', *European History Quarterly*, vol. 33 (2003), pp. 451-92.

Pax Christi – Basisgruppe Osnabrück und dem Antifaschistischen Arbeitskreis Osnabrück, eds, *SpureNsuche: Osnabrück 1933-1945* (Osnabrück, 1995).

Peiffer, Lorenz, 'Das Amt "K" und seine nachgeordneten regionalen Dienstellen: Kreissportlehrer im Regierungsbezirk Osnabrück: Ein Beitrag zur Alltagsgeschichte des Schulturnens im Nationalsozialismus', in Wolfgang Buss and Arnd Krüger, eds, *Sportgeschichte: Traditionspflege und Wertewandel* (Duderstadt, 1984), pp. 197-211.

Poppe, Roswitha, 'Denkmalspflege in Osnabrücker Raum während und nach dem Kriege', *Mitteilungen des Vereins für Geschichte und Landkunde von Osnabrück*, vol. 62 (1947), pp. 221-32.

Recker, Klemens-August, *'meinen volke und meinen Herrgott dienen...': Das Gymnasium Carolinum zwischen partieller Kontinuität und Resistenz in der NS-Zeit* (Osnabrück, 1989).

Recker, Klemens-August, *'Wem wollt ihr Glauben?' Bischof Berning im Dritten Reich* (Paderborn, 1998).

Reiter, Raimond, 'Das Erbgensundheitsgericht Osnabrück und die Sterilisationsverfahren nach dem "Gestz zur Verhütung erbkranken Nachwuchses" vom 14. Juli 1933', *Osnabrücher Mitteilungen*, vol. 110 (2005), pp. 211-22.

Reiter, Raimond, '"Heimtücke" und "Volksschädlinge": Osnabrücker vor dem Sondergericht Hannover in der NS-Zeit', *Osnabrücker Mitteilungen*, vol. 103 (1998), pp. 267-76.

Rickling, Matthias, *Der Tag, an dem Osnabrück Unterging: 13. September 1944* (Gudensberg-Gleichen, 2004).

Robben, B., *Die Herz-Jesu-Kirche in Osnabrück: Enstehung, Zerstörung, Wiederaufbau* (Osnabrück, 1955).

Schachtebek, Rudolf and Zimmer, Wendelin, *'die uns kein Teufel rauben kann': Vier Jahrzehnte Demokratie in Osnabrück seit 1945* (Bramsche, 1991).

Schipper, Uwe, ed., *400 Jahre Ratsgymnasium Osnabrück* (Bramsche, 1985).

Schroeder, Edgar, *Osnabrück: So Wie Es War*, 3 Volumes (Düsseldorf, 1981-1987)

Schroeder, Edgar, *Osnabrück im 19. Jahrhundert* (Düsseldorf, 1995).

Schubert, Stefan, *Sainsonarbeit am Kanal: Rekrutierung, Arbeists- und Lebensverhältnisse ausländischer Arbeitskräfte beim Bau des Mittelandkanals im Osnbrücker Land 1910-1916* (Frankfurt, 2005).

Seegrün, Wolfgang, 'Bischof Berning von Osnabrück und die katholischen Lainverbände in den Verhandlungen um Artikel 31 der Reichskonkordats 1933-1936', *Osnabrücker Mitteilungen*, vol. 80 (1973), pp. 151-82.

Segschneider, Ernst Helmut, 'Not kennt kein Gebot: Formen der Nahrungsbeschaffung nach dem Zweiten Weltkrieg im Raum Osnabrück', *Rheinisch-westfälische Zeitschrift für Volkskunde*, vols 34-5 (1989-90), pp. 205-38.

Segschneider, Ernst Helmut, 'Osnabrück im "achten Kriegsjahr": zwei Skizzen nach Zeitzeugenberichten', in Nils-Arvid Bringéus, ed., *Wandel der Volkskultur in Europa*, vol. 2 (Münster, 1988), pp. 855-65.

SPD Osnabrück, *1933-1983: Machtergreifung der Nationalsozialisten in Osnabrück* (Osnabrück, 1983).

Sportverein Eversburg, *75 Jahre, 1894-1969* (Osnabrück, 1969).

Spratte, Wido, *Im Anflug auf Osnabrück: Die Bombenangriffe, 1940-1945* (Osnabrück, 1985).

Spratte, Wido, Zwischen Trümmern: Osnabrück in den Jahren 1945 bis 1948 (Osnabrück, 1990).

St Ursula Osnabrück, *Festschrift zum Hundertjähriges Schuljubiläum* (Osnabrück, 1965).

Steinwascher, Gerd, 'Dr Johannes Petermann – Burgermeister und Regierungspräsident von Osnabrück', *Osnabrücker Mitteilungen*, vol. 106 (2001), pp. 247-59.

Steuwer, Carsten, 'Das Deutsche Nationaltheater in Osnabrück: Die Integration des Osnabrücker Theaters in die Nationalsozialistische Propagandamaschine', *Osnabrücker Mitteilungen*, vol. 106 (2001).

Thierbach, Dirk, and Blömer, Thomas, eds, *Vom Deutschen Metallarbeiterverband zur Industriegewerkschaft Metall: Texte und Dokumente aus der Geschichte der Metallarbeiter in Osnabrück* (Bramsche, 1990).

Uhrmacher, Heinrike, "'Resistenz oder Akzeptanz? Die evangelische Kirche in Osnabrück während der Zeit des Nationalsozialismus', *Osnabrücker Mitteilungen*, vol. 100 (1995), pp. 229-50.

van Kampen, Wilhelm, and Westphalen, Tilman, eds, *100 Jahre SPD in Osnabrück, 1875-1975: Ausgewählte Kapitel zur Geschichte der Arbeiterbewegung in Osnabrück* (Osnabrück, 1975).

Wegmann, Günter, *Das Kriegsende zwischen Ems und Weser* (Osnabrück, 1983).

Wienhold, Günter, *150 Jahre Osnabrücker Sportclub* (Osnabrück, 1999).

Wolf, Wilfried, ed., *Die Gründerzeit Osnabrücker Kunst* (Bramsche, 1986).

2. Select List of Publications on German History, 1929-49.

Abel, Theodore, *Why Hitler Came into Power* (Cambridge, MA, 1986 edition).

Abels, Kurt, *Ein Held War Ich Nicht: Als Kind und Jugendlicher in Hitlers Krieg* (Cologne, 1998).

Abelshauser, Werner, *Wirtschaft in Westdeutschland, 1945-1948: Rekonstruktion und Wirtschaftsbedingungen in der amerikanischen und britischen Zonen* (Stuttgart, 1975).

Allen, William Sheridan, *The Nazi Seizure of Power: The Experience of a Single German Town, 1922-1945* (London, 1966).

Angermund, Ralph, *Deutsche Richterschaft, 1919-1945: Krisenerfahrung, Illusion, politische Rechtsprechung* (Frankfurt, 1990).

Angermund, Ralph, "'Recht ist, was dem Volke nutzt': Zum Niedergang von Recht und Juztiz im Dritten Reich', in Karl Dietrich Bracher, Manfred Funke and Hans-Adolf Jacobsen, eds, *Deutschland, 1933-1945: Neue Studien zur nationalsozialistischen Herrschaft* (Düsseldorf, 1993), pp. 57-75.

August, Jochen, 'Die Entwicklung des Arbeitsmarkts in Deutschland in den 30er Jahren und der Masseneinsatz ausländischer Arbeitskräfte während des Zweiten Weltkrieges', *Archiv für Sozialgeschichte*, vol. 24 (1984), pp. 305-53.

Aust, Stefan and Burgdorff, Stefan, eds, *Die Flucht: Über die Vertreibung der Deutschen aus dem Osten* (Stuttgart, 2002).

Ayaß, Wolfgang, *'Asoziale' im Nationalsozialismus* (Stuttgart, 1995).

Bade, Klaus J., ed., *Fremde in Land: Zuwanderung und Eingliederung im Raum Niedersachsen seit dem Zweiten Weltkrieg* (Osnabrück, 1997).

Bagel-Bohlen, Anja, *Hitlers Industrielle Kriegsvorbereitungen, 1936-1939* (Coblenz, 1975)

Bajohr, Frank, *'Aryanization' in Hamburg: The Economic Exclusion of Jews and the Confiscation of their Property in Nazi Germany* (Oxford, 2002).

Balderston, Theo, *The Origins and Course of the German Economic Crisis, 1923-1932* (Berlin, 1993).

Bankier, David, *The Germans and the Final Solution: Public Opinion Under Nazism* (Oxford, 1992).

Bankier, David, ed., *Probing the Depths of German Antisemitism: German Society and the Persecution of the Jews, 1933-1941* (Oxford, 2000).

Baranowski, Shelley, *Strength Through Joy: Consumerism and Mass Tourism in the Third Reich* (Cambridge, 2004).

Bark, Dennis L. and Gress, David R., *A History of West Germany: From Shadow to Substance, 1945-1963*, Vol. 1, 2nd edn (Oxford, 1993).

Barkai, Avraham, *From Boycott to Annihilation: The Economic Struggle of the German Jews, 1933-1945* (Hanover, NH, 1989).

Barkai, Avraham, *Nazi Economics: Ideology, Theory and Policy* (Oxford, 1990).

Bastian, Till, *Homosexuellen im Dritten Reich: Geschichte einer Verfolgung* (Munich, 2000).

Bastian, Till, *Sinti und Roma im Dritten Reich: Geschichte einer Verfolgung* (Munich, 2001).

Beck, Earl R., *Under the Bombs: The German Home Front, 1942-1945* (Lexington, 1986).

Bellon, Bernard P., *Mercedes in Peace and War: German Automobile Workers, 1903-1945* (New York, 1990).

Benz, Wolfgang, ed., *Die Juden in Deutschland: Leben unter nationalsozialistischer Herrschaft* (Munich, 1993).

Benz, Wolfgang, ed., *Die Vertreibung der Deutschen aus dem Osten: Ursachen, Ereignisse, Folgen* (Frankfurt, 1995).

Benz, Wolfgang, *Von der Besatzungsherrschaft zur Bundesrepublik: Stationen einer Staatsgrundung, 1946-1949* (Frankfurt, 1984).

Benz, Wolfgang, Paucker, Arnold and Pulzer, Peter, eds, *Jüdisches Leben in der Weimarer Republik* (Tübingen, 1998)

Benz, Wolfgang and Pehle, Walter H., eds, *Encyclopedia of German Resistance to the Nazi Movement* (New York, 1997).

Benzenhöfer, Udo, and Eckert, Wolfgang E., eds, *Medizin im Spielfilm des Nationalsozialismus* (Tecklenburg, 1990).

Bergen, Doris L., *The German Christian Movement in the Third Reich* (London, 1996).

Berlekamp, Brigitte and Röhr, Werner, eds, *Terror, Herrschaft und Alltag: Probleme einer Sozialgeschichte des deutschen Faschismus* (Münster, 1995).

Berliner Geschichtswerkstatt, ed., *Alltagsgeschichte, Subjektivität und Geschichte: Zur Theorie und Praxis von Alltagsgeschichte* (Münster, 1994).

Besier, Gerhard, *Die Kirchen und das Dritte Reich: Spaltungen und Abwehrkämpfe, 1934-1937* (Munich, 2001).

Besier, Gerhard, and Vollnhalls, Clemens, eds, *Repression und Selbstbehauptung: Die Zeugen Jehovas unter der NS und der SED Diktatur* (Berlin, 2003).

Bessel, Richard, *Political Violence and the Rise of Nazism: The Storm Troopers in Eastern Germany, 1925-1934* (London, 1984).

Bessel, Richard and Schumann, Dirk, eds, *Life After Death: Approaches to a Cultural and Social History of Europe During the 1940s and 1950s* (Cambridge, 2003).

Bethlehem, Siegfried, *Heimatvertreibung, DDR-Flucht, Gastarbeiterwanderung: Wanderungsströme und Wanderungspolitik in der Bundesrepublik Deutschland* (Stuttgart, 1982).

Betts, Paul and Eghigian, Greg, eds, *Pain and Prosperity: Reconsidering Twentieth Century German History* (Stanford, CA, 2003).

Blackburn, Gilmer W., *Education in the Third Reich: Race and History in Nazi Textbooks* (Albany, NY, 1985).

Blaich, Fritz, *Wirtschaft und Rüstung im Dritten Reich* (Düsseldorf, 1987).

Bloxham, Donald, *Genocide on Trial: War Crimes and the Formation of Holocaust History and Memory* (Oxford, 2001).

Bock, Gisela, *Zwangssterilization im Nationalsozialismus: Studien zur Rassenpolitik und Frauenpolitik* (Opladen, 1986).

Böddeker, Günter, *Die Flüchtlinge: Die Vertreibung der Deutschen im Osten* (Berlin, 1997).

Boelcke, Willi A., *Der Schwarzmarkt, 1945-1948: Vom Überleben nach dem Krieg* (Brunswick, 1986).

Borsdorf, Ulrich, and Jamin, Mathilde, *Überleben im Krieg: Kriegserfahrungen in einer Industrieregion, 1939-1945* (Hamburg, 1989).

Boyens, Armin, et. al., *Kirchen in der Nachkriegszeit: Vier Zeitgeschichtliche Beiträge* (Göttingen, 1979).

Bracher, Karl Dietrich, Sauer, Wolfgang, and Schulz, Gerhard, *Die Nationalsozialistische Machtergreifung: Studien zur Errichtung der totalitären Herrschaftsystem in Deustchland, 1933/4* (Cologne, 1960).

Brandenberg, Hans-Christian, *Die Geschichte der HJ: Weg und Irwege einer Generation* (Cologne, 1968).

Broszat, Martin, *The Hitler State: The Foundation and Development of the Internal Structure of the Third Reich* (Harlow, 1981).

Broszat, Martin, Henke, Klaus Dietmar and Woller, Hans, eds, *Von Stalingrad zur Währungsreform: Zur Sozialgeschichte des Umbruchs in Deutschland* (Munich, 1988).

Buddruss, Michael, *Totale Erziehung für den totalen Krieg: Hitlerjugend und nationalsozialistische Jugendpolitik*, 2 Volumes (Munich, 2003).

Bruss, Regina, *Die Bremer Juden unter Nationalsozialismus* (Bremen, 1983).

Burgdorff, Stephan, and Hobbe, Christian, eds, *Als Feuer vom Himmel Fiel: Der Bombenkrieg in Deutschland* (Munich, 2003)

Burleigh, Michael, *Ethics and Extermination: Reflections on Nazi Genocide* (Cambridge, 1997).

Burleigh, Michael, *The Third Reich: A New History* (London, 2000).

Burleigh, Michael and Wippermann, Wolfgang, *The Racial State: Germany 1933-1945* (Cambridge, 1991).

Caplan, Jane, ed., *Nazism, Fascism and the Working Classes: Essays by Tim Mason* (Cambridge, 1995).

Clemens, Gabriele, *Britische Kulturpolitik in Deutschland, 1945-1949* (Stuttgart, 1997).

Connelly, Mark, *Reaching for the Stars: A New History of Bomber Command in World War II* (London, 2001).

Conway, J. S., *The Nazi Persecution of the Churches, 1933-45* (London, 1968).

Crew, David F., '*Alltagsgeschichte:* A New German Social History "from Below?"', *Central European History*, vol. 22 (1989)

Crew, David F., *Germans on Welfare: From Weimar to Hitler* (Oxford, 1998).

Crew, David F., ed., *Nazism and German Society* (London, 1994).

Cuomo, Glenn, R., ed., *National Socialist Cultural Policy* (New York, 1995).

Dabel, Gerhard, *KLV: Die erweiterte Kinder-Land-Verschickung: KLV-Lager, 1940-1945* (Freiburg, 1981).

Diem, Carl, *Der deutsche Sport in der Zeit des Nationalsozialismus* (Cologne, 1980).

Długoborski, Waclaw, ed., *Zweiter Weltkrieg und sozialer Wandel* (Göttingen, 1981).

Döring, Hans-Joachim, *Die Zigeuner im nationalsozialistischen Staat* (Hamburg, 1964).

Durth, Werner, 'Vom Überleben: Zwischen Totalem Krieg und Währungsreform', in Ingeborg Flagge, ed., *Geschichte des Wohnens*, Vol. 5, *1945 bis Heute: Aufbau, Neubau, Umbau* (Stuttgart, 1999), pp. 17-79.

Ecker, Paul, *Ernährungskrise und Nachkriegsgesellschaft: Bauern und Arbeiterschaft in Bayern, 1943-1953* (Stuttgart, 1990).

Eicholtz, Dietrich, *Geschichte der deutschen Kriegswirtschaft*, 3 Volumes (Berlin, 1971-96).

Eichholtz, Dietrich, ed., *Krieg und Wirtschaft: Studien zur deutschen Wirtschaftsgeschichte, 1939-1945* (Berlin, 1999).

Eitner, Hans-Jürgen, *Hitlers Deutsche: Das Ende einer Tabus* (Gernsbach, 1991).

Engbring-Romang, Udo, *Marburg. Auschwitz: Zur Verfolgung der Sinti in Marburg und Umgebung* (Frankfurt, 1998).

Engels, Marc, *Zwangsarbeit in der Stadt Aachen: Ausländereinsatz in einer westdeutschen Grenzstadt während des zweiten Weltkrieges* (Aachen, 2002).

Engelsing, Tobias, *'Wir Sind in Deutschland und nicht in Russland': Eine Alltagsgeschichte der Volksschule in den Jahren 1933-1949 am Beispiel der Stadt Radolfzell am Bodensee* (Constance, 1987).

Erbe, Dirk, ed., *Gleichgeschaltet: Der Nazi Terror gegen Gewerkschaften und Berufsverbände, 1930 bis 1933* (Göttingen, 2001).

Erker, Paul, *Vom Heimatvertriebenen zum Neubürger, 1945-1955* (Wiesbaden, 1988).

Eschenberg, Theodor, *Jahre der Besatzung, 1945-1949* (Wiesbaden, 1989).

Evans, Richard J., *The Coming of the Third Reich* (London, 2003).

Evans, Richard., *The Third Reich in Power, 1933-1939* (London, 2006).

Evans, Richard J., and Geary, Dick, eds, *The German Unemployed: Experiences and Consequences of Mass Unemployment from the Weimar Republic to the Third Reich* (London, 1978).

Falter, Jürgen W., *Hitlers Wähler* (Munich, 1991).

Fest, Joachim C., *Staatsreich: Der Lange Weg zur 20. Juli* (Berlin, 1994).

Finker, Kurt, *Der 20. Juli 1944: Militärpolitik oder Revolution* (Berlin, 1994).

Fischer, Conan, *The German Communists and the Rise of Nazism* (London, 1991).

Fitzgibbon, Constantine, *Denazification* (London, 1969).

Focke, Harald and Reimer, Uwe, *Alltag unterm Hakenkreuz: Wie die Nazis das Leben der Deutschen veränderten* (Hamburg, 1979).

Frevert, Ute, *Women in German History: From Bourgeois Emancipation to Sexual Liberation* (Oxford, 1989).

Fricke-Finkelnberg, Renate, ed., *Nationalsozialismus und Schule: Amtliche Erlasse und Richtlinien, 1933-1945* (Opladen, 1989).

Friedlander, Saul, *Nazi Germany and the Jews: The Years of Persecution, 1933-39* (London, 1997).

Friedrich, Jörg, *Der Brand: Deutschland im Bombenkrieg 1940-1945* (Munich, 2002).

Fürstenau, Justus, *Entnazifizierung: Ein Kapital deutscher Nachkriegspolitik* (Berlin, 1969).

Galius, Manfred, *Protestantismus und Nationalsozialismus: Studien zur nationalsozialistischen Durchdringung des protestantischen Sozialmilieus in Berlin* (Cologne, 2001).

Gall, Lothar, and Pohl, Manfred, eds, *Unternehmen im Nationalsozialismus* (Munich, 1998).

Gansmüller, Christian, *Die Erbgesundheitspolitik des Dritten Reiches* (Cologne, 1987).

Garbe, Detlef, *Zwischen Widerstand und Martyrium: Die Zeugen Jehovas im 'Dritten Reich'* (Munich, 1993).

Garrett, Stephen A., *Ethics and Airpower in World War II: The British Bombing of German Cities* (New York, 1993).

Gellately, Robert, *Backing Hitler: Consent and Coercion in Nazi Germany* (Oxford, 2001).

Gellately, Robert, *The Gestapo and German Society: Enforcing Racial Policy 1933-1945* (Oxford, 1990).

Gellately, Robert, and Stolzfus, Nathan, eds, *Social Outsiders in Nazi Germany* (Oxford, 2001).

Gießmann, Thomas, and Marciniak, Rudolf, *'Fast sämtliche Kinder sind jetzt Weg': Quellen und Zeitzeugenberichte zur Kinderlandverschickung aus Rheine, 1941-1945* (Münster, 2001).

Goldhagen, Daniel John, *Hitler's Willing Executioners: Ordinary Germans and the Holocaust* (London, 1996).

Gollancz, Victor, *In Darkest Germany* (London, 1947).

Grab, Walter and Schoeps, Julius H., eds, *Juden in der Weimarer Republik* (Stuttgart, 1986).

Grayling, A. C., *Among the Dead Cities : Was the Allied Bombing of Civilians in WWII a Necessity or a Crime* (London, 2006).

Gregor, Neil, *Daimler Benz in the Third Reich* (London, 1998).

Gregor, Neil, 'A *Schicksalgemeinschaft*? Allied Bombing, Civilian Morale and Social Dissolution in Nuremberg, 1942-1945', *Historical Journal*, vol. 43 (2000), pp. 1051-1070.

Griech-Polelle, Beth A., *Bishop von Galen: German Catholicism and National Socialism* (London, 2002).

Gries, Rainer, *Die Rationen-Gesellschaft: Versorgungskampf und Vergleichsmentalität* (Munich, 1991).

Groehler, Olaf, *Bombenkrieg gegen Deutschland* (Berlin, 1990).

Grosse, Alfred, *Geschichte Deutschlands seit 1945: Eine Bilanz* (Munich, 1974).

Grube, Frank, and Richter, Gerhard, ed., *Flucht und Vertreibung: Deutschland zwischen 1944 and 1947* (Hamburg, 1980).

Gruchmann, Lothar, *Justiz im Dritten Reich, 1930-1940* (Munich, 1990).

Grunberger, Richard, *A Social History of the Third Reich* (London, 1991).

Gurland, A. R. L., Kirchheimer, Otto and Neumann, Franz, *The Fate of Small Businesses in the Third Reich* (New York, 1975)

Habe, Hans, *Im Jahre Null: Ein Beitrag zur Geschichte der deutschen Presse* (Munich, 1966).

Hachtmann, Rüdiger, *Industriearbeit im 'Dritten Reich': Untersuchungen zu den Lohn- und Arbeitsbedingungen in Deutschland* (Göttingen, 1989).

Hake, Sabine, *Popular Cinema of the Third Reich* (Austin, TX, 2001).

Hall, Daniel Stuart, *Film in the Third Reich: A Study of the German Cinema, 1933-1945* (Berkerley and Los Angeles, 1969).

Hamilton, Richard F., *Who Voted for Hitler* (Princeton, 1982).

Hampe, Erich, *Der Zivile Luftschutz im Zweiten Weltkrieg: Dokumentation und Erfahrungsberichte über Aufbau und Einsatz* (Frankfurt am Main, 1963).

Hansen, Rainer, *Das Ende des Dritten Reiches: Die Deutsche Kapitulation, 1945* (Stuttgart, 1966).

Harsch, Donna, *German Social Democracy and the Rise of Nazsim* (London, 1993).

Hastings, Max, *Bomber Command* (London, 1979).

Hearnden, Arthur, ed., *The British in Germany: Educational Reconstruction after 1945* (London, 1978).

Hehemann, Rainer, *Die 'Bekämpfung des Zigeunerwesens' in Wilheminischen Deutschland und in der Weimarer Republik* (Frankfurt am Main, 1979).

Hehl, Ulrich von, et. al., *Priester Unter Hitler's Terror,* 2 Volumes (Paderborn, 1996).

Heinemann, Elizabeth D., *What Difference Does a Husband Make? Women and Marital Status in Nazi and Postwar Germany* (London, 1999).

Heinemann, Manfred, ed., *Erziehung und Schulung im Dritten Reich,* 2 Volumes (Stuttgart, 1980).

Heise, Sabine, and Harenbrock, Gerburg, eds, *Geschichte und Gespräch: Kriegsende 1945 und Nachkriegszeit in Münster* (Münster, 1997).

Held, Jutta, *Kunst und Kunstpolitik in Deutschland, 1945-49: Kulturaufbau in Deutschland nach dem 2. Weltkrieg* (Berlin, 1981).

Helmreich, Ernst Christian, *The German Churches Under Hitler: Background, Struggle and Epilogue* (Detroit, 1979).

Hellfeld, Matthias von, and Klönne, Arno, eds, *Die betragene Generation: Jugend im Faschismus* (Cologne, 1985).

Herbert, Karl, *Kirche zwischen Aufbruch und Tradition: Entscheidungsjahre nach 1945* (Stuttgart, 1989).

Herbert, Ulrich, *A History of Foreign Labour in Germany, 1880-1980: Seasonal Workers/Forced Workers/Guest Workers* (Ann Arbor, MI, 1990).

Herbert, Ulrich, *Hitler's Foreign Workers: Enforced Labour in Germany under the Third Reich* (Cambridge, 1997).

Hermand, Jorst, *Als Pimpf in Polen: Erweiterte Kinderlandverschickung, 1940-1945* (Frankfurt, 1993).

Heuzeroth, Günther and Petrich, Johannes, eds, *Unter der Gewaltherrschaft des Nationalsozialismus, 1933-1945, Vorgestellt an den Ereignissen in Weser-Ems,* Vol. 1, *Verfolgte aus politischen Grunden* (Osnabrück, 1989).

Hilberg, Raul, *Perpetrators, Victims, Bystanders: The Jewish Catastrophe, 1933-1945* (London, 1993).

Hilger, Andreas, *Deutsche Kriegsgefangene in der Sowjetunion, 1941-1956: Kriegsgefangenenpolitik, Lageralltag und Errinerung* (Essen, 2000).

Hillmann, Jörg, and Zimmermann, John eds., *Kriegsende in Deutschland* (Munich, 2002).

Hirschfeld, Gerhard, ed., *The Policies of Genocide: Jews and Soviet Prisoners of War in Nazi Germany* (London, 1986).

Hohmann, Joachim S., *Geschichte der Zigeunerverfolgung in Deutschland*, 2nd edn (Frankfurt, 1988).

Homze, Edward L., *Foreign Workers in Nazi Germany* (Princeton, NJ, 1967).

Hong, Young-Sun, *Welfare, Modernity and the Weimar State, 1919-1933* (Princeton, NJ, 1998).

Horchem, Hans Josef, *Kinder im Krieg: Kindheit und Jugend im Dritten Reich* (Hamburg, 2000).

Hull, David Stewart, *Film in the Third Reich: A Study of the German Cinema, 1933-1945* (Berkeley, 1969).

Huttenbach, Henry, *The Destruction of the Jewish Community of Worms, 1933-1945: A Study of the Holocaust Experience in Germany* (New York, 1981).

Institut für Zeitgeschichte, *Alltagsgeschichte der NS-Zeit: Neue Perspektive oder Trivialisierung?* (Munich, 1984).

Jacobmeyer, Wolfgang, 'Jüdische Überlebende als "Displaced Persons": Untersuchungen zur Besatzungspolitik in den deutschen Westzonen und zur Zuwanderung osteuropäischer Juden 1945-1947', *Geschichte und Gesellschaft*, vol. 9 (1983).

Jacobmeyer, Wolfgang, *Vom Zwangsarbeiter zum heimatlosen Ausländer* (Göttingen, 1985).

Jahnke, Karl Heinz, *Hitlers letztes Angebot: Deutsche Jugend im sechsten Kriegsjahr, 1944/45* (Essen, 1993).

Jahnke, Karl Heinz, and Buddrus, Michael, eds, *Deutsche Jugend, 1933-1945* (Hamburg, 1989).

Jannsen, Gregor, *Das Ministerium Speer: Deutschlands Rüstung im Krieg* (Berlin, 1968).

Jarausch, Konrad H., and Geyer, Michael, *Shattered Past: Reconstructing German History* (Princeton, 2003).

Jellonek, Burkhard, *Homosexuellen unter dem Hakenkreuz: Die Verfolgung Homosexuellen im Dritten Reich* (Paderborn, 1990).

Johnson, Eric, *The Nazi Terror: Gestapo, Jews and Ordinary Germans* (London, 1999).

Jordan, Ulrike, ed., *Conditions of Surrender: Britons and Germans Witness the End of the War* (London, 1997).

Kaiser, Ernst and Knom, Michael, *'Wir Lebten und Schliefen zwischen den Toten': Rüstungsproduktion, Zwangsarbeit and Vernichtung in den Frankfurter Adlerwerken*, 3rd edn (Frankfurt, 1998).

Kallis, Aristotle A., *Nazi Propaganda and the Second World War* (Basingstoke, 2005).

Kalt, Robert, *Rationierung der Nahrungsmittel und Schwarzer Markt in der Kriegswirtschaft* (Fribourg, 1951).

Kaminsky, Annette, ed., *Heimkehr, 1948* (Munich, 1998).

Kaplan, Marion A., *Between Dignity and Despair: Jewish Life in Nazi Germany* (Oxford, 1998).

Kater, Michael H., *Hitler Youth* (London, 2004).

Kater, Michael H., *Doctors Under Hitler* (London, 1989).

Kater, Michael H., *The Nazi Party: A Social Profile of Members and Leaders, 1919-1945* (Oxford, 1983).

Kater, Michael H., *The Twisted Muse: Musicians and their Music in the Third Reich* (Oxford, 1997).

Kauders, Anthony, *German Politics and the Jews: Düsseldorf and Nuremberg, 1910-1933* (Oxford, 1996).

Keinemann, Friedrich, *Sieben Entscheidende Jahre: Hamm, 1928-1935* (Bochum, 1991).

Kenrick, Donald, and Puxon, Grattan, *The Destiny of Europe's Gypsies* (London, 1972).

Kershaw, Ian, *Hitler, 1889-1936: Hubris* (London, 1998).

Kershaw, Ian, *Hitler, 1936-1945: Nemesis* (London, 2000).

Kershaw, Ian, *The 'Hitler Myth': Image and Reality in the Third Reich* (Oxford, 1987).

Kershaw, Ian, *Popular Opinion and Political Dissent in the Third Reich: Bavaria 1933-1945* (Oxford, 1983).

Kettenacker, Lothar, ed., *Ein Volk von Opfern? Die Neue Debatte um den Bombenkrieg, 1940-45* (Berlin, 2003).

Kitchen, Martin, *Nazi Germany at War* (London, 1995).

Klaus, Martin, *Mädchen im 3. Reich: Der Bund Deutcher Mädel* (Cologne, 1998).

Klee, Ernst, *'Euthanasie' im NS-Staat: Die 'Vernichtung lebensunwerten Lebens'* (Frankfurt, 1985).

Klee, Katja, *'Im Luftschutzkeller des Reiches': Evakuierte in Bayern, 1939-1953: Politik, soziale Lage, Erfahrungen* (Munich, 1999).

Kleßmann, Christoph, ed., *Nicht nur Hitlers Krieg: Der Zweite Weltkrieg in Deutschland* (Düsseldorf, 1989).

Klinksiek, Dorothee, *Die Frau im NS-Staat* (Stuttgart, 1982).

Klönne, Arno, *Jugend im Dritten Reich: Die Hitlerjugend und ihre Gegner* (Cologne, 1999).

Knopp, Guido, *Hitler's Children* (Stroud, 2000)

Koch, H. W., *The Hitler Youth: Origins and Development* (London, 1975).

Koch, Horst-Adalbert, *Flak: Die Geschichte der deutschen Flakartillerie und der Einsatz der Luftwaffenhelfer*, 2nd Edition (Bad Nauheim, 1965).

Kock, Gerhard, *'Der Führer sorgt für unsere Kinder': Die Kinderlandverschickung im Zweiten Weltkrieg* (Paderborn, 1997).

Kolb, Eberhard, *The Weimar Republic* (London, 1988).

König, Ulrich, *Sinti und Roma unter dem Nationalsozialismus: Verfolgung und Widerstand* (Bochum, 1989).

Koonz, Claudia, *Mothers in the Fatherland: Women, the Family and Nazi Politics* (London, 1987).

Kramer, Michael, *The West German Economy, 1945-1955* (Oxford, 1991).

Krause, Michael, *Flucht vor dem Bombenkrieg: Umquartierung im Zweiten Weltkrieg und die Wiedereingliederung der Evakuierten in Deutschland* (Düsseldorf, 1997).

Kruedener, Jürgen Baron von, ed., *Economic Crisis and Political Collapse: The Weimar Republic, 1924-1933* (Oxford, 1990).

Kuhn, Annette, ed., *Frauen in der Deutschen Nachkriegszeit*, 2 Volumes (Düsseldorf, 1984-6).

Kuhn, Annette, ed., *Frauenleben im NS-Alltag* (Pfaffenweiler, 1994).

Kurowkski, Franz, *Luftkrieg über Deutschland* (Düsseldorf, 1977).

Kwiet, Konrad, 'The Ultimate Refuge: Suicide in the Jewish Community under the Nazis', *Leo Baeck Institute Year Book*, vol. 29 (1984), pp. 135-67.

Lange, Irmgard, *Entnazifizierung in Nordrhein-Westfalen: Richtlinien, Anweisungen, Organization* (Siegburg, 1976).

Larass, Claus, *Der Zug der Kinder: Die Evakuierung 5 Millionen deutscher Kinder im 2. Weltkrieg* (Frankfurt, 1992).

Lauber, Heinz and Rothstein, Dirgit, *Der 1. Mai unter dem Hakenkreuz: Hitlers 'Machtergreifung' in Arbeiterschaft und in Betrieben* (Gerlingen, 1983).

Lehmann, Albrecht, *Gefangenschaft und Heimkehr: Deutsche Kriegsgefangene in der Sowjetunion* (Munich, 1986).

Lehmann, Albrecht, *Im Fremden ungewollt zuhaus: Flüchtlinge und Vertriebene in Westdeutschland* (Munich, 1990).

Lemberg, Eugen and Edding, Friedrich, eds, *Die Vertriebenen in Westdeutschland: Ihre Eingliederung und ihr Einfluss auf Gesellschaft, Wirtschaft, Politik und Geistleben*, 3 Volumes (Kiel, 1959).

Lessing, Alfred, *Mein Leben im Versteck: Wie ein deutscher Sinti den Holocaust überlebte* (Düsseldorf, 1930).

Levi, Erik, *Music in the Third Reich* (Basingstoke, 1994).

Lewy, Guenter, *The Catholic Church Under the Nazis* (London, 1964).

Lewy, Guenter, *The Nazi Persecution of the Gypsies* (Oxford, 2000).

Lissina, Hartmut E., *Nationale Sportsfeste im nationalsozialistischen Deutschland* (Mannheim, 1997).

London, John, ed., *Theatre Under the Nazis* (Manchester, 2000).

Longerich, Peter, *Die Braune Bataillone: Geschichte der SA* (Munich, 1989).

Longerich, Peter, *Politik der Vernichtung: Eine Gesamtdarstellung der nationalsozialistischen Judenverfolgung* (Munich, 1998).

Löwenthal, Richard, and von zur Mühlen, Patrick, eds, *Widerstand und Verweigerung im Dritten Reich, 1933-1945* (Berlin, 1982).

Lucassen, Leo, *Zigeuner: Die Geschichte eines polizeilichen Ordnungsbegriffes in Deutschland, 1700-1945* (Cologne, 1996).

Lüdtke, Alf, ed., *The History of Everyday Life: Reconstructing Historical Experiences and Ways of Life* (Princeton, NJ, 1995).

Lüttinger, Paul and Rossmann, Rita, *Integration der Vertriebenen: Eine Empirische Analyse* (Frankfurt, 1989).

Lutzerbäck, Rolf, *Die Bildungspolitik der Britischen Militärregierung im Spannungsfeld zwischen 'Education' und 'Re-Education' in ihrer Bezatzungszone, insbesondere in Schleswig-Holstein und Hamburg in den Jahren 1945-7*, 2 Volumes (Frankfurt, 1991).

McElligot, Anthony, *Contested City: Municipal Politics and the Rise of Nazism in Altona* (Ann Arbor, 1998).

Mallmann, Klaus-Michael, *Kommunisten in der Weimarer Republik: Sozialgeschichte einer revolutionären Bewegung* (Darmstadt, 1996).

Mallmann, Klaus-Michael, Paul, Gerhard and Hermann, Hans-Walter, eds, *Widerstand und Verweigerung im Saarland, 1933-1945*, 3 Volumes (Bonn, 1989-95).

Manwell, Roger, and Frankel, Heinrich, *The July Plot: The Attempt in 1944 on Hitler's Life and the Men Behind It* (London, 1964).

Margalit, Gilad, *Germany and Its Gypsies: A Post-Auschwitz Ordeal* (Madison, WI, 2002).

Marschalck, Peter, *Bevölkerungsgeschichte Deutschlands im 19. und 20. Jahrhundert* (Frankfurt, 1984).

Marßolek, Inge, and von Soldern, Adelheid, eds, *Zuhören und Gehörtwerden: Radio im Nationalsozialismus* (Tübingen, 1988).

Mason, Timothy W., *Social Policy in the Third Reich: The Working Classes and the 'National Community'* (Oxford, 1993).

Matthias, Erich and Morsey, Rudolf, eds, *Das Ende der Parteien 1933: Darstellungen und Dokumente* (Düsseldorf, 1960).

Mazur, Werner, *Das Dritte Reich: Alltag in Deutschland von 1933 bis 1945* (Munich, 1998).

Meehan, Patricia, *A Strange Enemy People: Germans under the British* (London, 2001).

Merkatz, ed., Hans Joachim von, *Aus Trümmern wurden Fundamente: Vertriebene, Flüchtlinge, Aussiedler* (Düsseldorf, 1979).

Merkl, Peter H., *Political Violence under the Swastika: 581 Early Nazis* (Princeton, 1975).

Meyer, Beate, *'Jüdische Mischlinge': Rassenpolitik und Verfolgungserfahrung* (Hamburg, 1999).

Meyer, Michael, *The Politics of Music in the Third Reich* (New York, 1991).

Meyer, Sybille, and Schulze, Eva, eds, *Wie Wir das Alles Geschafft Haben: Alleinstehende Frauen Berichten über ihr Leben nach 1945* (Munich, 1988).

Michalka, Wolfgang, ed., *Der Zweite Weltkrieg: Analysen, Grundzüge, Forschungsbilanz* (Munich, 1989).

Middlebrook, Martin and Everitt, Chris, *The Bomber Command War Diaries: An Operational Reference Book, 1939-1945* (London, 1985).

Milward, Alan S., *The German Economy at War* (London, 1965).

Moeller, Robert G., *War Stories: The Search for a Usable Past in the Federal Republic of Germany* (London, 2001).

Moeller, Robert G., ed., *West Germany Under Reconstruction: Politics, Society and Culture in the Adenauer Era* (Ann Arbor, 1997).

Montgomery, Sir Bernard Law, *Normandy to the Baltic* (London, 1947).

Mühlberger, Detlef, *Hitler's Followers: Studies in the Sociology of the Nazi Movement* (London, 1991).

Mühlfenzl, Rudolf, ed., *Geflohen und Vertrieben: Augenzeugen Berichten* (Königstein im Taunus, 1981).

Müller, Klaus-Jürgen, ed., *Der Deutche Widerstand, 1933-1945*, 2nd edn (Paderborn, 1986).

Neillands, Robin, *The Bomber War: Arthur Harris and the Allied Bomber Offensive, 1939-1945* (London, 2001).

Nicholls, A. J., *The Bonn Republic: West German Democracy, 1945-1990* (Harlow, 1997).

Nicholls, A. J., *Freedom with Responsibility: The Social Market Economy in Germany, 1918-1963* (Oxford, 1994).

Niethammer, Lutz, *Entnazifizierung in Bayern: Säuberung und Rehabilitierung unter amerikanisher Besatzung* (Frankfurt, 1972).

Niethammer, Lutz, and Plato, Alexander von, eds, *Lebensgeschichte und Sozialkultur im Ruhrgebiet 1930 bis 1960*, 3 Volumes (Bonn, 1983-5).

Niewyk, Donald L., *The Jews in Weimar Germany* (Baton Rouge, LO, 1980).

Nitschke, Asmus, *Die 'Erbpolizei' im Nationalsozialismus: Zur Alltagsgeschichte der Gesundheitsämter im Dritten Reich* (Opladen, 1999).

Noakes, Jeremy, 'The Development of Nazi Policy Towards the German-Jewish "Mischlinge", 1933-1945', *Leo Baeck Institute Year Book*, vol. 34 (1989), pp. 291-354.

Noakes, Jeremy, *The Nazi Party in Lower Saxony, 1921-1933* (Oxford, 1971).

Noakes, Jeremy, and Pridham, Geoffrey, eds, *Nazism, 1919-1945: A Documentary Reader*, 4 Volumes (Exeter, 1983-1998).

Norden, Günther van and Wittmütz, Volkmar, eds, *Evangelische Kirche im Zweiten Weltkrieg* (Cologne, 1991).

Nowak, Kurt, *Euthanasie und Sterlization im 'Dritten Reich': Die Konfrontation der evangelischen und katholischen Kirchen mit dem Gesetz zur Verhutung Erbkranken Nachwuchses und der 'Euthanasie'-Aktion* (Göttingen, 1984).

Nyssen, Elke, *Schule im Nationalsozialismus* (Heidelberg, 1979).

Ohr, Dieter, *Nationasozialistische Propaganda und Weimarer Wahlen: Empirische Analysen zur Wirkung von NSDAP Versammlungen* (Opladen, 1997).

Oltmer, Jochen, *Migration und Politik in der Weimar Republik* (Göttingen, 2005).

Oltmer, Jochen, '"Schutz des nationalen Arbeitsmarkts": Transnationale Arbeitswanderungen und protektionistische Zuwanderungspolitik in der Weimarer Republik', in Jochen Oltmer, ed., *Migration Steuern und Verwalten: Deutschland vom späten 19. Jahrhundert bis zur Gegenwart* (Göttingen, 2003).

Ottweiler, Ottwiln, *Die Volksschule im Nationalsozialismus* (Weinheim, 1979).

Overy, Richard, *The Air War, 1939-1945* (London, 1980).

Overy, Richard, *Interrogations: The Nazi Elite in Allied Hands, 1945* (London, 2001).

Overy, Richard, *War and Economy in the Third Reich* (Oxford, 1994).

Panayi, Panikos, ed., *Weimar and Nazi Germany: Continuities and Discontinuities* (London, 2001).

Patch, William L., Jr, *Heinrich Brüning and the Dissolution of the Weimar Republic* (Cambridge, 1988).

Patel, Karin Klaus, *'Soldaten der Arbeit': Arbeitsdienst in Deutschland und den USA* (Göttingen, 2002).

Pätzold, Kurt and Runge, Irene, *'Kristallnacht': Zur Pogrom 1938* (Cologne, 1988).

Paucker, Arnold, ed., *Die Juden im nationalsozialistischen Deutschland* (Tübingen, 1986).

Paul, Gerhard and Mallmann, Klaus-Michael, eds, *Die Gestapo: Mythos und Realität* (Darmstadt, 1996).

Pehle, Walter H. ed., *November 1938: From 'Reichskristallnacht' to Genocide* (Oxford, 1991).

Peiffer, Lorenz, *Turnunterricht im Dritten Reich: Erziehung für den Krieg* (Cologne, 1987).

Pendas, Devin O., *The Frankfurt Auschwitz Trial, 1963-1965: Genocide, History and the Limits of the Law* (Cambridge, 2006).

Petropoulos, Jonathan A., *Art as Politics in the Third Reich* (London, 1996).

Peukert, Detlev J. K., 'Das "Dritte Reich" aus der "Alltags"-Perspektive', *Archiv für Sozialgeschichte*, vol. 26 (1986), pp. 533-56.

Peukert, Detlev J. K., *Die Edelweißpiraten: Protestbewegung jugendlicher Arbeiter im dritten Reich* (Cologne, 1988).

Peukert, Detlev J. K., *Inside Nazi Germany: Conformity, Opposition and Racism in Everyday Life* (London, 1993).

Peukert, Detlev J. K., *Die KPD im Widerstand: Verfolgung und Untergrundarbeit am Rhein und Ruhr 1933 bis 1945* (Wuppertal, 1980).

Peukert, Detlev J. K., *The Weimar Republic: The Crisis of Classical Modernity* (Harmondsworth, 1993).

Pfahlmann, Hans, *Fremdarbeiter und Kriegsgefangene in der deutschen Kriegswirtschaft, 1939-1945* (Darmstadt, 1968).

Pine, Lisa, 'Creating Conformity: The Training of Girls in the *Bund Deutscher Mädel*', *European History Quarterly*, vol. 33 (2003), pp. 367-85.

Pinson, Koppel S., 'Jewish Life in Liberated Germany', *Jewish Social Studies*, vol. 9 (1947).

Plant, Richard, *The Pink Triangle: The Nazi War Against Homosexuals* (Edinburgh, 1987).

Platen-Hallermund, Alice, *Die Tötung Geistkranker in Deutschland* (Bonn, 1993 reprint).

Plato, Alexander von and Meinecke, Wolfgang, *Alte Heimat – Neue Zeit: Flüchtlinge, Umgesiedelte, Vertriebene in der sowjetischen Besatzungszone und in der DDR* (Berlin, 1991).

Poljan, Pavel Marković, and Zajončkovskaja, Žanna Antonovna, 'Ostarbeiter in Deutschland und Daheim: Ergebnisse einer Fragenbogenanalyse', *Jahrbücher für Geschichte Osteuropas*, vol. 41 (1993).

Proctor, Robert, *The Nazi War on Cancer* (Princeton, 1999).

Proctor, Robert, *Racial Hygiene: Medicine Under the Nazis* (London, 1988).

Pronay, Nicholas, and Wilson, Keith, eds, *The Political Re-Education of Germany and Her Allies After World War II* (Beckenham, 1985).

Raem, Heinz-Albert, *Katholischer Gesellenverein und deutsche Kolpingfamilie in der Ära des Nationalsozialismus* (Mainz, 1982).

Read, Anthony, and Fisher, David, *Kristallnact: Unleashing the Holocaust* (London, 1991).

Recker, Marie-Luise, *Nationalsozialistische Sozialpolitik im Zweiten Weltkrieg* (Munich, 1985).

Reemstma, Katrin, *Sinti und Roma: Geschichte, Kultur, Gegenwart* (Munich, 1996).

Reichardt, Sven, *Faschistische Kampfbünde: Gewalt und Gemeinschaft im Italienischen Squadrismus und in der deutschen SA* (Cologne, 2002).

Reiter, Raimond, *Psychiatrie im Dritten Reich in Niedersachsen* (Hanover, 1997).

Richards, Denis, and Saunders, Hilary St George, *Royal Air Force, 1939/1945*, 3 Vols (London, 1953).

Richarz, Bernhard, *Heilen, Pflegen, Töten: Zur Alltagsgeschichte einer Heil- und Pflegeanstalt bis zum ende des Nationasozialismus* (Göttingen, 1987).

Richter, Ludwig, *Die Deutsche Volkspartei, 1918-1933* (Düsseldorf, 2002).

Riecken, Andrea, '"Der Kranke Flüchtling": Die gesundheitliche Behandlung von Flüchtlingen und Vertriebenen in Niedersachsen', in Klaus J. Bade and Jochen Oltmer, eds, *Zuwanderung und Integration in Niedersachsen seit dem Zweiten Weltkrieg* (Osnabrück, 2002), pp. 101-30.

Rosenhaft, Eve, *Beating the Fascists: The German Communists and Political Violence, 1929-1933* (Cambridge, 1983).

Rosenhaft, Eve, 'Links gleich Rechts? Militante Straßengewalt um 1930', in Thomas Lindenberger and Alf Lüdtke, eds, *Physische Gewalt: Studien zur Geschichte der Neuzeit* (Frankfurt, 1995).

Rothenberger, Karl-Heinz, *Die Hungerjahre nach dem Zweiten Weltkrieg: Ernährungs- und Landwirtschaft in Rheinland-Pfalz, 1945-1950* (Boppard, 1980).

Rumpf, Hans, *Das War der Bombenkrieg: Deutsche Städte im Feuersturm* (Oldenburg, 1961).

Rüther, Martin, *'Zu Hause könnten sie es nicht schöner haben': Kinderlandverschickung aus Köln und Umgebung, 1941-1945* (Cologne, 2000).

Sachse, Christoph and Tennsedt, Florian, *Der Wohlfahrtstaat im Nationalsozialismus* (Stuttgart, 1992).

Sander, Peter, *Frankfurt. Auschwitz: Die nationalsozialistische Verfolgung der Sinti und Roma in Frankfurt am Main* (Frankfurt, 1998).

Schaffer, Ronald, *American Bombing in World War II* (Oxford, 1985).

Schenk, Michael, *Rassismus gegen Sinti und Roma: Zur Kontinuität der Zigeunerverfolgung innerhalb der deutschen Gesellschaft von der Weimarer Republik bis in die Gegenwart* (Frankfurt, 1994).

Schieder, Theodor, ed., *Dokumentation der Vertreibung der Deutschen aus Ost-Mitteleuropa*, 4 Volumes (Bonn, 1954-1961).

Schlegel, Martha, *Von der Nordseeküste in die Kinderlandverschickung, 1940-1945* (Oldenburg, 1996).

Schmiechen-Ackermann, Detlef, *Nationalsozialismus und Arbeitermilieus: Der nationalsozialistische Angriff auf die proletarischen Wohnquartiere und die Reaktion in der Sozialistischen Vereinen* (Bonn, 1998).

Schmuhl, Hans-Walther, *Rassenhygiene, Nationalsozialismus, Euthanasie*, 2nd edn (Göttingen, 1987).

Schneider, Michael, *Unterm Hakenkreuz: Arbeiter und Arbeiterbewegung 1933 bis 1939* (Bonn, 1999).

Schneider, Wolfgang , ed., *Alltag unter Hitler* (Berlin, 2000).

Schoenbaum, David, *Hitler's Social Revolution: Class and Status in Nazi Germany, 1933-39* (London, 1967).

Scholtz, Harald, *Erziehung und Unterricht unterm Hakenkreuz* (Göttingen, 1985).

Schubert-Weller, Christoph, *Hitler-Jugend: Von 'Jungsturm Adolf Hitler' zur Staatsjugend des Dritten Reiches* (Weinheim, 1993).

Schulz, Günther, *Wiederaufbau in Deutschland: Die Wohnungspolitik in den Westzonen und der Bundesrepublik von 1945 bis 1957* (Düsseldorf, 1994).

Schulze, Winfried, ed., *Sozialgeschichte, Alltagsgeschichte, Mikro-Historie: Eine Diskussion* (Göttingen, 1994).

Schumann, Dirk, *Politische Gewalt in der Weimarer Republik, 1918-1933: Kampf um die Straße und Furcht vor dem Bürgerkrieg* (Essen, 2001).

Schwarzwälder, Herbert, *Die Machtergreifung der NSDAP in Bremen, 1933* (Bremen, 1966).

Schweitzer, Arthur, *Big Business in the Third Reich* (Bloomington, IN, 1964).

Seeber, Eva, *Zwangsarbeiter in der faschistischen Kriegswirtschaft* (Berlin, 1964).

Siebenborn-Ramm, Kerstin, *Die 'Butenhamborger': Kriegsbedingte Migration und Ihre Folgen im und nach dem Zweiten Weltkrieg* (Hamburg, 1996).

Silverman, Dan P., *Hitler's Economy: Nazi Work Creation Programmes, 1933-1936* (London, 1998).

Smelser, Ronald, *Robert Ley: Hitler's Labour Front Leader* (Oxford, 1988).

Sofsky, Wolfgang, *The Order of Terror: The Concentration Camp* (Princeton, NJ, 1997).

Sollbach, Gerhard E., ed., *Dortmund – Bombenkrieg und Nachkriegszeit, 1939-1948* (Hagen, 1986).

Sons, Hans-Ulrich, *Gesundheitspolitik während der Besatzungszeit: Das öffentliche gesundheitswesen in Nordrhein-Westfalen, 1945-1949* (Wuppertal, 1983).

Stachura, Peter D., *The German Youth Movement, 1900-1945* (London, 1981).

Stachura, Peter D., ed., *Unemployment and the Great Depression in Weimar Germany* (London, 1986).

Steinberg, Günter, *Die Bevölkerungsentwicklung Deutschlands im Zweiten Weltkrieg* (Bonn, 1991).

Steinert, Marlis G., *Hitler's War and the Germans: Public Mood and Attitude during the Second World War* (Athens, OH, 1977).

Steinweis, Alan E., *Art, Ideology and Economics in Nazi Germany: The Reich Chambers of Music, Theatre and the Visual Arts* (London, 1993)

Stephenson, Jill, *The Nazi Organization of Women* (London, 1981).

Stephenson, Jill, 'Triangle: Foreign Workers, German Civilians and the Nazi Regime: War and Society in Württemberg', *German Studies Review*, vol. 15 (1992), pp. 339-59.

Struve, Walter, *Aufstieg und Herrschaft des Nationalsozialismus in einer industriellen Kleinstadt: Osterode am Harz, 1918-1945* (Essen, 1992).

Stüber, Gabriele, *Der Kampf gegen den Hunger, 1945-1950: Die Ernährungslage in der britischen zone Deutschlands, insbesondere in Schleswig-Holstein und Hamburg* (Neumünster, 1984).

Tebbutt, Susan, ed., *Sinti and Roma: Gypsies in German-Speaking Society and Literature* (Oxford, 1998).

Tewes, Ludger, *Jugend im Krieg: Von Luftwaffenhelfern und Soldaten, 1939-1945* (Essen, 1989).

Thalmann, Rita, *Frausein im Dritten Reich* (Munich, 1984).

Traverso, Enso, *The Origins of Nazi Violence* (London, 2003).

Trippe, Chrristian F., *Konservative Verfassungspolitik, 1918-1923: Die DNVP als Opposition in Reich und Ländern* (Düsseldorf, 1995).

Trittel, Günter J., *Hunger und Politik: Die Ernährungskrise in der Bizone (1945-1949)* (Frankfurt, 1990).

Ueberhorst, Horst, *Frisch, Frei, Stark und Treu: Die Arbeitersportbewegung in Deutschland, 1893-1933* (Düsseldorf, 1933).

Uphoff, Rolf, *Als der Tag zur Nacht wurde - und der Nacht zum Tage: Wilhelsmhaven im Bombenkrieg* (Oldenburg, 1992).

Wagner, Johannes Volker, *Hakenkreuz über Bochum: Machtergrreifung und Nationalsozialistische Alltag in einer Revierstadt*, 3rd Edition (Bochum, 1993).

Webster, Sir Charles, and Frankland, Noble, *The Strategic Air Offensive Against Germany, 1939-1945*, 4 Vols (London, 1961).

Wehler, Hans-Ulrich, *Deutsche Gesellschaftsgeschichte*, Vol. 4, *Vom Beginn des Ersten Weltkrieges bis zur Gründung der beiden deutschen Staaten, 1914-1949* (Munich, 2003).

Weidisch, Peter, *Die Machtergreifung in Würzburg, 1933* (Würzburg, 1990).

Weindling, Paul, *Health, Race and German Politics Between National Unification and Nazism, 1870-1945* (Cambridge, 1989).

Welch, David, *Propaganda and the German Cinema, 1933-1945*, 2nd edn (London, 2001).

Welch, David, *The Third Reich: Politics and Propaganda* (London, 1993).

Weyrather, Irmgard, *Muttertag und Mutterkreuz: Der Kult um die 'deutsche Mutter' im Nationalsozialismus* (Frankfurt, 1993).

White, Osmar, *Conqueror's Road: An Eyewitness Report of Germany, 1945* (Cambridge, 2003).

Wildmann, Daniel, *Begehrte Körper: Konstruktion und Inszenierung des 'arischen' Männerkörpers im 'Dritten Reich'* (Zurich, 1998).

Wildt, Michael, *Der Traum vom Sattwerden: Hunger und Protest, Schwarzmarkt und Selbsthilfe* (Hamburg, 1986).

Winkel, Harald, *Die Wirtschaft im geteilten Deutschland, 1945-1970* (Wiesbaden, 1974).

Winkler, Dörte, *Frauenarbeit im 'Dritten Reich'* (Hamburg, 1977).

Winkler, Heinrich August, *Der Weg in die Katastrophe: Arbeiter und Arbeiterbewegung in der Weimarer Republik, 1930 bis 1933* (Berlin, 1987).

Winkler, Heinrich August, *Weimar, 1918-1933: Die Geschichte der Ersten Deutschen Demokratie* (Munich, 1998).

Zayas, Alfred de, *Anmerkungen zur Vertreibung der Deutschen aus dem Osten*, 2nd Edn (Stuttgart, 1987).

Zayas, Alfred Maurice de, *The German Expellees: Victims in War and Peace* (London, 1993).

Zimmermann, Michael, *Rassenutopie und Genozid: Die nationalsozialistische 'Lösung der Zigeunerfrage'* (Hamburg, 1996).

GLOSSARY AND ABBREVIATIONS

Alltagsgeschichte	History of everyday life
Altstadt	Old town (usually referring to the city cetre)
Anschluss	German unification with Austria
Antifaschistischer Arbeitskreis	Antifascist Working Group
BA	*Bundesarchiv* (Federal Archive)
BAOS	*Bistumsarchiv* Osnabrück (Archive of the Osnabrück Bishopric)
BDM	*Bund Deutscher Mädel* (League of German Girls)
Berufsbeamtenring	Professional Employees Circle
Bezirk	Region
Bizonia	Joint British and American zones of occupation
Blockleiter	Leader of a block of flats during the Third Reich
Bund der Kinderreichen	League of Parents with More than Three Children
Caritasverband	Roman Catholic charitable organization
CDU	*Christlich Demokratische Union* (Christian Democratic Union)
Central Verein Deutscher Staatsburger Jüdischen Glaubens	Central Organization of German Citizens of Jewish Faith
DAF	*Deutsche Arbeitsfront* (German Labour Front)
DDP	*Deutsche Demokratische Partei* (German Democratic Party)
Deutsches Berufserziehungswerk	German Educational Training Works
DFW	*Deutsches Frauenwerk* (German Women's Enterprise)

DM	*Deutschmark*
DNVP	*Deutschnationale Volkspartei* (German National People's Party)
DVP	*Deutsche Volkspartei* (German People's Party)
Einsatzgruppen	Special task forces involved in racial persecution in eastern Europe
Eiserne Front	Iron Front (SPD defence organization)
Ernährungshilfwerk	Nutritional Relief Organization
Festsaal	Banqueting hall
Freikorps	Right wing paramilitary volunteer units
Führer	Leader
Gau	Nazi administrative region
Gauleiter	Head of regional administration
GDO	*Gemeinschaft der Ostvertriebenen* (Community of Eastern Expellees)
Gestapo	*Geheime Staatspolizei* (Secret State Police)
Gleichschaltung	Nazi term meaning co-ordination, i.e. nazification, of state and society
Heimat	Homeland
Heimtücke	Treachery against the homeland
Hilfswerk Mutter und Kind	Relief Organization Mother and Child
Historikertag	Historians Day (annual conference of German historians)
HJ	*Hitler Jugend* (Hitler Youth)
IMIS	*Institut für Migrationsforschung und Interkulturelle Studien* (Institute for Migration Research and Intercultural Studies)
JM	*Jung Mädel* (Young Girls: Hitler Youth group for girls between 10 and 14)
Jungvolk	Young People (Hitler Youth group for boys between 10 and 14)
Kaiserreich	German Empire of 1871-1918
KDF	*Kraft Durch Freude* (Strength Through Joy; sub-group of the DAF)
Kinderreich	Rich in children. Nazi description used for parents with more than three children
KPD	*Kommunistische Partei Deutschlands* (Communist Party of Germany)
Kreis	District
Kreisamtsleiter	District office leader
Kreisleiter	District leader
Kriegs-Chronik	War Chronicle

Kristallnacht	Night of the broken glass, antisemitic pogrom of 9-10 November 1938
Kulturkampf	Cultural struggle (between the Roman Catholic Church and the state)
Landesfrauenklinik	Regional women's clinic
Landkreis	Rural district
Landtag	Provincial parliament
Lebensraum	Living space
MA	*Militärarchiv* (Military Archive)
Marienhospital	St Mary's Hospital
Mischling	Person of mixed 'German' and 'Jewish' blood
NHH	*Niedersächsisches Hauptstaatsarchiv Hannover* (Main Archive of Lower Saxony in Hanover)
NS	National Socialist
NSBO	*Nationalsozialistische Betriebszellenorganization* (National Socialist Factory Cell Organization)
NSDAP	*Nationalsozialistische Deutsche Arbeiter Partei* (National Socialist German Workers' Party)
NSF	*Nationalsozialistische Frauenschaft* (National Socialist Women's League)
NSLB	*Nationalsozialistischer Lehrerbund* (National Socialist Teachers' Association)
NSO	*Niedersächsisches Staatsarchiv Osnabrück* (Lower Saxon State Archive in Osnabrück)
NSV	*Nationalsozialistische Volkswohlfahrt* (National Socialist People's Welfare Organization)
NWSM	*Nordrhein-westfälisches Staatsarchiv, Münster* (North-Rhine-Westfalian State Archive, Munster)
Ortsgruppenleiter	Local group leader
OKD	*Osnabrücker Kupfer- und Drahtwerk* (Osnabrück Copper and Wire Works)
Ost	East (symbol worn by eastern European workers)
Ostarbeiter	Eastern European worker
Rathaus	Town hall
Regierungsbezirk	Regional administrative division
Regierungspräsident	Regional president heading a *Regierungsbezirk*
Reich	Empire
RM	Reichsmark
Reichsbanner	Imperial Banner (Social Democratic defence organization)

Reichsbund der deutschen Beamten	Imperial League of German Civil Servants
Reichskammer	Imperial chamber
Reichskulturkammer	Imperial Chamber of Culture
Reichsminister	Imperial minister
Reichstag	Lower house of German parliament
RFSSSuChdDtPol	*Reichsführer SS und Chef der Deutschen Polizei* (Reich SS Leader and Chief of the German Police)
RSHA	*Reichssicherheitshauptamt* (Reich Security Head Office)
SA	*Sturmabteilung* (Nazi Storm Troopers)
SAPD	*Sozialistische Arbeiter Partei Deutschlands* (Socialist Workers Party of Germany)
SHD	*Sicherheitsdienst* (Security Service)
SPD	*Sozialdemokratische Partei Deutschlands* (Social Democratic Party of Germany)
Sportsplatz	Sports ground
SS	*Schutzstaffeln* (police and security organization)
Stadt-Chronik	City Chronicle
Stadthalle	City hall
Stadtwächter	City guard (Osnabrück political party and eponymous newspaper at the end of the Weimar Republic)
Stahlhelm	Steel Helmet (short name for right wing First World War veterans association)
Stahlwerk	Steel works
Verein	Organization
Völkisch	racist-nationalist
Volksgemeinschaft	People's community
Volksschädling	Racial Pest
Wehrmacht	Armed forces
Weltanschauung	Worldview
Weiße Wehr	White Defence (Osnabrück political party at the end of the Weimar Republic)
Winterhilfe	Winter help
WHW	*Winterhilfswerk* (Winter Relief Organization)
Widerstand	Resistance
Zentrum	Centre (Catholic Centre Party)

INDEX